The Origin of

John Hayberry
Edited by Angela Zilverburg et al.

Now that liberal socialist Democrats (L.S.D.ers, for short) are beginning to see that nothing of any value came out of all these years of President Obama's administration and the politics of psychopathology, some of them appear to be on the verge of realizing that there may actually be something wrong with their way of thinking. But few of them will probably ever admit it, even to themselves. So all of us should be aware that some people of poor judgment might seek revenge on society, especially on family-oriented, conservative Republicans and Tea Party Republicans, whom they wrongly consider their enemies and not their friends. Some liberal jerks may even attempt to harm their fellow man by doing such things as posting offensive photos of them or their wives and children on the Internet. Therefore, we should all be very careful what we do, not only in public but also in the privacy of our own homes. We should always be cautious where we travel, whether it be to another person's residence or through an unfamiliar neighborhood or to another city via a public conveyance, because there is just no telling what some Third World-thinker types are going to do if the theories in this book are accepted by the world as true. This is a new technological age in which we all live, and spying equipment, including such things as Google glasses, miniature Chinese cameras, small video recorders with low-light sensitivity and/or sound-and-motion-detecting capabilities, along with miscellaneous 1950s C.I.A.-quality devices, can be easily purchased on the Internet, which should be illegal. Some of these people may even go so far as to use telescopic cameras to peer into open bedroom windows. Dedicated liberals with access to social media Web sites may also use their smartphones with text messaging and G.P.S. capabilities to play a dire game called "Pop the Weasel," in which mini flash mobs of participants suddenly appear as directed in order to annoy a targeted person anywhere and everywhere that he or she travels, including public restrooms. The goal, of course, is to cause their chosen target to have an anxiety attack. Liberal techies high on marijuana may even burn CDs of dogs barking and then sporadically play the sound through a speaker at night to keep waking an enemy up. If their target eventually calls the police and no dog is found, he or she will looks like some kind of nut. If anyone (other than comedy writers) disagrees with anything in this book or has any additional information that they believe affects our national interest and should have been included, please send a United States Postal Service postcard (4" x 6" only) to our National Security Agency, Attention: Complaint Department, 9800 Savage Road, Fort Meade, Maryland 20755-6711. No envelopes will be accepted. Thank you.

Copyright © 2014 by John Hayberry
All Rights Reserved.

No part of this publication may be reproduced, stored in a retrieval system, or transmitted, in any form or by any means, electronic, mechanical, photocopying, recording, or otherwise, without the written permission of the author.

THE INFORMATION IN THIS BOOK WAS PUBLISHED UNDER THE AUSPICES OF THE FEDERAL BUREAU OF INVESTIGATION (F.B.I.) AND WITH THE PERMISSION OF THE NATIONAL SECURITY AGENCY/CENTRAL SECURITY SERVICE (N.S.A./C.S.S.). THE ACCESS DATES FOR ALL INTERNET WEB SITES THAT WERE REFERENCED HEREIN HAVE BEEN DOCUMENTED AND WILL BE SENT TO ANY U.S. GOVERNMENT AGENCY UPON REQUEST.

The Heritage of American Halfwits is a conservative class-action think tank dedicated to the immediate downsizing of the National Debt by reducing wasteful government spending. Our workshop is located at the following Internet Web site: humandevolution.biz. Thousands of Internet users have joined our group discussions and some of them have proved to be amazingly knowledgeable.

Dog Ear Publishing
4010 W. 86th Street, Ste H
Indianapolis, IN 46268
www.dogearpublishing.net

ISBN: 978-1-4575-2091-4

Library of Congress Control Number: has been applied for

All rights reserved under Berne Copyright Conventions. Under the "fair use" rule of copyright law, the intellectual property cited in this book was used to advance a new theory. The technological advances now being made with computerized electronic devices and subliminal audio equipment require the following disclaimer: No one involved in the writing, editing, copyediting, or proofreading of this book can be held personally responsible for any inadvertent errors. This project includes input by a group of volunteers. Some names have been changed or withheld to protect those persons' identities. Dr. Californigula, Professor Hiram Q. Kneebish, Theodorus Q. Abraham Wallieskurinsky, Jr., and Dr. Marvin Q. Yoickman are fictitious people. Legal information regarding intellectual property and/or the rights of all citizens of the United States of America to print the truth is available on the Internet at westlaw.com. This book was published in the interest of National Security.

This book is printed on acid-free paper.

Printed in the United States of America

This book is dedicated not only to all of the fallen soldiers in World War I, World War II, the Korean War, the Vietnam War, the Persian Gulf War, the War in Afghanistan, and the Iraq War but to all brave American men and women, who, after everyone reads this book, may never have to fight another war in a foreign country again.

"PLEASE DON'T FEED THE ANIMALS (INCLUDING THE NEANDERTHALS)" —Humorous warning painted on a plywood sign at a traveling amusement park in Peoria, Illinois.

Contents

Preface: The Politics of Psychopathology   ix
Introduction   xi

Part One
Fantasy Addiction Disorder (F.A.D.)

Chapter 1: What's Wrong With Them?   2

    On Psychosis and Miscellaneous Delusions   2
    Nonbizarre Delusional Disorder   6
    Folie à Plusieurs (The Madness of Many)   8
    Unspecified Type   10

Chapter 2: Are They Using Drugs?   12

    Pro-choice Drug Addiction, California Style   12
    Left-wing "Leisure" Drugs   16
    More-on Drugs   19
    Euphoria as a Left-wing Way of Life   24

Chapter 3: Why Aren't They Like Us?   27

    Don't Worry, "Be Happy"?   27
    Moron Liberal Fantasizing   28
    Political Puppetry   29
    Losing the Key to a Compartmentalized Delusion   34

Chapter 4: What Makes Them Act Like That? ... 36

    An Inexplicable Fondness for Dissociative Amnesia ... 36
    Liberal Addiction to Political Fiction ... 39
    Dopamine ... 42
    A Brief Review of What We Know So Far ... 47
    The Biological Behavior System ... 54
    The Proposed Psychiatric Diagnosis and Code ... 55

Chapter 5: Is It Really True? ... 57

    Psychiatry 101: Drug-Fueled Paranoid Schizophrenia ... 57
    How on Earth Can a Mass Mental Disorder Be Possible? ... 66

Chapter 6: Why Do They Act So Silly? ... 75

    Understanding Liberals in Sixty Seconds ... 75
    The Tea Party Protest against President Obama's Policies ... 76
    Five Methods that L.S.D.ers Use to Ignore Facts ... 79
    Projection ... 86
    The Orenthal James Simpson Double-Murder Case ... 88

Part Two
The P.E.T.S. Hypothesis

Chapter 7: Why Do They Act So Funny? ... 94

    Darwinian Psychiatry: The Evolution of Mental Disorders ... 94
    The Prehistoric Beginning of Fantasy Addiction ... 112
    Tinbergen's Four Questions ... 118

Chapter 8: What Happened To Them? ... 124

    P.E.T.S. (People Enabled to Survive) ... 124
    The Evolutionary War ... 132

Chapter 9: What Else Do We Know About Them? — 138

    Death Can Be Very Disadvantageous — 138
    The Liberal Peace Sign — 142
    Normalcy Bias — 143

Chapter 10: Where Did They Come From? — 145

    The Side Effects of the Written Laws of Men (and Women) — 145
    Unintended Human Evolutionary Engineering — 149
    Dominant and Subordinate Males — 152
    Ethnic Stereotypes? — 153
    Wild Animals and Domesticated Pets — 157
    A Brief Note on Facial Expressions — 160
    Shh! . . . Human Dysgenics — 162
    Mentalizing (for Fun and Profit) — 165

Chapter 11: Why Don't They Like Other People? — 172

    Compassion Used as a Personal Stress Reliever — 172
    Words That Are Worth a Thousand Pictures — 178
    The United States of Pilfered Piggy Banks — 178
    Liberals First and Scientists Second — 191
    The Ancient Kilawabo: "White Man Bad" — 197
    Interview with a Democrat — 203
    Racism! — 205

Chapter 12: Are They Really Our Friends? — 210

    The Vietnam War: Liberal Privates Exposed — 210
    Red States and Blue Dress States — 219
    All the News That's Print to Fit — 222
    Liberal and Conservative Opinions Are *Not* Equally Valid. — 223
    Liberal White Lies — 227
    Frequently Asked Questions — 228

Part Three
The Origin of Our Left-wing Species

Chapter 13: Why Aren't They Nice To People? — 232

    The Descent of Liberal Man — 232
    A Timeline of the History of Slavery — 234
    The #1 Jackass Political Tactic — 241
    The Little-Known U.S. Presidential "Legacies" — 244
    Trojan Donkeys — 245
    A Human Slave (or "Puppet") Gene? — 248

Chapter 14: Why Do They Look So Funny? — 259

    The Neanderthal Enigma — 259
    The Descent of the (Liberal?) Neanderthal — 268

Chapter 15: Why Don't They Tell Their Own Children The Truth? — 269

    Hollywood, California, Brainwashing Techniques — 269
    The Boob Tube: How Liberal Propaganda Works — 272
    Mindless Art and Music — 277
    Human and Animal Kin Selection — 280

Chapter 16: Do They Belong In A Zoo? — 299

    Anthroposuboptimality: The New Normal — 299
    The Difference between Males and Females — 307

Chapter 17: What Should We Do? — 309

    The Dilemma of the Good Samaritan — 309
    What (the Hell) Does the Future Hold? — 310
    The Final Piece of the Puzzle — 315
    Woolly Mammoth Resurrection — 317

Afterword — 319
Addendum — 320

Preface

According to the *Occam's razor principle,* simpler explanations are, with all other things being equal, generally better than explanations that are more complex. As any law enforcement officer will affirm, factual explanations are easy to understand but lies are difficult. So readers of this book can decide whether what is contained herein is true. You'll find a wealth of pertinent quotes by mostly intelligent people, along with *carefully researched proof* of certain startling conclusions pertaining to the human-mindedness that we call liberalism. Believe what you read or don't believe it; the choice is yours. However, before you make that decision, you should be aware that the behavioral and cognitive sciences, compared to most other branches of human knowledge, are in a stage of relative infancy. For that reason, they are vulnerable to any radical new theories, such as *fantasy addiction disorder,* that may come along.

So much remains unknown about the convolutions of the human mind that even textbooks written by renowned psychologists, psychiatrists, and neurologists often contain information that they'll be the first to admit is clearly debatable and subject to future change. Nevertheless, everything that appears in this book is based on the best and most current scientific research. That means anyone can easily verify what is stated. As far as we can tell, it's all accurate, but of course, mistakes can be made. If, in rare instances, these writings seem to digress from that which is known to be factual, then it has been made clear that it's only speculation.

Readers should also bear in mind that there's no such thing as a statement, even in basic arithmetic, that's always correct under any and all circumstances. Exceptions of one kind or another invariably exist with regard to any declaration of fact. For example, if I were to say that 1+1 equals 2, this would be true—but not *always* true, because in a binary numeral system, 1+1 equals 10. And if I were to say something like "If it's a bird, it has wings, feathers, and a beak," this would also be true—but not *always* true, because the creature might be an unknown species of some kind, or a duckbill platypus, or perhaps even a genetically engineered chicken. Exceptions to rules always exist. That's why exceptions also apply when discussing *Homo sapiens sapiens.* (Sapient, by the way, means intelligent, wise, and perceptive.)

You see, individuals are in a constant state of learning and change—hopefully for the better. There are so many types and varieties of men and women with overlying or similar characteristics, both mental and physical, that no statement can ever be made that applies to any specific individual, much less a group, that is consistently true in all cases. A *general hypothesis* is exactly that.

Introduction

Some mysterious things are going on in the world that most people never suspected and cannot even imagine. One of those things concerns human evolution. Why, for example, do so-called *liberals* think, speak, and act as they do? This mystery has baffled conservative Americans—the vast majority of whom are just normal people — for decades. One prominent stand-up psychiatrist analyzing liberalism has even offered a detailed etiology that is surely valid in many cases but does not adequately explain, in our opinion, all of the symptoms that we continue to observe. In fact, no one, to our knowledge, has ever gone so far as to seriously diagnose liberalism for what it really is: a *disease*. (The *Oxford American College Dictionary* defines the word disease as "a disorder of structure or function in a human, animal, or plant.") Some conservative writers continue to enlighten us by documenting the childish, hypocritical, and illogical things that liberals say and do, but unfortunately, they fail to explain liberal behavior and the *politics of psychopathology.*

Now finally, that will end.

The theory of *Human (D) Evolution* clarifies everything about liberals and the consequences of allowing them to serve in a governmental capacity that so many people have wondered about. *Fantasy addiction disorder* (F.A.D.) explains liberal thought, and the *P.E.T.S. hypothesis,* concerning people enabled to survive, explains liberals' origin and inherent behavior. Both the F.A.D. and P.E.T.S. hypotheses are, for the most part, ideas that are independent of one another, which means that each of these postulates can stand, or fall, on its own. Human beings are fascinating to study and learn about, and they are the subject matter of this project. All of us, no matter what race, color, or creed, were born with certain strengths and weaknesses. However, understanding people of the liberal persuasion will require a crash course in *psychiatry.* That's because some familiarity with abnormal mental function is a necessity, so please carefully study all of the information that this book contains. Some readers will be truly amazed by what they read and will undoubtedly want to continue thinking about it, so peer between the lines. Insight will come first, then *revelation.*

In 1775, some forty years after the first edition of Linnaeus's *Systema Naturae,* Johann Blumenbach of Göttingen published his controversial dissertation,

On the Natural Varieties of Mankind. Blumenbach did not stop with the features of the foot. Although he criticized Linnaeus for relying too much on dental characteristics in his diagnoses of species, he did not reject prominent, adult male buckteeth as important. Imagine a cross between John Wayne and Bugs Bunny. (President Obama does not fit into this category. His teeth are merely larger.)

Furthermore, *speciesism*, which comes into play here, is defined as "the assumption of human superiority leading to the exploitation of animals" (the *Oxford American College Dictionary*, Oxford University Press, copyright 2002, G. P. Putnam's Sons, New York). Speciesism may help many of us understand the enigmatic meaning of the word prejudice. For example, are liberals "prejudiced" when they call all conservatives extremists?

In the book *Extinct Humans,* the authors state that by the late 1940s, the picture of human evolution looked for all the world like that of other animals: different genera and species, some going extinct and, in the case of humans, only one surviving (Ian Tattersall and Jeffrey H. Schwartz, *Extinct Humans,* 2000, Westview Press, Boulder, Colorado, pp. 31 46).

As with that of other organisms, mankind's evolutionary past resembles a many-branched bush of diversity, with numerous species coming into existence and almost as many suddenly disappearing. Speciesism, by definition, means that a person is "prejudiced" toward all animals—such as monkeys, wolves, mice, two-headed frogs, Chihuahuas, or wild African donkeys (all of which are covered in this book).

In his *On the Origin of Species,* British naturalist Charles Darwin had what was essentially a religious and thus social/political problem. Why? Because it flustered religious liberals. Darwin's theory is that all living organisms are related by descent and natural selection from an increasingly remote series of common ancestors that were originally black-skinned, angry, and three feet tall.

That accounts for all of modern man's 1001 heritable characteristics, some of which are discussed in this book. Seven of them are as follows: (1) MF, or "male factor" (i.e., killer instinct), (2) FF, or "female factor" (i.e., sensitivity and caregiving instincts), (3) JF, or "Jewish factor," (4) LF, or "liberal factor," (5) HF, or "homosexual factor," (6) NF, or "Neanderthal factor," and (7) EF, or "evil factor" (i.e., murder-, rape-, and greed-related instincts), all of which every single person on earth has to some small measurable extent—without exception. Why? Because if mankind's ancestral roots are traced back far enough, we're all related. This is clearly what is stated in the *Holy Bible* (for those who believe it), and that book was, of course, written long after human beings evolved from apes.

Analyzing human beings, however, is like analyzing the leaves on a tree. The factors listed above can be applied on a scale of 1 to 5, with the number five being the most applicable. (Example: Neville Chamberlain—MF3, FF1, JF2, LF5, HF1, NF1, EF?) Each person is different. Characteristics overlap. Everyone's JF, or Jewish factor, for example, includes traces of an Arab heritage. However, as they say, "We are all God's children." That includes everyone—all of our liberal friends, too.

Darwin's argument was simple. In each generation, more living organisms are produced than survive to maturity, at which point the survivors are able to reproduce themselves. Those that succeed (i.e., the "fittest") carry inherited and thus heritable features that aid in their survival, characteristics that may then be passed along to their offspring. In Darwin's view, natural selection is nothing more than the sum of all those factors that act to promote the reproductive success of one individual and not another. Over time, and many generations, advantageous variations are predicted to become common in the population. However, what Darwin did not realize at the time, but probably suspected, because it wasn't increasingly as obvious to everyone as it is today, is that, because of human interference and influence over the laws of nature, *disadvantageous variations* are not only predicted to occur but to become established. These physical and mental changes in mankind may be distasteful, repugnant, and perhaps even horrible.

Examples of negative human anomalies include such things as arrested mental development, a predilection for illegal drug use, and the dragging of one's feet like a sloth while wearing oversized Nike "Black Flips"—even among relatively normal white Anglo-Saxon Protestants (W.A.S.P.S.). Further examples include long twisted hair, big corn rolls, or three-foot-long Rastafarian dreadlocks that reek of marijuana. So what's next, free government E.B.T. cards that can be used to purchase designer drugs and crack cocaine? Let's hope not.

Remember, the United States of America is already *$18 trillion in debt.* (Here's the actual amount owed: $17 trillion, 632 billion, 487 million, 325 thousand, and two hundred and three dollars.)

But why is everyone so mad at President Obama? He hasn't done anything—except play golf, throw White House parties, and give daily teleprompter speeches. He even seems to be acting like former president Bill Clinton sometimes, what with that contrived, *I'm thinking about women, children, and families* look on his face. He, too, has squandered trillions of dollars of our children's future federal income-tax payments, which negatively affects the personal security of all Americans. Why? To promote himself and pay off supporters? The situation has gotten so bad that some labor unions have now become little more than D.N.C. front groups. But it's even worse than that. Some foreign interests are beginning to set up front groups in the United States of America because they know that liberal socialist Democrats can be played like pianos. To top it off, L.S.D.ers are suddenly appearing on everyone's television sets—and computers—in taxpayer-funded government ads and commercials, wanting all young, healthy patriotic Americans to help pay for the president's "legacy": Obamacare—sometimes referred to as the (Un)Affordable Care Act. Who do these shysters think they're fooling? Are they on a tax revenue-funded White House payroll? Are their mouths dripping wet from drinking from the public trough? Is our hard-earned tax money being used to prop up the man we elected to run the government and make him look good? If not, then why is he still campaigning to be president when he already is? He was elected in 2008—six years ago. Isn't everyone's tax money supposed to be used to make the American people's lives easier? Apparently not. Instead, it's being used hand over fist to make President Obama popular.

Now, the United States of America is a huge house of cards ready to collapse under its own weight.

One of the hypotheses that you will read about pertains to the possible existence of a human slave gene. However, be forewarned: Although this theory seems to make perfect sense, that doesn't necessarily mean that it is correct. The evidence for a human slave gene may be, in fact, paralogistic. In other words, just because something appears to be obvious does not necessarily mean that it is true. For example, the Earth is not flat, even though to the naked eye it may seem to be. The Sun does not orbit the Earth, even though it seems to. Therefore, we should always be careful about what we conclude based only on those things that seem superficially apparent.

The societal effects resulting from the identification of a heritable (liberal) slave gene—if such even exists—could be enormous, so we should always be cautious when discussing this subject. If anyone finds anything in this book offensive, please ask yourself this question: Is it better to tell a blind man (e.g., the people of the United States of America) about a coiled rattlesnake *lying* in his path or to allow the snake to rear back, strike, and bite him? Well, unfortunately, we've already been bitten and the poison is flowing. So, as liberals like to say, "Let the healing begin."

In the early twentieth century, Darwin's theory of evolution made the religious hierarchy look ridiculous, especially during the Scopes Monkey Trial of 1925. (So here we go again.) Somewhere along the line, "religious" liberals managed to adopt Darwin's theory as their own in order to make their political enemies, Christian conservatives, look bad. In many cases, those liberals succeeded. One way they did it was by comparing dominant conservative military types to ancient Neanderthal man. But, at the same time, liberal paleoanthropologists refused to admit that early Neanderthal man, who was essentially a black-skinned human ape, may have continued to evolve throughout the last ice age and/or survive genetically. Instead, paleoanthropologists claimed that the Neanderthal went extinct, even though he has clearly evolved and become what we sometimes refer to today as an uneducated *liberal* union member and supporter of the left-wing socialist Democratic Party. Why do most paleoanthropologists continue to deny that half-breed Neanderthals still exist? What did they all do, eat one another?

So what's wrong with these people?

Human (D) Evolution

In the nineteenth century, the dictionary definition of the word liberal was as follows[1]:

> **LIB'ERAL,** *adjective* [Latin liberalis, from liber, free.]
>
> 1. Of a free heart; free to give or bestow; not close or contracted; munificent; bountiful; generous; giving largely; as a *liberal* donor; the *liberal* founders of a college or hospital. It expresses less than profuse or extravagant.
> 2. Generous; ample; large; as a *liberal* donation; a *liberal* allowance.
> 3. Not selfish, narrow or contracted; catholic; enlarged; embracing other interests than one's own; as *liberal* sentiments or views; a *liberal* mind; *liberal* policy.

Today, that nineteenth-century definition seems to fit most conservatives much more closely than it does those who we identify as "liberals." Apparently, somewhere along the line, the word liberal was hijacked for political purposes. That's the problem with obfuscating definitions and the true meaning of words. You'll note that the word *liberal* sounds much better than what everybody around the world has historically called them before.[2] The new and precise definition of a liberal, in my opinion, is this:

> **Lib·er·al** (noun) a non-conservative; a naïve male or female, or L.G.B.T. (lesbian/gay/bisexual/ transsexual), afflicted with juvenile fantasy euphoria addiction; a person with a genetic predilection for

---

[1] This is according to Noah Webster (1758–1843), who compiled the *American Dictionary of the English Language* in 1828. He read a dissertation entitled "The Supposed Change in the Temperature of Winter" before the Connecticut Academy of Arts and Sciences in 1799. Noah Webster was one of a long line of Websters and should not to be confused with Daniel Webster (1782–1852), who was a U.S. statesman, a lawyer, and a leading American senator from Massachusetts during the period leading up to the Civil War. Daniel Webster's increasingly nationalistic views and his effectiveness as a speaker made him one of the most famous orators and influential Whig leaders of the Second Party System. Daniel Webster (as opposed to Noah Webster) was the author of *The Rights of Neutral Nations in Time of War* (1802), and he was one of the nation's most prominent conservatives. He led the opposition to Democrat Andrew Jackson and the Democratic Party. (Be skeptical of any ugly photos of Daniel Webster that you find on the Internet. They may have been doctored by L.S.D.ers to make him look bad.)

[2] Remember when the leader of the South American country of Venezuela, Hugo Chavez, called President George W. Bush "el diablo"? Maybe Chavez (now deceased) was referring, instead, to himself and his short-lived dictatorship. (See "Projection," page 89.)

anarchy, promiscuity, and illegal drug use that often extends into old age; an immature human being with illogical social views stemming from a diminished capacity to understand what other people are thinking, and thus the world; a socialist/communist (potential traitor); a political puppet.

Anthropology. Today's dysgenic liberals are the unanticipated byproduct of decades of worldwide humanitarian efforts by governments and religious groups. Liberals are the close ancestors of multiracial enslaved populations that included criminals, drug addicts, and prostitutes, who would have done practically anything for fermented grapes, coca leaves, poppies, peyote, marijuana, or food. Liberals bear the genes of the extinct five-foot-three-inch-tall early black-skinned Neanderthal, a slothful, unintelligent hominid who was the object of random miscegenation with prehistoric modern man but who is said not to have survived the last ice age.

Theology. Liberals are followers of religious cults based on fads invented by charismatic con artists; Wiccans, or "witches"; worshippers of Mother Earth, stars, planets, unicorns, pyramids, wild animals, and "pot"; spiritual mediums with crystal balls, shifty-eyed palm readers, and streetwise "channelers" of the dead; (rare) solitary satanic "folks" or cult members with primeval polytheistic worldviews who practice magic (i.e., the *black rites)* or voodoo.

Now, as anyone can clearly see by reading these two definitions, they are very different. That's because each definition applies to very different types of people. One is obviously good, and one is obviously not so good. The first definition of a liberal applies to old-time liberals who had faith in God and believed at least most of what is stated in the *Holy Bible,* whereas the second definition describes the liberals of today. Most of today's liberals appear only to pretend to have faith, for various reasons, some of which are as follows: (1) A religious persona may be good for their political careers because it helps them seem to be normal mainstream citizens; (2) a religious personality may help attract the opposite sex by making them seem caring and compassionate; (3) a religious facade helps hide their true agenda; (4) pretending to be religious or to suddenly "get" religion can help reduce a court judgment or prison sentence, and it can get them released from incarceration more quickly; (5) the contents of the Bible may even help to enhance some other ancient religious belief.

Re: Definition 1: This first group normally only does things that are good for people, but sometimes those things, much to everyone's surprise, turn out to be not so good. Why? Because the things that they do may have hitherto unknown negative long-term consequences.

Re: Definition 2: This second group does things repeatedly (despite protestations from conservatives) that are bad for everyone, even themselves. Why? Because they have an inherent psychosis and are unable to acknowledge any proven fact that conflicts with their—often drug-fueled—reality. For that reason, members of group two are generally unable to honestly and permanently change their opinion about anything that may be detrimental to the long-term well-being of other people, and thus to the *evolution of the entire human race.*

However, most human beings can change their ways.

Part One

Fantasy Addiction Disorder (F.A.D.)

Chapter 1

What's Wrong With Them?

On Psychosis and Miscellaneous Delusions

The word *psychosis* comes from the Greek *psyche,* for mind/soul, and *osis,* for abnormal condition. Psychosis means a severely irregular condition of the mind and is a generic psychiatric term for a mental state that is often described as involving a loss of contact with reality.[3] Those who suffer from a psychosis are said to be *psychotic.* People experiencing psychoses may report hallucinations or delusional beliefs and may exhibit personality changes and thought disorder. Depending on the severity of the psychosis, which of course may range from mild to extreme, the psychosis may involve (1) simply having difficulty with social interaction, (2) some impairment in carrying out daily life activities, and/or (3) episodes of unusual or bizarre behavior.

    A wide variety of central nervous system "diseases," from both external poisons and internal physiological illness, can produce symptoms of psychosis; however, many people have unusual, unshared, distinct experiences of what they perceive to be different realities *without fitting the clinical definition of psychosis.* For example, there are those in the general population who have experienced hallucinations related to religious, paranormal, or extraterrestrial occurrences. That is because the human brain, like a faulty computer, is capable of extraordinary and sometimes inexplicable things. For that reason, it has been argued that a psychosis is simply an extreme state of consciousness that falls beyond the norms experienced by most people. In this view, individuals who are clinically found to be psychotic may simply be having intense or distressing experiences.

---

[3] An example of a psychosis might be the humorous term "Bush derangement syndrome," which, after President Bush left office, was superseded by Sarah Palin hysteria.

Human (D) Evolution

A *delusion* is a fixed belief that is false, fanciful, or derived from deception. Psychiatry defines the term more specifically as a belief that is pathological (i.e., the result of an illness process). Delusions typically occur in the context of neurological or mental illness, although they are not tied to any particular disease and have been found to occur in many pathological states, both physical and mental. However, they are of particular diagnostic importance in psychotic disorders, especially in schizophrenia, paraphrenia, manic episodes of bipolar disorder, and psychotic depression.[4]

Lack of awareness of one's own illness is a mental state called *anosognosia* (for more, see page 69.)

> "Any human guinea pig who voluntarily submits to an experiment that involves artificially induced or pharmaceutically induced peripheral sensory input misperception, and thus symptoms of delusional antisocial thought, speech, and behavior, in a controlled laboratory setting—with medical doctors, pretty registered nurses, and research scientists present—would immediately be convinced beyond a shadow of a doubt that his normal thinking processes are capable of malfunctioning *without him realizing it or even believing that it's possible!* That person would then be capable of understanding that so-called liberals have a genetic mental disorder." —Dr. Marvin Q. Yoickman, Ph.D., head researcher at the Institute of Anti-Psychedelic Sciences, January 31, 2010[5]

Although nonspecific concepts of madness have been around for several thousand years, the psychiatrist and philosopher Karl Jaspers was the first to define the three main criteria for a belief to be considered delusional. In his book *General Psychopathology* (1917), he lists the following:

1. certainty (held with absolute conviction),
2. incorrigibility (not changeable by compelling counterargument or proof to the contrary),

---

[4] "Psychopathological signs and symptoms are distinct from 'normalcy' by degree, not by kind." For example, depression is not simply sadness, paranoia is not simply suspiciousness, and illogic is not simply erroneousness. These "signs and symptoms" reflect extremes of variation that have become dysfunctional because of their abnormal frequency, intensity, or appropriateness (Martin Brüne, *Textbook of Evolutionary Psychiatry,* 2008, Oxford University Press, New York, N.Y., p. 7). Some Democrats reportedly experienced severe depression following the 2000 presidential election, when Gore (D) lost to Bush (R).

[5] The Institute of Anti-Psychedelic Sciences acts as a consultant for the American Heritage Group, a nonprofit organization dedicated to the restoration of financial losses suffered by all legal citizens of the United States of America in the name of "social justice."

3. impossibility or falsity of content (implausible, bizarre, or patently untrue).

These criteria still apply in modern psychiatric diagnoses, and today, the American Psychiatric Association defines a delusion as

> A false belief based on incorrect inference about external reality that is firmly sustained despite what almost everybody else believes and despite what constitutes incontrovertible and obvious proof or evidence to the contrary.[6]

The DSM-IV-Text Revision states:

> Clinicians assessing the symptoms of Schizophrenia in socioeconomic or cultural situations that are different from their own must take cultural differences into account. Ideas that may appear to be delusional in one culture (e.g., sorcery and witchcraft) may be commonly held in another.[7]

The DSM-IV-Text Revision also says:

> Some prodromal and residual symptoms are relatively mild or subthreshold forms of the positive symptoms specified in Criterion A. Individuals may express a variety of unusual or odd beliefs that are not of delusional proportions (e.g., ideas of reference or magical thinking).[8]

Delusions are categorized as *bizarre* or *nonbizarre* and as either mood-congruent or mood-neutral. A bizarre delusion is a delusion that is very strange and completely implausible. An example of a bizarre delusion would be that aliens (from outer space, not Mexico City) have removed the affected person's brain. A nonbizarre delusion is one whose content is *definitely mistaken but is at least possible*. An example of a nonbizarre

---

[6] American Psychiatric Association, *Diagnostic and Statistical Manual of Mental Disorders*, 4th edition, Text Revision (DSM-IV-TR), Washington, D.C., 2000, p. 821.
[7] Ibid., p. 306.
[8] Ibid., p. 302. "Positive symptoms" refers to indications of schizophrenia. Magical thoughts, of course, may revolve around imaginary animals, such as talking unicorns.

delusion would be that the affected person believes that he or she is under constant police surveillance.

A mood-congruent delusion is any delusion whose content is consistent with either a depressive or a manic state. For example, a depressed person may believe that television news anchors highly disapprove of him or her, or a person in a manic state might believe just the opposite and think that he or she is a powerful deity, messiah, or savior of some kind. A mood-neutral delusion does not relate to the sufferer's emotional state. For example, a belief that an extra limb is growing out of the back of one's head is neutral to either depression or mania. According to the DSM-IV-Text Revision:

> Delusions (Criterion A1) are erroneous beliefs that usually involve a misinterpretation of perceptions or experiences. Their content may include a variety of themes (e.g., persecutory, referential, somatic, religious, or grandiose). Persecutory delusions are most common; the person believes he or she is being tormented, followed, tricked, spied on, or ridiculed. Referential delusions are also common; the person believes that certain gestures, comments, passages from books, newspapers, song lyrics, or other environmental cues are specifically directed at him or her. The distinction between a delusion and a strongly held idea is sometimes difficult to make and depends in part on the degree of conviction with which the belief is held despite clear contradictory evidence regarding its veracity.
>
> Although bizarre delusions are considered to be especially characteristic of Schizophrenia, "bizarreness" may be difficult to judge, especially across different cultures. Delusions are deemed bizarre if they are clearly implausible and not understandable and do not derive from ordinary life experiences. An example of a bizarre delusion is a person's belief that a stranger has removed his or her internal organs and has replaced them with someone else's organs without leaving any wounds or scars.[9]

In addition to the above categories, delusions often manifest themselves according to a consistent theme. Although delusions can have any theme, certain themes are more common than others are. The following are five delusions well known to modern psychiatry, but there are many more.

1. *Nihilistic delusion* centers on the nonexistence of oneself or others, or parts of oneself, or all of humanity, and may include the false belief that the world is ending.

---

[9] Ibid., p. 299.

2. *Erotomania* is the false belief that another person is in love with you.[10]

3. *Grandiose delusion* is a belief in which one is convinced that he or she has special powers, talents, or abilities and may actually believe him- or herself to be a famous person.

4. *Persecutory delusion* involves the theme of being followed, harassed, cheated, poisoned, drugged, conspired against, spied upon, attacked, or obstructed.

5. *Religious delusion* is any delusion with a religious or spiritual content; this may be combined with other delusions, such as a grandiose delusion—e.g., the belief that one (the affected person) was chosen by God.[11]

Interesting parallels exist between F.A.D. and schizophrenia. For example, F.A.D. includes delusions, and so does schizophrenia. A delusion is defined as "an idiosyncratic belief or impression that is firmly maintained despite being contradicted by what is generally accepted as reality, typically a symptom of mental disorder." Let us tentatively label liberal delusions "Naïveté Type."

Nonbizarre Delusional Disorder

The following, from the DSM-IV-Text Revision, is important to understand, so it is included here in its entirety:

> The essential feature of Delusional Disorder is the presence of one or more nonbizarre delusions that persist for at least 1 month (Criterion A). A diagnosis of Delusional Disorder is not given if the individual has ever had a symptom presentation that met Criterion A

---

[10] "To love is to cherish. But the act of love should never be referred to as 'making cherish' because the woman will immediately think that you're an idiot." —Billy Bob
[11] For example, a liberal African American "messiah" with a shady birth certificate.

for Schizophrenia (Criterion B). Auditory or visual hallucinations, if present, are not prominent. Tactile or olfactory hallucinations may be present (and prominent) if they are related to the delusional theme (e.g., the sensation of being infested with insects associated with delusions of infestation, or the perception that one emits a foul odor from a body orifice associated with delusions of reference). Apart from the direct impact of the delusions, psychosocial functioning is not markedly impaired, and behavior is neither obviously odd nor bizarre (Criterion C). If mood episodes occur concurrently with the delusions, the total duration of these mood episodes is relatively brief compared to the total duration of the delusional periods (Criterion D). The delusions are not because of the direct physiological effects of a substance (e.g., cocaine) or a general medical condition (e.g., Alzheimer's disease, systemic lupus erythematosus) (Criterion E).

Although the determination of whether delusions are bizarre is considered to be especially important in distinguishing between Delusional Disorder and Schizophrenia, "bizarreness" may be difficult to judge, especially across different cultures. Delusions are deemed bizarre if they are clearly implausible, not understandable, and not derived from ordinary life experiences.... In contrast, nonbizarre delusions involve situations that can conceivably occur in real life (e.g., being followed, poisoned, infected, loved at a distance, or deceived by one's spouse or lover).

Psychosocial functioning is variable. Some individuals may appear to be relatively unimpaired in their interpersonal and occupational roles. In others, the impairment may be substantial and include low or absent occupational functioning and social isolation. When poor psychosocial functioning is present in Delusional Disorder, it arises directly from the delusional beliefs themselves. For example, an individual who is convinced that he will be murdered by "Mafia hit men" may quit his job and refuse to leave his house except late at night and only when dressed in clothes quite different from his normal attire. All of this behavior is an understandable attempt to prevent being identified and killed by his presumed assassins. In contrast, poor functioning in Schizophrenia may be due to both positive and negative symptoms (particularly avolition). Similarly, a common characteristic of individuals with Delusional Disorder is the apparent normality of their behavior and appearance when their delusional ideas are not being discussed or acted on. In general, social and marital functioning are more likely to be impaired than intellectual and occupational functioning.[12]

The DSM-IV-Text Revision also states:

> The differential diagnosis between Schizophrenia and Delusional Disorder rests on the nature of the delusions (nonbizarre in Delusional Disorder) and the absence of other characteristic symptoms of Schizophrenia (e.g., hallucinations, disorganized speech or behavior, or prominent negative symptoms).[13]

In conclusion, only one criterion, that of delusions, is required for a diagnosis of schizophrenia, but only if the delusions are bizarre.

Folie à Plusieurs (The Madness of Many)

There is another delusion that we haven't yet discussed that came to prominence more than a hundred years ago: *folie à deux,* which is French for "a madness shared by two." It's considered a rare psychiatric syndrome in which symptoms of a delusional belief are transmitted from one individual to another. The American Psychiatric Association (APA) refers to it as Shared Psychotic Disorder. The same syndrome shared by more than two people may be called *folie à trios, folie à quatre,* or *folie en famille.* Furthermore, *folie simultanée* describes a situation in which two people who suffer independently from psychosis can influence the content of each other's delusions so that the content becomes identical or strikingly similar.

Do you see where this is leading?

You may be surprised to learn that the field of psychiatry also recognizes another term: *folie à plusieurs,* which means "the madness of many." *Folie à plusieurs* is a communal psychiatric disorder that involves many persons consumed by shared delusional beliefs.

---

[12] American Psychiatric Association, *op. cit.,* pp. 323–324.
[13] Ibid., p. 310.

We've all heard of *mass hypnosis*.[14] Well, liberalism is not exactly mass hypnosis; instead, it is a kind of *mass psychosis* in which the people who are subject to it worldwide structure their entire lives to conform to erroneous convictions.

Liberal grand delusional beliefs require an *unimpeachable* or controlling authority to disseminate and thus reinforce misinformation—say, for instance, a liberal president of the United States of America.[15] They also likely require daily doses of propaganda from a liberal news media. Today, the most important examples of controlling authorities are (1) TV news channels, (2) major news organizations, such as the Associated Press, (3) newspapers, such as the *New York Times*, (4) news reports on Internet browsers, (5) radio news reports, and (6) the president's speechwriters.[16]

"Newspapers can put an idea in ten thousand minds in one day. . . . Television can put an idea in hundreds of millions of minds instantaneously." —*Awake!*[17]

Folie à plusieurs arises when many recipients are willing—and, perhaps, even eager—to share such beliefs. Erroneous ideas, no matter how dishonest, amoral, flawed, and specious, know no bounds and will always find a place to dwell in receptive and/or empty minds.

The A.P.A.'s manual of mental disorders states that a person cannot be diagnosed as being delusional if the belief in question is one "ordinarily accepted by other members of the person's culture or subculture" (e.g., "Poor people are good, and rich people are bad"). It is not clear at what point that a belief considered delusional is dropped from the *folie à* . . . diagnostic category and becomes "legitimate" because of the number of persons holding it. When a large number of people come to believe obviously false things based purely on hearsay,

---

[14] Question: Are liberals more susceptible to hypnosis than conservatives? Has anyone done a study?
[15] Please note that the correct name of our country, the "United States of America," has been used whenever possible throughout this book. The shortened versions, "United States," "U.S.A.," and "U.S.," are also acceptable. However, the abbreviation "US" (that curiously looks a lot like "UN") minimizes our country's importance because instead of being a shortened version of words that have meaning, it becomes trite. Coincidentally, so does the abbreviation "I.Q." The use of "US" should be recognized as just another liberal fad. Hopefully, the perpetually bankrupt *New York Times*, which somehow keeps finding enough cash on hand—or some imaginary liberal money tree—to stay in business, will be able to afford to print the extra dots. It'll require more ink.
[16] To avoid liberal propaganda, most conservatives watch FOX News and *The Sean Hannity Show*, read the "Drudge Report" on the Internet, or read books by Ann Coulter, or listen to *The Rush Limbaugh Show* on AM radio (many other conservative talk shows also come on before and after his, all day long).
[17] *Awake!*, Watchtower Bible and Tract Society of New York, Brooklyn, N.Y., May 22, 1991, pp. 4–5.

those beliefs are not considered clinical delusions by the psychiatric profession; instead, they are labeled *mass hysteria*.[18]

"Washington, D.C., is out of touch with reality." —Anonymous Politicians (3)

The *folie à . . .* delusions are defined as a rare pathological manifestation and are not often discussed in general psychology textbooks, being relatively unknown outside of abnormal psychology, psychiatry, and psychopathology. Aside from the delusional beliefs themselves, *the behavior of those who hold them is usually not otherwise odd or unusual.* This disorder is usually chronic, and individuals seldom seek treatment.

Unspecified Type

The DSM-IV-Text Revision lists six types of delusions as subtypes: (1) Erotomanic, (2) Grandiose, (3) Jealous, (4) Persecutory, (5) Somatic, and (6) Mixed. It also lists one more:

> Unspecified Type. This subtype applies when the dominant delusional belief cannot be clearly determined or is not described in the specific types (e.g., referential delusions without a prominent persecutory or grandiose component).[19]

---

[18] The global-warming scare is one example. FOX: "In fact, global warming is the most widespread mass hysteria in our species' history. . . . In centuries hence the global warming boogeyman will be seen for exactly what it is—The Great Delusion. Future generations will wonder how so many people could have believed something so suicidally ridiculous" ("Global Warming—the Great Delusion," FoxNews.com, February 17, 2012). Another clear example of mass hysteria is the 9/11 Truth Movement, in which adherents claim that the U.S. government was involved in causing the Twin Towers of the World Trade Center to collapse by controlled demolition after al-Qaeda terrorists managed to crash two Boeing 767s into them. Some liberal "Truthers" still believe (erroneously) that former president Bush actually planned the attacks as a pretext to going to war in the Middle East.

[19] American Psychiatric Association, *op. cit.,* p. 325. The delusion widely held by liberals in the United States that "Peace on Earth" can be achieved simply by being nice to our enemies—some would call it naïveté type—would seem to fall into this unspecified category. As someone once said, "You don't get peace by making a V sign with your fingers. You get it by grabbing your enemy in a headlock."

Human (D) Evolution

According to the DSM-IV-Text Revision:

> Social, marital, or work problems can result from the delusional beliefs of Delusional Disorder. Ideas of reference (e.g., that random events are of special significance) are common in individuals with this disorder. Their interpretation of these events is usually consistent with the content of their delusional beliefs. Many individuals with Delusional Disorder develop irritable or dysphoric mood, which can usually be understood as a reaction to their delusional beliefs. Especially with the Persecutory and Jealous Types, marked anger and violent behavior can occur. The individual may engage in litigious behavior, sometimes leading to hundreds of letters of protest to government and judicial officials and many court appearances.[20]

Liberals inarguably hold their views with "delusional intensity," as do people with a delusional disorder. That may be because liberals have a certain hitherto undefined weakness. You see, liberal socialist Democrats (L.S.D.ers, for short) do not seem to listen to their subconscious voices. Instead, they apparently listen only to the voices of their friends. The opinions of others, they frequently treat with matter-of-fact indifference.[21] Anyone who has witnessed the absurd ravings of various Democratic Party[22] politicians, pundits, and operatives can have no doubt about this. Why are people who have the most ridiculous *notions* so unalterably certain of their ideas? Can liberals be accurately diagnosed as simply having a delusional disorder—in other words, a verifiable *psychosis*—or is there something previously unknown to science involved here?

---

[20] Ibid., pp. 325–326. Dysphoric mood is a state of unease or general dissatisfaction with life.

[21] Our halfwhite African American president, Barack Hussein Obama, is a perfect example of matter-of-fact indifference and self-importance. His chosen first name is Swahili, which has its root origin in the Arabic language and means *blessed* (ﻇﻜﺮاﺑﻌﻞ). You don't believe it? Check out About.com.Islam, "What Does Barack Obama's Name Mean?" 2014 --and Microsoft® Translator. Many people in Third World countries are considered blessed if they have half a fried dog-and-cheese sandwich to eat for lunch. (Usually, dill pickles and potato chips are available only for the tourists.) The president's middle name, Hussein, means *good* --which is how an Indonesian dude probably feels the next day if, after eating a stray mongrel, he doesn't contract ptomaine poisoning. The president's last name, Obama, is common in the Dhoulou language of southwestern Kenya and is believed by some Americans --especially Republicans in Congress --to mean *pooh-pooher of everyone and everything*, including the Bill of Rights and the United States Constitution. Incredibly, multiple examples would lead us to believe that Barack Hussein Obama is the first president in American history who, when discussing matters of economics, is virtually 100 percent clueless. President Pooh-Pooh seems to know about as much about capitalism, supply and demand, *laissez-faire*, and the free-market system as Peter Pan knows about soul food.

[22] Although the long-accepted term Democratic Party is used throughout this book, it's actually not a real political party at all. Why? Because the Democratic Party's existence depends primarily on the support of the federal government. Without money from taxpayers, it wouldn't survive. Maybe it's just a different *kind* of party.

Chapter 2

Are They Using Drugs?

Pro-choice Drug Addiction, California Style

The almost religious-like affinity that liberal socialist Democrats (L.S.D.ers) have for illegal drugs, notably cannabis, is well known, documented, and beyond dispute, especially for anyone familiar with the '60s and all of the slow-talking, dull-eyed sluggards with baggies full of marijuana and assorted medicine-cabinet pills.[23] If conservatives were similarly enthralled with alcoholic beverages, they would carry flasks of whiskey in their back pockets, liquor stores would pop up on every street corner, and beer would be sold at K-Mart in vending machines. Tetrahydrocannabinol (THC), the active ingredient found in cannabis, is not the only psychoactive chemical that some liberals worship like a god. There are many more: Addictions of all types and kinds run rampant today in the great state of California. Drugs such as cocaine, heroin, methamphetamine, and marijuana are smuggled into that new Mecca of displaced Mexicans from—where else?—Mexico. (Note: Ordinary low-grade Mexican marijuana should never ever be confused with premium *medical marijuana*, which is now legal in many states and can be enhanced medicinally by liberals, who lace it with PCP, cocaine, methamphetamine, or pencil shavings and/or dip it in embalming fluid.)[24]

---

[23] Most left-wing loons prefer smoking marijuana. It's their drug of choice. Why? Because it can make them oblivious to the world and they can carry joints in their wallets. But why do they need oblivion? Don't they *like other people?*

[24] "Progressive" liberal Third World attitudes continue to spread unchecked and have even infected our nation's capital. In Washington, D.C., any resident with a one-hundred-dollar bill can apply for a medical marijuana card and legally buy from soon-to-open dispensaries in the city ("D.C. Residents Can Apply for Pot Card," WTOP, Washington's only all-news radio station, June 13, 2013). According to the application form, no Social Security number is required—which, like voting in our presidential elections, makes it easier for illegal Mexican aliens, convicted felons, and Chinese tourists. People who qualify as poor can file with twenty-five bucks.

Human (D) Evolution

Crystal meth and marijuana are also produced and cultivated in large quantities within California state lines. The San Diego/Los Angeles area, for example, is the principle transshipment zone and distribution center for a variety of illegal drugs smuggled across the border by the squat, crudely tattooed descendants of Spaniard/Indian/African/Mayan peasants and slaves whose personal habits and contraband are destined for widespread distribution in major metropolitan areas across the United States. Unfortunately, one of the most difficult things to find in the City of Guys Named Angel is the fence for the zoo. But don't worry about it, they all *love* one another.

The northern half of the state is said to be riddled with rural methamphetamine laboratories, and methamphetamine use is considered the major threat, although heroin remains the preferred drug of abuse by the (sometimes shockingly nude) inhabitants of San Francisco. Heroin and crack cocaine are also very big in Oakland, and various methamphetamine recipes (no doubt available at libraries and most local bookstores) provide powerful drugs that are consumed in large quantities in and around the capital city of Sacramento. The increased availability of high-purity heroin that can be snorted and used without the discomfort or inconvenience of standard paraphernalia—tourniquet, spoon, syringe, and bent dirty needles—encourages new younger drug users to try it, whereupon they quickly become addicted.

California law enforcement officials regularly encounter ethnic West African and Southeast Asian nationals (often referred to as "tar babies" and "chinks") involved in the distribution and transportation of Asian heroin, but Mexican black-tar heroin is most often what is seized throughout the state.[25] Methamphetamine is the primary drug threat, even though an ample supply of LSD is available because of the number of supplementary hidden laboratories operating in remote areas of the north.[26] Northern California has been known to be the center of LSD production since the 1960s, when the drug's popularity among members of the counterculture may have helped protesters endure long hours of heat, thirst, hunger, and boredom by providing them with vivid sexual hallucinations while they demonstrated against the Vietnam War.

Today, "mind-blowing" marijuana is cultivated by California's upper class (to use the term loosely), along with other members of the Democratic Party intelligentsia, in secret, beautiful, and elaborate hydroponic gardens throughout the

---

[5] Southeast Asian heroin is produced in Burma and shipped to the United States from China (CIA.gov, "Heroin Movement Worldwide, Southeast Asia," January 3, 2012).

[26] LSD, lysergic acid diethylamide, first synthesized in 1938, was wildly popular with liberal hippies. In fact, many members of the sixties' magic-mushroom subculture claimed spiritual benefit similar to that obtained from attending a church service—by running down neighborhood streets at night, butt-naked, glassy-eyed, and shrieking.

state.²⁷ Of course, not all drug use is done in seclusion. Left-wing "shotgunning," for example, is a procedure in which two marijuana smokers exchange big lungfuls of smoke and one of them, perhaps, inhales the breath of a feral Mendocino County hippie who hasn't brushed his teeth since 1984. Reportedly, another big problem in liberal circles is the illegal sale and distribution of prescription drugs by health-care professionals and other licensed workers, so now you know why, in many parts of the world, drug smugglers are hung by their necks until dead.²⁸

> "Marijuana cookies are what [liberal] child molesters often use on kids." —Anonymous Woman Police Officer

Unbelievably, there are 1,623 drug-and-alcohol rehabilitation centers listed for the state of California.²⁹ It is a national disgrace! But on the plus side, the rehab centers, medical-marijuana head shops, and hospital ambulance services are a reliable source of much-needed tax revenue. Luckily, "rehab loans"—normally advertised for renovating houses—are now available throughout California and to any Hollywood cocaine addict with a verifiable job history and a few personal references from cocaine-using friends.

Notable Liberal Quote:

"A preseedent like Pooh-Pooh Bear don't hav'ta worry 'bout bein' whachacall in-peached. He too entertainin'! It kinda like watchin' a po' little Monko-loid chil' try ta put a square peg inna roun' hole or somepin'. Who'd want dat snowy beef jerky Biten ta be pres'dent, ennaway? Things'd get even wourse 'cause he dumber! Do he be a Haaarvard graduate, too? Maybe we oughta elect a plain ol' donkey ta be pres'dent, den we'd all be glued to da TV set when he give a

---

[27] Northern California's Emerald Triangle is now said to be the marijuana capital of the United States. The pot business in Mendocino County, for example, much of it now legal under state law, makes up close to two-thirds of the local economy, generating up to $1 billion a year for those who haven't moved away. As much as 60 percent of that county's populace is thought to be involved in the marijuana industry. The pot is often shipped via FedEx and U.P.S. (CNBC.com, "Marijuana Inc., Inside America's Pot Industry," January 23, 2009).
[28] This fact may also help answer the often-asked question "Why are there no Democrats in the Middle East?" —Mr. Ed, the talking horse editor
[29] Treatment-centers.net, state-by-state directory, n.d. To its credit, Quincy, California, has only one treatment center. Los Angeles, on the other hand, has an incredible 136.

speech! He sure a lot funnier dan Preseedent Pooh-Pooh—and a whole lot smarter, too! Uh donkey don't needa tellee-prompter to tell 'im what ta say, do he? *Hee-haw. Hee-haw.* We cud even tie strings to da donkey's hands 'n' feet and see if we cud git 'im to sign Pooh-Pooh-Cares agin or some udder stupid law dat makes all duh white people so mis'rable dat dey don' gimme no tips. Pooh-Pooh Bear and I are ol' friends! He prob'ly don't remember me, but I'm da nigga he din't ever wanna play wit or fucks aron wit 'cause he knew I uh frienda da Hawaii-five-oh po-leece. Heh."
—Anonymous African American comedian

Actually, things have changed for the better. Today, when a man or woman enters a rehab center, it's no longer the source of ignominy, shame, and embarrassment that it was years ago—back when people in nice restaurants didn't scratch between their legs. Now, even periodic lifetime visits to drug rehab centers, especially for major Hollywood celebrities (or the beautiful creeple), is considered to be no more than a routine choice on par with that of seeing a hairstylist, rather than the humiliation that it ought to be. Of course, it's not all bad. Now, more quality time can be spent by the rich and famous (but mentally non-proportionate) in relaxing—with a severe case of the shakes—poolside at wonderful luxury resorts like Serene Center Long Beach, Hope by the Sea, Luxury Drug Rehab, and Sunset Malibu. (Welcome to the twenty-first-century liberal version of civilized society: trembling, sweating, empty-headed dopes covered with hives, constantly vomiting up their prescription methadone.)

It should come as no surprise that the poppy is California's state flower—but, thankfully, it is not the same type grown in Afghanistan. California is known as the Golden State, although there has been some talk of its annexation by Mexico after that nickname is officially changed to "IOU Territory." Here's a better idea: Instead of Mexico taking over the *Estados Unidos,* why doesn't the United States of America just take over *México* (or "M xihco") instead and turn it into a parking lot?

California is also the birthplace of our thirty-seventh president, Richard Nixon (R), who resigned from that office in Anglo-Saxon (people of no color?) disgrace, as is customary, when faced with impeachment for his connection to a single break-in by operatives at the Democratic National Committee (D.N.C.) headquarters. Apparently, President Nixon, a man somewhat familiar with the ideology and behavior of the Left Coast crowd, felt that, for the benefit of mankind, liberals had to be stopped at all costs. Many people thought of Nixon as a "crook" because of his demeanor, but still, most of us liked him—or at least tried to—because he had conservative family values and only did things that were in the best interest of the United States of America.[30] The only mistake he made, as many people said at the time, was in being caught—a well-known fact that you probably will not find mentioned today in any Common Core-approved history books.

Anyway, that's enough about California. Let's move on to a discussion of *liberal family values*.

Left-wing "Leisure" Drugs

Opiates, such as morphine, heroin, and codeine cough syrup (referred to as "purple drank" by long-haired unshaven lopsided hicks and other odd-looking liberal country bumpkins), directly stimulate chemical receptors in the brain that dissolve pain and cause a person to feel relaxed and blissful. Stimulant drugs (or "uppers"), such as cocaine, amphetamine, ephedrine, nicotine, caffeine, and Ecstasy, bind to other chemical receptors in the brain that cause a sense of mental alertness, confidence, and well-being.[31] Sedative drugs ("downers"), such as benzodiazepines and barbiturates, work on yet another chemical receptor in the brain and replace anxiety with tranquility. Scientists do not yet know precisely *which* effects of alcohol on

---

[30] Although Nixon initially escalated America's involvement in the Vietnam War, he subsequently ended U.S. involvement by 1973. Nixon's visit to the People's Republic of China in 1972 opened communications between the two nations and eventually led to the normalization of diplomatic relations. He initiated détente and the Anti-Ballistic Missile Treaty with the Soviet Union the same year. Domestically, his administration generally embraced policies that transferred power from Washington to the states. Among other things, he launched initiatives to fight cancer and illegal drugs, imposed wage and price controls, enforced desegregation of Southern schools, implemented environmental reforms, and introduced legislation to reform healthcare and welfare. Though he presided over the lunar landings beginning with Apollo 11, he replaced manned space exploration with shuttle missions. He was reelected by a landslide in 1972.

[31] Ecstasy, or MDMA (3,4-Methylenedioxymethamphetamine), is suspected to cause neurotoxic damage to the central nervous system and is criminalized in most countries under a United Nations agreement. Hundreds of deaths have occurred, too numerous to mention other than that of a fifteen-year-old girl who sank into a coma and suffered organ failure in June 2010 at the Los Angeles Memorial Coliseum during the 14th Annual Electric Daisy Carnival. Experts at the Multidisciplinary Association for Psychedelic Studies, based in Santa Cruz, California, stated that the drug was "sufficiently safe," apparently not taking into account the mental condition of the liberal consumer or the possibility of street lab impurities (MAPS, "Research: MDMA," 2011). Ecstasy is also available online—at the time of this writing—at numerous foreign-based Web sites catering to any kid with his parent's credit card number and who can use a keyboard. The stimulant effects of Ecstasy pills can include involuntary teeth-clenching, nausea, muscle tremors, blurred vision, chills, and sweating, as well as seizures, and Ecstasy can enable users to dance for extended periods before crapping in their baggy pants.

the brain cause people to feel relaxed and giddy—or for that matter, to suddenly become loud, obnoxious, and in-your-face, gutturally cheering, "OGGUPIE WALL STREET!"[32] The precise long-term physical and mental results—i.e., permanent side effects—of so-called leisure drug mixing are unknown but highly suspected not only by all conservative Americans but by the vast majority of foreign doctors, researchers, and scientists throughout the world.

Notable Liberal Quotes:

First e-mail: "Our Presiden Obama's relative, a nice African people, whose name I can't say or spell work at a liquor store. That's kinda nice. I also sorta heard that you kin make a long island Ice T with whisky. I wondering if the president of our USA had ever tried to chew a hole pack of Kool menthol or did he ever taste a bottle Jeremiah Weed. I were only wondering. I jus wanna make friends with peoples thats all. Heh, heh." —Walliesmileyface123456

Second e-mail: "Why didn't you mail me back my Email? What do you think I is some kinda NUT??? Never mind. Neder mind. I don't wanna be your friend afterall. Goodbye forever. You're never gonna hear from me again. I can promise you that. This is it." —Walliesmileyface123456

Third e-mail: "You MoTHrfukKA. I'm gonna FuKC up you!!!!!!! . . . ." —Walliesmileyface123456

Fourth e-mail: "Okay, oaky, okay, Im sorry I did that can you just please load me some money so I can buy my meds. I promised never to bother you again." —Walliesmileyface123456

---

[32] Additional information on hardcore drugs will be forthcoming and made available to the public at some future date.

<u>Fifth e-mail:</u> "It's been all most halve a day and I stilllll have not heard back from yu. Please talk to me before I start crying. On my salty crackers. I already ate the free soup I got." —Walliesmileyface123456

<u>Sixth e-mail:</u> "I'm gonna either KILL You or IM GoING to KiLL Myself dead right now. Maybe I making a great big BOMB or something. Don't you talk to strangers? Huh? What do you tink I am human trash?" —Walliesmileyface123456

<u>Seventh e-mail:</u> [Blank] —Walliesmileyface123456

The following day, a smoldering human corpse was reportedly discovered in a small garage apartment in New York City. The man appeared to have died from natural causes: spontaneous combustion. All that was left of his belongings was a small piece of his voter registration card, his gray ponytail, and some homemade plastic marijuana pipes. His desktop computer was melted. Traces of methamphetamine residue were found in his oven. His name was Theodorus Q. Abraham Wallieskurinsky, Jr. He was born and raised in Six Forks, Massachusetts. He was a distinguished 65-year-old retired professor of sociology and a graduate of an Ivy League community college. He was a liberal socialist Democrat beloved and respected by all who knew him. Some even considered him a kind of genius. He was a perfect example of a *left-wing loon.*

And then, of course, there are the so-called "designer" drugs. (To be continued.)

Human (D) Evolution

More-on Drugs

All other drugs, including hallucinogens, marijuana, and volatile substances such as women's hair spray, fingernail-polish remover, or premium gasoline, cause users to feel high in some manner, so users are eager to get back in their cars or on their motor scooters or skateboards and go buy more.[33] (So far, no reports have been received from San Luis Obispo of anyone inhaling uranium dust.) Most, if not all, drugs also stimulate the release of the chemical *dopamine* in parts of the brain that reinforce habitual behavior. Dopamine produces the desired effect of euphoria, calmness, or relief from anxiety. When such a brain system is established over time, it becomes very difficult for the person to stop "using." In laboratory experiments, for example, mice will stop eating and drinking to continue pushing a lever that electronically stimulates those areas of the brain that produce pleasurable dopamine. This experiment, apparently, has not yet been duplicated on any human subject despite all of the eager volunteers at Berkeley.

And then, of course, there is *euphoric recall*.[34]

In their book, *Darwinian Psychiatry*, authors Michael McGuire and Alfonso Troisi state:

> For persons who lack social skills, and who are addicted to drugs influencing the opioid system, such as heroin, the self-induction of pleasure by means of drugs may be a way of attenuating persistent feelings of personal isolation (Panksepp, Siviy, and Normansell, 1985). Clinically, the opposite point also holds: Persons who are addicted to pleasure-inducing drugs are less inclined to engage in bonding behavior than persons not using these drugs. For example, new mothers who are addicted to opiates bond less intensely with their offspring. These findings permit the following interpretations: Endogenous opioids are part of the neurochemical reward system for social attachment (Schino and Troisi, 1992);

---

[33] According to California Highway Patrol (C.H.P.) data, nearly 1000 deaths and injuries each year—in that state alone—are blamed directly on drugged-up drivers. Law enforcement puts much of the blame on medical marijuana use ("More Accidents with Drugged Drivers as Medical Marijuana Use Grows," The Blaze, July 3, 2011). Of course, a serious injury may also occur if a user leaps off the roof of a medical marijuana clinic while tied to a kite string—especially if he/she accidentally lands on one of the Girl Scouts out front who are now, reportedly, selling cookies.

[34] The regular use of alcohol or any other mood-altering chemical substance by either an addict or non-addict increases that person's capacity for *euphoric recall*. (For more, see page 58.)

the pleasurable quality of optimal social relationships is associated with endogenous opioid release; and the subjective feelings of distress associated with minimally adaptive or undesired social events (e.g., social ostracism) are associated with CNS opioid dysregulation. The street drug "ecstasy" might also be mentioned here. Users report that it increases a sense of general social affiliation as contrasted to dyadic affiliation, and this feeling of "group-belonging" is one of the principle attractions of the drug.[35]

Perceptive readers may have begun to discern that with liberals, as with any other animal that seeks safety in numbers—sardines, flamingos, lemmings—there is really nothing more important than group belonging. Popularity rules liberals; peer popularity in a saloon or crack house rules liberals absolutely.[36] A liberal's every word and deed is calculated not with logic but with the primary goal of social acceptance by the multicultural community (i.e., herd). It is almost as though they're all reading from the same bad Hollywood script or misguided behavior instruction book. With liberals, genuine independent thought is rare, perhaps nonexistent. That is why the opinion of any Democratic Party politician or pundit should probably always be treated, at the very least, as highly suspect, if not simply ignored and dismissed altogether.

Now, let us return to the subject of liberals' *Cannabaceae* family values.

Because, by definition, illegal drugs are grown, or manufactured, and purchased *illegally*, those involved in their sale, distribution, and abuse (i.e., "users") are more likely to have criminal tendencies and thus *asocial* or *antisocial* personality traits. Rates of drug and alcohol addiction are three to four times higher among the mentally ill than in people considered normal. Liberals, predictably, will scoff, but the overuse of so-called recreational drugs, including foot-long marijuana cigars, goes hand in hand with psychotic disorders, and this fact is well known in the psychiatric community.[37]

You don't believe it? Read on.

---

[35] Michael McGuire and Alfonso Troisi, *Darwinian Psychiatry*, 1998, Oxford University, New York, N.Y., p. 113. Dr. McGuire is a professor of psychiatry and a member of the Brain Research Institute at the University of California, Los Angeles. Dr. Troisi is a research psychiatrist in the Medical School of the University of Rome, Tor Vergata.

[36] Some drug-addled liberals manage to shake their addictions, whereas others are unable.

[37] If CBS News is to be believed (and it is debatable), recreational drug users have even been known to eliminate themselves from the human gene pool (CBS Detroit, "Police: Man Rips off Penis During Drug-Fueled Craze," June 24, 2013). Reportedly, he had eaten some unidentified mushrooms.

The A.P.A.'s DSM-IV-Text Revision says:

Psychotic Disorders can occur in association with intoxication with the following classes of substances: alcohol; amphetamine and related substances; cannabis; cocaine; hallucinogens; inhalants; opioids (meperidine); phencyclidine and related substances; sedatives, hypnotics, and anxiolytics; and other or unknown substances.[38]

In addition, the following two diagnoses appear in Appendix F of the same A.P.A. manual under "Numerical Listing of DSM-IV-TR Diagnoses and Codes":

292.11 Amphetamine-Induced Psychotic Disorder, With Delusions[39]
292.11 Cannabis-Induced Psychotic Disorder, With Delusions

Why this fact is not more widely publicized and discussed is beyond all human understanding. Illegal drugs, including marijuana—and even some F.D.A.-approved over-the-counter drugs—are indisputably a public health hazard, especially when they are *used at the same time*.[40] You see, when drugs—both legal and illegal—are combined, they can have unpredictable adverse side effects.[41] This is a very bad thing for everyone, liberals and conservatives alike. Genetics always plays

---

[38] American Psychiatric Association, *op. cit.*, p. 340.

[39] Amphetamines (speed) have a high risk of psychological dependence, and regular users may develop—without realizing it—delusions, hallucinations, and feelings of paranoia that can progress into *permanent* paranoid psychosis (i.e., symptoms of full-blown paranoid schizophrenia). Methamphetamines can have a similar effect.

[40] A surprising example is nasal spray and beer. Ordinary beer can shrink the sinuses, making it difficult to breathe. Nasal sprays such as oxymetazoline, which are used to open the sinuses, can also cause "psychological disturbances; prolonged psychosis (e.g., paranoia, terror, delusions)" (eAnswers, Facts & Comparisons®, "Nasal Decongestants: Adverse Reactions," Wolters Kluwer Health, 2010, www.factsandcomparisons.com/facts-comparisons-Online.aspx). "Unfortunately, sleeplessness is another side effect of nasal sprays --and both alcohol and nasal sprays can be addictive. That may be one reason why so many people take sleeping pills. It's an endless cycle. All drugs cause problems that other drugs must be used to cure." --Anonymous pharmacist

[41] "Why are consumers being subjected to so many pharmaceutical ads on television that use music, artwork, glitz, glamour, and special effects to make prescription drugs seem like they're wonderful? Every man-made drug has a negative side effect. In fact, man-made drugs don't belong in the human body any more than apple juice belongs in a car engine." --A. D. C. Impersonator

a role in a person's susceptibility to various drugs' side effects, which can sometimes prove to be devastating. But whenever there are enormous profits to be made, big political contributions follow, and so does government corruption.

> "The reason that some pharma companies don't print the worst possible side effects on the packages of over-the-counter drugs they manufacture is that they sell more of their product that way. They make such incredible amounts of money that they disregard the cost of any future lawsuits, or lobbying, or presidential campaign donations. It's merely the cost of doing business." —Bill

Maybe one day, the U.S. Congress will put a stop to this problem. Nevertheless, the politicization, ignorance, functional incompetence, and lack of respect for the American public—let's just be nice and call it "pharmaceutical correctness"—has taken hold of the F.D.A. According to *The Wall Street Journal*:

> A group of scientists at the U.S. Food and Drug Administration on Wednesday sent a letter to President-elect Barack Obama's transition team pleading with him to restructure the agency, saying managers have ordered, intimidated and coerced scientists to manipulate data in violation of the law.[42]

But there's more. According to CBS News:

> FDA managers who have failed to protect the American public, who have violated laws, rules, and regulations, who have suppressed or altered scientific or technological findings and conclusions, who have abused their power and authority, and who have engaged in illegal retaliation against those who speak out, have not been held accountable and remain in place.[43]

And according to the *New York Times*:

---

[42] "FDA Scientists Ask Obama to Restructure Drug Agency," *The Wall Street Journal*, January 8, 2009.
[43] "FDA 'Corruption' Letter Authenticated: Lawyers, Start Your Engines!" CBS News, MoneyWatch, March 12, 2010.

Members of Congress, an internal F.D.A. whistleblower and prominent medical journals have said the agency is incapable of uncovering the perils of drugs that have been approved and are in wide distribution.[44]

The use of legal or illegal drugs can also indirectly affect people who do not even use them. The shooting of Arizona Congresswoman Gabrielle Giffords by a twenty-two-year-old kid described as a "left-wing pothead" is a typical example.[45] The major role that illegal drugs play in *causing*—or simply aggravating—serious mental disorders seems almost to be a closely guarded secret. But why? You would think this would be a major topic of concern among our overly "compassionate" liberal friends, especially those who work in the television news media and whose self-appointed job it is to look out for the public's welfare. Why isn't MSNBC, for example, hashing out ways to fix, or crank down, smack around, and smoke out all of the inarguably dangerous illegal drug users among their swaying, dull-faced, half-lidded-eye viewers?[46] The degree of liberal propaganda on MSNBC has now become a source of humor even among that television station's liberal media peers.[47] All they would have to do is provide a little more info about the mental health side effects of psychoactive chemicals. It would certainly serve the public better than them constantly denigrating popular conservative females.

Notable Liberal Quote:

"My advice to people today is as follows: If you take the game of life seriously, if you take your nervous system seriously, if you

---

[44] "At F.D.A., Strong Drug Ties and Less Monitoring," the *New York Times* Health, December 6, 2004.
[45] James King, "Jared Loughner, Alleged Shooter in Gabrielle Giffords Attack, Described by Classmate as 'Left-wing Pothead,'" *Phoenix New Times*, January 8, 2011. Rep. Giffords (D-Arizona) was shot in the head and lived; a federal judge was murdered; five bystanders, including a child, were killed; and thirteen others were wounded. Loughner reportedly had been using a hallucinogenic drug, salvia—from the psychoactive plant *Salvia divinorum*, which can cause episodes that mimic a psychosis ("Jared Loughner Used Legal Hallucinogen Salvia," *International Business Times*, January 18, 2011).
[46] MSNBC, by the way, stands for "Make sure nobody believes conservatives."
[47] When the liberal media puts men and women known to be villainous in the best light possible on television, and even makes them out to be celebrities—which, of course, they aren't—such people and others who resemble them in physical appearance and/or attitude immediately become attractive to the opposite sex, which markedly increases their breeding capabilities. The same thing happens when the liberal media props up losers and tries to make them look like winners. Why do members of the liberal media do this? Don't they know the difference between *good* and *evil*? (Maybe they just don't care.)

take your sense organs seriously, if you take the energy process seriously, you must turn on, tune in, and drop out." —Dr. Timothy Leary (1920–1996), writer, psychologist, 1960s counterculture icon, and campaigner for psychedelic drug research and use[48]

"Drop out" of what? Junior high school? Is there anyone over the age of sixteen who does not recognize this for what it is: *left-wing liberal hogwash?*

Euphoria as a Left-wing Way of Life

Mania is defined as a "mental illness marked by periods of great excitement, euphoria, delusions, and over-activity." Euphoria is one of the characteristic features of mania. When experiencing mania, many will drink or use drugs to enhance the euphoria.[49] Euphoria is a good feeling, a feeling of being on top of the world. A person naturally feels euphoric in certain circumstances: when he or she is falling in love, or when spiritually inspired, or when something wonderful happens, like finding his car keys and his pipe right before a job interview. With euphoria, a person *feels* optimistic, confident, and cheerful. He interprets things in a positive manner. He *feels* generous and loving. Everyone seems to be his friend. He may reach out to strangers. He may even think he looks better than ever. It is as though he poured himself a glass of water and took a *happy* pill.

Drug intoxication can also cause euphoria. Some drugs and hallucinogens can induce a euphoric feeling of being at one with humanity, or the center of the universe, or indistinguishable from God (in which case, a net may be required). Other drugs induce a blissful or lethargic state. Essentially all substances of abuse cause some variety of euphoria, some sort of high.

Euphoria is the *opposite of depression*. Euphoria is also one of the early signs that mania is developing. Psychiatrists refer to this stage as hypomania because it is not yet serious enough to be considered mania. This is a pleasant state to be in, so

---

[48] What Leary said, of course, is bullshit. President Nixon called Leary "the most dangerous man alive" (*The War on Drugs: An International Encyclopedia*, 1999, ABC-CLIO, Santa Barbara, California, p. 118).

[49] Sometimes, the things people do to themselves with illegal drugs are difficult to comprehend.

it is no surprise that people rarely seek help. Generally, a person who is experiencing euphoria will not be troubled by it at all and will probably resist having it treated, which is perfectly understandable. After all, who wants to feel less carefree and happy?

> "Liberals live in a child's soap bubble." —Angela Zilverburg

Miscellaneous Marijuana Facts (a Compendium)

1. Marijuana makes ugly, smelly dopers with red eyes and dull smiles walk around with their legs spread wide apart so that they don't lose their balance and fall down in a pile of dog shit.

2. So-called "mind-blowing" marijuana can affect a user's unborn children, who may grow up to be "bad seeds" and set the house on fire while everyone is sleeping.

3. Never, ever, trust a marijuana smoker to pack your parachute. You may die screaming.

4. Probably the biggest problem with marijuana is that it makes dull, stupid people more dull and more stupid (i.e., "tetrahydrocannabinol dudes").

5. Buying marijuana benefits members of Mexican drug cartels who have decapitated tourists.

6. Marijuana is called a "gateway drug" to the use of other, more dangerous, drugs, and from there to homosexuality, bestiality, incest, and pedophilia.

7. Most conservative adults don't realize this, but the marijuana available today is said to be "ten times as potent" as it was in the 1960s, so it is much more addictive and liable to make users sick.

8. Some female marijuana smokers will break up with their lovers if they find somebody else with better "weed."

9. Some male marijuana smokers never have to pay for their drugs, as long as their female love interests are willing to turn tricks.

10. Marijuana smokers who ride choppers are not really the best guys for women to date or marry because, chances are, the women are either going to end up widows or rolling around in wheelchairs.

11. Some marijuana is so intoxicating now that a smoker will cough and hack for days. That is one way that prospective employers spot users who may die in six to eight months.

12. Always be careful who you kiss. With the price of marijuana getting higher and higher, hippies and their one-night stands may soon take to smoking dried animal feces.

Chapter 3

Why Aren't They Like Us?

Don't Worry, "Be Happy"?

Even psychiatrists can find it difficult to distinguish a patient's abnormal delusional beliefs from normal but perhaps unusual beliefs. People tend to be most *irrational* when thinking about and discussing topics that are very emotional, such as their weaknesses, hopes, or desires, or people they love or admire.[50] Sometimes, abnormal beliefs are referred to as *fantasies*. Fantasy is defined as "the faculty or activity of imagining things that are impossible or improbable; the product of this faculty or activity; a fanciful mental image, typically one that reflects a person's conscious or unconscious wishes; an idea with no basis in reality." When a normal person discusses his fantasies with others, he can usually accept realistic feedback. That is because normal people are able to apply logic to determine whether their fantasies are realistic or just wishful thinking—or a dream. That is the difference between fantasy and delusion: A delusion persists in spite of all feedback: facts, figures, expert opinion, and the like. The process of testing a person's belief to see if it responds to evidence and rational criticism is called reality testing, and anyone who watches the evening news regularly knows that the vast majority of devout liberal pundits, guest speakers, and hosts—nearly 100 percent of them—simply can't pass it.

---

[50] "Don't count on rationality with the Democrats." —Charles Krauthammer, Pulitzer prize-winning syndicated columnist, political commentator, and former psychiatrist. He said this in his appearance on *The O'Reilly Factor,* February 17, 2010. Krauthammer earned an M.D. from Harvard Medical School in 1975 and worked as a psychiatrist at Massachusetts General Hospital. His psychiatric work, referenced twelve times in *Manic-Depressive Illness,* is currently the standard textbook for bipolar disease. Bipolarism is marked by alternating periods of elation and depression—much like President Obama's face during his 2014 State of the Union address. (He looked like Daffy Duck on psychiatric medication.)

John Hayberry

Moron Liberal Fantasizing

Liberal fantasy is a preconceived notion.[51] It doesn't require any imagination. It's the liberal version of what is good and bad, right and wrong. In other words, it's whatever makes a liberal happy. You see, all liberals have the ability to think, but apparently only some of them have the ability to imagine. Liberals rarely foresee anything bad happening, so they are not often, if ever, bothered by any predictions by conservative Americans of dire consequences—until they happen. Liberals, in general, just don't seem to worry very much about anything that hasn't happened yet, even if what's going to happen is as obvious to other people as the nose on their own face. So that's why liberals can be so dangerous. That's also why, when bad things do occur, liberals often act so surprised. But it's only when something awful happens and people start complaining about it that liberals even begin to think like normal human beings. You see, liberals are *reactionary*. That means that they only start to understand *why* bad things happen *after* the bad things occur. Liberals apparently also have a very short memory, because they tend to forget what things they have done very quickly—usually after only a few months. That is why liberals do not ever seem to know what's going to happen next to themselves or to anyone else. Liberals also tend to speak in puzzling tongues—called Liberalspeak, or political correctness—without ever knowing, apparently, what they look like to others or what others think about them. The most foolish of liberals often speak idiotically, repeating themselves, seemingly without realizing how ridiculous they look.[52]

As we know, pets can sometimes read human beings' body language. Some smart pets can even read the expressions on human beings' faces, but their abilities are very limited. Many liberals appear to be the same way. Why, half the time, they just do not seem to know what's going on at all. In fact, some liberals are so bad off that they speak and gesture with wide eyes and jerky movements much like

---

[51] "Fantasy is their reality." —Rush Limbaugh. He is a nationally known conservative and bestselling author who has the highest-rated talk-radio program in the country. It airs on Premiere Radio Networks and is broadcast at over 600 stations nationwide (AM, 12–3 p.m. EST). He comes from a family of lawyers and calls himself America's Truth Detector. A November 2008 poll by Zogby International found that he is the *most trusted news personality* in the United States of America.

[52] Many liberal politicians love to talk automatically by moving their lips and tongues and vibrating their vocal chords.

automatons—especially after they all voted together for the (Un)Affordable Care Act, then announced, crying with despair, *"Oh, no, we made a big mistake!"*[53]

They are like the stringed terra-cotta figurines in ancient Greek marionette shows.[54]

Political Puppetry

by Charles Graveley

Puppetry is a form of *showbiz* that involves the manipulation of puppets, marionettes, dolls, and dummies for various purposes. Puppetry is very ancient, and its aboriginal history is not completely known. Primitive puppetry is believed to have originated more than 5,000 years ago.[55] Puppets are some of the oldest man-made objects in the world. Ancient Greek terra-cotta puppet dolls have been found from the fourth and fifth centuries B.C. The Greek word for "puppets" is   , or *neurospasta*, which literally means "string-pulling," from *nervus*, meaning either sinew, tendon, muscle, string, or wire, and from *span*, to pull. Aristotle referenced pulling strings to control heads, hands and eyes, shoulders and legs. Archaeologists have unearthed terra-cotta dolls dating back to 2500 B.C. with detachable heads capable of manipulation by strings. Evidence also exists that puppets were used in Mesopotamia and Egypt, when string-operated human figurines of wood were manipulated to perform the toiling action of kneading bread. The Greek puppets, made of brownish-red clay, had moving limbs that lifted up

---

[53] One thing you can be sure of is that the current liberal Democratic administration is going to throw away as much taxpayer money as it can to its liberal Democratic supporters via Obamacare before the president eventually leaves office, especially to all multicultural shysters with the abbreviation "Dr." in front of their names. Is it just a coincidence that free medical information that included home remedies for common ailments has now all but disappeared from the Internet? For some reason, the Web sites are suddenly charging fees. Why? So neighborhood witch doctors will have more patients?

[54] Which also used fake Greek columns.

[55] "Puppets can probably be traced back to some types of religious ceremonies, as many ancient cultures would use figurines that could be moved in the worship of their gods" (Thinkquest.org, "The Global History of Puppets," Bibliography). Human slaves were probably used for such ceremonies prior to the advent of puppetry.

when a string was pulled. (Many of today's political puppets also have mouths that open and close, as though *imitating* a normal person when he or she tells the truth.) Hieroglyphs describe "walking statues" being used in Ancient Egyptian religious dramas. Archaeologists who have studied ancient Egypt and China have found the remains of puppets. The Egyptian puppets, found in tombs, were wire-controlled articulated puppets made of clay and ivory. The Chinese puppets were made from the remains of animals: donkey, sheep, water buffalo, or fish skin. Within some ancient cultures, puppet societies existed that, for some reason, were very secretive and exclusive. Early Africans, Indians, and Chinese people used puppets to act out their ancient tales of gods and demons, and who knows what else? Puppets are known to have existed in Iran more than 1000 years ago. Some ancient puppets were undoubtedly depictions of slaves, just as many rock paintings are.

Puppets have been employed as a means of entertainment since the earliest times, and some historians believe that puppets were used before actors in theatre. Marionettes were popular with aristocrats. Puppets were also used *instead* of humans. Puppets can range in size all the way from tiny finger puppets to larger-than-life puppets—i.e., those in which an adult can fit. In fact, Shakespeare's plays were sometimes performed using marionettes instead of actors, and some actors, of course, fiercely complained. Marionette puppet theatre can be traced deep into the early Middle Ages, when puppets were probably used primarily to make people laugh. They were also used to act out *morality plays,* behaving in ways that aren't appropriate for human beings. In Europe, many serious plays, like *Doctor Faustus,* in which a deal is struck with the Devil, were performed with many different types of colorful, wooden humanlike puppets—young and old, black and white, ugly and pretty, "evil" and "good."[56]

Puppet shows are so much fun! They're so very entertaining. The painted, bright-eyed, blank-faced puppets dance around madly like humans who have the communal psychiatric disorder called *folie à plusieurs,* which involves many people full of shared delusional beliefs (see p. 30). Children love puppets. Oddly enough,

---

[56] Which came first, the chicken or the egg? The answer is the *egg.* Why? Because chickens *always* hatch from eggs, but eggs can be laid by a wide variety of creatures: birds, fish, reptiles, insects, and even mutated dinosaurs. So clearly, the egg came first. Now, here's another question: Which came first, "progressive" liberals or Evil (e.g., *ancient greed)?* Well, that's difficult to say because Evil is untold thousands of years old. Evil is defined as "profound immorality, wickedness, and depravity," so Evil does not exist in animals, only in human beings. Evil is an unchecked primal instinct that originates in the hindbrain. (Bear in mind that the primal instincts of a spider originate from cells the size of a dot.) Where did Evil come from? It's simple. During the course of human evolution, men and woman developed what is called a *conscience* and stopped behaving like a wild animals. A conscience is defined as "an inner feeling or voice viewed as acting as a guide to the rightness or wrongness of one's behavior." So that's when it all began. You see, having a conscience means understanding, respecting, and sympathizing with the feelings of *all other living things*—and not causing them undo harm—so evil did not begin to exist until human beings began to realize the difference between right and wrong. Therefore, Evil came first, and then "progressive" liberals hatched from it. So "progressive" liberalism is not Evil, per se; it's just a *psychiatric disorder.* But its symptoms include a childlike ignorance of evil, which allows evil to flourish.

adult imbeciles love puppets, too. Puppetry—just like midnight at Halloween—probably gives enigmatic liberals, such as "witches" and "wizards" a chance to unwind, come out of the darkness, and act out their inner urges—i.e., be themselves. Pinocchio, as we know, is the most famous and best-loved puppet of all time. Chucky the killer doll is probably the most feared. That's because puppetry involves storytelling (i.e., outright lies—which, in politics, can be detrimental to the United States of America. Normal people just do not like being *forced* by others to act like buffoonish puppets, but for some reason, liberals don't seem to mind it at all. The important question here is this: Are all Washington, D.C., politicians—Democrats or Republicans—who allow their political strings to be constantly yanked, tugged, and pulled daily really *liberals at heart?* It certainly seems so.

You see, the way political puppetry works is this: "Constituents"—i.e., friends, relatives, associates, special-interest groups, and various other supporters—donate money to a politician's election campaign in the expectation of some favor in return, often a government job. Political puppetry also involves politicians promising to vote *yay* or *nay* on some piece of potentially lucrative legislation and/or some pet project, which, if it's approved, will receive government funding. As you can see, political puppetry involves different forms of bribery, such as "kickbacks" and "payoffs." This is commonly referred to as *influence pedaling*. Special-interest groups and corporations also donate money under the table or make promises behind closed doors to politicians in return for senatorial or congressional votes needed to pass legislation that's financially beneficial to them. That is why easily influenced politicians who regularly make money on the side are called *political puppets*. They may even do the bidding of the White House. (Then they all shake hands.) Their minds are blank slates waiting for someone to write down instructions.

Everyone loves puppets. They make children laugh and giggle. Aren't pup-P.E.T.S. funny?

Notable Liberal Quote:

"I'm not at liberty to say what I think." —Secretary of State John Kerry (D-Mass)[57]

---

[57] John Kerry was the Democratic presidential candidate in 2004 but lost the election to George Bush. President Obama has appointed him Secretary of State. He got the job after Hillary Pandora Clinton took responsibility for what happened in Benghazi, Libya, then resigned from that office in disgrace. John Kerry reportedly served admirably in the military during the Vietnam War, but threw all of his medals away—over the White House fence—except for three Purple Hearts, which are medals of honor awarded to brave soldiers who are killed or wounded in the line of duty. Kerry has recently been described as someone who lives in a "parallel universe."

We Americans should also face the fact that most women—and, not surprisingly, members of some Third World ethnic groups—instinctively act like vulnerable puppets to attract mates and thus survive financially in the complicated world in which we all live.[58] (Generally, conservative Anglo-Saxon men and women don't need to do that because they can easily take care of themselves.) That's the reason every nation on earth needs to drastically limit not only the size and scope of its central government but also the extent of female influence in its political affairs. If the United States of America, which is the world's recognized leader and defender against tyranny and evil,[59] and humanity's only bastion of hope and freedom because we are the country that defeated the Nazi enemies of the Jewish people in World War II, ever fails to do this, we'll someday cease to exist!

A Korean War veteran contributor--who specialized in "repairing radios" in the Air Force--submits the following:

> "A famous sage once described the basic philosophies of three of the world's great religions towards the rest of humanity as follows:
>
> Your problems are *your* problems says the Muslim. We cannot help you solve them.
>
> Your problems are *my* problems says the Christian. We will help you in any way we can.
>
> My problems are *your* problems says the Jew.[60] You must help in all our endeavors, even to sacrificing your blood and treasure, in order to help us defeat our enemies.
>
> As a consequence of this kind of thinking, the entire Middle-East mess must be laid at the doorstep of the Jewish Lobby—both in the United States and Britain. What possible reason for us Americans to ingratiate ourselves with the likes of Saudi Arabia, whose political system, especially with regard to women, is on par with the Spanish Inquisition? Can it be to keep the rich Saudis from joining the fray against Israel? They secretly supply the necessary cash to the others anyway. Of course, we mustn't forget the oil!

---

[58] "One reason that our lives are so complicated here in America is that foreigners are now designing and manufacturing practically everything we own, so we spend all of our time either modifying it or repairing it—or, in the case of electronic equipment, trying to figure out how to use it. When we call tech support, an Indian or a Chinaman answers the phone." —T. N. T.

[59] Evil is like a tree because it has three roots: (1) the love of money, (2) religious fanaticism, and (3) contempt for the Ten Commandments. It should also be noted that so-called liberalism, which is a genetic mental disorder, appears to have the same outcome as all three of these things. This proves true every time a liberal socialist Democrat is elected to government office and obtains a position of power.

[60] Millions of other people around the globe think that it's the duty of the UnitedStates of America to protect each one of them, too.

And why is the United States so fearful of the Iranians obtaining a couple of nuclear bombs. For God's sake! The Pakistanis, still essentially a medieval society, have the same things, as does the Fascist regime running North Korea. Both nations are far more dangerous than Iran, but no plans to attack either are being openly discussed every day on cable TV.

Why did we invade Iraq. Some say because Sadaam tried to assassinate the elder Bush. The real reason: They were a threat to Israel because of Sadaam's large and well-organized army.

The socialist administration currently running the United States appears to be no friend of Israel. Strangely enough, the middle name of the president, which is Hussein, is identical to the surname of the prophet Mohammed. Due to our leader's inactions, Afghans, Syrians, Pakistanis, Iraqis and others are hell bent on forming a World Caliphate, which could ultimately cause Israel's demise."

Some Vegan Food for Thought: What kind of sick person, political party, or country would defend, and thus encourage, the use of Palestinian women and children for use as human shields in the ongoing sixty-six-year-old Israeli-Palestinian war?[61] (Some Democrats have done so on television.)

Liberal socialist members of the Democratic Party need to give up their *silly notion* of ever appointing a liberal socialist female or overt homosexual as U.S. Secretary of Defense, much less elect him or her President of the United States of America, and thus Commander in Chief. To the average everyday commonsense conservative, the very idea is *fantastical.* It would put our country and others in harm's way.

Okay, now, let's get back to the subject of liberal (i.e., adult child) psychiatry. By the time you've finished reading this book, you'll probably agree that the term liberal, as popularly used, is inaccurate and misleading. A much better, more accurate, term would be *delusionist.* Trying to convince delusionists that they

---

[61] The Israeli-Palestinian conflict is actually a hundred years old. In the year 3000, it will be two hundred years old. In the year 4000, it will be three hundred years old. In the year 5000, it will be four hundred years old—unless the Palestinians are given some free food and property on the Moon. Then maybe we can all watch something more entertaining on TV.

should stop ignoring reality is like trying to convince teenagers that they should stop thinking about the opposite sex. There is little or no chance of it ever happening. For anyone who might think that liberals differ from conservative Americans only in their opinions on political and social issues, think again. Liberals are different in other ways, too. For example, are liberals—our delusionist friends—*addicted* to the euphoria experienced when fantasizing? If so, they have F.A.D.

Losing the Key to a Compartmentalized Delusion

Compartmentalization is an unconscious psychological defense mechanism used to avoid *cognitive dissonance,* a mental uneasiness and anxiety caused by a person's having conflicting values, cognitions, emotions, and beliefs within him- or herself. Compartmentalization lets these conflicting ideas "coexist" by inhibiting direct or explicit acknowledgment of *illogic*. You see, the human brain simply cannot conceive of itself thinking illogically (i.e., going nuts). If it did, then that same brain would immediately begin to "flip-flop" and conclude that something is wrong with it because what it is thinking cannot be happening and is not true. That's the initial cause for the lack of awareness of one's own illness.[62]

In *Darwinian Psychiatry*, McGuire and Troisi state:

> From the perspective of functional units, psychic defenses have several critical features in common: (1) They minimize the effects of certain types of information; (2) they preserve functional systems and facilitate strategy execution in the presence of information that, if recognized, might compromise strategy enactment;

---

[62] Lack of awareness of one's own illness is similar to the situation with HAL, the computer that was preprogrammed with a corrupt and/or cracked disk in the movie *2001: A Space Odyssey* (1968), an epic British-American science-fiction film. The story deals with a series of encounters between primitive humans and mysterious black monoliths in ancient "Africa" 4 million years ago that are apparently affecting human evolution. A voyage is made to the planet Jupiter in order to trace a signal emitted by an identical monolith found buried in Earth's moon. HAL 9000 is the intelligent onboard speaking computer who begins to exert full control over the spaceship. (Maybe the Democrats programmed it.)

and (3) they increase the possibility of social participation and goal achievement. Thus, psychic defenses can be viewed as internal functions for controlling and limiting the potentially negative or destabilizing effects of information. Compartmentalized delusions may be viewed in a similar way: They represent a "last-ditch" effort to maintain infrastructural and functional integrity when one or more infrastructures is compromised.[63]

The common ingredient of this type of delusion is a false belief that is maintained in the face of strong evidence to the contrary—or despite conventional thinking—that suggests logical alternative interpretations. (Consider the widely held belief by Democrats that the higher a government raises tax rates, the more money it will automatically receive. It does not work in a democracy because members of an intelligent populace will always find novel ways—some legal, some barely legal, some illegal—to avoid being victimized.) Compartmentalized delusions may manifest themselves as atypical thoughts about oneself, or others, or inanimate objects, or ideas. These delusions may be persecutory, somatic, systematized, or bizarre.[64] Such delusions seldom extend to all forms of cognition or emotion.

To summarize, our liberal friends appear to be just normal, average, everyday people, despite their psychosis, because some types of information processing remain relatively normal.[65] Thus, we have an explanation for liberal *denial of the facts*.[66] It is a psychic defense mechanism.

---

[63] McGuire and Troisi, *op. cit.*, p. 100.
[64] Ibid., p. 99 (attributed to T.C. Manschreck 1989, 1992).
[65] Ibid., p. 99.
[66] Re: *Liberal Denial of the Facts:* The liberal continues to reject that which is obviously true. No matter how much evidence is presented that is contrary to widespread liberal belief and opinion, those on the far left (i.e., all of them) refuse to admit it. One classic example of this is the vital role that coerced interrogation techniques (e.g., waterboarding) have played in obtaining information that was crucial in locating Osama bin Laden, leader of al-Qaeda and mastermind of the September 11, 2001, attack on the World Trade Center. The usefulness of waterboarding was verified by a former Democratic Secretary of Defense, along with a former Director of the Central Intelligence Agency (C.I.A.), and verified by two former C.I.A. Chiefs, a former C.I.A. Counterterrorism Chief, a former National Security Advisor, and a former Secretary of Defense. Still, to this day, liberals say it did not happen. Is any more proof of *liberal denial of the facts* necessary?

Chapter 4

What Makes Them Act Like That?

An Inexplicable Fondness for Dissociative Amnesia

Dissociative amnesia is a disorder typically brought on by a traumatic event, such as (1) having your gross incompetence suddenly revealed to the American people, (2) being examined suspiciously as the illegal beneficiary of a shaky financial deal, or (3) stupidly voting for, or signing, an extremely bad piece of legislation and then, later, having an angry populace demand to know why.[67] (Liberal legislation is like artificial cheese. It looks good until you get a taste of it.) The main symptom of this primarily liberal Democrat disorder is the sudden inability to remember any relevant details about anything at all. This usually occurs when the liberal male or female automatically blocks things out, leaving him or her unable to recall the obvious because it is simply too embarrassing. The liberal male or female may also appear unduly confused and reportedly suffer from depression and/or anxiety. You

---

[67] Obamacare is just one example of liberal pathological political "madness." All of the Democrats voted *for it*. But now they are all *against it*. The same thing happened with the Defense of Marriage Act (D.O.M.A.). A long list of Democrats all lined up to applaud the Supreme Court decision to strike down D.O.M.A.—despite having *voted for it* when it passed in 1996. Even former president Bill Clinton (D), who *signed* the Defense of Marriage Act bill into law—get this—heralded the Supreme Court's decision. So what are all the Democrats doing in Washington, D.C.? What are they doing, just playing around? Or figuring out ways to funnel money to people who make campaign donations? Here's what Bill Clinton said in a statement that was also signed by his wife: "By overturning the Defense of Marriage Act, the Court recognized that discrimination towards any group holds us all back in our efforts to form a more perfect union" ("Dems Voted for DOMA, Cheered Its End," *Politico*, June 26, 2013). First they're for it, then they're against it. Yada, yada, yada. Why do we even bother to listen to these people?

see, liberal dissociative amnesia is not the same as simple amnesia, which is usually a result of disease or injury to the brain. Liberal dissociative amnesia, especially in the case of self-serving Democratic politicians, both male and female, frequently represents a knee-jerk response to the overwhelming stress caused by one or more (i.e., a series of) incorrect decisions, especially if one of them resulted in complete and utter *disaster*.

Evidently, a genetic link exists to the development of liberal dissociative amnesia, because persons with this disorder often have close relatives who make frequently suspicious similar claims. Curiously, dissociative amnesia seems to be more common in liberal females than in liberal males. One possible explanation for this may be the fact that men generally tend to think things through first, unlike women, who usually rely *entirely* on their female intuition—i.e., gender-based feelings.[68]

Men are genetically designed and built to fight and hunt wild animals, whereas women are genetically designed and built to attract the *opposite* sex in order to breed and bear children. As we all know, a woman instinctively protects her own offspring, and so she gathers foodstuffs—i.e., wild nuts and berries—just in case her chosen mate is unsuccessful and/or dies trying to kill a dangerous animal so that everyone in the family can eat rather than starve to death. This evolutionary arrangement has ensured the survival of our brave and noble (present-day) species *Homo sapiens sapiens* for the past 4.5 million years.[69]

What we all need to realize is that when our liberal friends and enemies vote, they vote according to their need. They do this because they have F.A.D., and thus they *always* vote based on their (gullible) "feelings" about the candidate. Sometimes, this may involve a "thrill" running up the leg. That is also why many liberals are so attracted to a particular politician's handsome face, big grin, deep-throated voice, pectoral muscles, or expensive clothing. Unfortunately, liberal men and women are very different, because liberals are apparently very unhappy people who understandably care more about their own well-being than about bad things happening to anyone else—sometimes even the men or women they profess to love the most.[70]

---

[68] The word intuition is defined as "the ability to understand something immediately without the need for conscious reasoning." It is also known that all human emotions are based on dopamine flow. (See "Dopamine," page 56.)

[69] Please note that the term *Homo sapiens sapiens* refers specifically to modern man. The term *Homo sapiens*—without the subspecies suffix—refers to the *primate species* to which modern man belongs, along with humanlike creatures not anatomically and behaviorally modern. Anatomical modernity, which can be determined by skeletal bones, began to appear about 100,000 years ago. Behavioral modernity, not so easily determined, probably occurred by 100,000 years ago (and may even have included the masculine greeting gesture of tipping of one's hat to the ladies).

[70] "Is it better to be the lover or the loved one? That depends on which one has the communicable disease." —Editor (three rat finks)

This is, of course, all very, very sad. That's why the United States government keeps giving our liberal friends (and even some of *their* liberal friends in foreign countries) lots and lots of free stuff—*over and over again*. Maybe someday they will stop asking for *more, more, and more*. It's almost as though liberals are trying to make us feel guilty about the fact that they're either too stupid or too lazy to feed themselves. Maybe liberal socialist Democrats just keep forgetting about all of the gifts we keep giving to them.

But why?

Can amnesia really be triggered when a person just wants to *avoid* stress? Consider, for example, our former liberal socialist Democrat First Lady/Secretary of State and the ongoing Benghazi cover-up. Is it the politics of concussions? (Or is it the politics of payola?) Remember what Ms. Former First Lady said after she was repeatedly called to testify before Congress? She spread her arms and cupped her hands and pointed both of her elbows down—as though she had secretly practiced those movements with others coaching her—then said loudly, "What difference at this point does it make?"

Many of our "celebrity" elected representatives seem to forget not only whom they work for—the American people—but also how they've cast their votes recently. Democrats, for example, forced the (Un)Affordable Care Act down the public's throat by passing it unanimously without anybody else's support, then later began to quietly back away from it like the metastasizing economic cancer that it is. Where is the money to pay for this monstrosity supposed to come from, anyway? Penniless college students? Our Chinese masters? Politicians like these liberal Democrats in the Senate, who were smiling and calmly watering their flowers, just didn't seem to care very much—and apparently, despite the rapidly accelerating National Debt, *they still don't*.

Is it just the rest of us, or is there something drastically wrong with these people?

According to McGuire and Troisi:

> Traumas are viewed not as accelerated instances of stress, but as experiences in which important goals are perceived as suddenly becoming improbable. . . . [A]mnesia rarely occurs unless high-priority goals are perceived as significantly jeopardized. . . . When adults develop disruptions of their consciousness of recent events, suboptimal automatic systems are implicated. . . . Mild instances of amnesia can be understood as attempts to adapt within constraints. . . . It is a strategy that leads to the decoupling of both

disconcerting (e.g., goal-compromising) information and structures, while potentially preserving the function of non-afflicted structures. Earlier, psychic defenses and compartmentalized delusions were explained in a similar way. . . . Further, in mild forms, amnesia elicits help from others.[71]

In "The Prehistoric Beginning of Fantasy Addiction," we will discuss how the signs of certain mental disorders, flaws, or weaknesses often elicit caretaking behavior and help from other human beings, increasing the evolutionary survivability of the genetic information of those who are afflicted.

Liberal Addiction to Political Fiction

What exactly is meant by the word *addiction?* This term commonly refers to the condition of a person physically and mentally dependent on a particular substance, thing, or activity. It is popular nowadays to loosely refer to all sorts of things as addictions: gambling, sex, tobacco, drugs,[72] alcohol, pornography[73], video games, shopping, exercise, overeating, anorexia, coffee, chocolate, television, radio, and even solitaire, just to name a few. As you can see from such common usage and habits, it is easy for a person to be "addicted" to several things at once or maybe even to be temporarily addicted to something at a young age and still not be considered abnormal. It would be easy to say that liberals are simply *addicted to fiction* and leave it at that. Undoubtedly, many readers would agree with that conclusion, but this book was not written to make unsubstantiated statements, so we are going to have to examine the underlying neurological mechanism by which liberal fiction addiction occurs.

The American Society of Addiction Medicine (A.S.A.M.) begins its detailed definition of the term *addiction* as follows:

---

[71] McGuire and Troisi, *op. cit.*, pp. 222–223.
[72] Many people who rationalize the smoking of marijuana are clearly not addicted.
[73] "A clean mind delivers power. A mind free of negatives produces positives. So why does our country have so many problems? Could it be because of the Internet?" —Anonymous

> Addiction is a primary, chronic disease of brain reward, motivation, memory and related circuitry. Dysfunction in these circuits leads to characteristic biological, psychological, social and spiritual manifestations. This is reflected in an individual pathologically pursuing reward and/or relief by substance use and other behaviors.[74]

As we can see from this definition, addiction is not simply a behavioral problem. Research indicates that addiction is the result of a chronic brain-chemistry disorder, often genetic in nature.[75] The past president of the Canadian Society of Addiction Medicine and chair of the A.S.A.M. committee on its new definition of addiction stated, "The disease creates distortions in thinking, feelings and perceptions, which drive people to behave in ways that are not understandable to others around them."[76] That is because addiction can result in altered judgment—i.e., it can make that which is wrong appear right. Although genetic inheritance plays a major role in the susceptibility of an individual to develop an addiction, other lesser factors contribute, too—and an argument can be made that they are all influenced by genetics. One of those factors is *neural adaptation,* which is a change over time in the responsiveness of the sensory system to a constant stimulus, such as repeated drug use. Another factor is *distorted values,* which affect one's thinking, attitudes, and behavior. Some addicts use alcohol or illegal drugs in a pathological pursuit of mindless euphoria, whereas others simply seek a state of joyous nirvana. Some addicts desire relief from dysphoria, which is "a state of unease or generalized dissatisfaction with life." Most addicts are clearly dysfunctional emotionally. The most notable feature of the addict is his or her obsession with a particular habit despite the adverse consequences. Such a person is said to have impaired control.

Unfortunately, the way our system works is that people with debilitating mental disorders, even if they are drug addicts, are permitted to *vote*. It's the American way.

---

[74] American Society of Addiction Medicine, "Public Policy Statement: Definition of Addiction," 2011, A.S.A.M., Chevy Chase, Maryland.

[75] According to the National Institute on Drug Abuse (N.I.D.A.), "Addiction has a moderate to high heritable component" (Substance Abuse Center, "Is Addiction Genetic?" March 14, 2008). The N.I.D.A. had to be dragged kicking and screaming to this conclusion even though it has long been known—especially in the days of the American frontier, the Wild West, the 1848 California Gold Rush, the Pony Express and the telegraph, and the gunfight at the O.K. Corral—that different ethnic groups, especially Mexicans and Indians, are very susceptible to alcohol and tobacco—and thus drug—addiction. What happened? Is somebody trying to redact American history?

[76] American Society of Addiction Medicine, A.S.A.M. News Release, "ASAM Releases New Definition of Addiction," August 15, 2011.

There seems to be a clear divisive line between true addiction and simple frequent repetition of something. Shopping addiction, for example, is not really an addiction; it's just a desire for and a habit of buying things that aren't necessary, sometimes with a soon-to-be-confiscated Visa card. It's a lot of fun to spend "free" money—as most congressmen who play games with our tax revenue will secretly affirm. Unfortunately, it's only when money is the result of an individual's *own* blood, sweat, and tears that he or she will think twice before spending it frivolously.

Spending too much of the public's cash should not be considered a true addiction. That is because if an out-of-control spender is deprived of the opportunity and forced to stop, it will not produce any real withdrawal symptoms, and a person questioned about his or her overspending habit probably will not go to extremes—like a heroin addict might—to deny it. (Although, come to think of it, maybe some congressional representatives deprived of his or her "earmarks" would.) We should always be careful about labeling something as an addiction, because the term becomes trivialized when applied to irresistible youthful urges that aren't substance-related—like, say, playing blackjack every day with unemployed friends for money. Use of the word addiction should be limited to describing a *recurring compulsion* by an individual to engage in some *dangerous* activity that may possibly result in harm to himself and/or others.

The applicability of the word addiction remains controversial, for there is no universal consensus regarding its appropriate use. Still, things such as video-game addiction, which don't quite fit the traditional meaning of the term (and may actually be better defined as an obsessive-compulsive disorder),[77] can nevertheless have serious withdrawal symptoms. Further understanding of neural science, the brain, the nervous system, human behavior, and affective disorders continues to reveal much about the effect of molecular biology on the development of "disease."

Here is something else to consider when contemplating the meaning of the word addiction: Most grandparents enjoy seeing their grandchildren regularly. Why? One reason is that it brings back pleasant memories by reminding them of when they were young. In many cases, it would be just as difficult to keep a grandmother or grandfather away from a favorite grandchild as it would be to keep a junkie away from a syringe, and attempts to do so could cause female hysterics, but grandparents are not addicts even though they may seem to be. Why not? Because their behavior has no harmful effect, and *that is what makes the big difference.* Grandparents are simply driven by instinct—a fixed pattern of behavior in humans and animals in response to certain stimuli—which involves complex chemical reactions in the brain. In an *imaginary* world where grandparents would constantly do harm to their children and grandchildren—say, stealing money from their plastic piggybanks or negatively affecting their future careers—the term "addiction" would clearly apply. *Negative consequences* are the key, so we should always be careful not to offhandedly label anything as an addiction

---

[77] An obsessive compulsion is considered an *addiction* only when it is dangerous or harmful.

unless (1) there is an identifiable substance involved,[78] (2) the behavior has negative consequences, and (3) the behavior is pathological.

Note that behavioral addictions are scheduled to be listed as a new class in the A.P.A.'s updated manual, DSM-5, but the only category included is gambling addiction. Sex addiction was rejected. Internet addiction will appear in the appendix.[79] You should also be aware that not all independent experts, college professors, and medical doctors agree on the exact nature of addiction or drug dependency.

In the book *Fifty Signs of Mental Illness*, the author states:

Sexual cravings are very similar to drug cravings. Drug users will often compare getting high on drugs to having sex. Some of the chemicals released in the brain during drug use likely are similar to those released during fantasy and orgasm.[80]

Yes, you read it right: *"chemicals released in the brain . . . during fantasy."*

Dopamine

Dopamine is a neurotransmitter produced in several areas of the brain, including the *substantia nigra* and the ventral tegmental area. Dopamine's chemical formula is $C_6H_3(OH)_2\text{-}CH_2\text{-}CH_2\text{-}NH_2$, and it has a structure similar to that of amphetamines and methamphetamine. Dopamine is also a neurohormone released by the hypothalamus, a region of the forebrain below the thalamus.[81] Dopamine has many

---

[78] An identifiable substance includes any chemical released in an addict's brain when he or she performs a harmful activity.
[79] The DSM-5 is the next (fifth) edition of the American Psychiatric Association's *Diagnostic and Statistical Manual of Mental Disorders*, which is, at the time of this writing, in consultation, planning, and preparation, and is scheduled for publication in May 2013 (Wikipedia, The Free Encyclopedia, "DSM-5"). Some believe that so-called sex addiction is really nothing more than a low-class human being acting like a dog. (But, then again, that person might not be acting.)
[80] James Whitney Hicks, M.D., *Fifty Signs of Mental Illness*, 2005, Yale University, New Haven, Connecticut, pp. 64–65.
[81] The hypothalamus is a portion of the brain about the size of an almond that controls, among other things, important aspects of parenting and attachment behavior. Hypothalamic function is responsive to and regulated by dopamine (Wikipedia, "Hypothalamus," April 30, 2013).

functions in the brain, including important roles in behavior and cognition, punishment and reward, motivation, working memory, and learning. Dopamine plays a part in voluntary movement, inhibition of prolactin production, sleep, mood, and attention. In the frontal lobes, dopamine controls the flow of information from other areas of the brain, and disorders in the frontal lobes can cause a decline in neurocognitive functions, especially with regard to memory, attention, and the ability to solve simple math problems.

Dopamine is most commonly associated with the reward system of the human brain, providing feelings of enjoyment and reinforcement to motivate a person to engage proactively in certain activities, such as doing the "dog dance" on a Saturday night behind a Sav-A-Lot. Dopamine is released in the brain by rewarding experiences such as those involving food, sex, drugs, and *neutral stimuli* that become associated with them. Pathological states associated with dopamine dysfunction are paranoid schizophrenia, autism, attention-deficit/hyperactivity disorder, and drug abuse addiction.[82] Drugs such as amphetamines, methamphetamine, and cocaine can increase dopamine levels by more than tenfold and can cause temporary psychoses. Dopamine has a diuretic effect, which means that, potentially, it can vastly increase urine output. Dopamine is also the natural substrate for bruised fruit-and-vegetable–browning enzymes in ripe yellow bananas. Dopamine is important in that it gives a person a drive to do things. Drugs that are abused increase dopamine in the limbic areas of the brain, and if we interfere with a drug's ability to produce dopamine, then that drug is no longer pleasurable. The ability to increase the production of dopamine is why some drugs are addictive and others are not. The mechanisms involving a dopamine signal have developed through evolution in the human/animal brain to ensure that the human/animal performs behaviors indispensable for the survival of its species, such as eating, or, in the case of some liberals, having sex in a filthy restroom at a gas station.

When a person uses a drug such as marijuana or cocaine, that person increases dopamine production. This is believed to trigger changes in the brain that will eventually lead—in an individual who is vulnerable—to a drug addiction. This means that the person loses control of his or her ability to decide when to take the drug and has an intense drive to use it compulsively. Not everyone becomes addicted. Research indicates that approximately 50 percent of a person's susceptibility to addiction is determined genetically, while the other 50 percent may depend on the contents of the liberal drug addict's "doobie."

---

[82] Interestingly, F.A.D. can, perhaps, also be understood as the antithesis of paranoid schizophrenia, for there appears to be a diminished (as opposed to increased) awareness of one's surroundings, and augmented (as opposed to decreased) trust of others.

The Dopamine Hypothesis of Schizophrenia

The dopamine hypothesis of schizophrenia (and of psychosis) is a model attributing symptoms of schizophrenia to a disturbed and hyperactive dopaminergic signal transduction. The model draws evidence from the observation that a large number of antipsychotics have dopamine-receptor antagonistic effects. This theory, however, does not state that dopamine excess is a *complete* explanation for schizophrenia and psychoses, because there seem to be other factors involved.

Genetic evidence suggests that genes or specific variants of genes may exist that code for mechanisms involved in dopamine function, which may be more prevalent in people experiencing psychosis or diagnosed with schizophrenia. Dopamine-related genes linked to psychosis in this way include COMT, DRD4, and AKT1.[83] Several risk factors seem to prefigure—that is, give an early indication of—mental disorder, the most notable of which are genetics and brain structure. Also, schizophrenia and psychoses occur along with changes in brain chemistry: specifically, excessive levels of dopamine. The dopamine hypothesis of schizophrenia states that the brain of a schizophrenic patient produces more dopamine than does a normal brain, and it is this increased dopamine level that is believed to be responsible for the symptoms of the "disease" (disorder). Although all of the research seems to indicate that dopamine is somehow involved in the production of psychotic symptoms, it is difficult to determine the exact way in which it is involved.

> "What's in the Neanderthal DNA of the far left that causes them to behave the way they do? We don't know. All of the research isn't in yet. Some researchers are still working with the *most reliable* samples. One of the samples came from Monica Lewinsky's blue dress." —Olive Oil

Self-Induced Dopamine Production

The cognitive state of the brain at any given moment can trigger the release of dopamine. Dopamine production can be prompted by a pleasant stimulus, either *physical* or *mental*. An example of a physical stimulus would be eating a juicy steak.

---

[83] "A Signaling Pathway AKTing up in Schizophrenia," *The Journal of Clinical Investigation*, 2008, American Society for Clinical Investigation, vol. 118, issue 6, pp. 2018–2021.

An example of a mental stimulus would be simply thinking about cooking the steak. The anticipation of something pleasant (the thought) and the direct stimulus (the eating) both increase dopamine levels. Other sensory stimuli may also be involved, such as smelling the steak as it cooks. What if the meat is spoiled rotten and stinks? Or what if the steak doesn't taste good because it's burned? Or what if you can't cook the steak and must eat it raw? In such cases, there would be little or no dopamine produced.

For much the same reason, *cognitive dissonance*, the psychological state of having inconsistent thoughts, beliefs, or attitudes, is not conducive to the release of dopamine. How things are represented in a person's mind (or how a person intentionally represents things to himself or herself) has an impact on the amount of dopamine released. Women are particularly sensitive to this in matters of sex—so if a boyfriend and/or husband hasn't had a job since the city garbage can pickups were improved and de-unionized, he should probably try to keep that information secret.

> "Why can't any liberal find a job after the government paid for their college tuition? What did they major in? Grassology? Or Being Offended? Where did they get their degrees, anyway? The Academy of the African Arts and Sciences?" —John Hayberry, Ph.D.[84] (2013)

Dopamine, amazingly enough, is central to the many choices we all make every day of our lives. Both liberals and conservatives decide what is rewarding (pleasant) and what is aversive (painful), not only for ourselves but also for others around us. We attempt to weigh our immediate choices against what may be rewarding long term (or short term) or aversive long term (or short term). Eating too many fast-food hamburgers, for example, would eventually make us fat, so, despite the fact that more dopamine will be released if we eat too many, we may choose to stop ingesting foods that have a negative result.

---

[84] The Ph.D. stands for professional hogwash detector. My motto is this: There's a valid explanation for everything.

Euphoric Recall

Can the act of deliberately thinking happy thoughts increase the flow of dopamine and other feel-good neurotransmitters? The answer is undoubtedly yes, especially if the thoughts involve sex, alcohol, food, or drugs. *Anticipation alone can elevate dopamine levels.* For example, an alcoholic[85] who simply drives by a bar may trigger dopamine release in his or her brain and cause an increase in "wanting." When a crack addict walks past an abandoned shack where he or she once got high, dopamine may be released. Mere anticipatory thoughts of things a person enjoys—like gambling or shopping—can also increase dopamine levels in conservatives.

The same applies to *political ideologies.*

The hippocampus plays an important part in the memory of previous euphoric (or dysphoric) experiences. Remembering pleasant sensations, including drug-induced highs, can cause a rise in the level of dopamine in the brain. Fantasizing (i.e., thinking about things that make one feel good) can also increase dopamine. Delusional beliefs can produce dopamine, too. Dopamine production is dependent on the person's state of mind and can therefore be self-induced. Examples of thought topics that may release dopamine include such things as peace, love, drugs, and flowers, but there are many more.

Overstimulation of dopamine production through the *liberal* use of drugs causes the brain to adapt. The brain does this by producing less of the neurotransmitter or by reducing the number of receptors in the reward circuit. As a result, the chemical effect on the reward circuit is lessened, reducing the liberal drug user's ability to enjoy the things that previously provided pleasure. That is one reason why cannabis is called a gateway drug. After a while, users are tempted to try harder, more dangerous drugs that require the liberal user to commit crimes to pay for them—unless, of course, he or she is as wealthy as the former *Saturday Night Live* wild and crazy tough-guy comedian John Belushi (an enigma), and now deceased.

Notable Liberal(?) Quote:

"I guess happiness is not a state you want to be in all the time." — John Belushi (1949-1982)[86]

---

[85] Question: Is there really such a thing as a conservative alcoholic? In fact, is any conservative really "addicted" to anything? If so, he or she must keep it to himself or herself much better than liberals do. Even the Betty Ford Center, established in 1982, helps *liberals*—not conservatives—overcome their addictions. To date, doctors have assumed that the response of a liberal's brain to alcohol is the same as that of a conservative's, but according to the more-than-obvious visual statistics, that is not the case at all.

[86] Famous last words. John Belushi was one of the original cast members of *Saturday Night Live*. He died at the age of thirty-three from a "speedball" shot, the combined injection of cocaine and heroin that was reportedly injected by a "drug queen," who was arrested and jailed and shall remain nameless.

Opioids

Along with dopamine are other neurotransmitters: opioids (opium-like compounds). Opioids are also involved with reward and are released in the brain during sex and eating. Opioids may actually be more important in the liking of a reward than is dopamine, which is believed to play a greater role in the preliminary wanting phase.

Opioid dependency is a medical diagnosis characterized by an individual's inability to stop using drugs containing opioids, even when it is clearly in his or her best interest to do so.

Examples of opioids are painkillers such as morphine, hydrocodone, oxycodone, and codeine. Opioid drugs being sold under brand names include OxyContin, Percocet, Vicodin, Kadian, and Avinza, among others.[87]

Heroin, illegal in all fifty states, is also an opioid.

A Brief Review of What We Know So Far

Now, let's review the facts that have been established:

- Schizophrenics cannot be convinced that the things they believe are wrong.
- Impairment of logic is characteristic of both liberalism and schizophrenia.
- Delusions are false ideas often believed by those with schizophrenia.
- A delusion is a fixed belief that is erroneous and/or fanciful.
- *Folie à plusieurs* refers to a delusional belief shared by many people.
- Selective or dissociative amnesia can help maintain a delusion.
- Illegal drugs stimulate the release of dopamine in the brain, a feeling that can be recalled.
- Addiction refers to a dependency on a particular chemical *substance, thing, or activity*.[88]
- Fantasy can normally be combated with logic, whereas a liberal's delusions cannot.

---

[87] National Institute on Drug Abuse, Prescription Drugs: Abuse and Addiction, "What are Opioids?" October 2011.

[88] The term *thing* refers to a pleasurable source of sensory input: primarily visual or auditory.

- Dopamine is released in the brain during fantasy.
- *Fantasy can therefore be addictive.*

On Liberal Addiction to Fantasy

Any reader who is still skeptical that a liberal who harbors delusions and/or dotes on fantasies can become hooked on the neurotransmitters that are being released in his or her brain, consider the residual effects of the dreams we all have during sleep. Both liberals and conservatives have pleasant dreams, which often involve a romantic interest, and then awaken from them feeling great, with that sensation lasting through much of the day. The difference is that liberals keep bumping into things. The reason that liberals and conservatives continue to feel good even though they know that what they dreamed wasn't real is that chemicals have been released as the result of *optimistic thoughts* and happy imagined experiences, and those chemicals can remain effective for hours.

Sometimes, later in the day, after the dream has faded and the chemicals have begun to wear off, people may even think back to that dream, *trying to recapture it* because it makes them feel good.

Well, try to imagine a person recapturing a particular dream—or perhaps a combination of dreams—with regularity, dreams that center on pleasant thoughts of make-believe, including happy elves and talking unicorns, that perpetuate the steady release of dopamine. After a certain period, there would come a point when a person could be accurately diagnosed as addicted, especially if the dream is harmful to that person or to others in some way. Imagine if that person's dream involved a fantasy belief in a nonexistent world of peace, love, and goodwill, with an absence of evil, even among all flawed men and backward nations of the world, and in places such as Central and South America, or the continent of Africa.

Notable Liberal Quote:

"When I was justa dum leetle kid walkin' aroun' town, I gotta job at a clothing store en New Yoke City makin' two-dollar-n-hour. Theen one day, my frieend Jeerome, a lacksadaisycal black kid abou' my age, smoked sum marryguana durin' his tree-hour lunch break. Whenny got back, he was yelled at by da boss for not movin' a clothing dummy quick enuff. After de scowlin' red-faced white dude was outta hearin' range, Jeerome slowly tuorned to me with a sad expression, den unhapp'ly told me somethin'. Jeerome sayd, 'He done blew myyy high . . . Ha!'" —Anonymous Mexican Negrito

Human (D) Evolution

TRANSLATION:
THE SHOCK OF REALITY CAN *"BLOW A LIBERAL'S HIGH."*

Now, to most people, the following may sound like it's way outside the realm of possibility: What liberals value most of all in life is staying "high" in order to *feel good*—so it's their main objective. It's sad, but true, so we should all try to be understanding. This mindless narcissistic goal explains an L.S.D.er's unhappiness and entire being. It is at least partially responsible for all of the sugary liberal claptrap and happy-faced ideology. It influences virtually everything that liberals say and do. It is the reason liberals choose to ignore disconcerting facts. Here are just a few examples: (1) "It doesn't matter *what* anybody says, no useful information is *ever* obtained by waterboarding"; (2) "Okay, so four Americans were killed. It happened two years ago—what difference does it really make now?" (3) "Don't worry—just keep waiting and waiting—eventually, you're going to *love* Obamacare."

Addiction to fantasy is the reason liberal minds can rarely be changed one iota. Here is another example: "Years of government data are *wrong*. Raising taxes on rich people will *always* produce more revenue. It doesn't make them leave the state or the country." Addiction to fantasy is the reason that, when legislation passed by liberal politicians causes our nation harm (impending bankruptcy[89] and an actual jobless rate of over 15 percent!), liberals try to blame the problem they caused on anything but socialism (anti-capitalism) and communism—and, of course, their own "mistakes" made out of self-interest.[90] For example, here are just a few examples of the excuses that liberals used when their policy of forcing banks—under threat of prosecution by the government—to loan money to high-risk minority members with low-paying jobs who obviously couldn't pay the money back *predictably* caused the U.S. housing market to collapse: (1) "Rich people caused it!" (2) "It was Wall Street's idea!" (3) "Banks did it!"[91] (4) "Our opponents are still obstructionists!" (5) "It's Bush's fault!" (6) "FOX News!" . . . and on, and on.

Liberal policies do not work, and they never have worked—ever. All of their legislation is *insolvent*. Practically everything they do is for *themselves,* not the American public. Self-serving liberal policies and opinions (e.g., *ancient greed*[92]) are

---

[89] Actually, independent countries don't go bankrupt. They just print more money to pay their debts, and thus lower the value of their currency, which, in turn, lowers the standard of living for everyone living there. Eventually, they become Mexico.

[90] The accuracy of U.S. government reports on such things as the jobless rate or the state of the economy is subject to politicization and manipulation. At the time of this writing, the information being supplied to us appears to be little more trustworthy than unsolicited e-mails from scammers in Nigeria.

[91] Banks would have been penalized if they had not done it—according to the law that liberals themselves passed!

[92] "Cursed he be above all others / Who's enslaved by love of money." —Aeschylus (525–456 B.C.), Greek dramatist

so old, they need to be carbon-dated. So why have we looked the other way for so long. Laziness? Disinterest? Or for the entertainment value? Is it because we like to watch liberals try to put square pegs in round holes? Why? So we can laugh at them? Or do we just like to feel smarter, morally superior, and more like adults—like when we see a children's puppet show? If so, it's time to stop enjoying ourselves and having so much fun, because it's not a laughing matter anymore. Far from it.

> Warning: L.S.D.ers in our federal government have been *wasting our money for decades now*—money that we did not give them, money that they do not have, and money that they are not supposed to spend! (Soon, all of that paper Monopoly money will have to be paid back, one way or another, by these liberal socialist Democrat puppets.)

As if that isn't bad enough, consider this: What if the apparently unalterable liberal belief that "there really is no evil in the world, so all that we have to do is be nice to tyrants and they'll like us and be our friends" suddenly resulted in a series of weak political decisions, awful policies, and chaos?[93] A catastrophic failure involving our National Security?[94] Guess what? It already happened once: the WikiLeaks document dump.[95] For some reason, after Jimmy Carter (D-Georgia) and then Bill Clinton (D-Arkansas) were elected to be our presidents, we all slowly began to let our guards down, and now we're all suffering the predicted global consequences.[96]

---

[93] *Re: Gun Control:* If liberals have their way, we'll all have to hunt pheasant with BB guns.
[94] Some of us still remember when National Security meant protecting our country from *government infiltration by 1960s liberals.*
[95] *Re: The WikiLeaks Document Dump.* In World War II, such a thing would have been inconceivable:
- 92,000 documents were made public on the Afghanistan War.
- 400,000 documents were made public on the Iraq War.
- 251,000 State Department documents were made public and available to our enemies.

The (alleged) culprit, P.F.C. Bradley E. Manning, a U.S. Army Intelligence analyst and devoted Lady Gaga fan, is said to have had "social difficulties" in the military that were attributed to his being homosexual. His subterfuge gives a new meaning to the phrase "Don't ask, don't tell." Did he vote for the Democrat Barack Hussein Obama—does anyone know? Or is he neutral politically? Maybe he doesn't vote at all. Or maybe he just writes in votes for Mary Poppins. Whatever the case may be, this is a prime example of how liberals view serving their country. They keep serving us up to our enemies on a silver platter. It's still an ongoing investigation.
[96] When former president Clinton signed the North American Free Trade Agreement (N.A.F.T.A.), it was just the beginning of our economic woes. But why did he do it? As predicted by conservatives, N.A.F.T.A. had the expected outcome of converting jobs for Americans into jobs for our poor Mexican neighbors. That's why so many of the things that we buy today come from Mexico, instead of here in the United States. Maybe Clinton did it because he wanted Mexican Americans to like him and vote for him and his wife and other members of the Democratic Party, despite the fact that virtually all citizens of the United States of America would suffer more hardship. Ya' think?

Those who live in the urban agglomeration called New York City, the omphalos (i.e., focal point) of *liberal civilization,* and of all liberal activity here in the United States, should of course pay special attention.[97] For a conservative American, staying relaxed and unconcerned 24/7—*like a liberal high on dopamine*—is simply inconceivable. What else is there left to say about the situation? As the old saying goes, "You can talk to a stupid person but you can't make him (or her) understand." Maybe we should all just give up and move to Africa.

Fantasy Addiction Disorder (F.A.D.)[98]

So here's the theory in a nutshell: *Liberals are fantasy addicts.* Facing the world as it really is does not appeal to them at all because reality does not make them feel good. Liberals (especially "progressive" left-wing loons)[99] are hooked like heroin

---

[97] The once-great state of New York is sort of like Kenya. It's a fun place to visit, but only a liberal would want to stay there. However, what we all need to understand, including committed skeptics, is that there is a certain fraction of a "caboodle" of LF (Liberal factor) and a bit of JF (Jewish factor) in *everybody.* This applies without exception to people all across the world, even Arab terrorists, and that is especially true for anyone who may have distant untraced ancestry back to the once-great state of New York, which is now loaded down with liberals. Furthermore, it is common knowledge in the South that many people have an Indian quotient and/or Negro quotient that is often visually almost imperceptible. The problem is that people with a larger fraction of the aforementioned quotients tend to be liberals. That is why "The Melting Pot" is now so heavily peppered with security cameras. (By the way, *omphaloskepsis* means the contemplation of one's navel as an aid to meditation. So N.Y.C. liberals and their politicians might want to *meditate* on the fact that, just recently—1975, to be exact—the famous New York City went bankrupt! The federal government of the United States of America decided to loan liberal socialist Democrats $2.3 billion to get back on their feet.)

[98] F.A.D. explains only the *fundamentals* of liberal thought and behavior. Traitors, criminals, anarchists, and even the typical everyday left-wing radical (i.e., extremist) have additional psychological issues, perhaps as a result of trauma(s) experienced in their early childhoods, or simply of an inherent disrespect for authority figures (i.e., anyone who make the rules and enforces traditional and customary behavioral guidelines) that runs like thickening sap in their decaying family trees. The attitudes of persons of the radical left-wing persuasion seem to be, for the most part, rooted in upbringings that engendered contempt not only for their own two parents (if both are known) but also for all other adults, and even more contempt for any imposing rules of law, including the Constitution of this country's fifty United States.

[99] "Progressive" is defined as a group or person "favoring or implementing social reform or new, liberal ideas." In other words, "progressive" is just another word for *liberal.* So who are these "progressives" and what is "progressivism?" Maybe they're only liberal extremists who want, for some inexplicable reason, to change their name. (See "Euphemisms and Obfuscation," page 84.) Is their goal future progress? It just doesn't seem very likely. Their goal seems to be government control—*of absolutely everything.* Maybe they would even like to modify instinctual human behavior, and thus control—i.e., reverse—human evolution and return society to the prehistoric Age of the Human Ape, when only dominant males and attractive females successfully "sowed their wild oats." That way, liberals could ensure *equality of outcome.*)

addicts on their childlike vision of life because they much prefer it to what is real. Liberals dislike reality—too many disconcerting facts to deal with. (With liberals, "facts" are defined as statements that are beneficial to oneself and thus promote the flow of dopamine.) Of course, as with any other addiction, the severity of F.A.D. can differ from one person to the next.

Generally, liberals tend to put their desire for personal pleasure above all else, including their own welfare—but only up to a certain point. This accounts for their well-known predilection for drugs—to use L.S.D.er jargon, *recreational* drugs.[100] That is why fantasy addiction, similar to drug addiction and other "addictions" that cause a release of dopamine in the brain, exists in people who are dependent on thoughts that cause feelings of euphoria. Those afflicted with F.A.D. act subconsciously to reinforce those thoughts despite the negative consequences for themselves and others. This euphoria can be maintained only as long as their fantasies remain undamaged—which explains their perpetual refusals to accept even the most trivial fact that may possibly conflict with those fictitious beliefs.

Liberals, who refuse to accept reality, will fight tooth and nail to maintain their biochemical bliss. This self-induced state of mind involves doting on the views of their collectivist Marxist "progressive" liberal ideology and/or, through simple recall, past personal use of hallucinogenic and mood-altering drugs. (Maybe that's why they so often look like they don't want to be friends with anyone.) But what are ideologues, anyway, but folks addicted to dogma, a set of "incontrovertibly true" principles that may or may not be correct, and may possibly even be fantastical in nature? Liberals' opinions are based solely on fantasy belief, delusion, and false premise—e.g., World peace is easily attainable by simply being nice to one's enemies. Left-wingers will never be convinced that what they feel and believe is wrong. (This lack of awareness of one's own disorder is also a feature of schizophrenia.)[101] You may as well be arguing with a wall of stone.

It's simply not possible, in most cases, for a liberal to accept that his or her internal logic, based on false assumptions that make him or her feel euphoric, has resulted in flawed conclusions. That's why they are known for ignoring facts and arguing endlessly 'round and 'round in circles. They also employ euphemisms and language that, although clearly inaccurate, help them maintain their erroneous visions of "humankind." Debating a liberal is an exercise in futility. Liberals refuse to acknowledge any bubble-popping fact, no matter how much evidence is presented and put on display. Becoming exasperated with their illogic is a complete

---

[100] Of course, it's probably just a coincidence, but the federal legalization of marijuana would be a boon to all voting child molesters, who could then freely procure it to use on potential victims. Liberals say they care about children. Are they lying about that, too?
[101] See anosognosia, page 69.

waste of time. Argument and frustration (and even yelling) accomplish nothing. You will never convince a liberal that he or she is wrong. Words rarely have any effect. The euphoria a liberal experiences by maintaining his or her fantastical vision of the world has taken over his or her reason, and, let's face it, a fantasy that is perpetually maintained—with no end in sight—is for all intents and purposes a delusion. Why? Because the two are indistinguishable. That is the reason that liberals are so often described as delusional, and liberalism, occasionally, as schizophrenic. Though exasperated conservative Americans have used psychiatric terms to describe liberals for decades now, probably few of them ever really suspected that some of the nomenclature they were using is fundamentally correct. Surprise!

Liberals are, indeed, the cryptic-human victims of a psychiatric zoological anomaly: *juvenile-fantasy-euphoria addiction disorder*, or F.A.D.[102] And reality "blows their high."

> "Conservatives, debating any topic, seem to experience a dopamine flow when they're *right* about something, whereas liberals seem to experience a dopamine flow when they're *wrong* about something. That must be why liberals smile and grin so much." —C. G.

Yes, unfortunately, the long-suspected, frequently alleged, and sometimes humorously postulated (yet still, I must admit, almost inconceivable) is actually true: *Liberals really do have a mental disorder.* Their opinions—whatever they may be—make them feel good. That is why they are and should be considered people of poor judgment, or P.P.J.s, for short. The enormous implications of this are clear, not the least of which is their influence, both directly and indirectly, on our criminal justice system.[103]

The recognized legal term, I believe, is *non compos mentis*.[104]

---

[102] Please note that these two terms are interchangeable. "Juvenile-fantasy-euphoria addiction disorder" is the full terminology.
[103] Maybe that's why every scandal involving the White House for the past five years is still "an ongoing investigation."
[104] I'm only joking, of course.
[105] McGuire and Troisi, *op. cit.*, p. 284.

The Biological Behavior System

The following is a simplified explanation of the relationship between behavior and the associated biochemicals that are released in the brain. The up arrows ( ) signify an increase, and the down arrows ( ) indicate a decrease in the associated factors or outcomes.

> Motivation-goal: MAINTAIN PHYSICAL AND MENTAL HEALTH
> Functional-psychological events: psychological regulation, satisfaction, self-esteem
> Physiological events: physiological regulation; stress-induced hormone activity;
> (*) norepinephrine, dopamine, and opioid activity
> Responses associated with goal-related failure: dysregulation, depression, anxiety;
> serotonin activity; enact alternative strategies to enhance health and minimize
> dysregulation; (*) norepinephrine, dopamine, and opioid activity[105]

The details of very few physiological-behavior relationships are fully understood, so they require further study. *Norepinephrine* is a stress hormone that affects large parts of the human brain where attention (alertness, or lack of it) and responding actions are controlled. This hormone triggers the flight-or-fight response—i.e., the way a human or animal reacts to threats either by standing its ground—and fighting—or by fleeing. Norepinephrine influences the reward system, or pleasurable effects. Also, *dopamine* is a neurotransmitter and precursor of other substances, including epinephrine—a hormone secreted by the adrenal glands, especially in conditions of stress, that increases the rate of blood circulation and breathing, along with the metabolism of carbohydrates (sugars, starch, and cellulose). *Serotonin* is present in blood platelets and serum that constrict the blood vessels and act as a neurotransmitter (i.e., transfers nerve impulses). *Opioid activity* refers to an opium-like compound (the chemical in illegal poppy plants) that binds to one or more of the three opioid receptors within the human body.

A Note on Endorphins

Endorphins are any of a group of hormones that are secreted within the brain and nervous system and have a number of psychological functions. Endorphins are peptides that activate the body's opiate receptors and resemble the opiates in their ability to cause an analgesic (relief from pain) effect and a feeling of well-being. Endorphins are produced by the pituitary gland and the hypothalamus during exercise, excitement, pain, consumption of spicy food, love, and sex. The term endorphin implies a pharmacological activity: *endo-* and *-orphin* are shortened forms of the words endogenous and morphine, intending to mean "a morphine-like substance originating from within the body."

In 2003, clinical researchers reported that the production of endorphins can also be triggered by relaxing in a float tank, with *little or no contact with the outside world.*

Notable Liberal Quote:

"A liberal mind is a mind that is able to imagine itself believing anything." —Max Eastman (1883–1969), writer, poet, political activist, and one-time socialist[106]

The Proposed Psychiatric Diagnosis and Code

Why has none of this been discussed on television? The public airways—no, excuse me, *cable*—is the method by which most everyone gets their news these days. This group of diagnoses is included in Appendix F of the A.P.A. manual under "Numerical Listing of DSM-IV-TR Diagnoses and Codes"[107]:

---

[106] Eastman, an atheist, was a supporter of socialism for many years and a leading patron of the Harlem Renaissance. He spent time in the Soviet Union and twice stood trial under provisions of the Sedition Act. He was an activist for liberal and radical causes but changed his views sharply later in life and became a free-market advocate and anti-communist (a metamorphosis that is commonly referred to as "growing up"). His sister was one of the founders of the American Civil Liberties Union (A.C.L.U.).

[107] American Psychiatric Association, *op. cit.*, pp. 857–858.

292.11 Amphetamine-Induced Psychotic Disorder, With Delusions[108]
292.11 Cannabis-Induced Psychotic Disorder, With Delusions[109]
292.11 Cocaine-Induced Psychotic Disorder, With Delusions[110]
292.11 Hallucinogen-Induced Psychotic Disorder, With Delusions[111]
292.11 Inhalant-Induced Psychotic Disorder, With Delusions[112]
292.11 Opioid-Induced Psychotic Disorder, With Delusions[113]
292.11 Other (or Unknown) Substance-Induced Psychotic Disorder, With Delusions[114]
292.11 Phencyclidine-Induced Psychotic Disorder, With Delusions[115]
292.11 Sedative-, Hypnotic-, or Anxiolytic-Induced Psychotic Disorder, With Delusions[116]

Perhaps the American Psychiatric Association should revise its DSM-5 to add one more diagnosis to it that pertains specifically to liberals: Dopamine Self-Induced Psychotic Disorder, With Delusions. However, for the sake of simplicity and clarity, maybe we had better just call it *fantasy addiction disorder*.[117]

Skeptics, quell your roar, and for the good of the country, please read on.

---

[108] Amphetamines, or "speed," are fatigue-reducing drugs sometimes used (illegally) by college students studying for exams.
[109] Cannabis is a "mildly" psychotropic drug often smoked in a greasy communal bong by hippies coughing uncontrollably.
[110] Cocaine is an addictive stimulant that is prohibited, for good reason, in virtually all parts of the civilized world.
[111] Hallucinogens are drugs like (sometimes mucho-contaminated) LSD.
[112] Inhalants are solvents breathed in by drug abusers who later develop perforated lungs.
[113] Opium is a narcotic used illegally by many people in Afghanistan (which explains the clouds of smoke in the skies of Kabul).
[114] "Unknown substances" can include things concocted by a nebbish with a Gilbert chemistry set.
[115] Phencyclidine (angel dust), a hallucinogenic veterinary anesthetic, is much preferred by sick liberal puppies.
[116] Prescription drugs such as these may be plucked by a sixty-five-year-old "flower child" from her neighbor's medicine cabinet.
[117] Or maybe dopamine-induced psychosis (D.I.P.) would be better.

Chapter 5

Is It Really True?

Psychiatry 101: Drug-Fueled Paranoid Schizophrenia

(The following is not meant to suggest that liberals are schizophrenics, for the vast majority of them, presumably, are not, even though some clear similarities exist between F.A.D. and schizophrenia. The facts presented here are intended only to help readers who are not conservative psychiatrists recognize a mental disorder when they see one. Everyone also needs to understand how illegal drugs and man-made chemicals of any kind can affect the human brain. The problem is that liberals sometimes do develop paranoid schizophrenia and then we hear about it in the news, but only after they commit some kind of hideous murders.)

Inarguably, the brain is the most complex organ that has ever evolved. It is the result of a multifarious evolutionary history spanning millions of years. There is much about how humans, animals, and insects think that is still a mystery or, at the very least, not well understood. Before anyone can even begin to comprehend the thought processes of our liberal friends, he or she must first have some basic knowledge of how the human mind can malfunction—i.e., flip-flop, flounder, flip out, fail, or lay a big fat egg. Perhaps the quickest way for anyone to achieve this understanding is to learn more about what is universally considered the worst of all mental disorders: *schizophrenia*.[118]

In his *Textbook of Evolutionary Psychiatry*, the professor of psychiatry at the University of Bochum in Germany, states:

> The term "schizophrenia" refers to a group of clinically highly heterogeneous psychotic disorders characterized by the presence of delusion, hallucinations, thought disturbances, disorganized behaviour, catatonic symptoms, and affective flattening or inappropriate affect.[119]
>
> Disorders within the schizophrenia spectrum are associated with widespread cognitive deficits in different domains. Executive control and social cognition, including the ability to reflect upon own and others' states of mind are most severely, perhaps selectively, compromised. One hallmark of all schizophrenia subtypes is impaired social competence, and such deficits are, by and large, best predicted by deficits in social cognition.[120]
>
> Furthermore, allelic variation of the catechol-O-methyl transferase (COMT) gene has been associated with increased vulnerability of psychosis, particularly in cannabis abusers. Finally, the cannabinoid receptor coding gene CNR1 has been hypothesized to be involved in the pathogenesis of schizophrenia, perhaps via its modulatory effects on dopaminergic and glutamatergic neurotransmission.[121]

---

[118] *Notable Liberal Quote:* "In our age, there is no such thing as 'keeping out of politics.' All issues are political issues, and politics itself is a mass of lies, evasions, folly, hatred, and schizophrenia." —George Orwell (1903–1950), English author, journalist, and liberal icon. He wrote *Animal Farm* and *Nineteen Eighty-Four*, the latter describing a frightening world in which the state controls thought and so misinformation is widespread—thus the term "Orwellian." He was a left-wing socialist Democrat who was suspected of being a communist, though that was not reflected in his writing. British Intelligence kept a file on Orwell for more than twenty years. Prior to his death, he spent eight months in a sanatorium.
[119] Martin Brüne, *Textbook of Evolutionary Psychiatry*, 2008, Oxford University, New York, N.Y., p. 185.
[120] Ibid., p. 188.
[121] Ibid., p. 190.

Undoubtedly, the psychological suffering of a schizophrenic cannot be fully comprehended by anyone sane. That is because people with full-blown schizophrenia may see, hear, say, do, and believe things that are incomprehensible to the rest of us.[122] Schizophrenics may perceive, for example, the faces of friends and relatives to be altering monstrously before their very eyes, like oil paintings by Picasso. They may even hear the queer otherworldly voices of "angels" or "demons" commanding them to do extraordinary things (throw cream pies, glitter, shoes, animal blood, human excrement, or other bodily fluids at people who disagree with them). Schizophrenics may also speak in strings of rapid nonsensical words, indicating thoughts and notions unfathomable to a normal mind.[123] Inexplicably, a schizophrenic may even wipe animal feces on meat and vegetables in a supermarket. Sometimes, a victim of schizophrenia is even convinced that invisible electrical wires are running from his or her brain to a flying saucer overhead that is piloted by (undocumented) aliens.

As you can see, the insanity of the afflicted literally knows no bounds, and suicide is not uncommon.[124] This can include the person intentionally putting his own life at risk by deliberately overdosing on drugs and alcohol, and it probably happens more often than we think. We should always remember that the behavior of a person with schizophrenia is internally logical, rational, and sound. The afflicted do things for reasons that, because of their disordered faculties and faulty thinking, *make sense only to them*.[125] That is why it is virtually impossible to convince a schizophrenic that what his or her brain is telling him or her is wrong. To an outside observer, the behavior may appear irrational or crazy, but to the schizophrenic, there is nothing crazy about it at all. As mentioned previously, this is called *anosognosia*. It is very difficult to understand, so here it is in black and white.

---

[122] Most of us would also consider incomprehensible a sitting U.S. president who declines to respond *instinctively and immediately* with force to an attack on a U.S. consulate. For example, the terrorist attack in Benghazi, Libya, began at night (3:40 PM Eastern Time) on September 11, 2012, and ended the next day. Those killed were United States Ambassador J. Christopher Stevens, Foreign Service Information Management Officer Sean Smith, and C.I.A. Security Officers and former Navy Seals Tyrone Woods and Glen Doherty. At the time of this writing (almost one year later), troubling questions remain unanswered, and much of what occurred—and did not occur—is still a mystery. Those who know are not talking.

[123] Some examples follow: (1) "No no no little yo yo yo maaan," and (2) "Yada yada yada, no weapons of mass destruction."

[124] "Insanity" is not a medical term but a legal one. It is characterized by extreme foolishness or irrationality. Insanity, according to Einstein, is "doing the same thing over and over again and expecting different results." However, Einstein was almost certainly referring to scientific research and not, say for example, a disastrous foreign policy, failed economic stimulus packages, unconstitutional acts and legislation, or intentional insult thrown at assorted doctors, police officers, entrepreneurs, C.E.O.s, and any conservative Republican who's the least bit successful.

[125] This statement also defines *liberal illogic*.

Anosognosia

The condition that psychiatry refers to as anosognosia is difficult for most of us to comprehend. After all, how can a person possibly not know that he (or she) is afflicted? In other words, how can a schizophrenic have no idea that he (or she) is schizophrenic? Here is the explanation: It is almost *impossible for the human mind to conceive of such a thing*. You see, if a person's intuition is faulty and it causes him (or her) to "feel and believe" things that are not true, then he (or she) is torn between the following realities:

1. the reality that he (or she) knows from a life of experience to be normal, correct, and logical, and

2. the false reality that his (or her) senses are incorrectly telling him (or her) is true.

In the overwhelming majority of cases, the patient will conclude that there cannot possibly be anything wrong with his (or her) brain—or way of thinking—so the patient concludes that the problem must be with others. [126] After all, how can your brain be malfunctioning if you are normal? In other words, if there is nothing wrong with your brain, but you are wrong about everything, then there must be something wrong with your brain. But there can't be anything wrong with your brain because if there is anything wrong with your brain, then what you are thinking doesn't make any sense. From the patient's point of view, this is inconceivable.

---

[126] Liberals, coincidentally, also believe this. For example, they believed back in 1992, when billionaire Ross Perot (I), Bill Clinton (D), and the first President George Bush (R) ran against one another in a three-way race for the presidency that our fast-growing $5 trillion National Debt could be paid off simply by raising taxes on "the rich people." It was *impossible!* But, today, liberals continue to speak, think, and behave as though it's not. The only reason Clinton won the election, by the way—and everyone knew it back then—is that Perot, a feisty conservative, split the Republican vote: Perot 18.9%, Bush 37.5%. Clinton, a liberal Democrat, was elected president of the United States with only 43% (less than half of the popular vote). It's a well-known flaw in our system that could be easily rectified—and the best thing about it is that it doesn't require different *political parties*. All that the United States of America has to do is hold one great big primary, then let the ten best guys run for president. Legally registered voters could make their choices in the order of their preference—10, 9, 8, 7, 6, 5, 4, 3, 2, 1—and we could add up each candidate's score. The one with the highest number becomes president because mathematically *he's the most popular*, and the runner up gets to be the vice-president. Simple, huh? So why don't we implement a new law as soon as possible—say, before New Year's Eve—instead of just standing around the Congressional House of Representatives in a three-piece-suit, looking important, and smiling about it?

Especially for a liberal. (Skeptics, please read on.)

Schizophrenia is a biological disorder—a "disease," by definition—that modern medicine does not fully understand. The only thing that can be said for sure is that there appears to be a genetic component, a susceptibility or predisposition. Schizophrenia is characterized by an abnormality of the mind that includes the inability to properly interpret incoming sensations—sight, sound, smell, taste, touch—resulting in an incapacity to respond appropriately to stimuli. An alteration of the senses exists that is referred to as over-acuteness. (Sensations can also be dulled, as well as enhanced.)

The human brain is a mysterious organ full of biological secrets—structural, chemical, and genetic—that scientists have only just begun to fathom. All sensory input into the brain passes through the *limbic area* in the lower portion of the brain. The limbic area is a complex system of nerves and networks that controls basic emotions and drives. The limbic system and thalamus filter this sensory input. The thalamus is either of two masses of gray matter lying between the cerebral hemispheres on either side of the third ventricle, relaying sensory information and acting as a center for pain perception. It is believed that with schizophrenics, there is a breakdown in the filter system. Normally, a person's mind filters out extraneous information coming in from all directions around it while that person performs daily activities. With schizophrenia, visual and auditory information located on the periphery of that person's awareness—information of little or no importance—enters the thought process and disturbs the consciousness. The brain's filtering system is said to be capable of becoming "permeated," and so it allows irrelevant information in.[127]

Many victims of schizophrenia also have structural brain changes, such as enlarged ventricles (four connected fluid-filled cavities), temporal lobe abnormalities (each of the paired lobes lying beneath the temples), and caudate nucleus defects (upper of the two gray nuclei of the corpus striatum in the cerebrum). The temporal lobes include areas concerned with the understanding of speech. The corpus striatum is part of the basal ganglia of the brain, which are a group of structures linked to the thalamus and involved in coordination of movement. The cerebrum is located in the front area of the skull and consists of two hemispheres responsible for the integration of sensory and neural functions and the initiation and coordination of voluntary activity.

In normal people, the brain functions in such a way that incoming information—or stimuli—is sorted and interpreted, then a correct response is chosen and sent back out. This process is believed to take place in the limbic system. The question is, what causes incorrect responses? Scientists still do not know for sure.

---

[127] Unanswered question: Can an "under-acuteness" of the senses occur when the filtering system in a person's brain gets "clogged" and keeps relevant information out?

The inability to interpret and respond appropriately to incoming information is at the very core of a schizophrenic's difficulties, including his or her ability to relate to other people.[128]

That is why many schizophrenics prefer to spend time in a room by themselves, withdrawn, staying quiet, and not communicating with others. Psychiatrists describe the schizophrenic's inability to respond to stimuli correctly as "an impairment of logic," and there are various degrees of severity—just as there are with alcoholism or marijuana dependency. In some milder cases, there is only a vagueness of thinking, lack of clarity, deficit of reasoning, and/or an evasiveness that defies precise psychiatric labeling. (Note that liberals may also exhibit these symptoms when they are on drugs.)

> "What nobody seems to understand is that, generally speaking, many, many people are nut cases *because they take drugs*. It's not the other way around. They don't take drugs because they're nut cases. They're just liberals." —Anonymous Psychiatrist

It may surprise many readers to know that delusions and hallucinations, although common symptoms, are *not* essential to a diagnosis of schizophrenia. In fact, no single symptom is required at all. Schizophrenia is a multifaceted "disease," and its mental features overlap those of other central nervous system (CNS) "diseases." Delusions, for example, are simply false ideas that are believed by the schizophrenic but not by other people—ideas that cannot be corrected by reason. They are usually based on some kind of sensory experience that the person misinterprets (which may possibly even be rooted in an ideological fantasy). Others often wonder where the delusional ideas in the affected person's mind are coming from.

Reasoning with an acute schizophrenic about his delusions will rarely achieve anything. (Note the similarity with liberals.) That person's mindset is based on an incorrect premise. You may as well be talking to someone whose ears are plugged. No matter what you say, no matter what proof you cite, no matter how convincing you are to others, that person probably will not believe you.[129]

As one psychiatrist wrote, "Reasoning with people about their delusions is like trying to bail out the ocean with a bucket"—a complete waste of time.[130] Over-acuteness of the senses, along with an impaired ability to logically interpret

---

[128] *The Liberal Mind*, copyright 2006, provides a detailed analysis of how liberals relate, and do not relate, to other people.

[129] Liberals, too, can be jungly in response to rational argument and often have little capacity for extended linear thinking.

[130] E. Fuller Torrey, M.D., *Surviving Schizophrenia*, 5th edition, 2006, HarperCollins, New York, N.Y., p. 26.

information derived from the eyes, ears, nose, tongue, and fingers, combined with a reduced ability to logically interpret thoughts, lies behind many of the delusions experienced by the schizophrenic mind.

Before we go any further, let me state once again that the vast majority of liberals are decidedly not schizophrenic—at least, not according to the strict definition or the generally accepted meaning of the word. That is just a description that many frustrated conservative Americans sometimes use when they are unable to understand or explain liberals' political behavior.[131]

Remember, liberals are human beings, too, and we should always treat them with respect.

Ethnic Groups

When examining a schizophrenic, one should always consider that person's culture, as it will affect that person's beliefs. For example, a schizophrenic man from a rural area of northern Iceland may actually be convinced that rosy-cheeked elves, subterranean gnomes, and flying winged fairies are spying on him. Or a Haitian woman may believe that she's being followed everywhere she goes by mindless zombies (the walking undead in a witch doctor's crude pharmaceutical trance) who intend to do her harm.[132] Or a hermit in Rachel, Nevada, a small desert town near Area 51 (now commonly known as "Homey" Airport), may believe that aliens from another planet are visiting his tarpaper shack at night and stealing his precious clumps of wild Mexican shit-weed before it's ready to smoke, sell, or trade for some toilet paper. Note that minority groups also tend to have a somewhat higher level of paranoia, based on historical persecution and discrimination. This, too, will affect schizophrenic beliefs.

---

[131] The liberal mental condition may warrant another new diagnostic term: *sociophantasmagoric pseudo-schizophrenia*, representing a much milder but similar form of "schizophrenia." Whatever the case, mental disorders are exacerbated by the use of drugs, so we will have to leave it up to medical researchers to decide what is wrong with these people. As mentioned in the Introduction, the reasoned arguments that this book contains may be paralogistic.

[132] Scottish psychiatrist R. D. Laing noted the link between social and cultural expectations and compulsion—forcing or being forced to do or submit to something—in the context of schizophrenia and other mental illnesses. He suggested that schizogenesis might account for some of the psychological aspects of zombification (as opposed to simple idiocy).

Severe Cases

Schizophrenics, as any psychiatrist will affirm, are usually not dangerous, despite the way they are often portrayed in books, in films, and on television. Victims of schizophrenia tend to be quiet and withdrawn, with poverty of thought (a psychiatric term) and lack of drive. Generally, schizophrenics are nonviolent. They are no more capable of harming others than is anyone else—with, of course, a few notable exceptions, such as murderers Jared Lee Loughner (2011), James Holmes (2012), and Juan Corona (1971). Schizophrenics also do not have multiple or split personalities, although people commonly believe this. Split personalities actually have nothing to do with schizophrenia. Today, most of the diseases of mankind have been identified, defined, and permanently labeled, but not schizophrenia.[133] That is because with most other diseases, evidence of their presence can be seen and measured. Mental disorders are very different. For example, with schizophrenia—even though abnormalities in brain structure and function may be present—there is nothing that can actually be put on a glass slide and examined with a microscope, then precisely labeled. For that reason, it is not a well-understood disorder. Its precise diagnosis and cause—and even its definition—are continually subject to modification and debate, and, occasionally, speculation.

Most mental disorders are genetic. Schizophrenia is genetic, too, but symptoms of schizophrenia can be triggered and/or aggravated by the use of illegal drugs. The same goes for some over-the-counter drugs, especially common cold remedies, which, of course, are available without a doctor's prescription. All drugs come with warnings. Some of those warnings are detailed and specific, whereas others are platitudinous: "If any problems occur, consult your doctor," for example.

Furthermore, some over-the-counter drugs cause fetal abnormalities. Such abnormalities may occur when a pregnant female fails to heed the printed warnings, either out of ignorance or because she can't read English—or perhaps even, in some cases, because she's hooked on an illegal drug of some kind and doesn't really care. All pregnant women should realize that different combinations of drugs can affect a developing fetus's brain, so they should always ask a pharmacist to run an Internet check on the side effects of any drug they purchase.[134]

---

[133] In medicine, the terms disease and disorder are often used interchangeably, but the vast majority of mental disorders are not "diseases," according to the layman's understanding and generally accepted usage of the term.

[134] Question: Why does anyone, especially a pharmacist, have to pay to access a medical Web site that lists all of the side effects of over-the-counter drugs? Why isn't the information readily available and free to anyone who buys the product? What happened to truth in advertising?

According to the American Psychiatric Association's *Diagnostic and Statistical Manual of Mental Disorders* (DSM-IV-Text Revision):

> The median age at onset for the first psychotic episode of Schizophrenia is in the early to mid-20s for men and in the late 20s for women. The onset may be abrupt or insidious, but the majority of individuals display some type of prodromal phase manifested by the slow and gradual development of a variety of signs and symptoms (e.g., social withdrawal, loss of interest in school or work, deterioration in hygiene and grooming, unusual behavior, outbursts of anger).[135]

The DSM-IV-Text Revision also states:

> Individuals with Schizophrenia are sometimes physically awkward and may display neurological "soft signs," such as left/right confusion, poor coordination, or mirroring. Some minor physical anomalies (e.g., highly arched palate, narrow- or wide-set eyes or subtle malformations of the ears) may be more common among individuals with Schizophrenia.[136]

Still, schizophrenics generally cannot be identified simply through observation—although the condition may certainly be suspected. A short, simple conversation with a psychiatrist is required before a positive diagnosis can be made. After determining that a patient is indeed schizophrenic, the next question the doctor usually asks is, "Do you use any drugs?" The reply may be, "Ahh, ahem, er, uh (cough) no. . . ." (The role drugs can play in the development and exacerbation of mental disorders will be examined later.)

Therefore, what we should try to understand is that the human brain, like any other electronic device, natural or man-made, is not always predictable. Computers, for example, are relatively delicate and easily capable of malfunction, not to mention complete failure. The human mind, like computers, also has the capacity to exhibit puzzling behavior.

---

[135] American Psychiatric Association, *Diagnostic and Statistical Manual of Mental Disorders*, 4th edition, Text Revision (DSM-IV-TR), Washington, D.C., 2000, p. 308. "Prodromal" refers to an early phase.
[136] Ibid., p. 306.?

How on Earth Can a Mass Mental Disorder Be Possible?[137]

You may have begun to discern that this is not a normal world in which we conservatives (i.e., normal people) dwell. This is a world in which a country full of intelligent people are deeply in debt as a nation because of politicians, yet we still have to argue vehemently with liberals about such an obvious thing as the necessity to stop spending money—even as our country falls over the edge of a fiscal cliff. This is a world in which unqualified politicians who are caught smoking crack, or stealing the public's money,[138] or taking bribes may be reelected to political office. This is a world in which medical doctors from prestigious universities cannot remember how to correctly treat, nor resuscitate, a patient. This is a world in which men and women who are obviously guilty of cold-blooded murder may be judged innocent despite overwhelming evidence. But why? It doesn't make any sense. Why are so many people so clueless? Is it because an estimated 20 percent of the public are liberal?

Never forget the old saying "There is nothing more deceptive than an obvious fact." Should we just continue to assume that the vast majority of the public are normal in their thinking? Or could liberals be afflicted with an inherent psychosis? It certainly would explain a lot of things, such as why overly relaxed liberals so often laugh, smile, and grin inappropriately when debating world politics and issues that are a matter of life and death—things that are of the utmost importance to the rest of us.

But how can some 20 percent of the population have a hitherto unknown mental disorder and no one realize it? Why, that's *more than sixty million people!*[139] No wonder we have spent ourselves into beggary. Virtually inconceivable, isn't it? The only explanation that I can offer is that the field of psychiatry is still in a relatively embryonic stage of development. Consider, too, the fact that 150 years ago, anthropology was in a similar stage. Then, suddenly, in 1859, people began to realize why they like eating bananas so much.

According to the National Institute of Mental Health (NIMH), mental disorders are common in the United States of America and internationally. An

---

[137] Illegal drugs can even cause brain abnormalities, according to some researchers.
[138] Question: Is our taxpayer money secretly being funneled to various organizations—with a wink and a nod—for the purpose of paying prominent politicians exorbitant speaking fees after they resign from (or are forced to leave) their positions? Or is it only to be used for campaign donations? Or is it just to keep their supporters happy, so they'll picket anything or anybody for TV news cameras?
[139] Based on a population of 315,666,110 (United States Census Bureau, "U.S. and World Population Clock").

estimated 26.2 percent of those people ages eighteen and older—about one in every four adults—suffer from *diagnosable* mental disorders in any given year, and about 6 percent suffer from diagnosed "serious" disorders.[140] When this percentage is applied to the 2010 U.S. Census residential population estimate, it translates to 61.4 million persons with mental disorders—and many of them suffer from *multiple* disorders. These are not my figures; they are the federal government's (and we all know how reliable *they* are). The field of mental health care has now become something of a core institution in our society.[141] Coincidentally, so have tattoo parlors[142], nudist colonies, and head shops.

On May 16, 2013, a new Centers for Disease Control (C.D.C.) report was released that describes, for the first time, federal activities that track children's mental disorders. This term means all mental disorders that can be diagnosed and that begin in childhood: for example, attention-deficit/hyperactivity disorder (A.D.H.D.), Tourette syndrome, behavior disorders, mood and anxiety disorders, autism spectrum disorders, and substance-use disorders. It has been estimated that 13 to 20 percent of children living in the United States—that could mean one out of five kids—experience mental disorders in any given year, and an estimated $247 billion is spent each year treating those disorders.[143]

Is this the same United States of America in which our parents grew up? It doesn't seem to be.

Notable Liberal Quote:

"Facts do not cease to exist because they are ignored." —Aldous Huxley (1894–1963), English novelist, author of *Brave New World*

---

[140] National Institute of Mental Health, Statistics/Prevalence/By Disorder: "Any Disorder Among Adults." The statistics depend on whom you ask, however. A mere 4.8 percent of the adult population suffer from a serious mental disorder, according to a report by the Substance Abuse and Mental Health Services Administration, based on that same year's data (www.samhsa.gov, "Mental Health, United States, 2010," p. 10).
[141] People being turned away from our nation's mental health care clinics because of lack of beds has become so common that the practice is called "streeting" (FOX News, December 9, 2013).
[142] Remember when you had to pay $1.50 for a ticket to see a tattooed woman in a circus? Now, they can be seen for free—they're all over the place.
[143] Centers for Disease Control and Prevention, "Children's Mental Health—New Report," May 17, 2013.

The *Brave* author again: "You shall know the truth, and the truth shall make you mad."[144]

Is the pervasiveness of mental disease a recent phenomenon? Let's go back half a century and take a look. General Lewis B. Hershey, testifying before House and Senate hearings after World War II, asserted that 856,000 men, representing 18 percent of all possible draftees, had been rejected because of mental illness.[145] (This figure no doubt included homosexuals.) Do the Dems have a lock on the loco vote? No, probably only about 75 percent of those with mental health issues vote Democratic—and they're all liberals. Unfortunately, there are no statistics to back this up because people diagnosed with mental problems—schizophrenia, for example—are not required to show their voter registration cards to psychiatrists, but certain facts can be gleaned from public information that *is* available. Consider the health data showing the prevalence of "poor mental health" by percentage in state populations. You may be interested to know that, of the top ten states listed—Utah, Nevada, Michigan, California, New York, Washington, Oregon, Delaware, Wisconsin, and Minnesota—*eight are blue* (i.e., they vote for Democrats).[146] Curiously enough, the only two states in this group that aren't blue—Utah (red) and Nevada (purple)—have large illegal-alien populations. (But that's probably just a coincidence, too.)

Here's another coincidence: the mental health statistics on state expenditures per capita. Of the top ten states listed—District of Columbia, New York, Hawaii, Pennsylvania, Vermont, Connecticut, Maryland, Montana, New Hampshire, and Massachusetts—*nine are blue*.[147] Curiously, the only state in this group

---

[144] Aldous Huxley, one of the most prominent and admired members of the famous Huxley family, was a humanist and pacifist well known for advocating and taking psychedelic drugs. He edited the magazine *Oxford Poetry* and was a Vedantist in the circle of Hindu Swami Prabhavananda. Later in life, he became interested in parapsychology and philosophical mysticism. (Don't most people grow out of such nonsense when they're teenagers? Yoga is for the birds, and the sacred Indian "om" sound—which is comparable to the Hebrew word Amen—isn't anything mystical. All it does is drown out all the noise when you're surrounded by crowds of people talking, so it helps a person who is suffering from lack of sleep to get some much-needed rest. Also, sitting for long periods of time with the legs folded, unmoving, is probably not good for a woman's hips.) Huxley lived in Los Angeles from 1937 to his death, but his application for United States citizenship was continuously deferred—i.e., it wasn't approved—because *he would not say that he would take up arms to defend the United States of America*. By the end of his life, he was considered in liberal academic circles to be a leader of modern thought and an intellectual of the highest rank—i.e., a rank intellectual. On his deathbed, unable to speak, Huxley made a written request for LSD (but he was reportedly given some catnip instead).
[145] Torrey, *op. cit.*, p. 418.
[146] StateMaster.com, "Health Statistics: Prevalence of Poor Mental Health (Most Recent) by State," 2013.
[147] Ibid. The mental health expenditures shown for the District of Columbia, a hefty $398.00 per capita, are more than twice that of any other state. And, curiously enough, before the Constitutional right to carry a firearm was taken away from everyone living in our nation's capital, Washington, D.C., it was also said to be the multicultural *murder capital* of the United States. Go figger.

that isn't blue—Montana (red)—also has a huge number of Spanish-speaking illegals.

Yet, the coincidences don't end there. Still another one lies in the curious fact that there are some 12,177 mental health clinics and counselors listed in our country's twenty-two blue states, whereas only 8,931 are listed in our country's twenty-two red states.[148] The difference—more than 25 percent—is significant.

It is also a fact that schizophrenia is much more prevalent in people who tend to congregate in overpopulated urban, rather than rural, areas.[149] This often includes African Americans, known to vote 85 to 95 percent Democrat (after being offered a free bus ride to the dance party).

So is it really that difficult to believe that liberals, who represent approximately one-fifth of the population in the United States of America, have a hitherto unknown, genetically inherited psychosis? Contrary to what most people may think, the human brain is just as likely to malfunction as any other bodily organ—the heart, liver, kidneys, bladder, or spleen. The only difference is that with brain dysfunction, there's a social stigma attached, which is why we rarely, if ever, hear a stranger describing weird thoughts he may have had or things he may have imagined (unless he's a drug dealer trying to con a user into paying big bucks for some common toadstools). Think of all the people you have met over the course of your life who acted in ways that you most definitely would not act, and ask yourself why. Did any of them have a psychosis? If so, could they also have had a problem with drugs or alcohol?

Statistics show that schizophrenia is increasingly on the rise. According to the A.P.A.:

> Schizophrenia has been observed worldwide. Prevalences among adults are often reported to be in the range of 0.5% to 1.5%. Annual incidences are most often in the range of 0.5 to 5.0 per 10,000. Incidence estimates beyond this range have been reported for some population groups—for instance, a far higher incidence for second-generation African Caribbeans living in the United Kingdom.[150] [By cracky, I wonder why that is!]

---

[148] The number of mental health clinics is based on listings available at YellowPages.com, "Mental Health Clinics Information, State by State." The labels "red states" and "blue states" are based on information available at Wikipedia.org, "Red States and Blue States."
[149] American Psychiatric Association, *op. cit.*, p. 308. What is not mentioned is the distinct possibility that an overabundance of noise and confusion, combined with the misuse of drugs, likely contributes to the onset and severity of a psychosis.
[150] Ibid. "Annual incidences" refers to yearly occurrences of schizophrenia.

In 2010, the *Los Angeles Times* reported that one in five Californians (almost five million adults) say they need mental health care.[151] This is especially worrisome, considering the fact that most undiagnosed schizophrenics believe that there is absolutely nothing wrong with them (i.e., anosognosia). The article was based on a survey released by researchers at U.C.L.A. About one million of those surveyed met the criteria for having "serious psychological distress." The study included more than 44,000 adults as part of the 2005 California Health Interview Survey, administered through the U.C.L.A. Center for Health Policy Research. However, don't get the wrong impression. The state of California isn't the only habitat for human loony tunes. It has been estimated that, worldwide, about 450 million people currently suffer from various psychiatric disorders.[152] The *vast majority* of those people are white liberals, black liberals, or half-white, half-black liberals who have used illegal drugs extensively.[153]

According to the aforementioned professor of psychiatry at the University of Bochum:

> Schizophrenia occurs apparently more often in urban environments compared with rural backgrounds, while the risk for schizophrenia is markedly increased by immigration, as well as through the use of illicit drugs, particularly cannabis. . . . Schizophrenia spectrum disorders comprise so many divergent findings at the clinical-behavioural, neuroanatomical, physiological, and genetic level that a unifying theory covering all facets of these disorders cannot be expected.[154]

The more research you do on schizophrenia, the more you begin to realize how little is really known for sure. The volume of work available on this subject is so overwhelming that much of the information is ignored by psychiatrists, if not forgotten altogether. Hopefully, someday, the search for a unifying theory will be successful.

---

[151] "One in Five Californians Say They Need Mental Health Care," *Los Angeles Times*, July 28, 2010.
[152] Brüne, *op. cit.*, p. 102.
[153] The president, for example, who admitted in his book that he has used cocaine in the past, may himself have symptoms of narcissistic personality disorder. For more information on this subject, read the A.P.A. handbook.
[154] Brüne, *op. cit.*, pp. 190, 192.

Some Vegan Food for Thought: Should a ponytailed, pot-smoking male psychiatrist who, being fully aware of the content of the American Psychiatric Association's mental health manuals, DSM-IV-Text Revision and others, continues to advocate for the legalization of "recreational drugs" and the easy public availability of "medical LSD," "medical methamphetamine," and "medical cocaine" have his license revoked? (Or should he be summarily executed?) No? What if Dr. Californigula happens to be the one treating a drugged-out liberal weirdo who eventually goes berserk and starts shooting at people?[155] There are different kinds of terrorists; some have pleasant voices, nice smiles, pipes, and cardigan sweaters—and brains the size of peas.

Liberals seem to view the world much differently than do those of us with normal (i.e., conservative) thinking processes. You may have also noticed that liberals tend to argue in circles. Anyone who tries to convince a liberal to change his or her opinion on matters of public policy is wasting his or her breath. Except on rare occasions, liberals seem immune not only to cold, hard facts and to the opinions of abstemious professionals but also to official government documents, verifiable scientific research, and irrefutable physical evidence provided by the Federal Bureau of Investigation (F.B.I.). Photographs, videotapes, films, eyewitness accounts, and expert testimony may elicit nothing more from a liberal than a mute stare and a slight shaking of his or her "puppet" head. Apparently, liberals don't want to believe what they don't want to believe, and nothing's going to change their minds. Proof contrary to liberal dogma is rarely, if ever, accepted by any of them for more than a few days. Incredibly, if the facts do not fit the popular preconceived narrative, a zealous liberal will try to ignore, twist, or spin even that which he or she has witnessed with his or her own two eyes. Liberals are also famous for their complete and utter disregard for the past when it warns against their goals for the future. That is why they constantly seek to manipulate, alter, or even erase many historical records (e.g., Trotskyism works great!).[156]

---

[155] Liberals dislike hypothetical-situation questions like this. Why? Because they loathe the correct answers.
[156] Psychologists are still unsure why liberals, in general, seem to prefer foreign leaders with wild unkempt beards, funny haircuts, and silly faces—Trotsky, Guevara, Chavez, Castro, Zedong, and others—or somebody like now-deceased Libyan leader Muammar Gaddafi, a transvestite who looked like he had been struck by lightning while shampooing a zoo animal.

As many of us know, there's virtually nothing that we can say or do to change a liberal's political opinion permanently.[157] Reality, it seems, has almost no meaning. Indeed, the old saying "You can talk to a stupid person, but you can't make him understand" likely drew its inspiration from debating a Democratic politician. But make no mistake, liberals are not stupid people. In fact, some of them are very intelligent (the ones whose ecologically friendly organic socks match). I would venture to say that in most conservative Americans' households, liberal illogic is a regular topic of discussion at the family dinner table, eliciting not only laughter and ridicule but also, on occasion, the angry physical dismemberment of a roasted lemon-pepper chicken. That's because liberals have unalterable opinions about things that continue to persist no matter how many times they're proven dead wrong, and liberals are well known for rejecting what a majority of the general public refers to as *common sense*. (This term, by the way, is one that left-wing radicals rarely use—probably because when they do, conservative adults roll their eyes knowingly and smirk.) It's almost as though liberals think they're in a movie and the plot has a secret twist or surprise ending or something.

Yes, a liberal is capable of ignoring anything under the sun (especially his or her own children). That's why a liberal politician, like a one-eyed narcoleptic flying a whirlybird in a typhoon, is so consistently risky and downright dangerous. With liberals, even proven facts and unbiased scientific research can go in one ear and out the other. When questioned, they often lie or say puzzling things in response that do not make a smidgen of sense.[158] It's almost as though liberals are living in some unknown dimension parallel to our own, because they don't seem to see, hear, or understand what everyone else does.

Never be fooled by an overly animated liberal who consistently frowns and pouts and shakes his or her head with disbelief, then raises his or her voice in anger, waving the arms in a display of exasperation, as though surrounded by people who don't understand anything at all. This is merely an attempt to portray oneself as a minority victim of the majority in order to conceal the utter erroneousness of one's logic.

It is a rare—but not unknown—occurrence when a liberal begins to break down and admit, not only to himself but also to others, that he or she may possibly be wrong about something with regard to anything political. It's as though his

---

[157] Sometimes, in fact, affable radio talk-show hosts make a career out of being 100 percent wrong about practically everything ("O. J. Simpson is innocent," for example). Some of them can be very entertaining (maybe because they used to be stand-up comics), but the problem is that liberal fans are susceptible to taking them seriously and thus will agree with everything they say. Remember how *folie à plusieurs* works?

[158] Sometimes, the FOX News channel proves this is true by interviewing liberal socialist Democrats who do a lot of pleasant smiling and disjointed talking, but then, afterward, they show a series of apposite excerpts.

or her view of the world has been molded and set in (premixed) Sakrete. When such an anomaly does occur and the liberal alters his or her opinion even slightly, he or she inevitably realizes the "mistake" and begins to backtrack immediately—especially if it means not being invited to some other liberal's (homosexual?) metrosexual cocktail party. Backtracking always occurs shortly after such inexplicable instances of carelessness—be it minutes, or a few days, or even a couple of weeks later—thus rectifying the liberal's temporary indiscretion.

In a detailed book *The Liberal Mind: the Psychological Cause of Political Madness*, the author, a forensic psychiatrist who has testified in numerous court cases, states:

> The liberal agenda fails this test [of the suitability of any political system for the regulation of human affairs] because its deeply flawed conceptions and the rules implied by them fail to protect the rights essential to the overall structure of liberty. Modern liberalism misconceives the nature of man, the nature of human relating, the nature of human development, the conditions in which relating and development must occur, and the ideals and institutions needed to promote and protect ordered liberty. These misconceptions foster economic irresponsibility, social conflict and political incoherence. By undermining capacities for self-reliance, voluntary cooperation, moral realism and informed altruism, they degrade the character of the people. When implemented in social policy they interfere with the acquisition of essential developmental achievements including basic trust, autonomy, initiative, industry, identity and competence. The liberal agenda upsets the balance of reciprocal influences between individual, family, community and government. The modern liberal mind generates these misconceptions because it suffers from systematic distortions in its perceptions of the world. It is a mind afflicted with madness.[159]

---

[159] Lyle H. Rossiter Jr., M.D., *The Liberal Mind: The Psychological Cause of Political Madness*, 2006, Free World Books, St. Charles, Illinois, p. 328 (www.libertymind.com).

You will be even more surprised when you read Part II, because not only do liberals have a genetically inherited mental disorder but you'll find out exactly *why* they have it and *where* it came from. Then you're liable to begin questioning everything you've always believed about the human race—including mankind's past, present, and future. You will probably even begin to wonder what the hell kind of world this is that you are living in. Prepare for a journey into the unimaginable. What you are about to read is going to open up a whole new can of wriggling earthworms in Darwin's theory of evolution.

Chapter 6

Why Do They Act So Silly?

Understanding Liberals in Sixty Seconds

On Guns: Liberals don't like guns because guns are not part of the liberals' fantasy world, so it doesn't matter if owning and using guns is right or wrong ("What difference does it make?"); guns don't release dopamine in liberals' brains, so guns don't make liberals *feel good!*

On the U.S. Military: Liberals don't like the United States military because the United States military is not part of the liberals' fantasy world, so it doesn't matter if having and using a military is right or wrong ("What difference does it make?"); the military doesn't release dopamine in liberals' brains, so it doesn't make liberals *feel good!*

On War: Liberals don't like war because war is not part of the liberals' fantasy world, so it doesn't matter if the war is right or wrong ("What difference does it make?"); war doesn't release dopamine in liberals' brains, so it doesn't make liberals *feel good!*

On the Laws of the U.S. Constitution: Liberals don't like the laws of the United States Constitution because the laws are not part of the liberals' fantasy world, so it doesn't matter if some laws are right or wrong ("What difference does it make?"); they don't release dopamine in liberals' brains, so they don't make liberals *feel good!*

On Reality and Morality: Liberals don't like reality and morality because reality and morality are not part of the liberals' fantasy world, so it doesn't matter if reality . . . Get it? . . . . Facing reality does not make liberals *feel good!*

The Tea Party Protest against President Obama's Policies

Maybe this will help quell the roar. Some readers may remember the CNN reporter who lost her cool—and, three months later, her job—while interviewing Tea Party members at a protest in Chicago on April 15, 2009.[160] The videos are still all over the Internet. The Tea Party demonstration was held on Tax Day only a few months after President Barack Obama's (NF3.5) inauguration.

The CNN reporter, along with other cheery Democrats across the United States—and no doubt in many Third World countries and certain parts of Europe, as well—was obviously still in a state of bliss over this wonderful new world leader, who was proclaimed by many enthusiastic African Americans to be "the smartest president this country has ever had!" (Now they know better.)

Like others of her political persuasion, this reporter now apparently felt that all was right with the world. The long-awaited, prophesied, low-swinging sweet Chicago chariot of a Democratic Party dream had finally come true. A beautiful acrylic painting of flowers, fruit, songbirds, and thick blades of green grass entitled *Hope and Change* had been elected the president of our new unknown Royal American Monarchy. His Holiness, Barack Hussein Obama, the Liberal King had been officially crowned.[161] The only thing missing was an elaborate vel-

---

[160] The word tea, by the way, stands for *taxed enough already*. Apparently, Tea Party members (especially the skinny ones) are fed up with paying other people's bills. For years now, the American people have listened to multitudes of Democrats who—virtually without exception—insinuated, labeled, or energetically denounced the Tea Party as racist. Those same talking heads inexplicably lost some movement in their lying tongues when, in 2012, Tea Partyers began to increasingly favor as a presidential candidate a conservative African American whose popularity among conservatives has helped eradicate a commonly held racial misperception caused by decades of incessant liberal propaganda.
[161] Micromanagement, the way African kings do it, just doesn't work very well. Ask anyone who works for a Fortune 500 health insurance company.

vet robe with matching loafers and a toy scepter. Peace on earth, Goodwill donations to men.

The Chosen One now reigned supreme—and with all of the toppings, including extra cheese, green pepper, and mushrooms. Liberals believed that their long-sought fantasy world, planet Nirvana, was finally coming into being and—at last!—all of their goals would be achieved. The cumulonimbus clouds parted, and a singing choir of heavenly angels could be heard above. It was the dawning of the Age of Entertainment.

Apparently, many strapped-for-cash college students thought that Barack Obama's election to the office of the presidency was going to mean that they would have a friend in the White House who was "one of them." They probably never dreamed in a million years that, after graduation, they would be forced to go back home and live with their alternately grinning and scowling parents. Unfortunately, fantasies can be difficult things to maintain in the face of reality, especially when real life takes the form of a seething multitude of increasingly angry middle-class citizens critical of their new debonair leader's lack of concern about other people's money.

So here was this poor unsuspecting CNN reporter, floating on cloud nine, suddenly confronted with hundreds of fuming, sign-waving terrestrials. How was she to know that they were only protesting our federal government's wasteful spending and the resulting huge National Debt (on that particular day, a mere whopping $11,218,863,034,278.70)?[162] How was she to know that protesters were particularly incensed by the $780 billion in green paper money that a Democrat-controlled Congress, with the president's blessing, had recently flushed down a Washington, D.C., toilet into a vast, complex cistern with multitudes of winding and curving underground pipes, some of which eventually led back to D.N.C. campaign coffers?[163] The worst thing was that those awful Tea Party people were saying such terrible things—the truth of which was apparent to most conservative American observers—about the liberal media's new big-eared, skinny, "godlike," fake-Greek-column hero.

---

[162] TreasuryDirect, "Debt to the Penny and Who Holds It," U.S. Department of the Treasury. This figure represents the total public debt to China and everyone else that was outstanding on April 15, 2009. Incredibly, during President Obama's first term in office, the faster the National Debt Clock accelerated, the more that liberal socialist Democrats believed they were winning some kind of economic-political lottery.

[163] Generally speaking, those of Jewish heritage are the only ones with any intelligence who willingly donate large sums of money to the liberal socialist Democrat Party. In fact, the Democratic Party probably wouldn't even exist without their help. The puzzling thing about this is, why would so many of them support the D.N.C.? Is it because liberals are much easier to manipulate than conservatives, so the Democratic Party is where the easy money can be made? Maybe we should ask the president's former campaign manager, David Axelgrease. Wouldn't it be nice if every American did what he or she knows is for the good of the country, rather than just good for themselves monetarily? Hopefully, someday we'll have real patriots working for us in Washington, D.C., rather than just a bunch of walking, talking, self-concerned political puppets.

This didn't seem to jibe at all with this particular CNN reporter's personal view of things. In fact, it appeared to be a major frontal assault on her senses. Suddenly, sarcasm changed to anger as she began arguing with people in the crowd, including a father with a two-year-old baby, whereupon she ended her report and signed off, arrogantly dismissing a *legitimate public protest* with several irrational statements: "[This is] anti-CNN," and "This is highly promoted by the right-wing conservative network FOX," and "This is not really family viewing." What on earth was this woman talking about?

Yes, apparently, this reporter felt that the Tea Party protest might upset the euphoric dreams not only of liberal adults but also of their children, so they should cover their eyes with their hands—that is, if any liberals had even the slightest idea where their litters were at the time. But what for? To prevent them from reading the obscene Tea Party words handwritten on the sign behind that reporter's head: "**T**o **E**very **A**merican: **P**oliticians **A**re **R**esponsible **T**o **Y**ou"?

Isn't *government accountability* what our forefathers and the framers of the Constitution intended?

Can you imagine even in your wildest dreams a nationally known conservative news reporter irately snapping at people and losing control of him- or herself while interviewing peacefully protesting liberals?[164] No, of course not. So what is going on? What's with this big difference between liberals and conservative Americans, anyway? Liberals are normal people, right? Let's hope so. They're all over the place. But, come to think of it, so are buzzing gnats, biting horseflies, and bloodsucking mosquitos.

The difference is this: Conservative Americans have no *childlike fantasy* to maintain. Conservatism, unlike liberalism, is rooted in reality, not wishful thinking. Individuals who are confident in the logic of their beliefs are not intellectually threatened by contrary opinion, especially when that contrary opinion is crystal-clearly *illogical*.

Internet bloggers, for simple lack of understanding, labeled that reporter a "psycho" and a "nut job," but actually, the poor woman is an award-winning news correspondent who has worked in radio and television broadcasting for more than two decades. She has had, for example, prime-time news anchor positions at several television stations. Her only inherent problem, over which she, like all other liberals, seems to have little or no control, is F.A.D. It rules their minds.

And the Tea Party continues, even to this day, to "blow their high."

---

[164] To paraphrase H. L. Mencken, the evidence of bogusness lies in the fact that a thing is insecure.

Human (D) Evolution

Five Methods that L.S.D.ers Use to Ignore Facts

Method 1: Euphemisms and Obfuscation

The old bumper-sticker phrase "ESCHEW OBFUSCATION" means *avoid confusion*, and confusion can be caused by sugarcoated facts.[165] Conservatives only sugar-coat facts occasionally, when they're talking to their children and don't want to upset them. Liberals, on the other hand, mix sugar with their words regularly to avoid offending other liberals with the truth—and they expect conservatives to act the same way. Liberals do this, apparently, to maintain in their own minds a high level of popularity. For example, saying that someone is "extremely odor challenged" when he or she stinks like a pig is a euphemism, and it doesn't make that person smell any better. Always be wary of anyone who employs euphemisms when writing or speaking, because for one thing, it's an indication that the person is being deceptive or trying to maintain in his or her own mind a false sense of reality. Caramelized, cooked-up, sugar-flavored words and phrases help liberals maintain a sense of personal security—just like a child who has candy. A few translations follow.

- *Fairness* (giving more money, against your will, to President Obama's supporters)
- *Diversity* (increasingly suboptimal populace)
- *Level the playing field* (tilt the field so all of the lazy boneheads will roll to the top)
- *Shared prosperity* (making hardworking Anglo-Saxons[166] pay goof-off's bills)
- *Wealth tax* (Gimme yo' money, mister.)
- *Multiculturalism* (a sly liberal method of increasing Democratic Party voter rolls)[167]

---

[165] The phrase *eschew obfuscation* is attributed to an aeronautical engineer with a good track record—i.e., a non-liberal.
[166] For lack of a more precise *general* term.
[167] Liberal multiculturalism is probably the reason for the recent vandalism to our national monuments. Now, baggage handlers at airports are being arrested for theft—i.e., stealing people's luggage and tearing it apart. Multiculturalism is likely also the reason that so many kids are being bullied in schools nowadays. Societal suboptimality is just another liberal legacy of which all L.S.D.ers can be proud.

- *Hate speech* (an objective analysis of liberals and their agenda)[168]
- *Social justice* (giving white people's money to black people)[169]
- *Tolerance* (letting liberals make your life miserable, rather than doing something about it)[170]
- *Family planning* (making an appointment with a licensed murderer to kill a fetus)
- *Conservatives* (orthodox, normal, respectable people)[171]
- *Liberals* (dysgenic domesticated pet-like *Homo sapiens*)

Liberals fear words greatly. Why? Because words transmit facts and information, their two mortal enemies. We've all observed liberals who, in discussions of politics, sigh deeply, shake their heads animatedly, and even bury their faces in their hands like ostriches in the sand, then display overt boredom, frustration, and anger. It's all a juvenile act—obfuscation—and an attempt to draw attention away from the truth and thus avoid a rational discussion. This kind of instinctual "mentally retarded" behavior helps preserve, in the liberal's own mind, the *legitimacy of illogic* and thus attain what the liberal really wants most of all: cotton candy.

"Why do liberals have to manipulate the English language in order to conceal uncomfortable truths?" —Anonymous television personality

---

[168] The offensive word "whitechickenniggerfucker," for example.

[169] The often-stated liberal desire to "spread the wealth" appears to originate in an unashamed abnormal urge to benefit oneself personally—monetarily, socially, and politically—at the expense of others: people the liberal doesn't know, doesn't want to know, and couldn't care less about (often, self-sufficient—orthodox—conservatives). Clearly, no one with the mental and physical ability to get dressed, brush his or her teeth, and go apply for a job at a McDonald's is entitled to anyone else's possessions—including his or her neighbor's checkbook—any more than that neighbor is entitled to theirs, yet the preposterous pseudo-compassionate noble-sounding rhetoric goes on.

[170] There comes a point when the tolerance of foolishness becomes foolishness in and of itself.

[171] Two more words that many liberals use to describe conservatives in order to muddy the water are *extremists* (normal commonsense people) and *denialists* (concerned patriotic Americans who simply do not believe a word that any liberal says).

Human (D) Evolution

Method 2: Circular Reasoning

Example 1: Liberals are never wrong, because liberals say so. Liberals say so because liberals are never wrong.

Example 2: Democratic Party politicians care the most about poor people, because Democrats say so. Why do Democrats say so? Because Democratic Party politicians care the most about poor people.

Example 3: Presdent Pooh-Pooh oughta be king uh da wuorld, because A.C.O.R.N. said so, and A.C.O.R.N. said so because Presdent Pooh-Pooh oughta be king uh da wuorld.[172]

Method 3: Omission of Information

1. LIBERAL (*adamantly*): "Guns kill people!" (But only when someone buys a gun, buys ammunition for the gun, and loads the gun, then walks up to another person and points it at that person's head and says, "Die, you bastard!" and pulls the trigger. Guns don't kill people; people kill people, and before guns were invented, people used spears, rocks, and knives.)

2. LIBERAL SOCIALIST (*accusatorily*): "He's a racist!" (A bicycle racist.)

---

[172] A.C.O.R.N., or the Association of Community Organizations for Reform Now, an extinct "antipoverty" organization whose headquarters were located in New Orleans, Louisiana, was not only operating in the United States of America but also served Argentina, Mexico, India, Canada, and Peru. In 2010, after A.C.O.R.N. had survived for some forty years, A.C.O.R.N. employees were discovered to be engaging in serial criminal activity, including Democratic voter-registration fraud. They were also filmed with hidden cameras and "outed" on national television. Incredibly, A.C.O.R.N. was *receiving* yearly taxpayer funding from our federal government! To top it off, the brother of the founder of A.C.O.R.N. reportedly embezzled almost $1 million. All of that wasted money, of course, is now part of our rapidly accelerating National Debt. The question is, what happened to all of the liberals that used to work for A.C.O.R.N.? Rumor has it that they now work for the N.A.A.C.P. (the National Association for the Advancement of Creole Puppets).

3. LIBERAL SOCIALIST DEMOCRAT (*smugly*): "My opponent said—*and I quote*—'I don't like poor black people!'" (The actual quote being, "I don't like poor black people always being tricked by Democrats.")

Method 4: Drowning out Opposing Views with Chanting, Rhyme, and Song

Example 1: "If the glove doesn't fit, you must acquit."
Example 2: "Bush lied; kids died!"
Example 3: "Hey-hey, ho-ho, so-and-so has got to go!"

"Liberals are impervious to rational discussion." —Betty Boop

Method 5: Lying

What exactly does it mean to lie? There are two kinds of "lie" in the English language: (1) the "lie" meaning to make an untrue statement with intent to deceive and (2) the "lie" meaning to assume a horizontal position in the morgue after being shot with a Saturday night special. The "lie" that we are talking about here, referring to a misrepresentation of facts, comes from the Old English *l ogan,* akin to the ancient German word *liogan*.[173] ("Lie" is also—just so you'll know—the abbreviation for "liberal in ecstasy.") Generally, an untruth attains the level of a lie only when it is deliberate and of some consequence. That is why today, anyone who accuses the president of the United States of lying is *technically incorrect,* because at this point, let's face it, no one but a mugged and clubbed victim waking up from a five-year coma would really believe anything that President Monkeyshine has to say, and so his rhetoric can be considered inconsequential.

In most cultures, there is no general law against lying, except to government officials and/or when placed under oath. If there were a law, everyone in the entire world would be incarcerated—and all liberal politicians would be bound, gagged, and held in maximum security.[174] When *orthodox* conservatives charge liberals with having no core

---

[173] Merriam-Webster.com.
[174] As any psychiatrist will affirm, *deception* is a common feature of persons with mental conditions.

beliefs, those liberals to whom their charges apply rarely—if ever—deny it, so clearly, even liberals believe that it's true.[175] Despite that, the advantage for those who have no core beliefs is (1) a diminished feeling of guilt and (2) a decreased inhibition against lying.

It wasn't so long ago, when times were tough, that any man caught lying to his friends, family, and neighbors was shunned or punished—and perhaps even killed—but today, most Americans consider politicians in Washington, D.C., who don't tell the truth to be standard fare in the political talking-dummy industry. Sometimes, lying politicians even appear to be admired for their hutzpah. Why? Because of *recognition*. You see, most people tell falsehoods at one time or another as a defensive measure, so when elected representatives do it, people see themselves. That's why lying politicians are now viewed as entertainment. But here's the big problem: Conservative Americans have core beliefs, but liberals don't—*everybody knows it*—and that's a very bad thing, because people with no core beliefs view the act of lying very differently from the rest of us. Liberals view lying not merely as an acceptable way of defending oneself but as a normal mode of behavior. That is why liberals are so quick to lie and tell untruths for miscellaneous other reasons, such as self-aggrandizement, monetary enrichment, and sex—even if it constitutes an act of criminality.

Notable Liberal Quote:

"I'm absolutely, one hundred percent, not guilty." —O. J. Simpleton, half-black football player

Our liberal friends love to lie; that's why they do *so much of it*. Liberals spontaneously lie to help maintain their fantasies. In fact, liberals are likely the ones referred to in ancient Eastern texts as "bearers of false witness."[176] It certainly seems probable. If

---

[175] The term orthodox means traditional and applies to many conservative Republicans just as it applies to many Democrats of the Jewish faith. Politically savvy members of both political parties will often vote in their own self-interests for the most easily manipulated and/or "bought-off" political puppets. That is when trouble ensues.

[176] Always be wary of smiling liberal Democratic Party politicians who invoke the name of Jesus, especially when most of them seem to believe that Jesus Christ is just a myth, much like Hercules or Zeus. The liberal will smugly ask, "If Jesus were alive today, would he be a Democrat or Republican?" as though the answer is obvious because Jesus cared so much for humanity, just like liberals keep saying that they do. (And the Kenyan American president so loved the world that he brought forth a Barbados American attorney general to sell AK-47s to Mexican drug cartels, who used them to murder hundreds of innocent people.)

so, that means liberals have been around for a long, long time. Are liberals the ones who caused the guiltless in times past to be punished, tortured, or put to death? The answer is yes. Just watch how they (liberals) behave on the evening news: jerking, bobbing, and weaving at almost every single question put to them—with their heads, arms, and legs all over the place, as they repeat some rehearsed gibberish. Sometimes the things that they say are so stupid, you would swear there was a ventriloquist hiding somewhere nearby. Listen carefully to what they keep saying repeatedly and decide for yourself. Are ancient liberals the ones who shamelessly pointed their fingers at innocent people and then called them murderers? The answer is *yes*. If you have any doubt about this, just ask former White House Deputy Chief of Staff Karl Rove or his bodyguards. Liberals ignore facts and continuously lie, lie, lie.[177] But why? The answer is simple. They do it because it makes them feel good, which helps them to function normally and survive. It's their way of obtaining unnatural and undeserved power, influence, and control over their more capable fellow man. To win elections and keep their jobs, liberals are forced to tell multiple falsehoods. If our big-shot political liberal friends were not allowed to lie, they would all be cleaning public toilets with plastic scrub brushes and/or mopping the floors at Toys "R" Us.

Notable Liberal Quote:

"What would Jesus do?" —Congressman Charlie Wrangler (D-New York)

Certainly not what Wrangler did with regard to House ethics rules and state and federal income tax laws.[178] Liberal politicians always try to paint their most popular opponents as uneducated and dumb even when the exact opposite is true. One reason for that, besides being unable to successfully dispute conservative American views, is that liberals seem to hold *personal popularity* dearer than

---

[177] *Notable Biblical Quote:* "This is the reason I speak to them in figures, because they see and yet cannot perceive; and they hear and yet do not listen, nor do they understand." —St. Matthew 13:13

[178] Democratic Party Representative Charlie Wrangler, in a discussion of the questionable wisdom of raising federal income taxes during a National Debt crisis, was implying that, yes, we should (FOX News, *Special Report,* July 10, 2011). Ironically, prior to this, following a series of allegations of ethics violations and failure to comply with state and federal income tax laws, Wrangler was forced to step down as Ways and Means chair, where *he was in charge of writing tax laws!* In November 2010, the House Ethics Committee found Wrangler guilty of eleven (11) counts of violating House ethics rules and later approved a sanction of censure against him.

life itself.[179] The very thought of not being invited to another liberal's multiethnic wine-and-cheese party and then chatting with oddly attired strangers named Jude, Mongo, or Abdul is simply more than any of them can take. (Oh, the unbearable shame!)

> "To a democrat any attitude based upon a concept of honor, dignity and integrity seems contemptible and offensive." —H. L. Mencken, humorous journalist, essayist, editor, critic, and one of the most influential writers of the first half of the twentieth century[180]

"Tell the truth!" sly far-left know-nothings often demanded back in the '60s when they argued with conservatives, thereby falsely insinuating that others were lying—and thus lying *themselves*. But fortunately, that tactic doesn't work very well anymore. Today, any liberal who demands that someone tell the truth is usually met with knowing smiles. Nevertheless, back in the '60s, during the Vietnam War, when left-wingers usually got away with spouting outright nonsense, most television viewers were never quite sure who was right and who was wrong. The Democrats? The Republicans? The Libertarians?[181] Even those politicians who were doing all of the debating did not seem to really know for sure. That's because there wasn't any easy way to check the facts back then. Now, with high-speed computers, things have changed considerably for the better. Now, up-to-date information is readily available at the punch of a keyboard, so for liberals, successfully lying to the public has become *all but impossible.*

---

[179] Note that when a conservative Republican woman is extremely popular with the public, that fact visibly drives liberals (especially the males with same-sex mates, for some odd reason) nuts! Some former members of the Obama administration, for example (which shall remain unnamed), quiver with unconcealed rage at the mere mention of, say, someone like the conservative female former governor of Alaska (R). What the heck has this woman done to liberals, anyway—except smile, look good, and speak? The way some liberal men act, you'd think she went hunting one night with a three-barreled elephant gun and shot their pussy cats!
[180] H. L. Mencken, *A Mencken Chrestomathy,* 1949, Alfred A. Knopf, New York, N.Y., p. 164.
[181] Many libertarians are non-conservatives (i.e., liberals) who have taken so many illegal drug "trips" and/or the wrong combination of drugs, that it has eaten away their minds.

JOHN HAYBERRY

Projection

Always beware of *projection,* the liberal Democratic art of watering down criticism of yourself by brazenly pointing a gnarled quivering finger at your opponent and publicly charging him or her with things that, in truth, you, the accuser—not the opponent—are guilty of. Remember a few years ago when House Majority Leader Nancy Polluti (D) snidely announced in 2006 that the Democrats were going to "drain the swamp"? Well, apparently, they drained the wrong people out of government, because just look at where we are today. It's awful: The United States of America is drowning in the deepest, thickest, blackest, most foul-smelling government corruption and incompetence that any of our country's forefathers, such as George Washington, Thomas Jefferson, and Benjamin Franklin, could've possibly imagined.[182] That's why projection is the liberal Democratic politician's most beloved of weapons. They adore it so much, in fact, that sometimes they even use it against one another. In the 2008 Democratic primary, we all saw Senator Barack Hussein Obama (D) of Illinois and former first lady Ms. Hillary Pandora Clinton (D) do this without hesitation *ad nauseam* for over a year.[183] The funny thing about it is that both their goals for the United States of America have always seemed to be indistinguishable from one another. Identical, in fact. What seems to be that goal? *Inflict maximum liberal carnage.*

> "Liberals should experiment with fresh prayer formulas." — Anonymous Religious Nut

> "They [liberals] are like arrogant little imps who—no matter who it hurts and no matter what the consequences—will never pass up an opportunity to poke truth tellers in the eye." —Anonymous

---

[182] So far, pinpointing the source(s) of corruption in the current administration has been like playing Pin the Tail on the Invisible Donkey. First, there was the 2008 New Black Panther presidential voting scandal, and now the constitutional improprieties, political corruption, and fiscal indecencies are simply too *numerous* to discuss.

[183] That is because normal people of good taste and breeding instinctively recoil at the sight and sound of a sly, smooth, unashamed, money-and-power-grubbing goofball telling matter-of-fact lies to benefit himself or herself. Perhaps, for answers as to why they do this, more scientific research needs to be done regarding saltwater iguana species.

Human (D) Evolution

"Remember when the Bill and Hillary Clinton administration left the White House in 2001? They reportedly trashed the place because they didn't like the new incoming Republican president, George Bush." —Mike

"Mommy, is President Clinton's wife the devil?"[184] —Anonymous Five-Year-Old

Well, we all know who won the 2008 presidential election. He does not want anyone to forget: He did. Barack Hussein Obama. Then he won reelection in 2013, followed by all of the disastrous consequences that *every single one of the conservative Republicans* predicted, but the Democrats are still using projection on a regular basis. In fact, we can figure out what they are up to just going by what they say about the Republican Party (G.O.P.).[185] You'd think everybody would have caught on by now.

Most of the examples are too trivial in this context to mention, but here's one of the very best. Believe it or not, this is what passes for political discourse these days on the other side of the aisle. In this case, it was former Congressman Alan Grayson (D-Florida), representing his state's 8th district at that time.[186] He stood before the U.S. House of Representatives with three big placards entitled "THE REPUBLICAN HEALTH CARE PLAN." He used the placards so that everyone would see him and understand, including, of course, C-SPAN viewers. Most people, I believe, remember this because it appeared on all the news channels. It occurred just prior to President Monkeyshine's controversial (apparently fraudulent) reelection when he went up against his Republican challenger. Printed on the placards was the following:

1. DON'T GET SICK

2. AND IF YOU DO GET SICK . . .

3. <u>DIE QUICKLY</u>

---

[184] We don't really think she is.
[185] G.O.P. stands for "Grand Old Party."
[186] A conservative journalist wrote a scathing column that called Grayson "America's worst politician" (Alex Eichler, "Is Florida's Alan Grayson Really So Bad?" October 25, 2010, The Atlantic Media Company, web.archive.org/web/201010270500 58/http://www.theatlanticwire.com/opinions/view/opinion/Is-Floridas-Alan-Grayson-Really-So-Bad-5519). The article includes a photo of Chucky the killer doll.

Did the good Congressman really believe the evil that was printed on these placards? Or did somebody ask/instruct him to hold them up and read them in front of the camera? Stunts like these are what won Obama his reelection. So now, here we are, fighting skyrocketing insurance costs with underfunded Obamacare. What are we supposed to do now, "DIE QUICKLY" and penniless instead? (Maybe everyone should just give up, buy sombreros, and pretend to be Mexicans.)

"Why are we still having problems with the V.A. [Veterans Administration] hospitals? Wasn't Obamacare supposed to take care of *everybody?* Or was it only supposed to take care of liberal socialist Democrats and get them to vote?" —Donald F., Political Analyst

The Orenthal James Simpson Double-Murder Case

Our increasingly foreign system of justice often leaves much to be desired. The American judicial system—which, of course, includes the Supreme Court[187]—has deteriorated in the same way that the rest of society has. I hesitate to use as an example of this the 1995 O. J. Simpson murder case, but it has been described as the "Trial of the Century" and it is a clear example of the negative influence of liberalism on our system of jurisprudence. Most people have an opinion about the Simpson case now, and it's not likely to change, but no example of liberalism run amuck seems more appropriate for this book.

It was a Hollywood production from beginning to end. Simpson, a black athlete, was a running back for the Buffalo Bills and then, later, the San Francisco 49ers. He was personable and charming, always smiling, and just about everybody thought that he was the greatest. Then he married an attractive white woman, a blonde. A few years passed, then there were charges of battery. After they broke up, she and a white male friend were "mysteriously" murdered. In the past, O.J. Simpson would have been executed without a trial, but that's not the way things are done in a civilized society. So here's what happened.

---

[187] Unfortunately, taken as a whole, the members of the Supreme Court of the United States (S.C.O.T.U.S.) are no longer considered to be, as they once were, people of exceptional judgment. Instead, they are looked upon by most people as just another group of political hacks. That's why they're so often the subject of derision and ridicule. (It's even rumored that the most recent addition works part time at Rent-A-Clown.)

The trial took place in a Los Angeles courtroom and there was a camera mounted on the wall. The female prosecuting attorney, sporting a new hairdo, seemed more concerned about the contention that a police detective had once used the word "nigger" than the fact that there was a murderer in their midst. Everyone on camera behaved as though they were actors making a Hollywood movie, so they followed the standard script: [Black man good, white man bad].

Many of us, I suspect, remember exactly where we were and exactly what we were doing when we first heard the depressing news that Mr. Simpson had been found not guilty of murder. It was the same day that liberals all across the United States feasted by eating chocolate brownies full of marijuana seeds and going hoarse from the celebration cheering. Some of us probably also remember our stunned next-door neighbors and their shaking heads and looks of disbelief, along with that sinking feeling of disappointment and numbness one gets at the sudden realization of how flawed our system of jurisprudence occasionally proves to be. The televised and much-watched Simpson murder show-trial was and still is an absolute national disgrace, as are the throngs of pathetic people in this country. The gut reaction of many of us to the verdict in the first Simpson trial was similar to the dispirited feeling any American patriot gets whenever he or she hears that a foreign enemy got lucky and outsmarted us in some way—in other words, whenever *evil* wins a battle over *good*.

There were two camps of opinion in the Simpson case: those who believed that Simpson, a celebrity African American, was automatically innocent, and those who believed that he was as guilty as could be—like a fleeing wild dog covered with blood, shit, and chicken feathers. Clearly, some people are right and some people are dead wrong. There's really not much room for half-right (or half-left, for that matter) opinion here. Either he did it or he didn't. Just take a look at the grisly crime scene photos and the corpses of his ex-wife, Nicole Simpson (a battered woman), who was nearly decapitated, and her friend Ronald Goldman, an aspiring male model, both with gaping knife wounds and both lying on the ground outside her condo. You would think they had been attacked by some kind of crazed demoniacal savage or wild beast. There were chunks of congealed blood all over the place.

Those of us who are convinced that Simpson is guilty have based our opinions on facts presented at the trial: (1) Simpson's blood at the crime scene, (2) the cut on his finger from the knife, (3) size-twelve shoe prints, (4) hairs and fibers, (5) bloody extra-large gloves, (6) bloody socks, (7) the bloody Bronco, (8) Simpson's violent past, and, most importantly, (9) clear motive.[188] Simpson is also said to have failed a lie detector test (either that, or one of his attorneys stopped it).

---

[188] Associated Press, "O. J. Simpson Civil Trial," *USA Today*, October 18, 1996.

Those liberals who, in their own muddled minds, are sure that he is innocent are just as adamant, basing their opinions on inner thoughts and personal feelings and such things as (1) perceived past injustices and discrimination, (2) the prior use of the word "nigger" by a police detective, (3) the popularity of the defendant, even among many whites, (4) the rhyming ability of a charismatic defense attorney, and (5) the distinct but highly improbable possibility that virtually all of the evidence in Simpson's trial had been faked and manufactured because none of the police officers who investigated the crime really gave a hoot about who had committed the murders. All they wanted to do was put an innocent black man in jail (you know, any innocent black man, or black woman, or black teenager, or black child—just like on TV).

Of course, readers can decide for themselves which group is more logical and in keeping with the concepts of truth, justice, and the American way. Readers can also decide for themselves which group is composed of sub-competent Third World-thinker types, who, if given a choice, would probably prefer to see the Constitution discarded so that they (liberal adult human babies) could be ruled by either a sheik or a tribal king of their own ethnicity. Unfortunately, the big multicultural genetic surprise for anyone who hasn't figured it out yet is this: People who don't look alike often don't think alike, either. (OMG!)[189]

"He's the true definition of a sociopath—in every respect." —The lead L.A.P.D. detective in the Simpson case.

In *DNA: The Secret of Life*, the author states:

In fact, DNA fingerprinting evidence presented in the Simpson trial pointed to the accused. A blood drop collected close to Nicole Brown Simpson's body, as well as other drops found on the walkway at the crime scene, were shown with virtual certainty to be his. With an equal lack of doubt, the blood staining the glove retrieved from his home was determined to be a mixture of

---

[188] Associated Press, "O. J. Simpson Civil Trial," *USA Today*, October 18, 1996.
[189] The use of illegal drugs can accentuate that difference. Is that why O. J. Simpson snapped? Did marijuana and/or cocaine trigger it? A long-haired "dude" was living with Simpson and his wife during happier times, but no one has explained why.

Simpson's and that of the two victims; the blood found on the socks and in the Bronco proved to match the blood of Simpson and that of his ex-wife.[190]

It should have been an open-and-shut case, but liberals turned things around by pointing out that DNA evidence is considered only as credible as the procedures for collecting, sorting, preserving, and presenting it. They also insisted that the police faked everything. Unfortunately, there was no way to prove that the DNA evidence was not tainted in the Simpson case—*or, for that matter, in any criminal court case before or since.* Convictions of criminals without genetic evidence has been going on for thousands of years. The growing problem with obtaining justice in our criminal court system is the fact that liberal losers in positions of authority love to stick their thumbs in the eyes of conservatives. Here's the reason why: Convicting nonconservatives (i.e., liberals, many of whom are registered voters) of criminality and/or serious wrongdoing doesn't advance the liberal agenda or outlook at all. In other words, the victim(s) of crime be damned—no matter who they are. Men, women, children. That's because the most important thing of all to liberals is this: *It doesn't make them feel good!* That's why the O. J. Simpson murder case turned out the way it did. In the mind of liberals, the plot had already been written, so it ended just like a made-for-TV movie: The "hero," O. J. Simpson, was found not guilty.

To conclude, F.A.D. is preventing murder convictions because dopamine addiction is obstructing justice.

> "Virtually *every single time* that new evidentiary material is suddenly discovered or made available to the public, it *proves* that our liberal friends were on the *wrong* side of a criminal case! It almost seems as though they might have some kind of psychological disorder." —Anonymous Conservative Analyst

Remember, everyone here in the United States has the right to vote, so our future is determined by not only what is right and what is wrong but by what the multicultural inhabitants of our declining country decide. Unfortunately, our way of life is not chiseled in stone and preordained by an all-seeing higher power. Our

---

[190] James D. Watson with Andrew Berry, *DNA: The Secret of Life*, 2003, Knopf, New York, N.Y., p. 270. Watson shared a Nobel Prize in 1962, following the breakthrough discovery of the structure of deoxyribonucleic acid (DNA).

Western culture is not something permanent that can just be ignored. That's because the only difference between America and, say, Armenia, is the number of people living in the United States who think like Armenians do (not that there's really anything wrong with having the *second worst economy* in the world).

Through legislation, the demographics of a country can literally be changed overnight—drastically. Just give the Democratic National Committee (D.N.C.) a chance. Also, be aware that when any criminal beats a rap, the problem is not only that he or she got away with breaking the law or that he or she may do it again to the detriment of someone else but also that the offending individual has the innate ability to *continue breeding*.

That means that suboptimality in today's judiciary will inevitably translate into the unsolved rapes and murders of tomorrow. Bleeding-heart liberals high on dopamine are methodically creating a world of inattentiveness to evil and technology-enabled evil hitherto unseen on earth.[191] Think about that the next time a few nebbishes from the A.C.L.U. sue for conjugal visits, one of the most blindly ignorant criminal justice system privileges ever conceived.

Oh, one more minor thing that no one seems to have noticed: The videotapes show Simpson donning latex gloves and then ostensibly attempting, with fingers stiffened, to pull the infamous bloody gloves on over the latex gloves. But, of course, he "couldn't." The female prosecutor failed to sternly ask him to do so, and the Asian judge didn't seem to care much about anything. Why didn't he order a couple of bailiffs to hold Simpson down and use a pair of pliers? Apparently, all that any of them could think about was their debut on the boob tube. Television cameras in a courtroom have the same effect as they do in the halls of Congress. Instead of concentrating on doing their jobs, everyone involved is more worried about how they are going to be perceived by viewers. The results will always be the same: disastrous.

Well, at least Simpson is locked up on unrelated charges now.[192] Good riddance.

---

[191] Many L.S.D.ers think that, because *"Everyone is friends,"* the details of every single piece of U.S. technology ought to be shared with the entire world.

[192] The white Ford Bronco in which O. J. Simpson rode while attempting to "escape" and threatening to commit suicide is now reportedly being rented for parties. Liberal partygoers must supply their own guns, passports, bloody shoes, and fake beards and mustaches.

Part Two

The P.E.T.S. Hypothesis

Chapter 7

Why Do They Act So Funny?

Darwinian Psychiatry: The Evolution of Mental Disorders

Everything in the universe has evolved.[193] That includes trees, birds, monkeys, automobiles, architecture, atoms, molecules, planets, stars, black holes, space, Earth's atmosphere, seawater, rocks, drugs, money, political parties, hats, hairstyles, peanuts, popcorn, and all types and varieties of *Homo sapiens*. These things, organic and inorganic, natural and man-made, are in constant motion and/or are altering with time. What exists at this very moment didn't exist in this exact state a week, a year, or a billion years ago, and it won't exist identically a hundred years from now (or maybe even after the next presidential election). All that we see, hear, smell, taste, and touch is continually transforming, either by chance or by design. Evidence of human evolution surrounds us all. It's everywhere. It's absolutely indisputable. It's apparent every day of our lives. It's staring us in the face (and holding a cardboard sign we can't read at the traffic light)—and cannot be denied. The Democratic National Committee (D.N.C.) is well aware of man's differences.

---

[193] Physicists tell us that not even subatomic particles existed prior to the Big Bang. As the universe expanded and cooled, atoms formed over a period of thousands of years. The universe may not continue expanding forever, however. If the expansion speed does not exceed escape velocity, then the mutual gravitational attraction of all matter could eventually cause the universe to contract. One theory predicts that the universe will collapse again into a black hole singularity. Then it may explode all over again. If it explodes and retracts an infinite number of times, an identical arrangement of atoms would be predicted to occur. Having no sense of time, a person who dies would be reborn immediately. If that happens, who knows, everyone might eventually live their same lives all over again. If not the first time, an infinite number of times later. (Of course, with black holes involved, there might be an infinite number of subtle variations—like having a mustache, for example.)

Human (d) Evolution

According to Wilmot Robertson, author of *The Dispossessed Majority:*

> Every man is like every other man in that he belongs to the same species, *Homo sapiens*. The seven-foot Watusi and the four-foot Pygmy, the milk-white Swede, the coffee-colored Latin American mestizo and the almond-eyed and almond-tinted Oriental are all capable of interbreeding. The idea of human likeness consequently has biological origins. So does the idea of human unlikeness. Every man differs physically and mentally from every other man, which accounts both for human individuality and group differences. . . . Race, as every American politician is well aware, goes far beyond the realm of the physical.[194]

The term *evolution*, contrary to popular perception, does not always mean progress. Darwin saw biological evolution as having no guidance or direction. To Darwin, evolution was merely the process of adaptation to a changing environment and an organism's means of continued existence. Darwin noted that variations favorable to a creature's survival tend to be preserved, and unfavorable ones destroyed. Step-by-step evolution caused by genetic mutation is no more preordained by a higher power than two-headed frogs are commanded to evolve by the multicultural liberal begetters of an accidental chemical spill.[195] Random changes are exactly that, and those changes are not usually favorable. Man himself makes

---

[194] Wilmot Robertson, *The Dispossessed Majority*, 1973, Howard Allen Enterprises, Cape Canaveral, Florida, pp. 3–4. Pygmies, by the way, are among mankind's oldest living ancestors, according to genetic researchers Cann and Wilson and their controversial human species family tree (1987). Their conclusion is based on an analysis of the patterns of sequence variation in human mitochondrial DNA, which is inherited only from the mother. Not surprisingly, it was one of the very few pieces of science ever to make the cover of the liberal rag *Newsweek*.

[195] It's important to note that some highly prominent conservatives, fighting an increasingly frustrating battle against liberalism, have allowed themselves to get caught up and entangled in discussions of religion, but the problem with liberalism is not one of theology; it's one of psychopathology, and we should never be confused about that. Theology is a crossbow armament best reserved for use against immoral adults, uneducated children, and heathens, not anesthetized pseudo-adults with a diminished capacity to understand how life works. Only scientific argument and mathematically based solutions can ever hope to quell the rising tide of liberalism. For those readers who believe that God created the Earth as it is on Day One and man as he is on Day Six, please try to temporarily suspend your belief and consider another possibility: that a higher power, rather than designing and creating every single thing that exists in nature, simply laid out the plan, creating the seed for all that is—i.e., space, time, matter, mathematics, chemistry, and the laws of physics—and left the rest to us. That way, He/She/It wouldn't have been so exhausted and had to rest on Day Seven.

many evolutionary choices—and, of course, women do too—but after *millions of years* of infrequent positive changes, the complex final products (for example, a human eyeball, or the echolocation system of bats) may appear wholly inexplicable. Darwin determined that *natural selection* directs the entire process of evolution. That means that the survivors of a particular environment are better adapted to the prevailing conditions of life. Darwin understood, too, the contributing factor of *artificial selection* as practiced by country farmers and animal breeders.

Of course, Darwin did not consider evolution to be an infinitely tall ladder that an automatically improving species continually ascends. On the contrary, Darwin saw evolution as being similar to a wild mulberry bush branching out in all different directions. That same bush, we should note, can be affected by ever-changing environmental factors such as water, sunlight, temperature, disease, hungry insects, or even a (conservative or liberal) human gardener, and the branches of that mulberry bush can grow downward as well as upward.[196] One Nobel Prize winner has even described evolution as a "tinkerer"—and so was the old man who made Pinocchio.

> "The fact—not theory—that evolution has occurred and the Darwinian theory as to how it occurred have become so confused in popular opinion that the distinction must be stressed." —George G. Simpson (1902–1984), American paleontologist, perhaps the most influential of the twentieth century

> "Nothing in biology makes sense except in the light of evolution." —Theodosius Dobzhansky (1900–1975), prominent geneticist and evolutionary biologist

Darwinian psychiatry, which began to take shape after *On the Origin of Species* was published in 1859, argues that evolutionary theory can and should serve as the theoretical framework for explaining and treating liberal mental disorders. The adoption of evolutionary-based ideas in psychiatry was encouraged by prominent neurologist John Hughlings-Jackson (1835–1911), along with psychiatrists

---

[196] Darwin's book *The Descent of Man* (1871) has an interesting title. By the word "descent," Darwin was referring to human origin and the transmission of characteristics to future generations through inheritance. Ironically, descent is also defined as the action of moving downward, dropping, or falling; a downward slope such as a path or track; and a moral, social, or psychological decline into a specified undesirable state. (Welcome to Detroit, Michigan.)

Human (D) Evolution

Emil Kraepelin (1856–1926) and James Crichton-Browne (1840–1938). A Swiss psychiatrist Adolph Meyer (1866–1950), who became well known as the president of the American Psychiatric Association and who is considered one of the most influential figures in psychiatry in the first half of the twentieth century, suggested that some liberal mental disorders, as well as some features of disorders, represent human evolutionary adaptations. Australian psychiatrist Aubrey Lewis (1900–1975), who undertook anthropological research on Aborigines, postulated that *depression,* because it often initiates caretaking behavior by others, is an evolved (mostly liberal) trait. Lewis believed that individuals who exhibit signs of a mental disturbance, like depression, may attract help from others, which *increases* their chances of survival.[197]

Think about that.

Evolutionary explanations started appearing in (conservative) psychiatric literature all the way from the 1930s to the late 1960s, so the idea of evolution playing a part in the origin of a mental disorder is really nothing new. By the 1960s, evolutionary theory had, itself, evolved into a complex system of theoretical formulations that could handle data and findings from all other fields of study, such as archaeology, anthropology, natural history, genetics, physiology, ethology, and part-time community organizing. That is when alternative theories of liberal mental disorders, developed by mostly conservative researchers in various disciplines, began gaining prominence.

Generally, psychiatrists are interested in four things: (1) etiology, (2) pathogenesis, (3) diagnosis, and (4) treatment of psychiatric disorders, but psychiatry, including psychiatric diagnosis, is far from an exact science. The field is still in a state of chaotic liberal primitivism. Even though conservative psychiatrists today have a much better understanding of the brain's structure and function and causes of disease than did doctors in the past, and even though drugs that control debilitating symptoms have been successfully developed, much remains unknown—and perhaps unsuspected—about liberal mental disorders. Because of the enormous amount of conservative research and the sheer volume of complex work published, many things that may have been known at one time are now either ignored or overlooked, or simply may have been forgotten.

Although psychiatry might seem to be a relatively new field, it has actually been around for thousands of years. In cultures as far back as 5000 B.C., for example, there is evidence of trepanning—drilling holes in the skulls of mental patients. Ancient "psychiatrists" apparently believed that some mental health disorders—probably the ones that involve hearing voices—were caused by demonic spirits and the only cure was to coax the spirits out of the poor victim's head. Even today, psychiatry has not yet agreed on the definition of mental illness, but most people can

---

[197] Depression is sometimes indicated by downturned eyes (with childlike sadness).

recognize a liberal disorder when they see it. (For example, still wearing a torn and faded "HOPE AND CHANGE" T-shirt after five years of unmitigated disasters might be an indication.) It is believed that psychiatric disorders don't discriminate according to age, gender, race, I.Q., or social status, so they're equal-opportunity employers.

It might seem that the process of human evolution would have largely eliminated mental disease over time and through natural selection, but, unfortunately, that's not the case at all. Remember, Darwinian evolution does not predict species perfection, only species change, with some genes and traits more likely to be preserved than others. We know that traits can emerge from gene-environment interactions. One fact that is often omitted from psychiatric literature, perhaps with the intention of avoiding an unpleasant truth, is that genes can also play a part in the *susceptibility* of a person to be adversely affected by his or her environment. For example: an illiterate liberal adult, who, because he or she had a poor education twenty-five years ago, still can't read the captions under the bloody crime-scene photos in the *Chicago Tribune*.[198] Liberals, curiously, just don't seem to like discussing certain subjects, such as I.Q. or genetics, which is why they rarely ever use such terms. But the human brain is undeniably a product of its history, and each of us has predispositions and genetically influenced traits derived from specific ancestral groups, along with their countries of origin. No amount of liberal political correctness and no feigned displays of shock or umbrage will ever change that fact. That's because any visible liberal DNA sequence variations won't be affected by uncontrolled anger, heated political debate, lawsuits, hurled objects, or screaming.

In the course of human evolution, those features that are preserved (from a psychiatric standpoint) are often far from ideal.

According to the textbook *Darwinian Psychiatry*:

> Diseases and disorders of all types are everywhere apparent in nature, and the vast majority of species (>95%) become extinct. Said another way, it is an error to assume that *Homo sapiens* has been selected to be mentally healthy. Such an assumption is riddled with contradictions, with misinterpretations about how evolution works, and with misunderstandings of its products.[199]

---

[198] The "progressive" liberal feel-good solution for minority illiteracy has been to lower the graduation standards in public schools to curb the never-ending problem with dropouts. This is, of course, comparable to adjusting the locker-room scales in high-school gymnasiums to lower obese pupils' body weights.

[199] McGuire and Troisi, *op. cit., ix*.

Human (D) Evolution

The *Textbook of Evolutionary Psychiatry* states:

> In other words, over eons, natural and sexual selection have shaped brain mechanisms through which an individual effectively communicates with his or her inner and outer environment. Mental life with all its facets is an adaptation to environmental conditions to which humans and their ancestors were exposed, and psychiatric disorders reside at the extreme of variation, rather than being qualitatively distinct from "normalcy."[200]

What this means is that a liberal politician who may appear normal to the naked eye might actually have extremes of some kind in his or her thought processes, including opinions that are contrary to what the vast majority of the population consider common sense. Humans have large, well-developed brains that contain traces of a long evolutionary past all the way from the reptiles through the mammals to the primates but that actually originated in creatures the size of amoebae. Predispositions are encoded within the human brain to think, feel, and behave in specific ways. Reptiles, you may note, have strong survival instincts and are usually more than capable of defending themselves, yet, surprisingly, some liberals today, unlike their distant reptile ancestors, seem almost devoid of many basic defensive instincts. Why? Well, to be quite frank, it's all very, very strange and almost beyond understanding. In fact, it really doesn't make any sense at all. (At least, not until you've completed reading this chapter.) The question is, what could possibly have occurred in mankind's evolutionary past that would rob any modern man or woman of his or her natural instincts and ability to survive, leaving that person so notably *unlike* more capable distant ancestors and even recent relatives of only a few hundred years past?

In their book, *Evolutionary Psychiatry: A New Beginning*, Anthony Stevens and John Price state:

> The limbic system includes the oldest and most primitive part of the evolving cerebral cortex—the so-called *paleocortex*. . . . In all mammals, including man, this part of the brain is, therefore, a

---

[200] Brüne, *op. cit.*, p. 1.

structure of the utmost complexity, controlling basic psychophysical responses and attitudes to the environment. An animal, deprived of its cerebral cortex, can still find its way about, eat, drink, and avoid painful stimuli, but it has difficulty in attributing *meaning* to things: a natural predator will be noticed, for example, but not apparently perceived as a threat.[201]

As most of us are well aware, a predator or enemy who is not perceived as a threat and is greeted with a display of manifest weakness—e.g., a silly grin, an overly exaggerated bow, a huge olive branch, or energetic bootlicking—will, nine times out of ten, sink its teeth into the foolish person's rump. So why don't Democratic politicians seem to get this? Obviously, liberals weren't born without cerebral cortexes (at least, not according to the latest MRI scans or X-rays). Weakness and laxity with regard to one's own safety and security are not normal in animals, nor should they be in adult human beings. So what's going on? Are liberals the meek who supposedly will inherit the earth? If so, who's going to feed, clothe, and protect them from one another?

Who's going to defend them from all of the sharp-toothed tyrants in the world so eager to smile and shake their hands but who wouldn't hesitate for a moment to beat them to death with their own protest signs? What kind of environment could possibly have produced liberals, anyway? It's all very difficult to understand, especially for anyone familiar with the behavior of the average wild duck. Why would any educated modern man or woman have a diminished capacity to recognize an enemy and be confused about how to act? Why would any human being have no sense of urgency in the face of clear and present danger? Is there any kind of natural—or even freak—environmental stimulus that could possibly account for such a thing? Certainly, nothing known to have been offered up by Mother Nature, who unmercifully eliminates with the efficiency of a mousetrap any organism that makes big mistakes with regard to its own personal protection.[202] In light of this, there can be only one conclusion: Any environment that results in the evolution of naïve human beings with a distinct proclivity for consorting with their own enemies (sometimes, it seems, the

---

[201] Anthony Stevens and John Price, *Evolutionary Psychiatry: A New Beginning*, 2nd edition, 2000, Routledge, Taylor & Francis, Philadelphia, Pennsylvania, p. 17.
[202] A rare exception to this rule might be the Galapagos Islands, an isolated wilderness and modern-day tourist destination. Darwin visited the Galapagos aboard the *H.M.S. Beagle* in 1835, as part of a five-year navigational mission to chart the coast of South America for the British Royal Navy. The animals—finches, boobies, tortoises, flightless cormorants, albatrosses—have no fear of humans—but possibly because everyone has been petting and feeding them.

devil)²⁰³ and leaving themselves vulnerable to personal harm—not only physical, but also financial and legal—must be *man-made*.

Begin thinking about that, too.

Darwinian evolutionary theory involves the replication of genes and the retention of genetically influenced traits with respect to appearance, thinking, and behavior from past environments through eons. The fossil record indicates that about 7 million years ago, chimpanzees, gorillas, and humans shared the same ancestor. Then, approximately 6.5 million years ago, the first primates began to appear. About 4.5 million years ago, bipedal hominoids were hopping around. And 1.8 million years ago, *Homo erectus* popped up. About 150,000 years ago is the estimated date for the appearance of *Homo sapiens*. About 50,000 years ago is the date for the arrival of *Homo sapiens* in Europe. Across the hominoid time span, our planet's physical environment underwent significant changes—e.g., the most recent ice age, droughts, floods, plagues, and earthquakes—so innumerable species became extinct, new species evolved, migrations occurred, and the genetic makeup of primates went through thousands of minor changes as a result of the process of natural selection.

Because of the influence of genetic information on traits, we humans—like other animal species—enter the world prepared and predisposed to (1) engage in certain behaviors, (2) react in certain ways to specific stimuli, and (3) pursue certain goals. This array of instinctual characteristics is a product of our evolutionary past and is carried in our genes. Other factors, such as experience, learning, and culture, also play a part. Whenever a conservative evolutionary biologist discusses predisposed traits, liberal nonscientists object to what they believe are highly insensitive and negative social implications involving such things as below-average learning ability, marginal governing capacity, illegal drug use, and criminal behavior. Some liberals worry, and rightly so. If ability and behavior are viewed as products of genes (which, of course, they are), efforts at social reform will be negatively affected and the current political practice of shoveling obscene amounts of the public's tax money into the pockets of future Democratic campaign donors in the name of *minority education* will come to a screeching halt. This would severely affect the power and influence of the "Democratic" Party (or, as they say in Texas, the Democrat Party), and that just

---

²⁰³ On July 2, 2013, pro-abortion advocates at the Texas State Capitol in Austin reportedly began shouting, "Hail Satan!" in an attempt to drown out the anti-abortion rendition of "Amazing Grace" when tensions ratcheted higher as protestors on both sides of the issue squared off. The governor of Texas had called for a second special session to pass an abortion law that would prohibit the procedure past the twentieth week of pregnancy, based on the idea that this is when the human fetus begins to feel pain ("Texas Abortion Battle Heats up as Activists 'Hail Satan!'" *The Washington Times,* July 3, 2013). Ten days later, police reportedly confiscated paint, glitter, bricks, tampons, condoms, and jars of urine and feces from protestors, who planned to throw these things at pro-life lawmakers before the final vote. A noted Houston seamstress also protested the abortion bill by making voodoo dolls of the governor and selling them with pins. She donated the proceeds to Planned Parenthood (KHOU.com, "Gov. Perry 'Voodoo Doll' Maker to Donate Sales to Planned Parenthood," July 17, 2013).

absolutely, positively, can never, ever be allowed to occur under any circumstances whatsoever. Why? Because if it did, liberal union bosses and their thuggish sycophants would have a fit. But in the United States, money grows on trees, so there's nothing to worry about—right?

For those of you unfamiliar with Darwinian psychiatry, rest assured that the evolutionary process of mental disorders is not a difficult thing to understand. Simply picture the human brain as a pumpkin in a farmer's patch. Pumpkins can grow to a wide variety of outlandish shapes and sizes. They can be ripe, overripe, green, diseased, or healthy. Also, if not protected, they can be damaged by hungry varmints. But in the end, on Halloween, people can choose which pumpkins they like best and decide whether they want them to look happy, sad, funny, stupid, or scary.

Liberal mental disorder evolution is almost as easy to grasp as that.

Before delving into the mystery of where liberals came from and trying to figure out why liberal thinking and behavior even exist in the first place, though, you should familiarize yourself with some terms and concepts that can help provide insight, so study the following subtopics carefully.

Minimal Selection Pressure

A decreased need for certain instincts or abilities in a given environment can cause the development of a dysfunction in the population. This is referred to as *minimal selection pressure*. (One example is dyslexia, a general term for disorders that involve difficulty in learning to read or in interpreting words, letters, or other symbols. Dyslexia appears to affect from 5 to 10 percent of the population but is said not to affect general intelligence, only learning ability. Minimal selection pressure is a possible evolutionary factor with a condition like dyslexia, which would go unnoticed

---

[203] On July 2, 2013, pro-abortion advocates at the Texas State Capitol in Austin reportedly began shouting, "Hail Satan!" in an attempt to drown out the anti-abortion rendition of "Amazing Grace" when tensions ratcheted higher as protestors on both sides of the issue squared off. The governor of Texas had called for a second special session to pass an abortion law that would prohibit the procedure past the twentieth week of pregnancy, based on the idea that this is when the human fetus begins to feel pain ("Texas Abortion Battle Heats up as Activists 'Hail Satan!'" *The Washington Times,* July 3, 2013). Ten days later, police reportedly confiscated paint, glitter, bricks, tampons, condoms, and jars of urine and feces from protestors, who planned to throw these things at pro-life lawmakers before the final vote. A noted Houston seamstress also protested the abortion bill by making voodoo dolls of the governor and selling them with pins. She donated the proceeds to Planned Parenthood (KHOU.com, "Gov. Perry 'Voodoo Doll' Maker to Donate Sales to Planned Parenthood," July 17, 2013).

in nonliterate societies, such as those that still exist in parts of Africa where there is no written language, only the spoken word.)[204] The question is, if minimal selection pressure played a role in the evolution of a disorder that makes it difficult to read words and symbols, could it also have played a role in the evolution of a disorder that makes it difficult to read an enemy and recognize subtle warning signs of danger? It certainly seems possible. Human facial expressions and other body language—just like words and symbols—must be recognized to be understood. The liberal inability to comprehend what another person is thinking or to predict with any accuracy what he or she is going to do can prove fatal. What kind of environment could have caused such a thing? What kind of society has ever existed in which the psychiatric vulnerability of its populace did not result in harm? How could nitwits of this type have avoided extinction?

Phenotypes

Environments differ and sometimes change. A trait that is advantageous in one environment may not be advantageous in another (e.g., skin pigmentation, body hair, or body size). Because numerous environmental factors affect, to some degree, a person's physical and mental characteristics—i.e., attitudes, abilities, and behavior—individuals are not only born with but also develop variant (abnormal) *phenotypes*. A phenotype is a set of observable characteristics resulting from the interaction of a person's genotype with the environment. Organisms are often classified based on their phenotypes. For example, many Scandinavians have blond hair and blue eyes, so those traits are considered two aspects of the Scandinavian phenotype. Someone with very dark skin, hair, and eyes might be considered an example of the African phenotype. The marked physical differences between various people's characteristics are related to the environments that their ancestors came from and are thus the result of untold centuries of evolution. Not all traits replicate equally well, and there may be a high degree of phenotype mortality in one environment and not in another. Of course, mating success also plays a role.

---

[204] The continent of Africa is widely considered to be the birthplace of man. Only limited written language existed in Africa prior to foreign influence, and for the past two hundred years, a large variety of writing systems have been created there. Today, most of the writing systems have been displaced by the Arabic or Latin alphabets. The total number of African languages is unknown and has been estimated to be anywhere from 800 to more than 1000, which may account for much of the animosity between tribes. The country of South Africa, for example, has eleven official languages: Afrikaans, English, Zulu, Ndebele, Sepedi, Sesotho, Swazi, Tsonga, Tswana, Venda, and Xhosa—and numerous unofficial languages, including Mo-Fu, Yada, Huh, and Unintelligiblese.

Adaptive Traits

In biology, any anatomical structure—including an organism's size—or any physiological or psychological process, or any behavior that makes an organism more likely to survive and reproduce is called an *adaptive trait*. Some of the liberal traits that are of interest to psychiatry include

1. the capacity to bond,
2. the ability to interpret information,
3. the ability to assess the costs and benefits of social interactions,
4. skill in building mental scenarios and developing strategies to cope with negative results, and
5. the ability to learn from one's own mistakes.

The manner in which a person speaks and what he or she says (often referred to colloquially as *attitude*) can have both survival and reproductive consequences and can influence the genetic makeup of upcoming populations. In fact, some possible new future age groups may include (1) the Beat-Up Generation (beatupniks), (2) Baby Bloomers (flowery Me-Me-Me's), (3) Generation Zero (lifelong penniless paupers), (4) Gen Rx^2 (mindlessly obedient, unoriginal, and high as a kite), and (5) Degeneration X (ignorant psychotic animalistic creeps).

Is lack of logic an adaptive strategy or an epiphenomenon (byproduct) of F.A.D.? Unfortunately, that is very difficult for anyone who is not actually a liberal to say. Whether illogic is used consciously or unconsciously by liberals to reduce undesirable effects on their mood can probably be ascertained only by highly trained Morganton mental health researchers administering a battery of tests in a clinical setting. It's certainly possible that liberal illogic is a secondary symptom that occurs simultaneously with F.A.D. but isn't directly related to it. My guess is that, in most cases, it's probably a little of both; however, there's no way of knowing for sure.

The term *liberal illogic*, of course, does not simply refer to the current list of Democratic Party talking points or to the decades-old dogma that they (liberals) espouse. It refers to their reasoning in virtually every situation and on any topic—political, social, or otherwise—in which some measure of satisfaction, power, or security is to be gained for *themselves personally*, thus increasing their pleasure. If something is known to be necessary for the benefit of us all (like working) but produces personal discomfort or reduced pleasure, a liberal will probably avoid doing that thing at all costs, perhaps even up to the point where he or she sustains a personal injury (like bedsores). It is only when the stark reality of poor choices can no longer be ignored that liberals will temporarily abandon their pleasure seeking and do what they must to end the pain that they have brought on themselves.

One thing is for sure: Whatever liberalism is, it's definitely not a result of normal brain activity.

Life is, unfortunately, very unfair. It's no one's fault. It's just the way things are. There's nothing anyone can do about it. Some humans are attractive, some ugly.[205] Some are tall, some short. Some are thin, some fat. Some are outgoing, some shy. Some are smart, some dumb. These variations are normal. But here's the big evolutionary mystery: Why are some people logical, some illogical? Is there any good reason for it? The answer is no. Why? *Because there is no natural environment on earth in which an illogical person is predicted to survive.*

Note that the difference between the words dumb and illogical is the same as the difference between (1) a person who stops his Jeep on a winding mountain road, gets out, and tries to follow or pet a wild grizzly bear and (2) a whistling, goateed trail-hiker who reaches into the back pocket of his trousers and tries to feed that same bear a handful of tutti-frutti. (This, according to a reliable etymologist, is the origin of the term half-assed.)

Some Vegan Food for Thought: If the inability to read and understand a book is considered a functional impairment, then is the inability of a liberal president to read the business community and understand that an unfriendly attitude exhibited by the federal government will reduce business expansion—*and thus jobs*—a functional impairment, too?

Genomic Change

1. Even though our exaggeratedly proud, nobly posturing, chin-elevated species, *Homo sapiens,* is still evolving, the rapid advancement of civilization has clearly exceeded the rate of genomic change. Genomic refers to the genetic material in an

---

[205] "But remember, beauty is a gift from God, so one should always be thankful, even if one's face was intended for a flounder." —Billy Bob

organism. Some conservative theorists have suggested that this delay has increased the probability of both psychological and physiological liberal dysfunction.

2. *Natural selection* gradually eliminates liberal (unfit) traits more than it promotes fit traits.

3. Liberal human beings propagate very quickly in societies in which there is absolutely no attempt at birth control.[206]

4. Liberal females with certain mental conditions are especially vulnerable to sexual advances and coercion by suboptimal males, who often have certain other mental conditions.

5. In our ancient past, when the earth was wild and when life was fraught with danger, any naïve liberal male was sure to meet with a quick demise, as was any naïve liberal female who made the fatal mistake of becoming his mate. This, of course, limited their joint breeding capacity. (Today, however, things have changed drastically for the worse. The safety and security provided to all American men and women regardless of their race, color, or creed—or I.Q.—ensure that even the most exceedingly inept liberals have the opportunity to propagate profusely, which means that in the modern world, successfully spawning from twenty to thirty children is not beyond the capability of any aggressive female nebbish. For better or for worse, suboptimal *Homo sapiens* are, for all intents and purposes, a federally protected species.[207]

---

[206] Some impoverished and downtrodden liberal females believe that society should *pay* for their birth control, too. Maybe that is not such a bad idea. L.S.D.ers, of course, aren't not the only ones who reproduce rapidly. A single female Chinese Himalayan rabbit, for example, can produce, in nine months, as many as 800 kits (children, grandchildren, and great-grandchildren). Fortunately, the human gestation period is much longer.

[207] Maybe some new birth control legislation needs to be passed by Congress to reverse the effects of their prior legislation.

Human (D) Evolution

Suboptimality versus Dysfunctionality

Suboptimal and *dysfunctional* traits are always distinguishable from one another. Suboptimal means "of less than the highest standard or quality." Dysfunctional means "not operating normally or properly." For example, a liberal male displays a suboptimal trait when he is too hebetudinous to use a toilet and pees in his pants, but he displays a dysfunctional trait when he walks up to a complete stranger and intentionally pees on that person's shoes.

Altruism

Altruism is the disinterested and selfless concern for the well-being of others (who are deserving of it). In zoology, it's the behavior of one animal that benefits another animal at the first animal's expense. Providing help to others can take many forms. Adoption, for example, which rarely occurs in the animal world—such as when a female dog nurses a kitten—is a cherished institution with human beings. In modern society, if the mother and father of, say, six or seven unwashed barefoot juvenile delinquents should accidentally lose both of their heads in a meth lab explosion, then neighbors, relatives, or strangers will adopt their orphaned brood. That means our human gene pool will not be denied the rich, high-quality contribution of two lawless, unskilled, drug-addled kitchen chemists. Things work differently in the savagery of the animal world, a realm in which any creature with instincts similar to those of a liberal (type F) personality simply will not survive. Orphaned animal offspring that cannot feed and care for themselves are doomed to die.

Institutionalized adoption is just one of several differences that exist between the evolutionary processes of lower and higher life-forms. *Reciprocal altruism theory* explains the "helping" behavior among non-kin. Person A will help person B if there is a high probability that person B will reciprocate. This human behavior can also be observed in some nonhuman species, including dogs, lions, dolphins, and bats. Reciprocal altruism theory is consistent with the principle of self-interest. Reciprocal behavior occurs in all known cultures. Certain attributes that a person may have can increase the likelihood of others offering their help. One of those attributes is childlike naïveté, as opposed to shrewdness and insightfulness. Another attribute is friendliness and goodwill toward all, as opposed to despising tyrants, crooks, and fools. Still another attribute is sadness, as opposed to constantly grinning from ear to ear. A person with all three of these attributes—

naïveté, friendliness, and *sadness*—would be much more likely to be helped by others than would a person who lacks them. Also, people with mental disorders have a diminished capacity to identify good and bad reciprocators, so they're more subject to being duped, fooled, and hornswoggled.

Kin Selection

Kin selection is natural selection that promotes one's relatives. It is based on the instinctual desire to increase the number of one's genes in subsequent generations. This goal is not restricted to simply having offspring, because close relatives share many of the same genes. Kin selection theory explains altruistic behavior toward kin despite the fact that clear benefits may not be forthcoming or even anticipated. Increasing the possibility of genetic replication is one reason why parents instinctively invest in both their offspring and their kin. This theory has even been successfully explained in terms of mathematical formulae involving the percentage of genes likely to be present in each kin (offspring, grand-offspring, cousin, etc.). *Certain paternity* is one investment-influencing factor. A grandmother, for example, is more certain of her genetic relatedness to her grandchildren through her daughter than she is through her son. A grandfather is less sure. That is why grandmothers instinctively invest more in the offspring of their daughters than in those of their sons.

Group kin selection is exhibited by individuals who want to promote the welfare of many, which normally includes themselves and others like themselves. For example, members of the National Association for the Advancement of Colored People (N.A.A.C.P.)[208] promote the taxpayer-funded welfare of all African American male and female liberal Democrats; members of the National Organization for Women (N.O.W.) promote the welfare of all male, female, and homosexual liberal Democrats[209]; and members of the American Civil Liberties Union (A.C.L.U.) promote the welfare of all queer-looking, humorless, gibbering, beady-eyed social rejects with foreign accents and/or speech impediments who will vote for any smiling two-tongued liberal politician who offers them lots of free stuff!

Joining the military to defend your country can also be considered an example of group kin selection, even though men and women may be prompted by

---

[208] It's really a mystery why so many African Americans seem to resent the Jews, because both of these ethnicities tend to vote Democratic. Is it because blacks somehow got the idea that the original organizers of the N.A.A.C.P. were Jewish puppeteers?

[209] Curiously, for some reason, the goals of liberalism and the new homosexual agenda seem to go hand in hand.

a wide variety of reasons to sign up. Clearly, some people have a much stronger soldierly instinct than do others, but remarkably, some able-bodied males and females refuse to fight for their country under any circumstance *whatsoever*—even if their own family homes are being targeted by Chinese D-5 missiles.[210] Often, these are the same men prone to throwing tantrums in public and arguing vehemently with little bitty children, waddling pregnant women, or handicapped senior citizens on slow-moving electric scooters. If a male, in particular, is lacking this protective group instinct, then there would seem to be only two possible reasons: (1) his DNA lacks a particular gene related to kin selection, or (2) he has no feeling of kinship because he doesn't consider himself a true member of the group (i.e., in his own mind, he's not really one of us).[211]

Here's an idea: How about if we make two years of military service mandatory for all citizens of the United States, including our protesting, peace-loving liberal friends. As it stands now, we are allowing the inept, apathetic, and suboptimal to breed at the expense of our nation's best—which would not be so bad if any of these dopey losers ever showed any gratitude. Exempting anyone from military service based on so-called conscientious objection—as opposed to what it really is: diminished survival instincts because of an inbred genetic abnormality—has a predictable evolutionary result. Liberals are the reason that the United States is in its looming bankruptcy predicament.[212] Many liberals, unfortunately, are *pusillanimous pussyfooters*. Make no mistake about it: Most liberal males would rather see abortion made illegal again and women lose the right to vote and Negro slaves pick cotton than have to go through nine weeks of basic training in the U.S. Marine Corps. The consensus of opinion among those in the know is that military service

---

[210] Interestingly enough, the Japanese don't seem to have much of a problem with patriotism, especially when considering the kamikaze pilots of World War II. However, here in the United States, on the opposite end of the spectrum, are people like Adam Gadahn (born Adam Pearlman), a homegrown "American" advisor for the terrorist group al-Qaeda and the first United States citizen charged with treason since Tomoya Kawakita in 1952. He's currently wanted by the Federal Bureau of Investigation.

[211] For more, see "Human and Animal Kin Selection," page 241.

[212] Actually, the United States of America has already gone bankrupt. You see, when a president spends every penny of our country's tax revenue that was collected by the Internal Revenue Service (I.R.S.), there's no money left over to pay the federal government's bills, so he has to authorize the printing of *money that doesn't exist*. How is that possible? It isn't. So, he sends economics experts around to sneak into every American's home at night and look for purses, piggy banks, and wallets. These economist burglars steal as much money as possible when none of us are looking, then they give it to the Federal Reserve. If, by chance, the economist burglars don't find enough money, they break into every bank vault in the country and haul out bundles of cash. (Sometimes they use wheelbarrows and/or pack mules.) The United States of America has held a public debt since the U.S. Constitution legally went into effect on March 4, 1789. That was the same year that George Washington was elected president. President Washington, who, as the story goes, never told a lie, admitted that he chopped down a cherry tree. But President Obama behaves as though he has secretly chopped down a jungle full of money trees. Where were they growing? In the Senate and the halls of Congress? Maybe the trees are being fertilized with R.I.N.O. (pronounced "rhino") dung.

helps build a feeling of camaraderie and thus real citizenship, which, of course, is preferable to being Americans in name only (A.I.N.O.s), so inarguably, it's *a good thing*. U.S. military service would promote the assimilation of not only unassimilated foreign Americans, but possibly even un-American liberal Americans and anti-American Americans. Unfortunately, today, there are *plenty* of them all.

The preceding may help us begin to understand the previously inexplicable, absolutely preposterous notion of many liberals, including those residing in San Francisco who sometimes dine at restaurants in the nude, that the U.S. military really isn't necessary at all.

Perhaps some of these liberal pseudo-adults would prefer speaking Russian or Chinese, or maybe even Arabic. If so, they should probably learn how to ask the following questions in the foreign language of their choice: (1) Officer, would you please remove this blindfold and untie my hands and feet? (2) Are you kidding? Death by firing squad for possession of a marijuana leaf? (3) What do you mean, I'm going to be shot for using pheromone cologne, skipping, and having a lisp?

Liberals apparently don't view the military as the protectors of this country and thus of their Constitutional freedoms. Most liberals, in fact, seem to regard the military as little more than an oversized, extremely annoying, grassroots conservative Republican organization full of mean stupid people whom they instinctively despise for their *courage, bravery,* and *heroism*. But why? The new liberal multicultural military includes an increasing number of Mexican Americans, Chinese Americans, Russian Americans, Korean Americans, Vietnamese Americans, Afghan Americans, Iraqi Americans, and Iranian Americans.

So what's the problem? Don't liberal socialist Democrats like "other peoples"? Maybe L.S.D.ers like only foreigners who are poverty-stricken coming to the United States of America, because they will most likely register to vote as Democrats. Why? Because most immigrants know what a democracy is, and that's why they came to the United States of America. But they don't know what a republic is. A republic has an *elected president,* rather than a monarch, ruler, emperor, or king.

Sorry, President B. O.

Human Genetic Characteristics and Early Environment

Characteristics, traits, preferences, and tendencies are rooted deep in our evolutionary past. For anyone to pretend that this isn't so, for the purpose of political correctness, is liberal foolishness of the highest order. The effects of adverse upbringing are also well documented and, with respect to liberalism, are now becoming more clearly understood, but what must be realized is that adverse upbringing is not something that necessarily occurs by chance. Curiously enough, it's more prevalent among *adverse* people and their families.

With both liberal human and nonhuman primates, unfavorable environments can have psychological, physiological, and cognitive consequences, some of which may continue to be detrimental throughout the person's life. With humans, *early and secure bonding* with both parents—i.e., one heterosexual man and one heterosexual woman, as opposed to, say, two flamboyant homosexual males, or a couple of lesbians, or two beaming bisexuals, or a pair of pedophiles, or a single self-absorbed asexual liberal female, like the fictitious 1990s *Murphy Brown*, is ideal. Such bonding has been shown to lead to better physical and mental health during impressionable children's adult years (which, for those who don't know or care, is considered a good thing). *Disrupted bonding,* in contrast, increases the chances of undesirable opposite outcomes—for example, a high-school student using facial implants, branding irons, and snake-scale tattoos to convert himself into a cross between Liberace and Godzilla. Never doubt the ability of television to spread propaganda, including the liberal habit and abomination of urging all Americans—including impressionable youngsters—to have sex with members of races other than their own. Never underestimate the brainwashing power of the boob tube. It is *enormous*.

Genetic Predisposition

A *predisposition* is a liability or tendency to suffer from a particular condition, to hold a particular attitude, or to act in a particular way. Can a foreign immigrant have a genetic tendency to favor specific environmental and cultural features that are foreign to our traditional American way of life? You better believe it. Can he or she have a fondness for things alien to the Declaration of Independence, the Constitution, the Bill of Rights, and the concept of life, liberty, and the pursuit of happiness? Don't doubt it for a minute. Genetic predispositions can pertain to practically anything, not the least of which is the desire to be ruled by an all-powerful king or queen—which may explain why liberals so often impart, by means of flowery language, storybook fantasy, and stretched logic, larger-than-life and even godlike qualities to their politicians. (Ah, yes, the wonderful world of the Kennedys . . .)[213]

An omnipotent ruler can provide an innate sense of security to liberal suboptimals. That's because a liberal king or divine superhuman has the ability to

---

[213] So as not to shock, depress, or anger anyone, no factual details about this famous liberal family and the fairy tales about their history are included in this book.

simply wave his or her hand and provide all bowing, lovesick, adoring subjects with the bare necessities of life—food (manna from heaven), shelter, and clothing, which can sure take a big load off a poor indolent schlub's mind. Things like *necessities* can be very annoying to have to worry about daily. Liberals don't like to worry about the future. Many of them prefer to lay back in lawn chairs at night, with their mouths hanging open, high on marijuana, and staring at another planet.

Human Attributes

Human evolution varies greatly because different cultures emphasize different attributes. For example, in undeveloped southern tropical, high-parasite environments, males and females involved in selecting mates are likely to put absence of diseases and the ability to escape predators above cognitive capacity and a pleasing physiognomy; however, in relatively safer, colder, northern, low-parasite environments, such factors may be substantially reduced in priority for choosing a mate. Some liberal and conservative individuals may be physically attractive and/or intelligent, while others may not be, but beauty is in the eye of the beholder. This applies to everybody, including big-eared, skinny, dark-eyed Kenyan zebras.

The Prehistoric Beginning of Fantasy Addiction

What caused F.A.D. to develop in the first place? One problem with grasping the evolution of a psychiatric disorder is that physical mutations and deformities are much more easily pictured in our minds than are mental ones. It is also very difficult to pinpoint the origin of something that may have developed over a period of hundreds, perhaps thousands, of years or more. The availability of relevant psychiatric data ranges from scant to nonexistent, so all anyone can really do is make an educated guess. Here are four possibilities to consider:

---

[213] So as not to shock, depress, or anger anyone, no factual details about this famous liberal family and the fairy tales about their history are included in this book.

Human (D) Evolution

Possibility #1: Incurring Empathy as an Adaptive Strategy

The Australian psychiatrist Aubrey Lewis postulated that the mental disorder we call depression, because it often initiates caretaking behavior by others, is an evolved trait. Depression can initiate a beneficial response, so it is theorized to be an adaptive strategy. This same deductive reasoning can be applied to juvenile-fantasy-euphoria addiction (once again, this term is interchangeable with F.A.D.). Adult men and women who have certain traits and attitudes that are normally exhibited only by children (such as crying and begging for free stuff) engender a similar caretaking parental-like behavior in others—who then begin to develop an increased tolerance for suboptimality in their fellow man. An adult displaying signs of childish naïveté would tend to incur empathy and assistance in the form of food and water, just as he or she would by displaying signs of depression. Viewed in this way, F.A.D.—like depression—can also be understood as an *adaptive strategy*. In fact, any mental disorder can incur empathy, as long as the person is not dangerous. That includes the debilitating "disease" known as schizophrenia.

Possibility #2: Adapting to Loss or Deprivation

F.A.D., like the psychiatric states of anxiety and depression, may also be understood as a *pathological exaggeration* of a biological condition that can possibly contribute to survival. To clarify, F.A.D. may be an adaptive reaction to personal loss or deprivation. How can such things as anxiety, depression, or the feelings that come with fantasizing contribute to survival? Well, exhibiting anxiety can contribute to survival because it elicits cries of distress, which can help prevent infant mortality. Anxiety and distress in adults and children cause them to be more alert and thus to respond more quickly to emergencies. Depression, which we have already discussed, can result in receiving help from others—an obvious survival factor. Fantasizing can also contribute to survival because it has a calming effect, thus enabling an individual to maintain not only a peaceful state of mind but also his or her sanity in a traumatic situation or environment that may include some form of physical torture. Clearly, fantasizing can help a person survive an awful situation and/or horrible life. It can enable a person to stay relatively tranquil and to maintain the appearance of biological normality.

In contrast, a captive slave or prisoner of war who is not acquiescent and goes berserk would be far less likely to survive the whole ordeal. He or she might even fight to the death to escape.

Fantasy addiction—like depression—evokes a socially unattractive state of passivity and submission. This generally helps to avoid serious physical attacks from dominant and more powerful individuals, which, of course, increases the *likelihood of survival* for liberal males. When enslaved, most liberal males and females come to terms with their circumstances. Kept in close quarters, increased breeding occurs. The big difference between liberals and conservatives is that the latter will often die trying to escape. Such people are considered heroes, especially when they return with friends, combatants, or soldiers and free the liberal men, women, and children.

Possibility #3: Displaying Naïveté and Thus Incurring Mercy

When captured in battle, any naïve and harmless-looking person having the physical and mental characteristics of a child rather than of a warrior would not be considered a threat, so his (and even her) life would be spared. Such a person, male or female, would likely be captured and released, or enslaved. Note that this applies only to humans, not animals, because the evolution of lower life-forms does not involve the survival of the naïve, stupid, and harmless. For this reason, F.A.D. can be best understood as an evolved (liberal) human trait. Obviously, any natural human or animal characteristic that helps avoid death is "positive" *evolutionarily*. Slaves, for example, have access to food, clothing, and usually shelter—which is, of course, preferable to starving, or freezing, or dying of thirst in Ethiopia. (Solution: "Cash for Castration"—see page 260.)

Another advantage to having a childlike aspect, which is often a feature of the mentally retarded, is the fact that slave owners prefer to have servants who are *acquiescent* in the vicinity of their homes, especially at night while they're sleeping. This goes double if the slave/servant has access to anything that can be used as a weapon. (Imagine the difference between trying to control someone like, say, all of the former members of our president's Choom Gang[214] as opposed to General Norman Schwarzkopf.)

It's also important to note that a captive's chance of being spared from death is also increased by his or her value as an entertainer—e.g., having the ability to sing, or dance, or play a musical instrument, or make people laugh, especially if he or she has attractive "cartoonish" (i.e., exaggeratedly friendly or puppet-like) facial features or characteristics—a comedian, or "comic."

---

[214] Choom is a verb that means "to smoke marijuana."

Human (D) Evolution

Possibility #4: Fantasizing to Survive Barbaric Treatment

The precise origin of any negative biological feature or characteristic is, of course, a chance genetic "abnormality," but the cultivating mechanism for fantasy addiction disorder (F.A.D.) is clearly *slavery*. Institutionalized slavery, which has been and continues to be prevalent throughout the world, can best be understood as a *deviation* from the norm that contributes to mankind's evolutionary development.[215] Communism, of course, with its lifelong oppression, is just another form of slavery. The effects of "enslavement" are easily apparent not only in people but in beasts of burden and livestock: domesticated cattle, mules, goats, etc. Primitive communism/slavery is where it all began, and until all forms of oppression are eradicated from the face of the earth, the human psychological characteristic that we call liberalism—with its F.A.D.—will never go away. Fantasy addiction disorder is the result of men and women being forced to live such grueling lives as captives and/or slaves under conditions so intolerable, painful, and degrading that only by fantasizing about a better world was any slave capable of surviving the ordeal. Without fantasy, under such circumstances, most human beings would go insane.[216]

Furthermore, any mistreated, imprisoned, or enslaved human beings, whether male or female, who manage to respond with acquiescence, the appearance of contentment, and artificial halfhearted smiles would likely evoke some feeling of sympathy in even the most ruthless and hardened of captors. That captor might even believe his captive to be insane, whereupon the victim's life would likely be spared and he or she might even be freed. This clearly has the potential to become an adaptive evolutionary strategy. In other words, F.A.D. is, like the response of sneezing to clear dust from one's sinuses, a predictable and inevitable—but hitherto unsuspected—human evolutionary feature.

You see, Darwin's theory of evolution actually predicts that what we refer to as liberalism would eventually develop in any *man-made* environment that includes barbarity and/or slavery—and it doesn't matter whether the captive is man or beast (e.g., a domesticated pig, turkey, or goat). Under extreme and barbaric conditions, only those human beings who are able to tolerate, with no hope for the

---

[215] Human barbarity—i.e., extreme cruelty and torture—is also a contributing factor, but "natural occurrences" such as cannibalism or plague are not, because all animals are subject to these factors.
[216] The 1978 film *Midnight Express* demonstrates (Hollywood style) how extreme cruelty can cause a liberal to go insane. It's based on the true story of a misguided young American citizen whose life became a living hell after he was caught attempting to smuggle hashish out of Turkey, whereupon he was sentenced to a Turkish prison for over thirty years.

future, having their minds and bodies violated repeatedly would ever have any chance of continuing to live and breed. All others would surely perish.

Fictitious author's note: Skeptics must do more than simply say they do not believe any of this. They must also explain, preferably in detail, how slavery—i.e., forced labor for the benefit of others (which includes political oppression)—and torture, neither of which exists in the wild animal kingdom but both of which drastically alter an organism's environment, do not affect human evolution. In other words, a disbeliever cannot simply claim that mixing yellow and blue paint does not give green paint; he or she must also say what color does result! All you have to do is compare wild animals to farm animals to see the stark difference. In fact, more readily available proof exists of the theories contained in this book than Darwin put forth to prove his theory.)

The authors of *Darwinian Psychiatry* state:

In summary, different psychological states, traits, and events have clinical signatures; we can make inferences about infrastructural functions and their possible contributions to conditions by observing these states and traits, and both *psychic defenses and compartmentalized delusions*, which are usually thought to be indices of conditions, may have adaptive value.[217] [italics added]

Human prehistory was replete with extreme environmental variables. Man did not originate in a lush garden of paradise; he emerged dripping wet from a savage and horrible soup. This conclusion is based not only on the written accounts and records of the past 5,000 years but on common sense. Man was not born civilized. Human behavior was originally like that of an animal, and his living conditions, compared to today's, were atrocious. But despite all the evidence to the contrary, many liberals seem to believe that long ago, the (aboriginal) world was one of peace and love. They apparently don't realize that what really existed in prehistoric times—and still exists in some parts of the world today—was mindless animalistic *human barbarity*. Some may prefer to think that, long ago, mankind was "at one with nature," but it's much more likely that prehistoric men and women cursed nature every day of their lives—if they dared to offend their primitive gods, to whom they sometimes offered up screaming human sacrifices. If anyone wants to see how our ancient ancestors really lived (and can stomach it), they should just look at the so-called *modern men* living in the Democratic Republic of Congo

---

[217] McGuire and Troisi, *op. cit.*, p. 100.

today. That is how ignorant barbaric human animals really behaved, not like the noble, loving, and compassionate larger-than-life fools in liberal legends, storybooks, and fairy tales.

"Peace" did not exist anywhere on earth prior to recorded history, except when conservatives were in charge of things.

Man's inhumanity to man is undoubtedly as old as the human race. Murder, cannibalism, and rape were much more prevalent in the ancient past. In some African and Polynesian societies (which includes the Hawaiian Islands), and especially during times of famine, enemies were probably even caged, herded, and eaten like beef cattle. Eyewitness accounts exist.[218] There can be no doubt such behavior occurred, because human beings will do whatever they have to in order to survive. As far as torture goes, it was just as physically painful in prehistoric times, even without the infamous devices of the Dark Ages. Imagine being staked out in the hot sun on a pile of ants. Temporary slavery, too, has undoubtedly always been the norm for anyone captured in battle.

Who manages to survive war and hand-to-hand combat? Usually, the strongest, smartest, and bravest (and luckiest)—and, of course, those who refuse to fight at all. Anyone physically and/or mentally incapable of doing battle, or who simply chickens out, might live to see another day if that person isn't executed as a traitor. Survival through meekness and/or weakness is primarily a human phenomenon that does not exist in the wild animal world. Any animal that is incapable or unwilling to fight for its own life doesn't normally retain the privilege of procreating, and yet human beings who lack these instincts often do. Many things other than fighting ability can possibly help someone survive a battle: hiding, consorting with the enemy, performing sex acts, or simply running away as quickly as possible. Also, anyone appearing mentally or physically weak—i.e., nonthreatening—may be ignored by an enemy as inconsequential, and thus, he or she may live to see another day. Various other factors can also play a part in determining whether a captive lives or dies. Exhibiting apathy is one of them. Willingness to convert to the religion of one's enemy is another. (Inexplicably, some people refuse to pretend to do this even when the consequence is death.) What that means is that having no strong core religious and/or moral beliefs can be conducive to having one's life spared. Still another factor might come into play in certain other situations by having a weak sexual identity. Anyone perceived by a captor or conquering enemy as sexually friendly would have a better chance of being taken as a mate. This is not at all how things work in the wild animal kingdom.

Clearly, additional factors that can positively affect human survival in captivity include being (1) antiwar, (2) nonreligious, (3) naïve, and (4) sexually indiscriminate, along with having the previously discussed predilection for fantasizing.

Did anyone just hear a bell ring?

---

[218] For further information, read Herman Melville's *Typee: A Peep at Polynesian Life* (1846)..

Most people captured in battle will attempt to escape. Some succeed, but more die trying. Even those who simply rebel against their captors are often killed. Sometimes, those who are enslaved and cannot cope with the loss of liberty, or the servitude, or being subject to the whims of someone more powerful, may commit suicide or go insane. It is simply not in some people's nature to live under such conditions. Many of us have a low tolerance for being forced to do anything, while others don't seem to mind it too much. Some can successfully cope with unjust treatment, but others cannot. People held in captivity and made to do what they do not want to do can ease their minds through fantasy, imagining themselves in a better world and a better place. Liberals' days may be spent dreaming and pondering such things as love, hope, peace, displaying compassion, and societal change—while chewing on poppies, odd buds, and flowers—anything that helps them avoid the stark reality of their own desperate lives. In other words, they can survive by simply pretending that everything's okay.

The *Textbook of Evolutionary Psychiatry* states:

> Apart from formal thought disorder, many aspects pertaining to the content of delusional beliefs appear to be tightly linked to scenarios that were selectively important in the human evolutionary past. This does certainly not preclude influences on delusion formation from an individual's personal background, but the uniformity of delusional content across cultures suggests that universal patterns relating to survival and reproduction are mirrored in delusions. . . . [H]appiness has probably never been a selection target of selection; however, the pleasurable state of mind associated with happiness perhaps has been.[219]

Tinbergen's Four Questions

Nikolaas Tinbergen (1907–1988) was a famous ethologist who shared a Nobel Prize in Physiology or Medicine for discoveries concerning organization and elicitation of individual and social behavior patterns in animals. Tinbergen is well known for his *four questions,* which he believed should be asked of any animal behavior, for they constitute the key components of a complete understanding of

---
[219] Brüne, *op. cit.,* pp. 197, 317.

both behavior and maladaptive traits. The answers to these questions are discussed here briefly with regard to F.A.D.

1. *What is the adaptation (the function)?*

In Darwin's theory of evolution by natural selection, the ultimate function of any adaptation is to increase the chances of gene survival. For instance, birds fly south in the winter to find food and escape the cold. This is a basic survival instinct. Birds are not too slothful to flap their wings. If they were, they would all freeze to death or be pounced upon by predators and eaten, so their genes would not survive. Also, birds don't sit hungry in nests all day long, simply wishing that their stomachs were full. If they did, they would soon starve. Wild animals do what is required to take care of themselves, as opposed to some people today who depend on handouts. Wild animals are survivors, as are most—but not all—modern human beings (e.g., the ones who rely on friends, neighbors, strangers, and the government to pay their bills). Gene survival is achieved through an unbroken chain of natural events: acquire a mate ⇒ bear offspring ⇒ raise offspring ⇒ some liberal offspring may reproduce like rabbits. As long as the chain remains unbroken, any dysfunctional lumpish set of genes can endure forever.

Adaptive value is the *benefit* the organism receives in its ability to sustain itself in a particular environment, but this does not imply that any psychopathological sign or symptom represents an adaptation. Illogic, for example, has no known benefit other than, perhaps, self-assuagement. Fantasizing can temporarily improve one's outlook and state of mind. It seems likely that synthetic tranquility or drug-induced mellowness in the face of harsh reality might even be found attractive, initially, to some members of the opposite sex (especially if they have the same problem). Females, for example, might easily mistake a sluggish, apathetic male's relaxed smile and manner for a kind of gentle inner wisdom.

Whatever else they are, most mental conditions are conditions of failed functions.[220]

To answer Tinbergen's first question with any reliable accuracy, we would first need to determine for sure what kind of environment and conditions and under what circumstances the primate species *Homo sapiens* was forced to adapt. Most mutations are disadvantageous, and copy errors of self-replicating deoxyribonucleic acid (DNA) are generally eliminated through negative selection. Positive selection may occur, however, if a newly developed trait increases an individual's

---

[220] McGuire and Troisi, *op. cit.*, p. 44.

reproductive fitness, which is determined by his or her attractiveness to the opposite sex and by the ability to survive and procreate. Of course, successful reproduction can depend on a wide variety of contributing factors, such as the easy availability of aspirin, silicone breast implants, hair plugs, stomach staples, plastic surgery, or Viagra. (All of these things are covered under Obamacare.)

There is clear deductive evidence that F.A.D., as a mood-regulating trait, was positively selected at some point during human evolution. It is also important to remember that mutations and the resulting adaptations that follow are not usually optimal by design and only represent random changes, some aspects of which may be very negative.[221]

Natural selection and *sexual selection* are separate aspects of the evolutionary process, and different traits emerge from each. Naturally selected traits are traits that help the organism to survive and are generally the same for both males and females (except when running from *Smilodon fatalis*, a big saber-toothed cat). Traits and characteristics that are dissimilar between males and females of the same species (for example, a forty-nine–inch bosom) are the product of sexual selection, which may also indicate "love." The most probable suspect for the origin of F.A.D. is man's inhumanity to man: slavery.

2. *What is the phylogeny (how did the dysfunction evolve)?*

Phylogeny is the branch of biology that deals with the evolutionary development and diversification of a species or group of organisms, or of a particular anatomical or behavioral feature (like F.A.D.). Evolution, which is determined by both *function* and *phylogeny*, results in the genes—the hereditary makeup—of a population. In 1871, Darwin proposed that man (i.e., all men, women, and children) is most probably of African origin and most closely related to the great apes.[222] Biochemical evidence now reinforces this conclusion and indicates that the divergence of

---

[221] DNA is constantly mutating, and certain genetic disorders tend to be more prevalent in specific countries or regions of the world than in others. This is particularly true in places that experience little to no immigration or emigration and, thus, no genetic drift. One such country is Cuba, which not only forbids its citizens from leaving the island but also allows few foreign visitors. The Cuban government has set up a genetics program and family registry to combat the resultant problem with genetic disorders—which include schizophrenia ("Genetic Abnormalities Found in People of Cuban Descent," Bright Hub, Inherited Traits & Mutations, July 13, 2011). Isn't communism a beautiful thing?

[222] That Darwin waited more than twenty years to tell anybody is not surprising. He could probably hardly believe it himself. Imagine living in the 1800s and thinking of man and animal as two completely different entities with no real hereditary connection, much less a common ancestral origin—and then being told that your uncle was, in fact, a monkey.

man's lineage from the African apes took place between five and eight million years ago. The earliest group of well-known and undoubted hominid fossils comes from Laetoli in Tanzania and dates from 3.7 million B.C. These belong to the genus *Australopithecus* and appear to have been confined to the continent of Africa. *Australopithecus* was a bipedal, small-brained hominid.

The earliest fossil remains that are classified as *Homo* and thought to be our direct ancestors come from the area of southwest Ethiopia and Kenya and are dated to two million B.C.[223] This species, named *Homo habilis*, had a somewhat larger brain than *Australopithecus* and appeared at approximately the same time as the earliest stone tools—prior to the discovery of fire. The evidence uncovered in Kenya in 1981 and in South Africa in 1988 suggests that the earliest known controlled use of fire by hominids dates from about 1.4 million years ago.

The successor to *Homo habilis* was the much more modern-looking *Homo erectus*, 1.8 million B.C., a species that eventually spread into Eurasia. Little is known about him, but he could probably walk much better (and maybe even rap, or break-dance).

Recent biochemical data suggest that *Homo sapiens sapiens* arose in Africa about 200,000 years ago. (Whether anyone had F.A.D. at this point is presently impossible to determine.)

New hominid species are frequently being discovered. In March 2009, the skull of *Australopithecus sediba*, which had very long arms and long legs, from nearly two million years ago—a somewhat mysterious period of human evolution—was dug up in deposits at Malapa.[224] The species is known from at least four partial skeletons discovered at this fossil site. It has been speculated that the remains are those of a (husbandless) female and a (delinquent) young male child who fell into a fifty-foot cave shaft while looking for water. No evidence of any prehistoric behavior that indicates the presence of F.A.D. has been found, nor should we expect to find any such evidence in early man, because he probably wouldn't have lived past puberty with F.A.D. Why a weakness such as F.A.D. exists in some human beings—but not in wild animals—will be discussed further. Suffice it to say for now that F.A.D. appears to be the relatively recent result of inadvertent *artificial* selection and breeding.

---

[223] This means that all of us may possibly be related to President Obama.
[224] Malapa is located near Johannesburg, the unofficial capital of South Africa, which has been described as the kind of city that could just as easily be found in the United States: towering skyscrapers, modern shopping malls, traffic jams, ghettos, heavily fortified white suburbs, lots of guns, and a high rate of black-on-black-on-black-on-black-on-black crime. For a real shocker, look up the crime statistics for Johannesburg on the Internet and you will find out things that liberal media outlets in the United States refuse to publicize. Even the city of Chicago, Illinois, pales in comparison. But the good news is that murder rates everywhere appear to be on the decrease—probably because surgeons are getting more adept at sewing dying victims back together.

3. *What is the proximate mechanism (the causation)?*

The physiological mechanism, along with the biological function, is discussed in detail in Part I.

4. *What is the ontogeny (when does dysfunction set in)?*

Ontogeny is the branch of biology that deals with the development of either an individual organism or an anatomical or behavioral feature from the earliest stage to maturity. Traditionally, the causes of psychiatric disorders and their signs and symptoms are believed to begin with possible disturbances during fetal development (you know, that nine-month-long period of pregnancy when liberals, in their wisdom, don't believe there's any human life kicking). After birth, any adverse events that occur during infancy, early childhood, or adolescence must be explored. An adverse event is one that has negative long-lasting consequences (for example, being raised by a mother who mistakes you for a sheepdog).

Many psychiatric professionals maintain that mental disorders are the result of adverse early experiences—i.e., environmental, rather than genetic. Others believe that the origin of disorders is primarily hereditary. Research and observations lead me to conclude that genetic and environmental causes both play a role, with the greater emphasis on genes, at a conservatively estimated ratio of about 75:25. This conclusion is based on the simple reason that today, in the United States, *environments rarely occur by chance*; they occur by choice, and each of us has a wide variety of environments from which to choose. All anyone has to do is get on a bicycle and go rent an apartment somewhere else. Even wild birds are industrious and smart enough to build their nests near a busy Burger King. We Americans have a wide variety of lifestyles, sports, weather, and housing from which to choose. The choices we make are, for the most part, the result of genetics.

Genes play a role in determining the traits of the individual, but those same genes were involved in determining the traits of the individual's natural parents. Moreover, those same parents decided what kind of environment(s) to which their offspring were exposed. For example, a drug addict who was raised in an adverse environment may have been frequently ignored as a child because both his mother and father were living, off and on, in a methadone clinic. As most of us know, the degree to which liberal parents actually *care* about their offspring can vary enormously. Consider the female crack addict who sells her baby for twenty dollars to buy a small amount of drugs. No mother in her right mind would even consider such a thing. Genes can also determine the *susceptibility* of an individual to be affected by a negative environment and his or her ability to overcome it. "Like father, like son" is not a phrase with no meaning.

The consensus now among biologists is that behavior is the product of gene-environment interaction. Although childhood trauma is often cited as the cause of the psychopathology of the far left and, no doubt, plays a large part, it's not prerequisite for a diagnosis of F.A.D.—the condition that causes a person *to be* a liberal in the first place.

The indications are that F.A.D., a mental disease of moderate severity, has a wholly genetic origin that includes an increased susceptibility to strong environmental components, particularly the use of illegal drugs.[225] Objective observations would indicate that extremely liberal attitudes, which often include illegal drug use, along with observable symptoms of F.A.D., generally develop in an individual between the ages of sixteen to twenty-one, as some individuals mature more quickly than do others. Naïveté, a universal characteristic of young people, should never be confused with liberal thinking, per se. Generally, young people grow more conservative as they get older, whereas liberal attitudes, with rare exception, do not seem to diminish in old age.[226] That is why so many octogenarian males have haircuts like Cinderella these days.

---

[225] It should go without saying that with F.A.D.—or any other genetic mental disorder, for that matter—*environment* always plays a part. That's because any mental disorder can be triggered and/or aggravated, or, in the case of liberals, encouraged by the person's environment, and thus the symptoms of the disorder make themselves known and become more apparent.

[226] By "old," I mean anyone who still remembers when, prior to about 1964 (coincidentally, the same year that America became involved in the war in Vietnam), white people who smoked marijuana were considered degenerate, or even human trash.

Chapter 8

What Happened To Them?

P.E.T.S. (People Enabled to Survive)

The *three* things that we can always count on are (1) death, (2) taxes, and (3) the fact that man's ancient prehistory will forever remain unknown. Archaeologists can piece together a few bits of our long, unrecorded past, but the details of practically everything that occurred prior to about five or six thousand years ago—the people, their names, deeds, accomplishments, romances, leaders, and wars—are gone, kaput. We will never know any of the particulars. All we can do now is use our imaginations and guess. The oldest known texts that can be considered historical records come from Egypt and Mesopotamia. No records exist of what humans did prior to the first Egyptian dynasty (beginning in 3100 B.C.), during which people and animals, such as the African ass, were sacrificed to various gods.[227] We know only a little about the ancient Egyptians and much less about man prior to the Stone Age. Apparently, our caveman ancestors could not spell the word cannibal, so they left no written accounts—just teeth marks. What this means is that today, literally 99 percent of human history is a permanent enigma. Even where historical records of any kind do exist, there are always huge gaps that must be filled, so all we can really do is speculate as to the approximate date that what we call liberalism actually came into being.

Liberal influence in academia is undeniable.[228] What many of academia's members lack in understanding and imagination, they more than make up for with

---

[227] The African wild ass *(Equus africanus)* is believed to be the ancestor of today's domestic donkey.
[228] Academia is defined as a small, socially regressive community in which aged students with disheveled unkempt hair, rumpled clothing, and all of their dusty out-of-date textbooks are referred to as "professors."

the capability to plagiarize. What you are about to read regarding evolution has never appeared in any textbook. If it has in any form, then the facts have certainly never been widely publicized or discussed, despite their monumental importance, with regard to not only our quality of life but also the very future of the human race. Let all skeptics be reminded once again that the information contained in these pages is based on nothing more than history, science, mathematics, and simple logic. There is little reason for speculation when verifiable and inarguable facts speak so loudly and clearly for themselves.

Most would agree that the two opposing behavioral thought processes that we refer to as liberalism and conservatism didn't just appear out of nowhere. Everything has an origin. Everything is also in a constant state of change. *Liberalism* and *conservatism* are terms used to describe two dissimilar sets of beliefs, values, and attitudes utilized by those who hold them to form their own personal opinions and to determine the way they act.[229] Note that the word *conservative* is defined in several ways: (1) "holding to traditional attitudes and values, and cautious about change or innovation, typically in politics or religion"; (2) in matters of dress or taste, "sober and conventional"; and (3) in estimation, "purposely low for the sake of caution." The vast majority of conservative Americans are Republicans. But these definitions are not exactly how Democrats describe their opponents, are they? ("They want old people to die!" "They want *children* to starve!" "They want polluted air and water!" "They want to end all life on the planet Earth!") That is why liberal vocalizations, in general, deserve all the respect due a tricycle horn.

There is a reason why this country, after more than two hundred years, is still mostly conservative. It's not just a fluke. It's because conservatism works. Conservatism makes sense. Conservatism is conducive to survival. Conservative principles allow people to live side by side with as much peace, comfort, and security as possible. Secure and comfortable living conditions promote efficiency and productivity, which results in having more food to eat—obviously a good thing. However, this book is about liberals, not conservatives. The truth is, if the book were only about conservatives, no one would want to buy it. After all, who wants to read about normal people who are described in dictionaries as "traditional," "cautious," "sober," and "conventional"? Liberals are much more entertaining. We'd all rather read about, say, a slobbering Rastafarian high on bath salts who ate a rotten possum, then jumped out and ran from a New Orleans police department helicopter when it crashed through the roof of a local Piggly Wiggly.

So, where did these liberals with their F.A.D. come from?

If F.A.D. does indeed exist, it can only be the result of some extraordinarily abnormal environmental stimuli. What conditions could possibly have produced such

---

[229] Conservatism is a tried-and-true method of survival, whereas liberalism is a proven way to get your ass kicked.

a thing? Human suffering? Cruelty? Man's inhumanity to man? Early Middle Ages brutality at the hands of conquering enemies? Medieval torture by tyrannical kings? Prehistoric cannibalism? The bubonic plague? Or is F.A.D. simply a side effect brought on by long periods of war, death, and destruction and years of extreme isolation in the darkness of dungeons and stone-cold prisons, anticipating death? Did fantasy addiction develop as a means of combating stress in some awful primeval setting, or did F.A.D. result from all of these things? Or none of them?

Maybe something else produced it: *slavery and lifelong political oppression.*

Darwin's theory of evolution, which revolves around the concept of survival of the fittest, is simple to understand—once he explained it to everyone. We are surrounded by the proof of evolution, and we can easily see it with our own two eyes. Evolution takes place every day of our lives. When someone squashes a cockroach on the kitchen floor but two or three (or 147) other quicker cockroaches manage to escape, that is survival of the fittest in action. The same thing occurs when a mother pushing a baby carriage manages to cross a busy eight-lane highway without being hit by a car. Examples are endless. Even if a person who simply uses good judgment in deciding whom to hang around with—to avoid being poisoned, stabbed, or shot in the back—is exhibiting the instincts of a fit survivor. The mechanism of survival of the fittest is something so basic and simple that virtually everyone understands it. Mental and physical characteristics that promote an organism's ability to survive are passed on from one generation to the next. That's why, eventually, the result is a wily fox that can evade a pack of baying hounds, or a raccoon that can figure out how to turn a doorknob and get into a kitchen, or an orangutan that can pick the lock of its cage with a small stick and let itself out (supposedly, this actually occurred). Many species of plant and animal did not survive the process of evolution and so became extinct; some estimates have even put that figure at 99.9 percent.

Few people, if any, consider Darwinian evolution to be so-called *settled science.*[230] Some things we still do not completely understand about the origin of life, biological development, and the fossil record. Darwin's theory, however, now more than 150 years old, provides a framework that appears to explain the basics satisfactorily—just like Pythagoras's theory that the Earth is round and Copernicus's theory that Earth orbits the Sun. Fortunately, for this book's purposes, the basics of evolution are all that we really need to concern ourselves with, so that keeps things simple.

---

[230] Actually, there is no such thing as "settled science." There never has been, and never will be. It's just a meaningless phrase that liberals use to end arguments. The ongoing debate about "global warming" is a perfect example. The truth is, liberal governmental policies to end "global warming" are nothing more than a Democratic scheme to funnel our tax dollars to D.N.C. supporters. One of them is former vice president of the United States of America Al Gore (D), a man who was once described by a flustered masseuse as a "crazed sex poodle." But maybe he's just a liberal wolf in sheep's clothing.

There is an aspect of the evolutionary process that has apparently gone unnoticed, however, and it is difficult to fathom why. This unnoticed dynamic is certainly not very complicated. It's as plain as day, yet the following fact appears in no textbook: *As the intelligence of a species increases, the influence of natural selection decreases.* Eventually, the effects of natural selection may even disappear altogether and the species automatically—whether it realizes it or not—may become the lord, headmaster, dictator, captain, or kingfish of its own evolutionary development.[231] That is because there is something very important that substantially affects only higher life-forms (i.e., humans): the ability to manipulate and control the evolutionary environments of themselves and others. Lower life-forms—animals and insects—can also affect the environments in which they live, but to a far lesser degree. Plants and microscopic organisms have virtually no ability to affect their environments intentionally, but man determines the course of his own evolution, both *mental* and *physical.* Sometimes, changes occur with our knowledge, but other times, changes occur accidentally. That's because control over one's own environment, and over the environment of others, involves a lot more than just light bulbs, heat, and air-conditioning. The term environment includes *every single external factor* that even minutely affects our lives.

And what affects human lives more than anything else? *Government.*

If that doesn't make you nervous, it should.

Will future man have hands that resemble centipedes, with more than eighty fingers—one for each symbol on his computer keyboard? Will he eventually look like something out of an H. P. Lovecraft story? Probably not, because such a change doesn't appeal to most of us, but physical changes are only half of the evolutionary process. Undesirable mental changes can also occur that are not easily discernible, so they are not so alarming. Man's increasing ability to control his life and his world (eventually his entire encompassment) is not something that should be ignored or taken lightly. In fact, this ability should be right up at the very top of our list—next to nuclear bombs—of the most dangerous things to keep an eye on. Why? Because this ability to control our frequently artificial environment has a drastic reciprocal effect on the evolutionary process that made us what we are today: *It has effectively turned natural selection on its head!* Yes, when intelligence increases in any developing life-form, then natural forces are drastically curtailed. That's when a big, secret, hush-hush, politically incorrect (unmentionable) thing gradually begins to occur:

---

[231] Natural selection, a cornerstone of modern biology, is defined as "the process whereby organisms better adapted to their environment tend to survive and produce more offspring." The theory of its action was first fully expounded by Darwin and is now believed to be the main process that brings about evolution. The term "natural selection" was introduced by Darwin in his *On the Origin of Species* and was described as analogous to artificial selection, the process by which plants and animals with characteristics considered desirable by human breeders are systematically favored for reproduction. Nothing was known of modern genetics at the time of Darwin's writings.

JOHN HAYBERRY

THE STRONG ENABLE THE WEAK TO SURVIVE.

As any Arizona old-timer or livestock farmer will tell you, coyotes tend to be very smart and wary of man-made traps. The reason is simple. In the past, coyotes that were not wary of traps were eliminated from the *Canis* gene pool, so this is an example of the survival of the fittest. Today, some cautious coyotes manage to kill cows, goats, and pigs without ever being caught. A million years ago, the environment of man was identical to that of coyotes and every other land animal, but now, things are very different. One major change is that modern man has developed the enhanced ability to help the weaker of his own species. Animals may sometimes have the desire to help others of their own kind, but rarely the ability. Modern man's capacity to help the suboptimal, weak, and defenseless takes three basic forms: *mercy, charity,* and *aid*.

To understand the consequences of this, imagine if coyotes had the same mental and physical abilities as humans. The *mercy* factor would come into play if the trapped coyote and his pack of varmint friends begged the farmer to let him go and not to shoot him with a rifle, and the farmer let the coyote live. The *aid* factor would come into play if other varmints rescued the coyote by releasing its leg from the metal jaws of the spring trap. And if there happened to be a hospital nearby, then medical care, including advanced surgical techniques, could be used by a veterinary doctor to treat the wound. The *charity* factor would come into play if the other varmints provided food and shelter to the limping coyote for the rest of its life because it could no longer catch prey. The result of all this would be that rescued coyotes, once destined to pay the ultimate price for lack of wariness, would now be free to continue breeding. Their genes would not have been eliminated from the *Canis* pool. So what does that mean? It means that eventually—say, one hundred years from now—untold thousands of stupid coyotes (possibly enjoying free health care just like today's illegal Mexican aliens)[232] would be roaming the rocks, fields, farms, and deserts of Arizona, and worn-out steel traps would be constantly snapping shut on their paws. Yelps, howling, and ambulance sirens would be heard all over the state.

---

[232] There is a very good reason, of course, why free professional medical services, prescription drugs, and surgery are not guaranteed by the U.S. Constitution, and now, unfortunately, the United States of America is on the verge of finding out the hard way what that reason is. (Hint: *Charity is the very lifeblood of liberal existence.*) The worst part about it, though, is that when liberals are provided with anything free by the government, they act as though society owes it to them. Liberals are too self-absorbed, narcissistic, and perpetually high on their own dopamine to tell any of us thank you.

Human (D) Evolution

Anyone in favor of the (Un)Affordable Care Act should understand the significance of this.[233] Even a liberal socialist Democrat with his or her head stuck in a feed bucket can plainly see that there is a stark difference between the evolutionary environment of ancient man or wild animals and the evolution of modern man. Wild animals, for the most part, have only themselves to depend on, whereas humans have a vast network of medical, humanitarian, and financial aid available.

The most important fact that must be faced here in the United States of America is this: By bravely, nobly, and generously endeavoring to protect weaker nations around the globe who continuously seek our help, we are inadvertently cultivating liberals and thus liberalism on a grand scale, notably in all Third World countries.[234] America needs to realize that whenever we attempt to aid foreigners, especially the mentally ill and physically incapable—i.e., the chronically financially distressed—we fool evolution into believing that members of those groups and/or entire populations that may prosper by the humanitarian efforts of the entire world have the most desirable human qualities and characteristics.

Animals live by the rule of survival of the fittest. Man once did, too, but no more. The environment in which we Americans now live allows us to let our guards down. We need not be as quick or wary as our ancestors once were. If a person makes decisions not conducive to his or her survival, there is always help available from others, including the government. Liberals live their lives swinging on a trapeze above a taxpayer-funded safety net. Our society will not let them die—generally speaking, of course. Compassion and the act of charity are basic human instincts. Most of us couldn't avoid being charitable to those who need help even if we were to try. After all, who can turn his or her back on a starving child? Or a starving adult with the brain of a child? No one that I know in the entire state of Texas.

Interestingly enough, the concept of government-sponsored, or *mandatory,* charity appears to be something with which our ancient ancestors, including early American settlers, Pilgrims, and our country's founding fathers, were completely unfamiliar. It is doubtful that primitive Native American Indians had ever heard of

---

[233] The irony of it all is that the successful treatment of various diseases, physiological ailments, and psychiatric problems can actually increase their prevalence and *promote their existence!* (Why haven't any doctors told us this?) We're already creating a new breed of Viagra dependents. Future generations of impotent teenagers may curse us. When the symptoms of various debilities are successfully treated or masked with drugs, the victims are more likely to attract mates successfully, and so those same debilities tend to increase in the human gene pool. Will the human race have to be renamed *Homo defectus?*

[234] The United States of America will become a Third World nation, too, if Republicans ever find out what's going on and move to another country. Remember, "The trouble with Socialism is that eventually you run out of other people's money." (That's why the Democrats are secretly paying illegal aliens, especially those who can speak English, to keep their mouths shut.)

it, either. In fact, if a liberal Democrat had tried to explain such a thing to our first United States president, George Washington,[235] in 1789, Washington probably would have scratched his head quizzically, glanced over his shoulder to make sure no one was sneaking up behind him, then squinted at the pantalooned nebbish suspiciously. Probably, without hesitation, he would have politely shown the nitwit the door, bolted it shut, and then checked his pockets and gotten his wife and children to count the silverware.

Apparently, liberals' opinions were not held in very high regard by our forefathers, for there are no liberals' signatures in the first Bill of Rights or the original Constitution.[236] Liberals, for example, don't believe that "all men are created equal." Instead, liberals believe that hardworking people should be forced to give money to all dumb animals—to make them *appear* equally hardworking and successful. Moreover, if relaxed, grinning, unproductive duds—excuse me, I mean unproductive *dudes*—and babbling, three-quarters-naked, fruitless loons as poor as Job's multi-feathered turkey eventually lose all that they are given (except Obamacare), they should automatically be provided with more.[237] And, if necessary, more and more.

What's going on today in Africa is a textbook example.[238] It appears that no amount of money will ever permanently solve the hunger problem. Is this an example of survival of the unfit? No, not quite, but it's close. All over the world, those who cannot successfully help themselves, defend themselves, or take care of themselves properly

---

[235] Supposedly, George Washington never told a lie, so he was elected first president of the United States of America because everyone knows that things tend to work from the top down. But when Bill Clinton—face full of liberal joy—was elected president, people took his cue, and so they began to *lie* and *cheat* on their spouses more. Then, when Barack Obama was elected president, people began to show contempt for the law and other people's money, and so they began to *steal* more. Now, the question is, what will happen if another liberal is elected president? What's left? Will people lie, cheat, steal, and commit more murders?

[236] America was originally populated and established by English settlers (not migrating Africans, Mexicans, or Polacks as is commonly taught to today's school children) who sought to escape the influence of tyranny and, of course, the associated liberalism. Today, drug-addled rabble from all countries are flocking here in hordes by airplane now that the coast is clear. They're like lost pets searching for a new owner to feed them. Let's be honest, did anyone, even in their wildest dreams, ever think they'd see a day when a sitting president of the United States of America would try to use votes from illegal aliens to help him take over the United States of America?

[237] Unbelievably, many people still believe that Obamacare, which is an outright government lie, is *affordable*.

[238] For decades now, millions of Africans have been said to be dying. The most prevalent diseases include malaria, dysentery, tuberculosis, whooping cough, typhoid fever, gonorrhea, and A.I.D.S. (acquired immune deficiency syndrome). Other serious health problems include bilharzia, yellow fever, syphilis, herpes, tetanus, hepatitis, and giardia. Bogus drugs, unproven remedies, and snake-oil medicines are common, but fortunately, Africa continues to receive educational, developmental, and humanitarian aid from a variety of charitable sources around the globe, and donations are expected to continue for at least the next half a million years.

by modern standards are often protected and supported by those who can. Clearly, this kind of evolutionary environment does not exist in the animal world—except when man gets involved and attempts to make improvements to livestock or to protect an endangered species. Mercy, charity, and aid are factors that affect, for the most part, only human evolution.

Despite our good intentions, the unfortunate consequences are inarguable and clear: We are paving a road—actually, a four-lane highway—to hell, and the name of that road is Ignorance.[239] Now, as far as the evolution of the human race goes, absolutely nothing can be said in defense of government-sponsored mercy, charity, and aid. It would be nice if we taxpayers heard an occasional "thank you" for handing over our cash to strangers, but instead, we hear nothing but mean-spirited criticism designed to make us feel guilty, along with shameless demands for more. That is because the future of mankind doesn't seem to worry liberals one iota. Why should it? Future bankruptcy, societal confusion, crime, anarchy, terror, war—none of these things affect any of them personally, so they don't care, yet liberals act like they deserve gold medals.

Human evolution is not something nebulous that is going to occur after everyone alive today is dead and gone. Evolution is already occurring. It's here now! Each of us can see it with our own two eyes. When a society instinctively helps those who cannot successfully maintain and defend themselves, that society, in effect, tricks Mother Nature into believing that the recipients of aid are fit survivors; thus the core precept of the P.E.T.S. hypothesis: *The milk of human kindness eventually curdles, becoming the lumpy cheese of hereditary ineptitude.*

In summary, an evolving life-form that achieves a certain high level of intelligence also becomes capable of successfully preventing the early demise of weaker members of its species. Mercy, charity, and aid—including advanced medicine and modern surgical techniques (and, of course, free health care)—help those who may be mentally and/or physically suboptimal to survive not only their environments (severe weather, geologic upheaval, accidents, predators, disease, and human enemies) but also poor life choices regarding their behavior and their finances. This produces an average *decrease* of optimality in the population, and the natural evolutionary law referred to as survival of the fittest not only ceases to apply but may, to a large degree, actually be reversed:

Survival of the unfittest?

---

[239] The road signs to hell are written in a language called Incremental Legality. The road has four lanes so that liberal socialist Democrats can travel back and forth in buses, and thus avoid creating a traffic jam.

Nowadays, members of our species who were formerly destined for early removal from the gene pool not only continue to contribute to it but are propagating exponentially (not generally considered a good thing).[240] What exists in the world today and continues to grow rapidly was unavoidable and inevitable: a vast sea of suboptimal individuals who still live and breathe because of mercy, charity, and aid given to them, just as it was given to their ancient ancestors—*people enabled to survive.* P.E.T.S.

The Evolutionary War

The U.S. Constitution guarantees citizens the right to "Life, Liberty, and the pursuit of Happyness," but liberals, in their childlike "wisdom," have attempted to take things one step further. The right to life means a person has the right to live—unless he or she forfeits that right by criminal behavior—and no one can legally take that right away from him or her. It doesn't mean that society—i.e., complete strangers—are required to get a second job and work nights to take care of anyone who slips on a banana peel after getting stoned out of his or her mind and breaks his or her neck. We all feel sorry for such a person, of course, and that's what charity is for, but the maintenance of a person's mind and body is ultimately his or her own responsibility—no one else's. That is because adult human beings are not society's babies or pets. But the problem is that whatever you do for someone out of kindness, they'll eventually want legislated by the bench—"Give somebody an inch and they'll take a mile," as the old saying goes. And the more you give some people—especially liberals—the more they want.[241]

---

[240] In the primitive human/animal world, creatures that look or behave strangely are usually attacked and killed by other members of its own species, and thus eliminated from the gene pool. But as man grew more civilized, he passed laws to protect those who are different (e.g., exhibit aberrant behavior), so liberals began to thrive. Now, big cash incentives—and perhaps free cell phones—offered by the United States government in exchange for *voluntary castration* may be the only answer.

[241] Our thoroughly ungrateful liberal friends want *free health care,* but instead—much to their chagrin—they got Obamacare, the so-called Patient Protection and Affordable Care Act. As usual, what the Democrats named this boondoggle is the opposite of what it really is: a huge, unsustainable mess. The best anyone can tell is that it is being run, at best, like some kind of enormous and sloppy automobile insurance agency. Untold billions of our tax dollars have already been spent just setting it up and promoting it. Where all the money is going, nobody really knows. Untold billions were also spent writing and passing the eternally damned legislation. Why did the Supreme Court of the United States of America allow this to happen? It was a very foolish mistake.

Human (D) Evolution

Whatever defect or weakness that man overcomes, he establishes as a characteristic. Chronic back problems, for example, likely did not exist in early man, but this flaw is prevalent in our species today because of our ability to utilize sticks, canes, crutches, and specific exercises to help us walk. We also employ additional methods to take the strain off our backs, such as wearing back braces, or using ropes tied to rafters to pull ourselves out of bed, or raising ourselves from sitting to standing positions by pushing on one knee. All of these methods help take stress off weak backs; thus, human beings with inherent back problems have managed to survive. Lower life-forms, however, can't do any of these things. An animal with a bad back has no ability to do anything about it. Unable to catch prey or elude predators, it simply dies.

This clearly and *significantly* demonstrates what happens when members of a species manage to overcome any physical—*or mental*—disability. People born with medically conquered sicknesses continue to thrive, so their ailments become established as the genetic heritage of future generations. Those who are incapacitated with a mental or physical problem are often also helped by others, who may provide them with food, shelter, or protection from their enemies. Inarguably, the more man is able to protect the mentally and/or physically inferior members of his species, the weaker his species becomes. A hundred thousand years ago, mentally and physically fragile individuals would have quickly perished in the wild or become some animal's (or enemy's) lunch.

Consider how this evolutionary fact may account, at least in part, for the prevalence of such things as mental illnesses, tooth decay, acne, and obesity. (How many pimpled, grossly overweight, toothless, inexplicably behaving wild animals have you ever seen?) The ability to overcome physical defects may even account for male pattern baldness, which, of course, can be concealed with hats, caps, cloths, wigs, or various other types of head ornamentation. Clearly, all of modern man's imperfections are at least partially due to the fact that he has learned to help not only himself survive but others, as well—including those with diminished intellects and instincts. If this had not occurred, man would, like most animals in the wild, have no inherent physical and mental abnormalities of which to speak. Nature has a way of making sure of such things. The human spine is not underdeveloped, as some have suggested. Instead, it is defective.

In light of that fact, consider the prevalence of "progressive" liberalism in society today.[242]

Of course, the test of any new theory is its ability to not only explain but also predict future events. You will find that when you apply the hypotheses of both

---

[242] "Progressive" liberals have even been placed in key positions throughout the current administration. That must have emboldened other "progressives," because reportedly, they are now trying to take over the National Football League. But why? Maybe they want the cheerleaders to tell the quarterbacks what plays to run.

F.A.D. and P.E.T.S. to any perplexing liberal political or societal riddle, it all becomes quite clear. The P.E.T.S. hypothesis, for example, explains why some cultures that are hundreds or even thousands of years old are still operating with suboptimal or unsuccessful forms of government. It also explains why it's so difficult, if not impossible, to create a successful stable democracy in many countries, even when the U.S. military—funded, of course, by taxpayers (who, by the way, are almost entirely conservatives)—helps establish and maintain order.

It's a sad thing to have to conclude, but the democratic freedoms we Americans are lucky enough to enjoy may be genetically inappropriate for the population of certain foreign countries, particularly those in Africa and the Middle East. Establishing a true democracy in some Third World countries, for example, is the equivalent of turning a kennel full of domesticated house pets (cats, dogs, gerbils) loose and expecting them all to survive on their own. It is impossible. They can't feed themselves, stay clean, remain healthy, and live long, happy lives. Unfortunately, freedom confuses many foreigners; they simply cannot cope with it, and *they do not want it.* That is because they are genetically coded to prefer a single, all-powerful, male iconic authority. They also want someone who looks like them and thinks like them. They want someone whom they can depend upon to take care of them, no matter what it may cost their fellow man. They want a ruler, a majesty, a dear leader, a czar, a chief, a sheikh, or an ayatollah, rather than a group of elected representatives serving in several branches of government, along with a temporary president having only limited powers (except when it comes to issuing constitutionally illegal executive orders).

Most of them look like the kind of people that you wouldn't even want living in your neighborhood, much less running the United States of America.

> "It looks like President Obama hired all of the nuts who have crazy ideas about pyramids, planets, and stars from Web sites on the Internet." —Donald Duck, Anonymous Contributor[243]

> "What does the White House employment application say: DO NOT APPLY UNLESS YOU'RE A WEIRDO? What kind of person are they looking for, SpongeBob with horns?" —C. G.

---

[243] All of the Disney cartoon characters mentioned in this book are pseudonyms—just in case anyone didn't know.

"Why do so many male and female Progressives resemble preprogrammed androids? What are they trying to do, imitate isolated sphere dwellers on the planet Uranus? Or some evil alien beings?"
—John Hayberry (2009)

The liberal point of view is easy to comprehend. It is the same as a child's point of view. The world is far too complicated for adult liberals to understand. Liberals prefer that others take care of everything for them. Liberal men and women want to be spoon-fed from cradle to grave. They don't like having adult responsibilities or having to make any kind of important decisions. It's way too much trouble. Liberals, like children, just want to have fun.

The fact is, liberals would prefer a *god* or *master* who promises to take care of all their worries, so they can relax and stay high. They are not hereditarily geared for "a government of laws and not of men." Some people are not hereditarily geared toward allowing one person or cabal to take charge and govern their lives in totality forever. If their leader or leaders choose to bend the law, reinterpret the law, or even act outside the law, they don't really care—as long as bad things happen only to other people and not to them personally.

"Don't worry, be happy."

A few years ago, an interesting documentary film clip began circulating on the Internet. It showed a sweating African man wrapping a thick piece of animal hide around his arm and then confidently crawling into a large hole in the ground while holding a burning handmade torch. Inside the hole, a huge snake with a head about as big as a medium-sized cantaloupe reared back and bit onto the animal hide, clamping its jaws tightly and hanging on as other villagers pulled the man out by his feet, dragging the enormous snake with him. Then they killed the snake—presumably with a club—and carried it back to their village to eat. It is a dramatic reminder of where we all came from and of the kind of life that our ancient ancestors lived. Probably the only real difference between this unnamed African tribe and prehistoric man is that all of their clothing is made in China and donated by the Peace Corps.

The question is, if the men and women of this particular tribe were given a choice, whom do you think they would prefer to rule over them, an all-powerful king who would insert himself into their lives and personally take charge of solving all of their problems, or a temporary four-year president with limited constitutional powers? It's laughable, isn't it?

Unfortunately, freedom is not what all men seek.

Like helpless infants, our liberal friends want someone to take care of them, and that someone is the *federal government*. The rule of the corrupt and powerful is what the original settlers of our country suffered great hardship and even risked death trying to escape from, and the accumulation of power by any controlling individual(s) is what our Constitution was designed to guard against. That is one reason why liberals have so little respect and often even ridicule for our forefathers and the Constitution. The goal of virtually all L.S.D.er politicians is not to uphold their oath of office but to actually *eschew* and *obfuscate* the laws of this land. That may be difficult to believe, but it's true. Using whatever devious and shady means possible, they twist the amendments to the Constitution and the laws passed by Congress into something almost unrecognizable, sometimes *clearly* the opposite of what was originally intended. Are you beginning to see why?

It is all because of genetics.

Is the human race doomed forever to be a chaotic, illogical, financially struggling species of perpetually poor judgment that is riddled with various physical ailments and mental abnormalities (i.e., a liberal socialist Democrat politician's dream)? The answer is an emphatic no. This apocalyptic evolutionary disaster is only in the short term, because, as common sense tells us, any society that is made up primarily of individuals with serious shortcomings will simply begin to collapse at some point, along with the man-made environmental stimuli (i.e., government) that supported and produced such a pathetic de-evolved population in the first place. The result of societal chaos is frustration and intolerance, followed by violence, with countries growing increasingly angry at one another, which could easily lead to another prolonged and terrible world war.

Unfortunately, signs of increasing international tension are growing stronger every day.

Please note that liberals, who seem to ignore world history because they consider it absolutely irrelevant, dismiss the silly idea of another world war occurring, even though two have already been fought in the past hundred years. The terms "World War I," "World War II," and "World War III" are simply not part of the liberals' lexicon. That's because on the various planets upon which our liberal friends dwell—whether Uranus, Mars, Pluto, the Planet of the Apes, or the Wonderful World of Disney—such a thing, in their minds, could never occur. However, there's always the possibility of an L.S.D.er nut case who, as a sitting president of the United States of America, wants to maintain his or her prestige, influence, and power, so would be eager to fire a first shot and start one—but that's something that, for now, is outside the parameter of this book.

As with all things in nature, a tipping point will eventually be reached. Are we there yet, or do we still have a long way to go? If so, how long? Five years? Ten years? Twenty? A hundred? The unavoidable truth and reality of the situation is that when negative mental traits, sexual abnormality, diminished capacity, lack of spirit, non-productiveness, poor reasoning powers, and bad judgment are eliminated as factors affecting our human species' ability to not only survive but also thrive, the evolution of *Homo sapiens* can no longer be viewed as a ladder of any kind whatsoever, nor even a bush. Instead, human evolution begins to resemble a greasy, downward-spiraling corkscrew. Can we remedy this situation with reasoned scientific discussion and calm political debate? Only time will tell. But it's not likely, given our history. Indeed, mankind may be headed for an *evolutionary war*.[244]

---

[244] Reportedly, an elaborate crown of horns and a handwritten scroll describing the biblical Apocalypse (sometimes pronounced "a-pack-of-lips") was discovered hidden in a plastic bag in the basement of the White House.

Chapter 9

What Else Do We Know About Them?

Death Can Be Very Disadvantageous

Now, let's get back to the subject of the Darwinian origin of fantasy addiction disorder (F.A.D.).

As far as reproductive success goes, death can be very disadvantageous. When threatened, some people may react by succumbing or by pleading for their lives (which can sometimes work), whereas others may refuse to surrender, instead fighting back (which may or may not work). Although submission and cooperation with more powerful captors may be the best temporary option, some people are simply not capable of it, especially in the long term. Imagine spending your life doing hard labor for the benefit of another and receiving no compensation for it—and occasional beatings with a stick. That's more than most of us can take without rebelling, but anyone able to maintain childlike fantasies and a hopeful outlook in the face of such horrendous circumstances is much more likely to survive the ordeal. Slaves who don't rebel aren't killed. That's how, under conditions of enslavement, acquiescence can improve the odds of a person eventually mating and contributing to the human gene pool, so any unique ability to ignore reality is then passed on to the next generation.

Barbarity, however, includes much more than just working for no compensation and feeling the sting of a lash. Consider long-term isolated imprisonment in a filthy cell while being forced with ropes to sit on a large pointed rock for days on end. That is just one of the milder examples. What about the thousands of men confined for decades in some of the most infamous prisons in recorded history, such as the Devil's Island penal colony of French Guiana (1852–1946), or the

French Goree Island prison off the coast of Senegal (1536–1848), said to have been the center of the West African slave trade? Or the Château d'If (circa 1580–1890), well known as the setting for the story *The Count of Monte Cristo?* What were the results of such treatment? A huge population of liberal socialists, perhaps?

According to *Darwinian Psychiatry:*

> Social interactions are no less important to adults, although they sometimes like to think otherwise. Adults need to talk, touch, and receive others' recognition; otherwise, dysregulating physiological and psychological changes occur (McGuire and Troisi, 1987a; McGuire 1988). The nearly total elimination of auditory and visual stimuli that characterized the sensory deprivation studies conducted during the 1960s (which used normal adult subjects) led to such a high prevalence of adverse psychological and physiological consequences in the subjects (dysregulated infrastructures) that the studies were discontinued (Schultz, 1965). And unusually well-controlled studies have shown that significant increases in depression, psychosis, and attempted suicide (behavior associated with extremely dysregulated infrastructures) occur in persons in penal institutions who are placed in solitary confinement (Volkart et al., 1983). When one is alone, pleasurable fantasies and meditation can partially regulate dysregulated states, but there are limits (McGuire and Troisi, 1987b). In effect, humans, like other primates, live in a world of conspecifics with whom they frequently interact, a world of social noise, visual stimuli, physical contact, thoughts, and feelings. It is not surprising that humans seek out and defend those who, because of the ways they interact, increase infrastructural regulation. Such interactions are as important to CNS homeostasis as glucose is to cell life. It is equally understandable that persons avoid social interactions that have dysregulating effects.[245]

Undoubtedly, many of those who were imprisoned were criminals of various sorts who had a habit of telling bald-faced lies. Once locked up, they were often treated like animals and, probably, in some cases, like inanimate objects, such

---

[245] McGuire and Troisi, *op. cit.*, p. 169.

as a chair, so they were, of course, broken mentally. Slavery is just another form of unjust incarceration. Sometimes, prisoners and slaves are released back into the population to intentionally dispirit other enemies of the state, but what's important to understand is that people who are enslaved and who cooperate with their captors rather than die fighting may then be shown mercy—by not being buried alive—and so, once again, they have the opportunity to propagate. The human gene pool is affected accordingly.

The big problem here is that the very behavior that was once entirely functional and beneficial to those individuals who lived in captivity, bondage, and subjugation is now dysfunctional and harmful to their *modern genetic descendants*. That is because, today, some of their modern genetic descendants live in a completely different environment—i.e., a free and civilized society in which men and women are masters of their own fate and not dependent on others to shelter, clothe, and feed them. It is simply not in some of their modern genetic descendants' blood to live in a society based on "the rule of law, not of men."

Darwinian psychiatry is a field of study still in its earliest stage, so undoubtedly, there is still much more to be discovered. This may also prove true for liberalism.

In the previously mentioned *Textbook of Evolutionary Psychiatry*, the professor/author discusses the evolution of subclinically depressed individuals, saying, "A certain level of seeing the world more positive than it actually is, could be adaptive."[246] Also, in discussing mild forms of hypomania, he says, "[This disorder] may even be reproductively advantageous, which could make a case for the selection of self-deceptive abilities."[247]

Furthermore, he states:

> Competition between selfish motives and altruism may be an important source of intrapersonal conflict. The emotions of shame and guilt may have specifically evolved through group-selection and to maintain reciprocal relationships. The induction of guilt and shame serve manipulative purposes to reinforce the cooperative behaviour of individuals who under specific circumstances are tempted to behave selfishly. However, the possibility to

---

[246] Brüne, *op. cit.*, p. 215.
[247] Ibid., p. 215. Self-deceptive abilities, of course, would include fantasy addiction disorder (F.A.D.). F.A.D. would be particularly advantageous under conditions of enslavement because, generally speaking, women don't want to have sex with men who are angry. Women prefer that men see the world more positively, as they do. That's because anger, even when justified, is not conducive to breeding. Anyone who thinks otherwise has been watching too many Hollywood movies.

act in selfish ways is enhanced by the cognitive ability to conceal one's real motives before the self, referred to as 'self-deception'. Self-deception may in the first place have evolved to enhance the ability to deceive others, because if an individual is unaware of his or her selfish motives, it is easier to send more convincing signals to others so as to disguise the individual's real intention. This assumption is intriguing because it suggests that natural selection has not favoured cognitive capacities to produce accurate images of the world, *but to systematically distort conscious awareness and to block inadvertent access to non-conscious information processing.* These mechanisms are active in distinct ways in healthy as well as disordered mental life, and play an important role in psychological problems and disorders requiring psychotherapy.[248] [italics added]

Overlapping signs and symptoms often exist among various psychoses, and for that reason, it is probably safe to assume—until the results of more research become available—that the same evolutionary processes that came into play during the development of one particular disorder may also explain the development of others. F.A.D., in my opinion, is clearly an adaptive mechanism that evolved to help many of man's ancient ancestors become capable of surviving traumatic experiences associated with human barbarity. This includes long periods of isolation and mistreatment that could be tolerated only by individuals who had the ability to ignore the hopeless reality of their situation and remain functional human beings. But is it really possible for someone to shut his or her eyes to truth, facts, and reality? The answer is *yes*—if that person is experiencing or has experienced something sufficiently awful.

Evidence indicates that the modern-day liberal response to any information that conflicts with their preconceived fantasies is similar to the human and animal response of turning one's head away from the sun and automatically seeking the shade of a tree—especially one with lots of thick, obfuscating leaves and branches. But it's not liberals' eyelids that close; instead, it's their minds. In the same way that a wandering barefoot beach bum uses sunglasses to keep bright light out of his eyes, liberals are prone to use recreational drugs to help keep reality out of their consciousness and to maintain a peaceful outlook.

Beginning to get the psychedelic liberal picture?

---

[248] Ibid., p. 307.

JOHN HAYBERRY

The Liberal Peace Sign

by D. Falcon, lexicologist

The peace symbol meant different things to different groups of people throughout history. It was once called Nero's cross, linking it to the notorious Roman emperor who persecuted Christians. Centuries later, it was discovered to be an Old Norse rune. Vikings called it *Toten Rune*, the death rune, while some Germanic tribes labeled it *Todesrune*, the rune of death. After World War II, it was found chiseled on the tombstones of certain Hitler SS troops and so was labeled the dead man rune. It was revived in the '60s by hippies and others who protested nuclear weapons, Western culture, and Christian family values.[249] It then became a worldwide symbol for a brave new age of global peace, unity, and Mother Earth worship. Many of today's "progressive" liberals (especially the ones dressed like grotesque heavy-metal rock fans) could have passed for Nero fans and would've used this symbol to mock their Christian enemies.[250] But a symbol alone has no power; it needs meaningful words backed up by meaningful action to sustain it. That is why the peace sign has no power. Because liberals don't want to join the military and fight for it.[251] What is happening in the United States of America today is nothing new or "progressive." The same thing happened in Sodom and Gomorrah.

---

[249] It's common knowledge that the Democratic Party pays union members and front organizations to carry pre-manufactured signs and then protest, shout, denigrate, and argue in order to vilify Republicans and their policies. It seems to happen over every little thing. The Democrats even transport by the busload and to the same locations those who are willing to protest, so that news reporters will put them on TV. But here's an important question: Are "atheists" also being paid by someone to protest Christian activities? Their extravagant anti-Christian undertakings seem suspiciously choreographed. If true, who could be behind such a thing? Iran? Militant liberal homosexuals? Some filthy wealthy liberal foreigner? Or the Devil himself?

[250] "VATICAN OFFICIAL: 'OBAMA'S POLICIES ARE HOSTILE TOWARD CHRISTIAN CIVILIZATION'" (FOX News, segment caption, March 28, 2014).

[251] During the Vietnam War, the hippie peace sign was called "the footprint of an American chicken."

Human (D) Evolution

Normalcy Bias

What psychologists refer to as *normalcy bias* (i.e., prejudice) is a mental state that all human beings have, each to an observable extent, when faced with a disaster. Normalcy bias appears to be more prevalent and severe among liberals—who, of course, have F.A.D.[252] Normalcy bias causes the average person to underestimate not only the likelihood of a disaster but also the effect of it, and so he or she prepares inadequately. The erroneous assumption that an individual can make is that because a particular disaster has never occurred in the past, it will probably never occur in the future, either. This results in an inability to successfully cope with that disaster when, eventually, it does occur.

Obviously, some people have a stronger normalcy bias than others. Many people, for example, have difficulty reacting to the possibility of something detrimental happening to themselves or to their country that they have never before experienced. Liberals, who tend to be the worst about this, will often interpret dire warnings in the most optimistic way possible, eagerly seizing on perceived ambiguities to infer a less serious situation. Some liberals have been known, for example, to refuse to leave particular locations even in the face of impending doom. By drastically underestimating the consequences of terrifying things that are predicted to occur, they still believe that they'll be fine, despite radio and television broadcasts, or books like this one, or nervous friends and neighbors who may cause them to wonder if they are, indeed, at risk. This is why liberals with their characteristic *cognitive dissonance* do not belong in government.

"Conservatives think about the future, but liberals think only about the here and now." —Angela Zilverburg

---

[252] At the time of this writing, for example, most liberals are still—unbelievably—in a complete and utter state of denial over the abject failure of the current administration. But that won't last long, considering the disastrous economic policies, the serial untruths, Benghazi, "fast and furious," the New Black Panthers voting scandal, Solyndra, the G.S.A. scandal, the I.R.S. violation of public trust, Obamacare, the nobody-knows-anything-about-anything attitude from the top down, the "I-can't-comment-because-it's-an-ongoing-investigation" excuse, the foreign-policy buffoonery, the deepening distrust of our allies, the out-of-control debt crisis, the looming world economic *apackalips* (is this what is meant by the ghetto term "Black Planet"?) . . . and the list goes on. It is the growing legacy of President Barack Hussein Obama, who appears to have stopped doing the job for which he was elected (running our government) in the early summer of 2013. If he was managing a Dairy Queen, he would have been fired.

Interestingly enough, normalcy bias has been theorized to be linked to the human instinct to remain still and play dead when overpowered by any predator, which may be considered an act of subjugation. Both subjugation and the refusal to accept facts are closely associated with F.A.D. Is this link just a coincidence? Further study may be warranted.

Question: What caused thousands of Hurricane Katrina victims not to evacuate, even though it was common knowledge in the greater New Orleans area after decades of studies by civil engineers that the levies might fail and the city would flood?[253] *Answer:* normalcy bias. This also explains why, during the rise of Nazism prior to World War II, hundreds of thousands of Jews unfortunately waited until it was too late to try leaving Germany.

Normalcy bias doesn't just affect minorities, however; it affects all of us to a certain degree (as does F.A.D.). Perhaps normalcy bias also helps explain those Democratic politicians who continue to throw our tax money away hand over fist to their grinning constituents (and also to drooling campaign supporters) despite a skyrocketing, out-of-control National Debt, as though such behavior has no real consequence.

Just look at what liberal socialist Democrats, along with a few counterfeit (liberal) Republicans, have done to us: Our nation is almost *$18 trillion dollars in debt*—and that amount is rapidly accelerating.[254] No wonder liberals and the people that they elect to represent them in government are so anxious to take all of the American people's guns away.

---

[253] To be fair, normalcy bias is not the only reason that many New Orleanians didn't leave that city before the eye of Hurricane Katrina hit. Some of them didn't have running automobiles and/or five bucks for gasoline.

[254] That number was only $15 trillion a few years ago. To help visualize our growing debt to China and others, try to imagine a stack of 18 trillion one-dollar bills reaching up into the sky. It would be about 1.21 million miles high—and that's taking into account *gravity and compression*. Scary, isn't it? The worst part about it is that more than a trillion of those dollars was paid to various liberal Democratic Party support groups to help make the president *look good*.

Chapter 10

Where Did They Come From?

The Side Effects of the Written Laws of Men (and Women)

> "Nature rewards success. Liberal policies punish success. That's why liberal socialist Democrats in government negatively affect human evolution."
> —John Hayberry (2010)

The more laws passed by government to protect people from making mistakes, the more *liberals* survive. Laws requiring people to buy automobile insurance, for example, are a major factor that influences human evolution. That's because the mandatory purchase of insurance policies helps protect people who make bad decisions and can't afford to pay for their mistakes (in most cases, they are liberals). This enables them to continue to survive financially. In other words, *mandatory auto insurance props liberals up*. In the untamed natural world, Mother Nature determines the course of evolution, but in a modern civilized society, human beings make these decisions instead.

Here is another example: In the wild animal world, forced mating occurs frequently, whereas among civilized human beings, men who commit rape are automatically jailed (except perhaps in Egypt). This has the positive effect of reducing rapists' contributions to the human gene pool. That decreases the number of males with a similar proclivity for forcing women to have sex in future generations, so, obviously, incarceration is a *good thing*. By legislating—*and enforcing*—the laws of the land, government can control and influence mankind's evolution in a positive way. Prison time and/or chemical castration (or the electric chair, firing squad, or hanging) help to decrease unwanted behavioral traits.

The problem here is that laws passed by Congress can also have *negative consequences*. Every act of legislation, no matter how seemingly insignificant, affects the way we live to some small degree. We should remember that environment is always the key because it defines the course that human physical and mental evolution will eventually take. Consider, for example, what kind of society we would have today if welfare policies beneficial to Neanderthals had been enacted during the sudden appearance of early *Homo sapiens* prior to the ice age. Undoubtedly, the world would be full of hulking, dimwitted cannibals unable to count the number of toes on one foot. So, as you can see, the written laws of men (e.g., the Constitution, the Bill of Rights, or any bastardized legislation rammed through Congress by liberal socialist Democrats who haven't read it) can be major determining factors in the evolutionary development of the population of the United States of America.[255] Here is the *unavoidable* reason why: Whatever government champions, it also propagates. For example, if a suboptimal liberal president champions suboptimality, he propagates crude thinking, taste, and behavior. It is inevitable. That is why today, we conservatives are so often treated to the irritating sight of a smirking homosexual erectile dysfunction patient, or a big fat water-soaked tampon, or the latest cheery diarrhea commercial on high-definition TV.

> "Things work from the top down. People began to think that it was all right to lie when Bill Clinton was elected president, so people began lying more. People have begun to think that it is all right to ignore the law now that Barack Obama has been elected president, so now people are breaking the law more. What will happen when the next liberal socialist Democrat is elected president? Maybe that it's all right to commit murder? Then what will

---

[255] The United States Congress consists of two houses: the Senate, with 100 elected public employees—i.e., representatives called senators—who have six-year terms, and the House of Representatives, with 435 elected public employees—i.e., representatives called congressmen—who have two-year terms. So how are so many of them becoming wealthy so quickly? Where's all the money coming from? Saint Nick? Why do we need 535 people to represent only *fifty union states?* We all know that too many cooks spoil the broth, so why does it take five-hundred-and-thirty-five smiling politicians to make such awful decisions for our country over and over again? We're all Americans, right? Then why is *gerrymandering* needed to make different groups of people living in our country artificially compatible and proportionate in power? Here's a better idea: Why doesn't anyone who doesn't like other people and isn't satisfied with just one, or two, or even three elected governmental officials from his or her own state of residence simply buy a plane ticket and return to their ancient ancestor's place of origin: the jungles of Africa (the Dark Continent)—i.e., Somalia, Namibia, Nigeria, Kenya, Detroit, the Democratic Republic of Congo, etc.—or perhaps, the ancient underground caverns of Eurasia, including the bottomless depths of the River Styx.

happen after that, when the next liberal is elected president, and the next, ad infinitum? . . . The long-predicted biblical Apocalypse?" —Angela Zilverburg

Imagine if tomorrow, a law were passed stating that every woman with red hair shall begin receiving $10,000 a month from the government. Dying hair red, of course, would probably then become a felony—even for a greedy male-to-female transsexual. The effects of such a head-hair preference would be enormous and easily observable a century from now. Red-haired men, women, and children would be running around all over the place. Blonde-haired, brown-haired, and black-haired people, of course, would then be a small minority—or extinct. That's because highly prized redheaded women would be considered the most desirable mates and every man would want one for his wife. Mothers would wish for red-haired daughters over sons, and attractive eighteen-year-old redheaded tomatoes would be in great demand. Then, under current law, any male or female human fetus *without* the much-preferred red hair follicles could be discarded in an abortionist's office for about $2.50—excuse me, I mean *$250.00*. (The price keeps going up and up—maybe someday it will reach *heaven.*)

See how man-made evolution works?

Imagine, if you will, what would surely happen if, tomorrow, Congress passed a law stating that redheaded women must always be given preference when hiring and must always be awarded government contracts—even if the woman applies for a job and cannot pass a standardized test. See what I mean? Such a policy is extremely dangerous, especially if she wants to be a New York City skyscraper crane operator. That's because any advantage given to a group of people based on their hair color increases their proliferation in society. (Please note that, in my opinion, there is nothing wrong with herds of redheaded women, but it's liable to bankrupt peroxide manufacturers.) Also, imagine if Washington, D.C., politicians, instead of just passing a few obscure laws benefitting red-haired females, enacted a whole panoply of so-called comprehensive legislation that benefits redheads—*3500 pages long*. A thousand years from now, redheaded Irish men and women would rule the earth. (So just imagine what would happen if we were talking about *Neanderthals* instead.)

Visa Lottery Winners

Consider the effects of liberal programs like affirmative action, lottery visas, food stamps, welfare, and free health care: All of these things have *predictable evolutionary consequences*. Lottery winners, for example, are, more often than not, PWT (poor white trash), so imagine how this translates to *visa lotteries* in a foreign country like Nigeria. Who in the name of hell is responsible for this? Why are we importing losers ("winners") to the United States? Don't we have enough of them already? Our federal government, in its politically correct liberal wisdom, holds a lottery each year, providing an extra 50,000 visas to any foreigners who apply and win. Many of the participants in the Diversity Visa Program are from Third World countries, and this bad-for-the-United States (B.F.T.U.S.) Democratic opportunity has actually been the means by which some Middle Eastern terrorists have entered the United States. Past lottery winners reportedly include a grateful Pakistani national who later pled guilty to conspiring to destroy electrical power stations, the Israeli consulate, a National Guard armory, and other targets in South Florida in pursuit of his jihad, or Islamic holy war. But, hey, what's more important, National Security or a steady stream of likely Democratic voters?

The Butterfly Effect

In chaos theory—a field of study in mathematics with applications in biology—the *butterfly effect* refers to a highly sensitive dependence on the initial conditions of events. Some believe that a small change at one point in time can result in enormous differences later. The name of this effect, which was coined by a meteorologist, comes from the theoretical example of a hurricane's formation on the east coast of the United States being somewhat dependent on whether a simple butterfly in Africa had flapped its wings several weeks before. That means that if just one more union member still living in Detroit eats a sloppy joe, dripping sauce on his cotton undershirt, future man may develop a lower lip the size of a lobster bib. You see, the rule of thumb is this: The more people who depend on the federal government to take care of them, the dumber and lazier they get. Fatter, too.[256]

Now, the president's supporters are demanding *free health care*.

---

[256] The national obesity problem may be due to the fact that, thanks to the federal government, many people can only afford to buy cheap TV dinners that are thirty percent animal fat.

Human (D) Evolution

Unintended Human Evolutionary Engineering

> "Liberals are what we'd get if we created life in a petri dish. Conservatives are what we'd get when it figured out how to escape." —John Hayberry (2010)

Inadvertent artificial (i.e., man-made) dysgenic breeding has been taking place for untold thousands of years, and probably in one form or another since the first appearance of *Homo sapiens* on this planet some 4.5 million years ago. So-called liberalism, an unrecognized feature of the human evolutionary process, can best be understood as dysfunctional genes, pure and simple. It's a clear case of *oblivious optimals promoting suboptimals* (O.O.P.S., for short). The big problem is that government-sponsored altruism causes the situation that exists with liberalism to keep getting worse.[257] In the context of enslavement by captors, the proliferation of suboptimal liberal adults is logically predicted to increase by Darwin's theory of evolution.

The Good, the Bad, and the Unproductive

No one is against charity. Why would they be? At one time or another, virtually all of us have participated in it. Providing help to those in need is an age-old human instinct. But what about compulsory charity? Taking from the rich and giving to the poor sounds noble, good, and worthy, doesn't it? Well, it certainly does to a nigritic Parisian gang of gypsy pickpockets. However, confiscating the work product of the productive and then donating it to the nonproductive is not something that occurs naturally in any known earth environment. The concept is unique to liberal ideology, so we should always bear in mind the most important law of unintended human evolutionary engineering:

> Rewarding *anything* breeds it.

---

[257] Altruism normally includes a return on the investment. But in the case of liberals, the only apparent return on our investment is the entertainment they bring to politics and news stations, then to television viewers who are intrigued by their adult male buckteeth, seesaw eyes, wide noses, speech impediments, unevenly distributed testosterone development, and asymmetrical eyebrows.

Whatever a government supports, promotes, protects, aids, or favors will automatically increase in number, including underdogs. That is why the more laws passed by government that protect people from making mistakes, the more liberals survive and the more *liberalism propagates*. Imagine, for example, if you had a dozen physically fit laboratory mice, and all but two of them were able to navigate a maze to find the cheese. (The two emaciated, unexceptional mice just sat and licked themselves all day long.) After a while, feeling sorry for that pair of hungry rodents, you might begin taking a few meals away from the other mice and begin hand-feeding the starving ones—*godlike*—so they wouldn't die. Does anyone want to take a wild guess what you would have ten years later? Here's what: Millions of ignorant, apathetic, scrawny, wild-eyed mice, and scars from bites all over your arms and fingers. This throws a whole new light on the 1964 Johnson administration's declared "War on Poverty," doesn't it? Exactly how long does it take to win a war against poverty, anyway? A time span approaching that of the Pliocene Epoch?[258]

Remember this:

The more you help idiots, the more they breed.
The more they breed, the more help they need.

Today, we have the American Association of Retired Persons (A.A.R.P.) Foundation's Drive to End Hunger, the United Nations' World Food Programme, Feed the Children, Freedom from Hunger, End Hunger Network, etc., and you'd have to be a cold, heartless bastard not to feel any sympathy for someone who's dying from lack of food. Of course, it's probably just a coincidence, and only a tiny thing, but all of these programs have the ultimate effect of boosting future L.S.D.er voter rolls. That's because, fortunately, there are no starving conservative Republicans—at least, none that anyone south of the Mason-Dixon Line has ever heard of. (After all, what does it cost to make a ham-and-cheese sandwich? Twenty-five cents?) If there are any, then they are very scarce. So what's the answer? There appears to be only one: Promote *decreased*, not *increased*, reproduction among those who are unable to fend for themselves. If anyone believes that he or she knows a better way, please, let's hear it (A.S.A.P.)—that is, if anything at all can be heard over the booming cacophony of liberal Democratic politicians' screams. In fact, I think I hear some angry hee-hawing already.

---

[258] It has been estimated that during the fifty years since President Lyndon Baines Johnson first promised to end poverty, the United States of America has wasted some $15 trillion.

Human (D) Evolution

That brings us to the biggest and most notorious problem with institutionalized charity: After a while, the people receiving handouts from taxpayers (many of whom are teenage kids working for the minimum wage) begin to think and act as though they're entitled to it, and if we don't keep giving it to them, they're liable to retaliate. Next thing you know, the whole city of Atlanta, Georgia, is on fire. So the consensus of opinion seems to be that it's better to spend $10 million now on various donations to P.P.J.s—people of poor judgment—living in dilapidated inner-city communities than to sustain $40 million in property damage later due to rioting, arson, looting, and random acts of vandalism, not to mention all of the senseless murders.

> "We ask why there is violence in our schools, but we have systematically removed God from our schools." —A former Republican state governor (name withheld)

> "In the past, anyone who said publicly that he or she doesn't believe in God was either ignored, shunned, beat up, imprisoned, exiled, or executed. Not today. In the United States of America, the A.C.L.U. gets involved." —Louis

The violence is just a backlash that's occurring because liberal socialist Democrats are breeding supporters by constantly rewarding them with lots of free gifts from their *political deck of playing cards:* (ace) nonsensical I.R.S. rebates; (deuce[259]) good-paying jobs through affirmative action hiring policies; (three) non-taxpayer tax refunds; (four) no-credit home loans; (five) free public housing; (six) Cash for Clunkers; (seven) unlimited cellular phones and monthly service[260]; (eight) first-, second-, and third-generation welfare checks; (nine) an endless river of unemployment checks; (ten) E.B.T. cards—i.e., credit cards—the new food

---

[259] "Deuce" is the number 2 in a standard deck of playing cards. The word is also informally used as a euphemism for "devil" in expressions of annoyance, impatience, or surprise—as in *"What the deuce!"*
[260] Imagine if the Democratic Party secretly sent the following text message to millions of freeloading Americans with no jobs and free government-supplied cell phones: "TODAY IS THE BIG ELECTION! VOTE FOR ALL THE DEMOCRATS! IF A REPUBLICAN IS ELECTED, HE WON'T PAY YOUR PHONE BILL!!!" But that would be illegal, wouldn't it? Let's hope so.

stamps; (jack) $7.25-an-hour minimum wage[261]; (queen) government child-care subsidies; (king) unearned college "scholarships"; (joker) free health care—and the list goes on and on.[262] It's just a big house of cards ready to fall down as soon as the next president takes charge.

Poor guy. We all wish him the best of luck.

Dominant and Subordinate Males

Nature, as we know, can be cruel. With many mammal species, the strongest and most aggressive male not only dominates the group but also mates exclusively with all of the females and remains in charge until he is defeated in a show of strength by a more powerful rival. In the animal world, subordinate males are often chased away, wounded, or killed by the dominant male. The dominant male serves as a ruthless and protective leader. For example, dominant male elephant seals keep a close eye on their harems and are quick to attack with their massive snouts and enormous weights. Dominant male lions, who are really nothing more than big pussycats, lie around doing nothing most of the day, then, later, after one of the other lions makes a kill, decide who eats and who doesn't eat. Sometimes, dominant male animals also sacrifice their own lives in defense of the group. Dominant-subordinate behavior can even be observed in some insects. Undoubtedly, these same instincts have also existed for millions of years with some uncivilized humans; however, modern man is quite different. Today, governmental legislation ensures that *subordinate* males have exactly the same rights as *dominant* males, including the right to breed.[263] But what, if anything, can ever be done about that? Maybe that's just the way things are intended to be.

---

[261] Why doesn't anyone call a spade a spade? When President Obama stands in front of a TV news camera and asks every business owner in the United States of America to raise his or her minimum wages, he's just trying to buy the votes of low-income workers for the Democratic Party—*with other people's money!* There's no such thing as a "minimum wage." There never has been and there never will be. Here's why: If business owners are forced to pay their workers more money, they either fire the workers or make them do more work. If business owners can't get any of their workers to do more work, then they fire everyone and rehire them as "independent contract employees," and burger flippers become burger-flipper engineers. Then the boss pays each of them a 2 percent commission based on some nebulous monetary figure that no one can possibly figure out.

[262] The serious question that needs to be answered is this: Should *government dependents* have unlimited reproduction rights?

[263] The effect of this legal right is particularly evident in certain areas of Pinellas County, Florida..

Human (D) Evolution

Ethnic Stereotypes?

All human beings are products of their ancestral environments. That's the way genetics works.

Liberals, in their perpetual intellectual dishonesty, would have everyone believe that traditional perceptions of ethnic groups, each of which has a unique heritage and corresponding colorful reputation, are all bald-faced lies. So who are we to believe—scowling liberals wagging their fingers, or our own ears and eyes? There was a time when ethnic characteristics, along with the differences between the sexes, were openly acknowledged and accepted good-naturedly. But sadly, no more. Now, the mere mention of such a thing as an ethnic characteristic may be met with a stranger's wide eyes and disbelief. Nevertheless, it's an inarguable fact that over the centuries, various environmental factors, immigration, and governmental legislation and religious laws, under which all of our ancestors lived, either by choice or coercion—including the degree to which beneficial laws were enforced—affected their evolutionary development, and thus ours. All of us have positive and negative physical and/or behavioral characteristics for that very reason.

In any discussion of evolution, *environment* is always the key. Every major population group has had a different ancestral environmental influence, causing people from that particular part of the world to think and behave differently. Sometimes, this even occurs among people who live in the same neighborhoods here in the United States of America, especially when the government treats them differently. So why do we allow reverse discrimination in a country where everyone is supposed to be treated equally?

Here are some brief ethnic histories for comparison (in alphabetical order).

African Americans

Has the evolution of African Americans been affected by decisions made by the United States Congress? By the Civil Rights Act of 1964? By the Civil Rights Act of 1865? By Southern plantation owners? By the Atlantic slave trade? By the Constitution? By the Declaration of Independence? By the Bakongo, Igbo, Mandé, Wolof, Akan, Fon, and Makua?

The Chinese

Has the evolution of the Chinese been affected by the enslavement of criminals and the incarceration of political prisoners? By Mao Zedong? By Chiang Kai-shek? By the Communist Party? By Soviet influence? By Sun Yat-Sen? By the abolishment of slavery in 1910? By hundreds of Chinese emperors? By the Zhou Dynasty? By the Shang Dynasty? By the Xia Dynasty? And the list goes on. . . .

The French

Has the evolution of the French been affected by World War II and by the Nazi occupation and the control of the Axis Powers?[264] By the country's rule by a monarchy? By Napoleon Bonaparte? By Charlemagne? By the Frankish king Clovis I? By the forces of the Roman Empire? By the Gauls, the Aquitani, and the Belgae? And the list goes on. . . .

Germans

Has the evolution of the Germans been influenced by the forced labor of Germans in the Soviet Union after World War II? By the division of Germany into democratic West Germany and communist East Germany, which were reunited in 1990? By denazification? By Adolf Hitler? By the Treaty of Versailles? By the Reichstag? Feudalism? Otto I? By the Alamanni, Franks, Bavarii, Chatti, and Saxons? And the list goes on. . . .

The Greeks

Was the evolution of the Greeks affected by the invasion and occupation by Nazi Germany in World War II? By the Greco-Turkish War and the population exchange between Greece and Turkey? By Ottoman rule? By the Byzantine Empire? By the establishment of Roman rule and the advent of Christianity? By Alexander the Great? By the Minoan civilization in Crete? By the Mycenaeans? By slavery in ancient Greece? And the list goes on. . . .

---

[264] France was conquered by Germany in 1940 and was liberated (i.e., everyone was freed from their jail cells and allowed to live their lives normally) by the Allied forces in 1944.

Human (D) Evolution

The Irish

Has the evolution of the Irish been affected by the Irish Free State, which ended in 1937? By the Act of Union? By the Penal Laws? By the Crown policy of plantation? By more than 700 years of direct English rule and, later, British involvement in their country? By chattel slavery in the British Isles? By the Christian missionary Saint Patrick? By Niall Noígíallach? And the list goes on. . . .

The Jewish Peoples[265]

Has the evolution of the Jews been affected by an atmosphere of fanaticism and Islamic intolerance? By the imposition upon them of Sharia law and the guidelines of the Qur'an by their Islamic captors? By the Old Testament? By the Ten Commandments? By Herod the Great? By an untold number of pogroms?[266] By the diaspora? By Roman rule? By the laws of the ancient peoples of Israel? And the list goes on. . . .

Italians

Has the evolution of the Italians been affected by Fascism? By Benito Mussolini? By the Vatican City State—a rare case of a nonhereditary monarchy? By the ban on capital punishment in 1889? By the Sicilian Mafia? By the Holy See? By the Roman Empire? By Caligula? By the Etruscan civilization? And the list goes on. . . .

Mexicans

Has the evolution of the Mexicans been affected by an estimated 25 million men, women, and children illegally crossing over into the United States? By N.A.F.T.A.?

---

[265] Judaism now includes hundreds of different populations and shares some of the characteristics of a nation, an ethnicity, a religion, and a culture. Many Jews are not religious.

[266] Pogroms are defined as "organized massacres." Because of all the pogroms their ancestors endured and somehow survived, many people today of Jewish heritage are exceptionally bright, gifted, and entertaining. In Hollywood, California, they also have a reputation of becoming "shameless self-promoters" because they so often stand out from the crowd. Some Jews are also monetary survivors to thepoint of it being a genetic psychosis. Investment advisor Bernie Madoff, for example, is now serving a 150-year sentence and forfeiture of over $17 billion for a Ponzi scheme believed to be the largest of its kind in U.S. history. (Comedienne Joan Rivers, a funny standup comic and fiscally conservative Republican "platypus," hadsomething to say about it: "I'm Jewish. I don't work out. If God had wanted us to bend over, He would haveput diamonds on the floor.") You see, it's all in the genes.

By Partido Revolucionario Institucional (a member of Socialist International)? By the hacienda system? By Maximilian I? By Spanish rule and enslavement? By the Aztecs? By the Maya? By the Toltecs? By the Olmecs? And the list goes on. . . .

The Poles

Has the evolution of the Poles been affected by the People's Republic of Poland's creation by the Soviet Red Army? By the Nazi invasion and occupation in World War II? By the Russian Empire, the Kingdom of Prussia, and the Austrian Habsburg Monarchy? By the Polish–Lithuanian Commonwealth? By the Jagiellon dynasty? By the adoption of Christianity? By the Piast dynasty? By the arrival of the Slavs? And the list goes on. . . .

Scots

Has the evolution of the Scots been affected by the rule of the kings of Scotland? By the ruthless Kenneth McAlpin? By the Christianity inaugurated by St. Columba? By the teachings and rituals of the ancient Druids, including possible human sacrifice? By the enslavement of the Alba and Picts? And the list goes on. . . .

The Swedes

Has the evolution of the Swedes been affected by the Swedish Social Democratic Party? By the immigration of more than one million Swedes to the United States (1850–1910)? By the Treaty of Nystad? By Gustav Vasa? By King Christian II of Denmark? By the Kalmar Union? By the abolishment of slavery and serfdom in 1335? By the Swedish monarchs? By the Viking Age? By the advent of Christianity in 829 A.D.? By King Adils? By the Suehans? And the list goes on. . . .

Human (D) Evolution

Wild Animals and Domesticated Pets

Pretend for just a moment that you are a wild fox standing face-to-face with a pet Chihuahua. Look into its eyes. What do you see? A friend? An enemy? A distant cousin?[267] A meal? Well, what a fox sees in the eyes of a Chihuahua is probably very similar to what a conservative sees in the eyes of a liberal (and vice versa): It's mutually incomprehensible.

Liberals, if my hypothesis is correct and human devolution has indeed occurred, are essentially the human equivalent of our favorite domesticated farm animals or beloved household pets.[268] Like the Chihuahua, liberals no longer have the keen survival instincts of wild animals. That is why a (conservative) fox does not understand the thinking of a (liberal) Chihuahua, and vice versa.

Fortunately, the increasing lack of parallel logic between conservatives and liberals makes each of them incapable of agreeing with the thinking process of the other, so both political parties are now at a stalemate in Washington, D.C. Both Democrats and Republicans are equally aware of the seemingly undefinable difference between them. When conservative and liberal politicians look into each other's eyes, they see people very different from themselves. They see people who talk (or bark, or yap) much like themselves but who will rarely agree with them. Still, people can communicate on many different levels, so as long as everything goes relatively smoothly, everyone gets along just fine. However, when things don't go smoothly, all hell breaks loose. Conservatives and liberals, just like the fox and the Chihuahua, live in two different realities. The fox lives in what he or she views as the real world of *danger*. The Chihuahua lives in what he or she views as the real world of *guaranteed entitlements*, which includes financial security, peace, love,

---

[267] "Sometimes, animal species are difficult to differentiate. The gray fox is a solitary hunter with the ability to climb trees, and its eyes in bright light have thin vertical-slit pupils similar to those of a cat. But it's not a pussycat. The gray fox is actually a member of the Canidae family, which includes domestic dogs, wolves, coyotes, dingoes, jackals, Lycaons (African wild dogs), and other lesser-known dog-like mammals, many of which are extinct." —Anonymous editor

[268] Publicly using the term "human farm animal" to describe any liberal male or female (no matter how oafish) is strongly discouraged, for it may qualify as hate speech.

comfort, and limitless food.[269] In the Chihuahua's little doggie world, all that he or she is required to do is eat and sleep, and everyone, including the *mailperson*, is a potential friend.

But a fox living in the wild sees things very differently. The fox sees his or her life as a constant struggle with potential threats hidden behind every tree. The fox is wary and self-reliant, but the Chihuahua is naïve. The fox has exceptionally sharp instincts, but the poor little Chihuahua's instincts are dull. The fox stays alert, but the Chihuahua prefers to relax and snooze. The fox has only itself to depend on, whereas the Chihuahua is dependent on its human master(s). The fox is well aware of predators, but the goofy Chihuahua does not even comprehend what a predator is—not until the flying predator swoops down like an American bald eagle from the wild blue yonder, snapping him or her up in its talons.

The fox considers humans to be its enemy until proved otherwise. The Chihuahua, on the other hand, considers everyone a potential source of love, cuddling, head petting, paw shaking, and treats. The fox stays on guard and will bite viciously when attacked, but the surprised Chihuahua yelps and runs around in circles. The fox conceals itself in the underbrush, carefully observing its surroundings. The Chihuahua often lies out in the open on a porch, a front lawn, or a busy street, sound asleep, dreaming about playing with Frisbees, and snoring—oblivious to the approaching Mack truck threatening to squash it. The fox knows what it must do to survive each day. The Chihuahua has no instinctual conception. If the fox is captured, it will tear frantically at its cage, doing whatever it can to escape. The Chihuahua, however, if locked up, will probably just whine for hours on end. The wild gray fox has a sense of urgency and knows what it must do to survive. The obese ten-pound Chihuahua has no sense of urgency at all—only excitement about being fed three times a day and taken for walks. The fox understands the real world; the

---

[269] The U.S. Department of Agriculture's food stamp information Web site states the following: "We help put healthy food on the table for over 40 million [actually about 50 million] people each month" (USDA.gov, Food and Nutrition Service, home page, June 1, 2011). It's the federal government under President Barack Hussein Obama run amok. The Supplemental Nutrition Assistance Program, or S.N.A.P., is the Obama administration's snappy new name for the Food Stamp Program, which, over the years, has developed (appropriately enough) negative connotations. Liberal projects always do. As a result, well over 15 percent of people living in the United States of America are dependent on the government—along with the contents of their taxpaying neighbors' wallets—for meals that provide all poor helpless starving souls with their basic food and nutrition. Through bartering, they also easily obtain much-needed liquor, cigarettes, money, and illegal drugs. Estimates vary, but food stamp recipients appear to collect, on average, about $150 per month. (When fraud is involved, the take is much higher.) Charitable and religious organizations such as the St. Anthony Foundation can also provide much-needed clothing, and groups such as Habitat for Humanity may offer to build shelters for those seeking true independence. Welfare checks illegally converted to cash also help pay for boxes of Kentucky Fried Chicken, fifths of Old Crow, and bleached-blond Negro prostitutes.

Human (D) Evolution

Chihuahua does not. That's because the conservative fox lives on planet reality but the liberal Chihuahua lives in the lyrics of a John Lennon song—and no cockeyed humming and singing liberal can comprehend what's wrong with that.

(Note: All readers should be aware that there are ferocious pet Chihuahuas out there that some wild foxes probably wouldn't dare tangle with. The human equivalent of such a rare beast would be, for example, a drug-running Oriental Californian who carries a malfunctioning .22-caliber pistol concealed in his or her breast holster. Also, a docile wild fox may slink into a backyard and eat any leftover food in a bird-dog bowl—just like the occasional Republican politician who surreptitiously feeds at the nearest public trough—but the analogy is still valid.)[270]

In his book *DNA: The Secret of Life,* renowned geneticist James D. Watson states:

> For now the power of genes to affect behavior is more evident in other species, whose nature we can actually manipulate using genetic tricks. One of the oldest, and most effective, of those tricks is artificial selection, which farmers have long used to increase milk yield in cows or wool quality in sheep. But its applications have not been limited to agriculturally valuable traits like these. Dogs are derived from wolves—possibly from wolf individuals that tended to hang around human settlements looking for a scrap and thereby conveniently assisting in garbage disposal. It is thought that they first laid claim to the title of "man's best friend" 10,000 years ago, roughly coinciding with the origin of agriculture. In the brief time since, the anatomical and behavioral diversity engendered by dog breeders has become literally a thing to behold.... But it is the behavioral differences that I find most impressive.[271]

---

[270] Stark visual examples of the conservative-fox-versus-liberal-Chihuahua analogy can be seen in debates between television show hosts and their guests, especially on the FOX channel. Film clips and videos are also available on YouTube.
[271] Watson, with Berry, *op. cit.*, p. 384. James D. Watson is also a molecular biologist and zoologist.

JOHN HAYBERRY

A Brief Note on Facial Expressions

Liberal socialist Democrats can often be visually identified by the fact that many of them, in debates, appear to be clueless about things that are obvious to most other people. They don't really seem to be thinking about much of anything at all. Instead, their lips move automatically while reciting their illogical opinions based on erroneous beliefs. Another sign of unthinking erroneousness can also be observed in that person's smile. A genuine smile, for example—known as a Duchenne smile—is characterized by the activation of the muscles around the eyes, which for most people are controlled involuntarily. Consequently, an individual attempting to mimic a *true* smile is unable to activate those muscles. Instead, he or she displays a *false* smile—which is often recognizable as such, particularly on the beaming face of a White House-employed TV *Obamapologist*.[272] What can it be? A primeval look of both ignorance and fear? Perhaps additional research by law enforcement is needed on this particular subject. Meanwhile, let's consider the following five typical human facial expressions (in alphabetical order):

1. Greed (primary interest is money and financial security)[273]
2. Ignorance (liberal, goofy, unable to "mentalize," puppetlike)[274]
3. Indifference/Apathy/Laziness (welfare recipient, juvenile delinquent, etc.)
4. Malevolence (evil, fanatic, terrorist)[275]
5. Understanding (intelligent, conservative, normal) detached

---

[272] Note that, generally speaking, when a conservative smiles, he or she appears to *understand things* and might be willing to be your friend. But when a liberal smiles, he or she looks pleased with him- or herself and doesn't really want to know you. When being interviewed, liberals also frequently address others by their first names in the same tone of voice that an adult (who is detached from reality) might address someone whom he or she considers to be nothing more than a silly child.

[273] In some cases, the money is needed to fuel a drug habit.

[274] To "mentalize" means understand what other people are thinking.

[275] Long ago, people who had malevolent or unfriendly faces, showed disrespect to others, or behaved strangely were thought—more often than not, rightly so—to be up to no good, so they were stopped and questioned by members of the community, but now such people are not even given a second glance. Instead, they are read their *Miranda rights* after they commit crimes. That is why there are so many criminals living among us today. It's a simple fact. We see such people so often now in movies, on television, and in advertisements—and even on the political scene in Washington, D.C.—that the younger generation has come to accept them as normal patriotic citizens of the United States, when, in fact, they are not—and they know it. Now, incivility, misbehavior, and contempt for the moral white majority is considered normal, too. That's probably why so many young people appear to discount the possibility that persons different from themselves can, under certain circumstances, turn out to be dangerous. So, unfortunately, some of them find out the hard way. This new computer age makes this situation even worse because everyone spends so much time staring at the screens of electronic gizmos or texting with smart (dumb) phones, rather than talking to peers face-to-face. This has resulted in a kind of *arrested development*. Today, the American public, taken as a whole, has a diminished capacity to recognize malevolence.

Human (D) Evolution

Most people, of course, have a facial expression that contains at least a trace of all five categories. It should also be noted that, occasionally, liberal socialist Democrats want to accomplish the same thing politically that conservative Republicans do, but on the rare occasion that this occurs, it almost always turns out to be for the *wrong reason*. That's because conservatives will refuse to pass legislation that is not beneficial to their country, whereas liberal politicians seem bent on passing laws that will either directly or indirectly benefit only *themselves*. Now we know one reason why: Liberals, because of fantasy addiction disorder, act purely out of self-interest. That makes it very easy, in most cases, to tell a liberal from a conservative: Observe the person's face carefully and ask yourself the following question: Would this man or woman fight to defend the United States of America, or would he or she be interested in only two things: money and himself/herself?

> "Look at the old film clips of the pleasant-looking people in the 1960s television comedy series *Laugh-In*, then compare them to the current occupants of the White House and see what you think." —Cogger

> "Why do so many Obama appointees look like some fiend from a monster movie has been training them to stare at people as though they were insects?" —C. G.

> "L.S.D.ers look at other people as though they don't really like them—either that, or they're on medication from another planet." —John Hayberry

> "Liberals look at you as though they are from another planet, and you don't matter." —Nancy

> "Anyone who watches the news and has trouble distinguishing the difference between a conservative and a liberal should just try to imagine if the person suddenly walked into your living room. Would he or she look like a friendly neighbor, or would he or she look like someone up to no good?" —Anonymous

"What the hell is the matter with so many people's eyes these days? They look like they've stopped *believing in God.*" —Angela

Shh! . . . Human Dysgenics[276]

In his *Textbook of Evolutionary Psychiatry,* Martin Brüne states:

> In the early 20th century, psychiatry failed to acknowledge the rediscovery of the rules of Mendelian inheritance. Moreover, many psychiatric authorities held the view that psychopathology was the result of a domestication-induced degeneration process, and proposed eugenic measures to control the (perceived) spread of mental illnesses.[277]

The author goes on to say:

> More importantly, however, during the late 19th and early 20th century, psychiatry was concerned by the observation of a large-scale increase in number of psychiatric in-patients. By the outgoing 19th century, thousands of patients across Europe and the United States were treated, or all too often merely institutionalized, in large asylums. The skyrocketing number of mentally ill patients led psychiatrists to conclude that the abolishment of natural selection had induced a degeneration of the population, a popular idea that curiously met the then prevailing cultural pessimism. On his journey to Java, Kraepelin observed, for example, that mental disorders were comparably rare in 'primitive' races, and that the prognosis of mental illness was more favourable than in the developed world, which Kraepelin interpreted as the result of

---

[276] Dysgenic is defined as "exerting a detrimental effect on later generations through the inheritance of undesirable characteristics." Human (D) evolution pertains to an affected population's ultimate choice of political systems, which, among the suboptimal, is *always* communism, rather than capitalism. In the United States of America, a suboptimal general electorate is indicated by the increasing success of the Democratic Party.

[277] Brüne, *op. cit.*, p. 4.

greater resistance against disease in people from developing countries. Kraepelin's opinion that mental illnesses were the result of a domestication-induced degeneration strongly influenced psychiatric nosology, which grossly neglected poverty, poor hygiene and lack of education as possible causes of psychiatric illness. Consequently, as effective pharmacological treatment of mental disorders was unavailable, many countries introduced eugenic measures to prevent further increase of prevalence rates of mental illnesses, including compulsory sterilization. Many psychiatric authorities who approved such means saw themselves as advocates of mental hygiene at the population level (with several clearly having racial hygiene in mind), rather than medical doctors who dealt with individuals.[278]

Modern man's intelligence has all but conquered the natural world. Now, as we navigate through the evolutionary routes of the twenty-first century, we are spinning the ship's wheel at the helm of multiple species, notably dog breeds, but inadvertent human dysgenic breeding has been taking place for hundreds, if not thousands, of years.[279] As our ability to protect the physically and mentally weaker of our species increases, so do the grinning beneficiaries of our benevolence.[280] In the P.E.T.S. hypothesis, this evolutionary process of *oblivious optimals promoting suboptimals* has had the predictable negative consequences. Whether modern man likes it or not, he is in control now. Important and difficult decisions must be made. One way or another, mankind will make them, either through conscious effort or through apathy, and the result of the latter choice is virtually guaranteed to be *abhorrent*.

Eugenics, the science of improving the human population through governmental incentives that promote positive breeding outcomes, is an idea that fell

---

[278] Ibid., p. 4.

[279] Dysgenic breeding in dogs has produced deformations such as the short hindquarters (hip dysplasia) of German shepherds and the flattening of the bulldog's face almost to the point of being cruel. The process has also contributed to the preservation of dumb dog breeds, such as the Afghan hound and basenji, and the creation of breeds with problematic personalities, such as pit bulls. When man interferes with natural selection, genetic changes can easily occur overnight.

[280] What the world has failed to realize up to this point is that having to deal with all of the daily problems caused directly and indirectly by liberal suboptimality, along with their multiculturalism, decreases the propagation rate of normal healthy individuals—i.e., married, conservative-minded men and women with jobs and/or children whom they need to care for and protect. These days, normal responsible people have to work longer hours to complete the same amount of work, and, in most cases, make less pay—all the while praying that they will be able to save enough money to retire someday. This situation, of course, is not conducive to looking for, much less finding, a mate if the person is single. It is also not conducive to having children if one is married. In fact, all of the data indicate that childbirth among conservatives is inversely proportional to the amount of money the government spends on liberals in the form of food stamps, welfare checks, and *fraud*—and to the corresponding increase of our National Debt. In other words, perpetually ignorant unemployed liberals and their political representatives are actually throwing up roadblocks that prevent conservatives from achieving their biological imperatives. Maybe it's time for some *real* change in Washington, D.C.

into disfavor only after the inhumanity of the Nazis. It's an admiral goal, of course, and no thinking person can deny it. Imagine, if you will, a world population made up almost entirely of reasonably intelligent, reasonably healthy, reasonably normal people, as opposed to lifelong food-stamp recipients; the born-to-be-incarcerated; and unwashed, unkempt, sporadically maniacal and rarely employed Occupy Wall Street types.[281] For one thing, think of all the money taxpayers would save on gasoline for city garbage trucks, police overtime pay, detective work, public defenders, trials by jury, and fifty-gallon drums of industrial-strength Lysol. Think of all the large-scale wars we would not have to wage against tyrants kept in power by the forever ignorant, backward, and judgmentally unsound.

If genetic improvement is good enough for edible plants and farm animals, then why isn't it good enough for *Homo sapiens?* The choice is ours and must be made *as soon as possible:* dysgenics or eugenics? Which shall it be? The ultimate decision has been dumped in our higher life-form laps. One thing is for sure: The current evolutionary path that we are on is inarguably the long dirt road to ruin. Liberals may not care about such irrelevant things as man's recent history or future, but conservatives certainly do.

Someday, man will have the ability, utilizing enzymes and ligase genetic manipulation, to control the evolution of the human race with precision—so who gets to decide? With all of the amazing new discoveries and advances currently being made, there is no doubt about it. Nature, in most respects has already been conquered (as long as an asteroid the size of Guatemala doesn't land on an Idaho potato farm). That means nature is no longer the major determining evolutionary factor. Laws passed by government are what most affect man's environment now. If mankind's attitude continues to be one of indifference or, even worse, political opportunism, then our unfortunate future descendants are guaranteed to be riddled with multiple physical deformities and severe mental disorders whose symptoms can be controlled only as long as the supply of psychotropic drugs holds out. Unfortunately, this is not mere speculation. It is already occurring. If you believe in the fundamentals of Darwinian evolution—as most people do—then you must accept the reality of *human devolution* as a cold, hard fact.

---

[281] Occupying a barbershop for a just few minutes would probably work better. At least that might help land a job.

Human (D) Evolution

Mentalizing (for Fun and Profit)

There is one major symptom of liberalism that cannot be directly attributed to F.A.D., and it is an important one. This symptom, or characteristic, exists at the very core of human development, so it ought to be examined carefully. Some prominent psychiatrists have noted publicly and privately that people of the liberal persuasion appear to exhibit a somewhat below-average ability to *mentalize*.[282] "Mentalizing" is a recognized psychiatric term that refers to an individual's aptitude to determine the mental state of others—i.e., to *figure out what other people are thinking*.

One reason for this inability may be that a person who has a job where he or she interacts with others on a regular basis better understands how other people think because that person does more *socializing*. Here is something else to consider: A person who drinks alcoholic beverages is much more conversational in a social setting than a person who is strung out on marijuana and/or other drugs. Also, ideas are exchanged among friends through coherent conversation. People who cannot talk generally do not learn anything.

As many of us know, liberals tend to be very naïve. But what is naïveté, anyway? In most cases, naïveté is simply childish ignorance, inexperience, or lack of sophistication because of a sheltered or isolated upbringing, but severe liberal naïveté can prove to be wartime catastrophe. For example, liberals' inability to comprehend what enemies of the United States, such as Iran, North Korea, Russia, China, and Cuba, are really thinking may result in a shower of missiles. Also, liberal political naïveté when it comes to overseas travel, wining and dining foreign dignitaries, along with broadly smiling, glad-handing, mentally unstable—even creepy—communist and socialist dictators can be very dangerous to us all and is best understood simply as liberal obliviousness to reality—i.e., ignorance of how the world really works. It almost seems as though President Monkeyshine would much prefer to be a dictator, too, even though the laws of our country do not allow it. Maybe all of the world's dictators should buy a tropical island in the Caribbean and form an elite private club.

As history has shown us, when a prominent world leader puts his own benefit, profit, and pleasure (e.g., recreational teeing on eighteen-hole golf courses) above the interests of his own country, it always leads to the same thing: economic catastrophe—and, potentially, a foreign war.

---

[282] In some cases, this inability to mentalize may be partially due to the exorbitant amount of time some people spend these days watching Hollywood movies, and watching the sugarcoated news presented on the liberal media, and communicating with computers, smartphones, etc., rather than talking to live people in person. This can result in a reduced capacity to recognize an enemy when they see one.

That's what we are witnessing here in America today.

Unfortunately, the chief problem with many of our liberal friends is that (through no fault of their own, actually) they have little or no ability to mentally *grasp*—much like a swinging arthritic orangutan—or hold onto, the things that other people may be thinking about them. Let's face it, many liberal politicians just don't know what the *hell* is going on. They're totally in the dark. That is why so many liberal men and women, along with their sometimes grotesque, facially ornamented broods, remain completely unaware of the outright lies, incompetence, corruption, narcissism, and stupidity in Washington, D.C.—even though virtually all exceedingly kind and tolerant conservatives see it so clearly.

Yet, apparently, because these liberal Democratic politicians are so entertaining—just like laughing women in New York City on New Year's Eve (or a puppet show)—our elected representatives have allowed it to go on.

Time for a change of guard.

"In my opinion, the words naïve, progressive, liberal, socialist, communist, and Democrat are all synonymous." —A conservative political analyst[283]

Both naïveté and the lack of capacity to mentalize are the reasons that candidate Obama was so convinced in 2008 that Mahmoud Ahmadinejad, president of the Islamic Republic of Iran, could be easily won over with much friendliness and chat. These are also the reasons that liberals believed with all their little red beating hearts that everyone was going to *love* Obamacare so much after that brainless, greased-up legislative nightmare—a clear and present economic danger (and a fraudster's dream come true)—was rammed like an oversized multi-trillion-dollar wax plug through the ear canals of the Democrat-controlled Senate and Congress. Then it was signed into law by the president himself. Lack of ability to mentalize is why liberals don't seem to know, even when everyone else does, how they appear to others when they pass idiotic laws like the (Un)Affordable Care Act, which tried to take over *one-sixth* of the United States economy!

Was this piece of liberal nightmare legislation, "A.C.A.," an economic deathblow? We will all know soon enough. The fiscal cliff has not yet disappeared; it's still there—growing, and waiting. It is waiting for all of us, including the federal government, to fall over it, screaming for more money. It was mindless for our federal bureaucracy to attempt to handle 17 percent of the U.S.

---

[283] Stated during a discussion of the president's untenable proposal that Israel return to its pre-1967 borders—followed by Prime Minister Netanyahu's absolute dismissal of the idea.

economy, especially when the country is already floundering in a *depression*. Who asked it (the liberal federal government) to, anyway? What does it (the liberal federal government) think gives it (the liberal federal government) the *right?* The United States of America has a government of laws, not of liberal people.

Lack of ability to mentalize is why liberals are also absolutely awful at predicting which way popularity polls will swing, except, of course, when the polls are artificially manipulated using tried-and-true liberal methods from their official fantasyland playbook (e.g., a slick president being photographed solemnly holding a bible upon leaving a church fish fry).

Poor mentalizers seem capable of only *generalizing* about the thoughts and feelings of others. The prevailing psychiatric theory is that this is because of emotionally unresponsive and/or unavailable parenting—which clearly plays a part. You see, the ability to mentalize and the degree of attachment a child has to a parent or caregiver are proportional. Early social relationships with primary caregivers—usually the mother—doubtlessly have lasting effects on an individual's attitudes toward social interaction and on the way that mentalities of others are appreciated. Adversely affected persons use immature defense mechanisms more often than do persons who, as children, developed secure attachment with their mothers and thus independent states of mind.

In *Textbook of Evolutionary Psychiatry,* the author states:

> Consequently, traumatized individuals are particularly vulnerable to making use of immature defense mechanisms. Due to their impaired ability to accurately represent own and others' mental states, they may have more difficulties in distinguishing inner and outer reality, be more intolerant of alternative perspectives or tend to construct mental images of the world that no longer resemble reality.[284]

The question is, what would explain why any liberal parent would behave in such a way as to traumatize his or her child in the first place? F.A.D., maybe? Also, how does a helpless liberal infant cope with insensitive parenting or when left alone for long periods of time by the mother? By fantasizing that he or she is not in danger, so nothing bad will happen, and there's no such thing as evil? Are we to believe that the psychiatric model of adverse childhood is the only possible one? Are

---

[284] Brüne, *op. cit.,* p. 309.

we also to believe that the only way liberal attitudes are passed down from one generation to the next is by each successive mother ignoring her own children, or pretending they don't exist, or dumping them on a foreign neighbor's doorstep—with no major genetic component(s) involved? No, that just doesn't seem plausible.

Liberalism is thought by some people to be nothing more than a learned set of erroneous values. But that's not true. If it were, then why aren't any liberals being successfully taught to think correctly and logically (even if it takes electroshock therapy) and—*Voila!*—changed into conservatives?

Experiments with some African simian lab animals have verified the lifelong psychological effects of isolating an infant from his or her mother—especially in a Third World country. However, we should be careful about assuming that we know the origin of a particular human mental illness just because we can duplicate some symptoms of it in another species. Constantly beating a dog, for example, can make it vicious and even turn it into a growling killer, but that doesn't mean that every human who commits a murder was beaten daily by his or her parents with a stick. The looks on many juvenile delinquents' faces simply defy nongenetic explanations.

Likewise, the playful antics of a (potentially cannibalistic) chimpanzee that likes to drink beer don't prove that 90 percent of the population has parents who are bartenders. Although the prevailing theories on this subject appear logical, it's difficult to buy the idea that millions of "adult" liberals—or about one out of every five people—who are the raging, pathological, organized force behind the disintegration of modern civilized society, which seems to achieve new lows almost daily, are nothing more than the product of mulish, disinterested, inattentive mommies.[285]

Also, note that people who experience insecure attachments with their mothers at a very young age frequently display enhanced suspiciousness and distrustful reactions.[286] But liberals generally display just the opposite: *decreased* suspiciousness and *increased* naïveté.

Many times, when we conservatives look into a devout Kool-Aid-drinking liberal's eyes, we don't see just someone with contrary opinions; we see a person whose brain is wired very differently, so we should at least consider the possibility that an individual's below-average capacity to mentalize has a partial genetic origin. The inability to understand other people, as with so many other human traits, is clearly heritable—although, perhaps, as a predisposition that is partially dependent on environment. Either that or it is simply the inevitable result of being raised by a family riddled with F.A.D.

---

[285] These are the same type of women who were once delicately referred to as "trash."
[286] Perhaps Oklahoma City bomber Timothy McVeigh is an example. He is the only known right-winger who behaved like a 1960s left-wing radical. That's why liberals are always holding *him* up as an example of a radical enemy of the United States. McVeigh's parents were divorced when he was only ten years old, and he lived with his father in New York near the Canadian border.

You decide.

Notable Liberal(?) Quote:

"Da reason a nigga bees a demonicrat is 'cause he sick or sompin' sos somethin' bees wrong wit 'im. Dat's science. Ya can't bees black and bees a demonicrat. It don' make no sense! An' smart peoples don' likem anyway. Da demonicrats cruel. Dey likes ta bees cruel. Ya know wha' I's sayin'? Dey ain't no whayacall inteelectuals. Dey bad. I wa' talkin' ta Zula awhil' back an' I wa' sayin' dat duh foist ting you gotta bees issa gotdam black assho' afore ya can bees a demonicrat. Ya gotta be a gotdam assho' ta beeleaves wha' dey do. Ya gots ta bee bad. I believes it gots somepin' ta do with dey limbic brain cells. I really does believe dat some people's limbic brain cells bad." —Anonymous Member Of The New White African American Community

See, liberals aren't *that* stupid.

It's likely that any infant of normal intelligence brought up by one or more illogical liberal idiots who don't seem to make much sense will have difficulty later on as an adult when trying to understand other people. In fact, this conclusion is really a no-brainer. But that doesn't mean that the inability to mentalize isn't genetic in origin. For example, subjecting monkeys, dogs, and laboratory rats to unpleasant environmental stimuli can probably create a psychosis of any kind desired, but that doesn't mean that psychoses and/or susceptibility to developing psychoses are not determined by DNA.

No doubt, genetic differences also account for varying sensitivity to social experiences during a child's early stages of development—like when the child's drug-addled mother accidentally leaves him or her to be dry-cleaned.

The author of the *Textbook of Evolutionary Psychiatry* states: "Similarly, attachment styles may be mediated by genetic variation, e.g. dopamine or serotonin receptor polymorphisms, such that insecure attachment may be more likely to occur under circumstances associated with both insensitive parenting and a specific allelic variant."[287] In other words, genetic variation may account for the fact that it is not unusual for brothers and/or sisters to experience an identical childhood trauma but for only one of them to develop a psychological problem because of it.

---

[287] Brüne, *op. cit.*, p. 99.

According to the authors of *DNA: The Secret of Life*:

> While the basis of most behavior is surely polygenic—affected by many genes—a number of simple genetic manipulations in mice reveal that changing even a single gene can have a major behavioral effect. . . . In 2002 Catherine Dulac at Harvard discovered that by deleting a gene from a mouse of her own she could affect the processing of chemical information contained in pheromones, the odors mice use to communicate. Whereas male mice will typically attack other males and attempt to mate with females, Dulac's doctored males failed to distinguish between males and females and attempted to mate with any mouse they encountered. Nurturing behavior in mice is also subject to sex-specific manipulation of a single gene. Females instinctively look after their newborns, but Jennifer Brown and Mike Greenberg at Harvard Medical School found a way to short-circuit this native sense by knocking out the function of a gene called *fos*-B. Otherwise entirely normal, a mouse so altered simply ignores her offspring.[288]

Here is a different, simpler, theory about the liberal inability to mentalize. Any person who is unable to understand fully what others are thinking about him or her is also unable to predict with any accuracy what others are going to do; thus, that person is much more likely to be tricked by his or her enemies and more prone to be captured and enslaved. A pet dog, cat, parrot, or squirrel monkey, for example, can observe what its master is thinking and doing today, but rarely is it able to deduce and correctly predict what its master will be thinking and doing tomorrow. Dumb animals, you see, are not especially good prognosticators of future events. Why? Because they have a very limited aptitude for connecting dots. Normal people—i.e., the vast majority of conservatives—have the capability to connect a series of dots, or bits of information (and also misinformation) that may include such things as another person's facial expressions, body language, haircut, scent, clothing, and tone of voice, and pertinent details of past experiences from one's prior relationships.[289] But liberals seemingly do not. (Perhaps they're just snoozing with their eyes open.) One can only conclude that genetically/mentally detached or enfeebled liberals either do not have the capacity or do not have the desire to

---

[288] Watson, with Berry, *op. cit.*, p. 385.
[289] Maternal and paternal bonding, for example.

understand what other people are thinking. Either that or, because of drugs, they simply do not care.

Liberal "compassion," by the way, which, over the past fifty years, has become a standard of Western thought, is now used routinely for political propaganda. In other words, it is a lie.

Suboptimal mentalizing ability, a condition that normally proves disastrous when it occurs in wild animals and so is constantly eliminated from affected gene pools, appears to have been unknowingly bred and cultivated in today's liberal *Homo sapiens*. In the opinion of some scholars, it just does not seem possible that present-day liberal attitudes, along with the characteristic liberal inability to mentalize, are entirely due to having bad mommies, who themselves had bad mommies, ad infinitum.[290]

But whatever the problem is, what's the solution?

---

[290] "Persons who are addicted to pleasure-inducing drugs are less inclined to engage in bonding behavior than persons not using these drugs. For example, new mothers *who are addicted to opiates* bond less intensely with their offspring" (McGuire and Troisi, *op. cit.*, p. 113; italics added). This fact accounts for the correct supposition by many psychiatrists that liberal thought and behavior result from adverse events—e.g., decreased bonding—that occurred in early childhood. Adverse events may also include being raised by a mother, father, or guardian with F.A.D., in which case, diminished bonding would almost certainly occur.

Chapter 11

Why Don't They Like Other People?

Compassion Used as a Personal Stress Reliever

The following was submitted by an associate employee and friend of A. H. G.:

Years ago, during a somewhat tense discussion at my office, one of my coworkers, a friendly African American woman who is a quick-to-protest Democrat (what else?) whom I occasionally joke around with over coffee and greatly respect, apparently resented the fact that I had unofficially figured out an obvious solution to our company's problem. Suddenly, she threw up her hands in despair and blurted out, *"What about Heartline?"* Her reaction was *bizarre* to say the least. None of us knew *what* she was talking about. It was only later that I learned that Heartline is a charitable organization for children with congenital heart disease that is based in Great Britain and had nothing at all to do with what we were talking about! After a brief silence with *no explanation* being offered by her, we resumed our discussion. It seemed to have been something that she had just blurted out—similar to a *knee-jerk reaction*—which, I guess, could probably happen to anyone under a lot of pressure because a person can be very unpredictable. But I found it very rude at the time because of the way she had suddenly transformed herself from someone who had no answers into someone *more caring and compassionate* than anyone else in the room—and so I guess that she thought that she was automatically morally superior. That incident bugged me for a long time, so I kept rolling it over and over again in my mind, but my husband and I were never able to understand it. . . . Do you have any idea?

—Teresa

Here's the answer: When liberal men and women are confronted with any situation or fact that may somehow conflict with their fantasy-based view of the way things are, or ought to be, the situation begins to cause them anxiety. When a liberal person's beliefs and logic are exposed as untrue, he or she can instantly relieve the pangs of angst by expressing deep concern and compassion for other human beings, whether that compassion is actually felt by him or her, or not.[291] The way it always works is this: Liberals can quickly go from feeling *bad* to feeling *good* about themselves. This automatic cerebral reaction helps shield them from the awful sensation of questioning their own ideology and, therefore, just about everything that they believe to be true. Liberals, in effect, throw up mental blocks and build a kind of wall. The "compassion-expressing" centers of the liberal brain, which are linked to the reward systems in the central nervous system (C.N.S.), offer them relief from anxiety. Liberals use compassion as a defense mechanism to comfort themselves.

If you don't believe this, try it yourself. Stop what you're doing right now, drop your arms limply to your sides—or better yet, put your hands in your pockets as though having nothing at all to do. Then sigh deeply, wag your head back and forth, and say with all the sincerity that you can muster, *"Oh, we need to be nice to everyone,"* and *"We need to be everybody's friends,"* and *"We have to stop fighting,"* and *"We need to feed all of the poor people. . . . Aaagh."* See how relaxing that can be?

This connection to the reward systems would also seem to account for a liberal's inability to stop expressing compassion, even when those who are the objects of his or her sympathy (1) don't *ask* for it, (2) don't *expect* it, and (3) don't *require* it. You see, essentially, it's done only for themselves. So the next time that you see a liberal automatically do such a thing—and in political debates, it occurs quite often—you'll know why.

It's called the *politics of compassion*.

---

[291] *Re: Liberal Compassion.* Democratic politicians frequently use handicapped supporters as "human shields" against criticism of themselves and their policies.

Notable Liberal Quote:

"Please try to be more kind to us instead of being so right about us all of the time. Do you really want to hurt us? Do you really want to make us cry?" —Democratic politician (Mr. something or other—the name was unreadable.)[292]

So who's more compassionate, liberals or conservatives? To answer that question, we must first define the term. Compassion is a "sympathetic pity and concern for the sufferings or misfortunes of others," and the adjective compassionate means "feeling or showing sympathy and concern for others." Clearly, as a group, liberals are more compassionate than conservatives are because they are constantly verbalizing (and thus showing) sympathy for others. Of course, whether a person actually *feels* sympathy is another matter altogether, and only that person and Heartline know for sure.

It's easy to see how the act of expressing deep sympathy for others can be used as a propaganda tool. It can also be used by anyone—a Republican or a Democrat—to promote him- or herself and his or her agendas, but our Democratic friends and enemies clearly have the act down pat. (Always be wary of any politicians or pundits who, when asked direct questions on national television, automatically respond like unthinking automatons, and especially if they use the hackneyed phrase "hungry children.") You see, here's how it usually works: If one politician is "more caring and compassionate" than another politician, it means that he or she must also be "morally superior." So how can anyone possibly question his or her sincerity, his or her motives, or the validity of his or her ideas? No one can, of course. In fact, anyone who *does* look at him or her skeptically risks being branded as uncaring and perhaps even mean and hateful. That is why both sincere and insincere expressions of deep compassion have been known to win political debates.

When a liberal uses this well-known tactic in an argument with a conservative, the liberal attitude always seems to be this: "It doesn't matter what you say or do, and it doesn't matter what the facts are, because I care more about all of the poor people than you do, so I'm more ethical—which makes me right and you wrong!" Well, that high-and-holy hokum smokum may have worked in years past, but not anymore. We're onto these two-tongued platitudinous con artists now. Liberal Democrats aren't morally superior to conservative Republicans any more than

---

[292] This request was received by us in a letter on September 15, 2014. The envelope was postmarked Washington, D.C. The words were written in pencil on a Kleenex.

juvenile delinquents who shoplift are morally superior to the cops who arrest them after making them give everything back.

It is called liberal *cafeteria-style compassion*. This is, of course, when a person carefully picks and chooses what to feel sad about, according to his or her own taste. That may include deciding on what group of people, or plants, or animals—either foreign or domestic—for which to show public empathy. This decision appears to be based almost entirely on what will be most beneficial to themselves politically. Note that cafeteria-style compassion does not occur very often in conservative ranks because conservative concern is genuine.

Still another type of compassion is *peacock empathy*, which includes shameless displays of exaggerated concern, sympathy, and tearful emotion—sometimes with eyes sporadically darting. This is plainly done out of self-interest for political gain, pure and simple—not real compassion at all. That is why such people occasionally even show hints of fear. Behaving in this manner clearly stems from the thought of losing his or her next election.

So here's the $64,000 question: Do liberals, in general, who constantly express compassion for other people yet apparently don't really understand what other people are thinking, actually feel real compassion for others? Or is much of their empathy *learned behavior* from childhood? Liberal compassion, one of the greatest myths of our time, has—with the help of the illegitimate liberal news media—become a virtually unchallenged standard of Western thought. Decades of cancerous liberal propaganda have resulted in this fairy tale being accepted by even some of our most popular conservative writers and political commentators. We have all been brainwashed into believing that liberals, as a group, are more kind-hearted and charitable toward their fellow man than are conservatives, which, of course, is ludicrous. It's true that liberals are usually more *publicly sympathetic* toward such things as whales, turtles, and trees, but we should note that all of these things can also give people pleasure to contemplate, and *feeling good* is what liberals, as we know, value the most. In addition, there is usually a hidden political agenda involved.

Warning: Mental and/or physical weakness is not synonymous with kindness.

"Have you ever noticed that sometimes when people die, most liberal socialist Democratic politicians don't really seem to care? Maybe it's because dead people can't vote anymore." —Charlie Lucy Brown, political consultant

Liberal "Love" for the Poor

Remember the mentally ill sixty-three-year-old woman who "loved" dogs so much that she ran a breeding operation and had emaciated animals in cages all over her property, not to mention the forty-three dead ones wrapped in plastic and hidden in her refrigerator? That's the same way many liberal socialist Democrats (and communists, too) appear to love the poor—and the more poor, the better! Of course, votes by poor people are what help keep most liberal socialist Democrat politicians in office, so anything that liberal socialist Democrats can do to superficially help the poor—like, say, raising the minimum wage to as high as $100.00 an hour—they'll try their best to achieve. Why? Because it makes liberals feel good. The only problem is that instituting price controls and artificially raising wages causes thousands of lower-income people to either lose their jobs or not be able to afford to buy anything new because the cost of everything keeps going up. Also, the lucky ones who manage to keep their jobs are forced to work long hours and two-and-a-half times as hard to make up for all the employees who were fired. Next thing you know, teenagers and college students all across the country are going to have premature heart attacks.

But don't worry. All Americans who, after five years (at the time of this writing), still do not have decent jobs can take heart in the fact that Prime Minister Raila Odinga of Kenya—a member of President Obama's father's tribe—personally approves of our president's policies and has even advised him to "stay the course."[293] The question is, "What course?" The golf course? Or the course taken by all of his policies floating together like a raft down the Pongola River toward precommunist South Africa? Another few years of carefully planted adoring crowds at President Obama's fundraisers and carefully written teleprompter speeches—in lieu of any true leadership—and "We the people of the United States" will soon be subsisting primarily on $45 watermelons.

Elections have *consequences,* so please commit the following to memory:

WHEN A COMMUNIST COUNTRY SENSES WEAKNESS IN THE UNITED STATES OF AMERICA, THAT COUNTRY IS EMBOLDENED TO INVADE OTHER SOVEREIGN

---

[293] According to Transparency International, Kenya ranks high among the world's most corrupt countries. Dishonesty and poor governance in that African nation have had a negative effect on growth, making it very expensive to do business there. Corruption thrives on confusion and secrecy. "When politicians don't make decisions that benefit the public, but rather themselves, this is corruption" (Transparency International, "Corruption Perceptions Index 2012"). The president promised us transparency in government, and we got it. Now we can all see right through him.

Human (D) Evolution

NATIONS. WHEN THAT OCCURS, THE SCOURGE OF COMMUNISM ALWAYS SPREADS, ALONG WITH WAR, DEATH, AND DESTRUCTION. THIS AFFECTS THE SECURITY OF THE ENTIRE WORLD.

The above is the opinion of America's allies and of geopolitical analysts all across the globe.

Unfortunately, liberals, just like that nutty old woman, don't really seem to care very much about the United States of America, only *themselves*. Do they think that everything they do that harms our nation's economy hurts only rich people because poor people don't have anything to lose? Apparently so, but it is the *reasoning of a child*. Here's how it *really* works: First, liberal Democrats pass legislation that sounds good to poor people but isn't. Then, shortly afterward, poor people begin losing their jobs, their cars, their homes, and, finally, their families because they're constantly squabbling about losing everything. But most of them never even suspect that their smiling buddies in the liberal Democratic Party are the ones who caused it. Do liberal politicians comprehend what they are doing? It seems impossible that they do not. Do they care so little about poor people's lives and only about those people's votes? Are they perpetuating abject lifelong poverty to benefit themselves politically, or do they just not understand people, economics, or the world that they're living in? All of the above seem to be the case. Instead of helping the poor, liberals hurt them in hundreds of elusive and unseen ways.[294]

Liberalism, unfortunately, also breeds *national disloyalty.*

That is one reason why the United States of America has no fear of a country like communist China. China's thoroughly oppressed population is full of men, women, and children who are little more than mindless liberal robots willing to put up with being shoved around by their government. The Chinese people will fight for their country only if they are *forced* to fight. That is why the Chinese government is so afraid of an island called Japan. That is also why the Chinese government's best friends are liars like Vladimir Putin, Mahmoud Ahmadinejad, and Kim Jong-un—you know, the obese little kid with bad breath who keeps giving idiotic speeches in North Korea, throwing himself around and acting like a horse's ass for the news cameras. We haven't heard much out of North Korea lately. Maybe President Obama promised to give their supreme leader some basketball lessons, a case of Yuengling, and a free bag of cell phones.

The United States of America, *"the land of the free and the home of the brave."*

---

[294] Are Democrats in Washington, D.C., afflicted with some unidentified form of Münchausen syndrome by proxy?

JOHN HAYBERRY

Words That Are Worth a Thousand Pictures

Most people have seen at least one photograph of an aborted human fetus.²⁹⁵ It is difficult for some of us to remain dispassionate when staring at a color picture of something that is in all reality—let's face it—nothing less than a bloody, mutilated human baby, but still, the inane arguments go on. Years ago, on *Meet the Press,* when former vice president Gore (D-Tennessee) was asked, "Would you favor postponing the execution of a pregnant woman?" this was his instinctive liberal response: "I'd have to think about it."²⁹⁶ *Think about what?* For most people, even children, this question is a no-brainer and the correct answer is immediate. Of course, you do not execute an innocent unborn baby. What if—God forbid—a little kid gets snatched up by a crocodile at the edge of a lagoon? Do you sit on a tree stump and scratch your empty liberal head, thinking about that, too? What kind of people are we electing now to run the country, anyway? The sharpest knives in the drawer? Or the plastic forks, wooden spatulas, and jelly spoons? And why are these mindless liberal wonderers being paid so much to harm our country? For the foreign entertainment value? Or because of their stature, deep voices, and the fact that their Pinocchio tongues and noses operate properly?

The United States of Pilfered Piggy Banks

Why in the name of God Almighty is a country like the United States of America, the leader of the free world, with all of its wonderful natural resources, modern educational system, technological advancements, and exceptional abilities, operating as though it's an economic Third World nation? Why are we $16 trillion—

---

²⁹⁵ Public opinion may be changing after the quiet moral indifference of many television news stations to seventy-two-year-old Dr. Kermit Gosnell, a Negro abortionist convicted of first-degree murder for routinely killing human babies born alive by clipping their spines with scissors. Now some have begun to question whether liberals, in general, really care about children at all. *The Daily Beast* reported that aborted fetuses were everywhere at Gosnell's West Philadelphia clinic: in the refrigerator, in cat-food containers, in orange-juice cartons. There was even a jar full of severed feet. Where's the liberal outrage?
²⁹⁶ *449 Stupid Things Democrats Have Said,* 2004, Andrews McMeel Publishing, Kansas City, Missouri, p. 52. On Election Day 2000, Gore came within a wild boar's ass hair of becoming the forty-sixth president of the United States.

excuse me, make that *$17 trillion,* no *$18 trillion*—no, make it *$100 trillion*—in debt? Are we really that fiscally maladroit? Why is our nation's quarter coin fast becoming the new penny, especially when, for so long, economist geniuses have been in charge? The reason is that there is a big difference between an economist and a mathematician. An economist is a person who studies the stock market, calmly gives his private advice, and relishes the growth of his personal investments while dreaming about retiring one day, buying a Rolls Royce, and vacationing in Acapulco, whereas a mathematician adds up the National Debt on a calculator, then begins cursing. (Actually, most calculators display only eight digits, not thirteen, which makes them inadequate for working with trillion-dollar government I.O.U.s that look like this: $1,000,000,000,000.) Another big difference is that mathematicians are rarely victims of *Ponzi schemes*.[297]

Never let skinny, curly-haired, darting-eyed economists clutching personal portfolios thick with stocks and bonds confuse you with phrases they memorized from their college textbooks, because both *money* and the *U.S. economy* are very easy things to understand. First of all, you don't have to be smart to make a lot of money. All you have to do is want it bad enough and try harder than anyone else. It also helps to have a little basic knowledge that should probably be taught in high school. That is as follows: The value of money is based on the value of gold.[298] So who sets the value of gold? Is it the Chairman of the United States Federal Reserve, Ben Shalom Bernanke? No, he only sets the interest rates.[299] It's five—count 'em, 5—squirrely guys in Great Britain.

> The London gold fixing or gold fix is the setting of the price of gold, determined twice each business day on the London bullion market by the five members of The London Gold Market Fixing Ltd, on the premises of N. M. Rothschild & Sons. It's designed to fix a price for settling contracts between members of the London

---

[297] "About forty years ago, everyone began to accept women running for political office because they were generally thought to be more honest than men. But things didn't get better. They got worse. Now, the United States of America has an administration so corrupt that they lie about everything with a smile. What happened to law enforcement?" —Ron

[298] *Re: Gold.* A long time ago, when men did not have gold, they got by just fine. Men worked hard and traded the products of their work with others. Then one day, someone discovered that if he showed a stranger something shiny and got a friend to pretend to admire it and say that it's very, very valuable, he could sometimes trick a sucker into giving him everything that he owns for it. This isn't nice to do to people. It's bad. Very, very bad—and so is the manipulation of the stock market and currency by price-fixing.

[299] Manipulating (i.e., raising and lowering) interest rates hides economic problems and causes the value of the dollar to fluctuate—historically, downward.

bullion market, but informally the gold fixing provides a recognized rate that is used as a benchmark for pricing the majority of gold products and derivatives throughout the world's markets. The gold fix is conducted in United States dollars (USD), Pound sterling (GBP), and the Euro (EUR) daily at 10.30am and 3pm, London time, via a dedicated telephone conference facility.[300]

The way it works is this: If you (or a government) don't make any money, you don't have any money to spend—*unless you're living on an allowance.* And if you're living on an allowance, then the money that you're spending is coming out of somebody else's pocket. The same rule applies to whoever is paying your allowance: If he or she doesn't make any money, he or she doesn't have any money to spend.

When we pay taxes to our federal government, we are giving it an allowance. The big problem, however, is that when politicians get to Washington, D.C., they seem to lose all perspective and become so impressed with themselves that they don't understand this concept at all. It must be all the big fancy buildings and marble statues that impress them and make them think they're more important than they really are. The truth is, there are hundreds—no, thousands—no, tens of thousands—of people who can probably do politicians' jobs as well *or better* than they can. Politicians are elected because we like them, along with their opinions, but we don't hire them to roll over us. We pay them to take care of things that we're generally not that interested in and consider boring, so we can have more free time and can concentrate on what we consider to be the important things in life. The fanfare and TV cameras, unfortunately, always seem to go to these politicians' heads.

Maybe to keep our Washington, D.C., politicians humble, we should make all of them reside at Holiday Inns or Motel 8s—or maybe bed and breakfasts—like most other people do when they're in town for only a short while. That way, senators and congressional representatives won't be so quick to forget that they were elected to serve the public—not to serve themselves to what *belongs* to the public. The problem is that the attitude of virtually all Democrats—and even some Republicans—seems to be that everyone's money is ultimately theirs (i.e., the federal government's) and that they are the ones doling out the allowance to us, rather

---

[300] Wikipedia, "Gold fixing," March 5, 2014, en.wikipedia.org/wiki/Gold_fixing. Furthermore, the price of gold has historically remained *remarkably stable*. For example, Sir Isaac Newton, as master of the United Kingdom Mint, set the gold price in 1717, and it remained *effectively the same* for almost two hundred years. The only exception was when the value fluctuated during the Napoleonic Wars.

than the other way around. The president, in particular, seems to have great difficulty comprehending this fact. Handling such large sums of money—more than twenty-five cents—must be making his head spin. Maybe someone—a small child, perhaps (or maybe the Supreme Court)—needs to explain the basics of how an allowance works to all of our big-shot Washington politicians and clarify how the U.S. Constitution limits their perceived powers here in the United States.

It's all really very simple.

Economic Judgment Day[301]

Okay, we've heard the talk about the economic collapse and why the United States is going bankrupt: the housing crisis, Wall Street, banks, big oil, financial institutions, the Democrats, the Republicans, Fannie Mae, Freddie Mac, Barney Frank, . . . and on, and on.[302] Well, one thing you can always count on: If an explanation from someone isn't simple, clear, and logical, then—almost without exception—that person is ill-informed, inept, or trying his or her best to hide something, so let's skip all of the peripheral political nonsense and go right to the heart of the matter.

First of all, no intelligent, hardworking individual with good judgment goes bankrupt—i.e., spends more money than he or she can pay back—unless that person is the victim of some unpredictable calamity beyond his or her control, such as a destructive hurricane, a severe car accident, a deadly disease—or the worldwide

---

[301] *Re: It's The Economy Stupid.* "How can the United States of America have what many people are now suspecting to be the most disingenuous White House administration in U.S. history and also have the highest Dow Jones Industrial Average ever (an astounding 17138.20 on July 16, 2014) at the same time? It just doesn't make any sense. The stock market should've taken a dive off a cliff back in 2009 as a result of all of our country's problems. Then it should have stayed there splashing around in the water because the problems have only gotten worse. So something fishy is going on. (Clue: Money, sex, or drugs are involved.) Some people believe that the president of the United States is being manipulated by "white handlers," and that they're "cooking the books" to make all of our country's economic news look good --instead of bad, which it is. But here's something even more important that we all need to consider. The National Debt keeps going up and up and up, especially with the interest payments. That means the *net worth* of the United States is going down. In other words, we may all be broke soon. So where'd all the money go? It didn't disappear. It had to go somewhere. Who got rich off of all our money (seven trillion dollars)? The JF5 Democrats maybe? One thing's for sure. When a fool is in charge, everybody parties." --You Know Who I Am

[302] *Believe it or not!* Incredibly, on April 2, 2013, the current administration proposed that all banks ease their requirements on home loans to customers—in other words, that they loan money to people who probably *won't be able to pay it back!* It's the same government-enforced policy that *caused* the housing crash in the first place! (Quick, somebody call Ripley's.)

effects of *liberal socialist Democrat governmental legislation*.[303] The reason why the United States of America is "on the verge of bankruptcy" today is an L.S.D.er-wrought disease called *propsupatitus* (props-up-a-ti-tus).[304] Fortunately, the cause and inception of this fiscally unhealthy creeping bug is easy to understand. According to the little-known First Law of Economic Motion, whatever goes up must come down, and whatever is propped up will fall down—*with a great big thud!*

The United States props up shady foreign governments who don't like us, by giving them money so they'll be our friends.

The United States props up countries that can't defend themselves, by giving them military aid.

The United States props up countries that can't feed themselves, by giving them food.

The United States props up citizens of Third World countries who can't take care of themselves properly so that we don't have to look at photos of them crawling with insects.

The United States props up people who can't support themselves, by giving them welfare checks and food stamps.[305]

The United States props up people who lose their jobs, by giving them unemployment checks.

The United States props up minority members who can't afford to go to college, by giving them "loans" that may never be paid back.

The United States props up people who can't pass tests, by making employers hire and promote them anyway and then suffer the consequences.

---

[303] On February 21, 2014, FOX News reported that, around the globe, many people involved with the investment of capital were suddenly committing suicide by jumping out of office buildings. But why is this happening? Is money that important? Maybe it is to someone who finances everything he or she owns, instead of paying cash for it. As the old saying goes, "Neither a borrower nor a lender be." That's a rule that our federal government should follow, too.

[304] Note that P.E.T.S. theory actually accounts for the onset of *propsupatitus,* which quickly develops after the P.E.T.S.—people enabled to survive—themselves get into the government and immediately begin doling out more mercy, charity, and aid to all of the other P.E.T.S. (Think about it. Funny thing, huh?)

[305] Some domestic programs have now developed into new sources of foreign aid. Hundreds of New York food-stamp recipients, for example, are reportedly shipping fifty-five-gallon barrels full of welfare-funded groceries—macaroni, evaporated milk, rice, beans, pasta, and sausages—to relatives in Jamaica, the Dominican Republic, and Haiti. Frosted Flakes, baby formula, juices, olive oil, and canned soup are reportedly being sold on the black market. Undoubtedly, the situation with the perpetually poor is becoming the same as it is with (all other) domesticated pets. They just sit and wait for another handout. You see, liberals are like soft-shelled crabs. After they've been fed gourmet shrimp with a shish-kabob stick, they just sit there and don't do anything at all, *hoping* they'll be safe, and waiting to *change.*

The United States props up unskilled laborers by increasing the minimum wage—which raises the cost of goods and services.

The United States of America props up people who can't afford to buy homes, by forcing banks to loan them money that—to no one's surprise—is never paid back.

The president props himself up by sending people unexpected $250 checks in the mail in hopes that they'll vote for him next time he runs for office.

The president props himself up by expanding government and giving all of his supporters jobs.[306]

The president props up unions by giving them lots of money to pay their bills and to donate to his next campaign.

The congressmen prop themselves up by "bringing home the bacon" to their districts.

The government props up various corporations considered "too big to fail," by loaning them lots of money that may never be paid back, even if they're a bunch of losers who keep making mistakes.

The government props up, props up . . . *ad infinitum.*

Guess what happens when the government spends more than its allowance. *Surprise!* Everything that it has propped up comes tumbling right back down again, and you can be sure that it's going to happen with our present-day economic house of cards. That's because propping something up is only a temporary fix. With propping, *no problem is solved.* Propping is only a temporary solution. When you prop up a rotten wooden fence, for example, it will last only until another bumbling cow comes along or a horse wants out. Suppose you had a big hole in your roof and you kept stuffing it with paper money instead of repairing it permanently with tar and shingles. The money patching could go on day after day, forever. This is the way the federal government behaves, and it's why we're going to be stuck with a staggering bill of $18 trillion (the approximate U.S. National Debt that is currently outstanding).[307]

Simple, clear, logical.

---

[306] "Since when do government employees get bonuses? They are public servants. Why are they being paid anything other than a salary to do their cushy jobs? It's just another way to funnel taxpayer money to supporters, while the rest of us eat pork and beans." —Billy

[307] It is only a drop in the bucket. As of August 1, 2013, the total amount of U.S. government unfunded liabilities was more than $125 trillion (www.usdebtclock.org). Unfunded liability is the amount of money the government knows it *does not have* to fund Medicare, the Medicare Prescription Drug Program, Social Security, the military, civil servant pensions, and other entitlement programs. In other words, it's the amount of money that the government knows it needs—*but will never accumulate*—in order to pay its (i.e., the American people's) bills. This enormous amount of money will, of course, have to be redefined—i.e., grossly transfigured—which means the bills will not ever *really* be paid!

Republicans and Democrats are both guilty, but it is the F.A.D.-riddled "Demonicrats" who *refuse to stop*.[308]

Question: Why would a Democratic president keep trying to compare himself to a Republican such as Ronald Reagan, our fortieth president? For years, we listened to an endless drumbeat of sarcasm from liberals regarding Reagan's trickle-down theory (i.e., supply-side economics), which is based on nothing more than ordinary common sense. Today, supply-side economics, generally considered to be the way things actually work, is still ridiculed by Democrats as something strange and idiotic. That is because nature's genetic couch potatoes aren't satisfied with having other people's money just trickle down to them. That's insulting. Their ultimate fantasy and goal is to have money, money, and mo' money gush in torrents from a taxpayer-funded geyser way up above their big heads, then splash down on their grinning faces, outstretched arms, and open mouths, showering upon them and overflowing from their pants pockets as they stand there bellowing with joyous laughter, cheerfully singing old Negro spirituals.

"A liberal is a person who believes that water can be made to run uphill." —Theodore H. White (1915–1986), American political journalist, historian, and novelist[309]

Can the United States of America survive any more of President Monkeyshine's Kenyanesian[310]—excuse me, I mean, *Keynesian*—economics? Probably, but only if each of us learns how to live on a budget and find new ways to save money (like peeing in the street so that we don't have to flush the toilet). Other societies have survived much worse, of course, such as erupting volcanoes, meteorites, swarms of locusts, the Black Plague, and army ants. Only time, and our devalued bank accounts, will tell. The U.S. economy is on its way to becoming a liberal socialist Democrat/Republican apocalypse.

---

[308] Don't forget that under the current administration, the value of the dollar in the United States of America has continued to drop precipitously. So try to be fair to those who voted for Obama the second time around. Be sure to always tip them at least 25 percent more than you normally would.

[309] White, who graduated *summa cum laude* from Harvard in 1938, was known for his wartime reporting from China and for his accounts of five presidential elections. His book *The Making of the President* (1960) won a Pulitzer. A week after the death of J. F. K., Jacqueline Kennedy is said to have summoned White to the Kennedy compound to "rescue" her husband's legacy. She proposed that White prepare an article for *Life* magazine drawing a parallel between her husband and King Arthur of mythical Camelot. Out of kindness, White obliged, and thus was born one of our nation's most enduring—and inaccurate—myths; Kennedy's time in office was transformed into "a magic moment in American history." White later admitted that his 1,000-word essay was a "misreading of history" and wrote that the magic had never existed. (Note that the so-called legend of King Arthur and the Knights of the Round Table was a tale of fantasy and the basis for hundreds of Monty Python skits.)

[310] Kenyanesian economics ("crony" capitalism). That's when you pay people off to get what you want.

> "When Obamacare and liberalism collapse, as they both eventually will, people are going to be wandering around aimlessly and willing to work for a lot less than the minimum wage. That's why liberalism, like water, always runs downhill—into a gutter." — Steven (U.S.M.C.)

Recessions and Depressions

Imagine what this country would be like if we stopped giving the average Joe Schmo on welfare his free money to pay the rent, his free cell phone, his free food, his free beer, and his free cigarettes. All hell would break loose. What we are in right now is called a *depression*. That's right, a depression. America has been in a depression for fifty years now—ever since the Johnson administration's declared "War on Poverty." (Why are the Democrats constantly declaring *war* against people and all kinds of things? Don't they like America?) Yes, that's when it all started, so we can't very well blame it all on the current president. Instead, we can blame it on Lyndon Baines Johnson, another Democrat who is said to have made it all the way to the office of the presidency of the United States of America utilizing fraudulent voting practices. (Isn't it time we put a stop to it?) How do you know when you are in a depression? Because you can remember when a hundred dollars a week was considered a *good-paying job*. You see, the word depression is defined as "a long or severe recession in an economy or market," and the word recession is defined as "a period of temporary economic decline." In other words, a recession and a depression are *exactly* the same thing. The only difference is that the word recession is a "nice" word and the word depression is a "bad" word, so calling what we are in a *recession* sounds much better. So, as you can easily see, this is just another example of our liberal friends playing games with the English language. We should all feel very sorry for the next president of the United States of America who inherits this mess.[311]

> "They [the Democrats] have been talking about an economic recovery—as though there is one—for many years now, but there is no recovery. A recovery is when you fall off a pier into the water

---

[311] *Re: Depression.* When we rely on economic experts to do the jobs that they were given in the federal government, they often spend all of their time just sitting at desks, looking around. They work on their personal portfolios instead and then try to fool us into believing that they have plenty to do. We, the American people, would be much better off if we simply administered polygraph exams to all potential government employees (with the exception of those who decline, get an attorney, and plead the Fifth). Remember how our country's first president, George Washington, passed his test when he was asked if he chopped down that cherry tree? If you have never heard that story, then you must have had only liberals for teachers.

and climb out right away so that you don't drown. It isn't splashing around helplessly for five days or more and screaming for someone to throw you a rope!" —Dudley Do-Right, Systems Analyst

"Why aren't the president and his administration doing anything at all that helps American businesswomen create jobs? Why? Why? What are they doing, spending all of their time engaged in vote-buying schemes?" —Margaret

A Few Survival Tips for Working People

1. For those of you who come home tired at the end of a long hard day at work and don't have the energy to clean your bathtub, try using a little charcoal starter, mineral spirits, or kerosene—whatever is the cheapest—to help remove the buildup of scum. (Sometimes even a little muriatic acid will do the trick.) Scrub it lightly with a hand brush and use a little dishwashing detergent mixed with water to scrub it again. For the shower curtains and tiles, mix some bleach and water in a spray bottle and spray it on any mold that may be present. But be sure to rinse the spray bottle nozzle by removing it and flushing it with water to prevent any metal parts inside it from rusting.

2. For a quick nutritious breakfast, put four large spoonfuls of grits and a dash of salt in a bowl and add about 2/3 cup tap water, then heat it in a microwave for about 3 minutes. Then add a fresh egg on top, along with pieces of a turkey hotdog wiener. Sprinkle a little salt and pepper on the egg. Then put a plate on top of the bowl and reheat it again for about a minute, and let it sit.

3. For a fancy gourmet dessert after dinner, crumble a cookie on some vanilla ice cream.

4. Buy food in bulk, but be sure to keep things that are sold in paper bags and cartons, like rice, sugar, and flour, in tightly

sealed jars and/or in the refrigerator. Otherwise, weevils and other insects will find a new home.

5. Buy a standard-sized box fan to cool your home, and be sure to buy a cheap air filter to place over the back of it to keep the outdoor air clean from such things as rotting oak tree particles or huge African dust clouds that sometimes blow all the way over to the United States from all of the out-of-control garbage burned, along with fields set on fire to flush out animals.

6. To help make your cheap foreign-made shirts and pants last longer, fill your bathtub with water, pour a little detergent in it, then wash and wring the clothes out. Either that, or set your washing machine on "delicate." Then string a clothesline outside and use wooden clothespins to let them dry. If you use an electric dryer, be sure to dry your favorite clothes separately, just a few at a time. Otherwise, they will wear out quickly because of the cardboard (wood cellulose fiber) that they were made with. If the clothes wear out anyway, they can be bleached or re-dyed.

7. Do a lot of fishing with earthworms and bread.

Exponential Growth

Amazingly, when it comes to discussions involving mathematics, liberal Democratic politicians seem to be making their calculations in some other dimension. They are either unable or unwilling to comprehend the meaning of the term *exponential growth*. (Take your pick: It's either normalcy bias or F.A.D., so it doesn't make them feel good.) Our National Debt is not just simply growing; the rate of growth, because of the interest rate, is *increasing rapidly*—snowballing.[312] The amount of

---

[312] *Re: $18 Trillion National Debt.* Imagine a snowball rolling down a steep mountainside. The bigger the snowball gets, the bigger it gets. And the bigger it gets, the bigger it gets. The snowball keeps getting bigger and bigger and rolling faster and faster. Then it reaches a point where no matter how many people run out in front of it, it just cannot be stopped. So it gets bigger and bigger and bigger until . . . BOOM! It hits the rocky bottom of the mountainside. Then the United States of America owes foreign interests everything—our money, our land, our homes, our wives, our children, our dogs, everything—lock, stock, and barrel!

money we now owe is quickly approaching a point where all of today's living Americans will be incapable of paying it off no matter what we do—other than print so much paper money that the value of the dollar bill will drop below its current value, which is now about equal to that of a nickel in 1894, thus becoming virtually worthless.[313]

> "The unfortunate thing about addition is that, no matter what anybody says and no matter how cheerful anybody acts, the numbers just keep adding up. The National Debt keeps getting bigger and bigger. Now, it's a monster that needs to be fed." —Matt

> "Today, it'll cost you at least twenty dollars to buy a *real* U.S. silver dollar. Does that give you any idea what's happening to our money?" —Anonymous

> "In the 1950s, a guy could go see a doctor and be treated for any minor ailment for ten to fifteen dollars. I still have the receipts in my attic. The doctor would even come to your apartment for a few dollars more. A shot in the arm might cost an additional fifty bucks. My wife delivered a baby at the best hospital in town for a hundred. So what happened? Why does everything cost so damn much? Hundreds and sometimes even thousands of dollars? Somebody's playing a shell game." —Anonymous Old Man

> "Few people realize just how much the value of the dollar has decreased because the quality, quantity, and size of the products that they buy has shrunk along with it. The good food that they would have eaten has gone into liberal mouths." —Anonymous

---

[313] In September 2011, the U.S. dollar was worth only about 1/90 of the value that it had prior to the 1960s (in gold). Before the Vietnam War (America got involved in 1964), the amount of gold that a dollar bill could buy had remained stable *for over a hundred years:* One troy ounce could be had for $18.90 to $35.27. But then guess what happened: After the (liberal) media began promoting the sixties "revolution" as something *positive*—with its foul language, shocking nakedness, and hallucinogenic LSD—liberals suddenly became respectable people to be admired and even emulated (e.g., the male "hippie," the female "flower child," and the "wiser-than-anyone-else Jewish underdog"). From there on, the value of gold began to go haywire like an out-of-control skyrocket! The value of the dollar, of course, began dropping precipitously. In 1960, for example, a bottle of Coca-Cola could be purchased for just 10 cents—and guess what: There was a 2-cent return on the bottle! !

Human (D) Evolution

"Why doesn't everyone know that when there is no money and people don't have enough food to eat, people kill innocent animals to eat? Sometimes they use rocks, bottles, spears, arrows, sticks, stones, darts, gigs, and clubs to kill crabs, manatees, sea turtles, catfish, frogs, squirrels, oysters, skunks, perch, bass, doves, moles, robins, sparrows, armadillos, pops, turtles, cottontail rabbits, deer, alligators, mice, cats, dogs, butterflies, snakes, pigs, hogs, cows, horses, ducks, quail, lizards, woodpeckers, pheasant, red snapper, pigeons, possum, moths, salamanders, raccoons, turkeys, bream, crickets, otters, grasshoppers, moose, owls, buffalo, worms, snails, redbirds, bluebirds, minnows, storks, sheep, goats, tadpoles, coyotes, chipmunks, geese, bear, salmon, crayfish, elk, tapirs, flowers, watermelons, gorillas, rats, and wild chickens. Then there is usually blood all over the place, so they carefully sprinkle dirt all over everything, so nobody ever finds out or knows for sure what they did." –Worried Boys and Girls, 5th Grade Class, Public School, State of Florida

"Democrats want to spend way more money than they have. Why? So they can pretend that the world is beautiful. Then, when their beautiful world comes crashing down, they will blame it on the Republicans." —Paul

"Everybody in theUnited States is having to work two jobs, double shifts, and extra hardnow in order to take care of all the liberals on welfare and unemployment. That's where all of the "stimulus" tax money is going to. Now, we're all going to have to live in cheap apartments for therest of our lives and drive to work on motor scooters. We won't ever be able to retire. Our money's going to be all gone." --ExhaustedTwenty-Nine-Year-Old

"The government doesn't want you to retire. It needs you to keep working and paying taxes so that it can spend more money. What they are doing now is making your retirement nest egg worth next to nothing. That way, if you retire, you'll have to go back to work and pay more taxes." —C. G. (2011)

"Nobody seems to understand this, so I'm going to spell it out for everyone: T-H-E U-N-I-T-E-D S-T-A-T-E-S O-F A-M-E-R-I-C-

"A D-O-E-S N-O-T H-A-V-E E-N-O-U-G-H M-O-N-E-Y T-O P-A-Y I-T-S B-I-L-L-S!" —G. B.

"We're going deeper and deeper into debt. We're robbing Peter to pay Paul. It's a Ponzi scheme." —Donald D.

"It all boils down to this. Your money is only worth what the government says it is." —Anonymous Political Analyst

"Do you remember comedienne Lucille Ball (a popular and funny liberal) in the chocolate factory when she was trying to wrap individual candies on an accelerating conveyor belt? She is what America is starting to look like—silly, frantic, and out of control—and you can be sure that everything is eventually going to turn into a big chocolate mess." —John Hayberry

"After four-and-a-half million years, women got the right to vote. Now, here we are seventeen-and-a-half-trillion dollars in debt and [women] are waiting for some guy to come along, fix everything, and pick up the tab." —Name Withheld, Pending Notice Of Next Of Kin

Why is it that as the value of stocks go up and up, the price of food at the grocery store goes up and up, too? Is the United States of America in good shape economically—like the liberal Democrats keep saying—or is the dollar bill just worth less? What are all of the Obama supporters on Wall Street going to do when it comes time to *pay the bill?* Retire to a foreign country permanently? If they're on the run, maybe they could hide out in India somewhere. An Indian rupee used to

---

[314] France is also the country that the Allied forces liberated from Hitler in World War II. In 1886, France gave the United States of America the masculine female Statue of Liberty ("Liberty Enlightening the World"; French: "La Liberté chocolate éclair soup de le monde"), a colossal neoclassical sculpture on Liberty Island in the middle of New York Harbor, in Manhattan, New York City. It was a gift: a robed female representing Libertas, the Roman goddess of freedom. It bears a torch and a tabula ansata (a tablet evoking immigration law) upon which is inscribed the date of the American Declaration of Independence, July 4, 1776. A broken chain lies at her feet. The statue is an icon of freedom and of the United States. But under the Democratic Party, the Statue of Liberty has become symbolic of an open-border policy, an invitation to untold millions of needy liberal foreigners from all lands.

buy something in Bangladesh, just like a penny used to buy something here in the United States. That's why rupees and pennies were invented in the first place: to buy things. Well, guess what? Today, one million increasingly worthless rupees are equal to about $10,000!

On Friday, August 5, 2011, for the first time in our nation's history, the top-tier AAA credit rating of the federal government was downgraded by Standard & Poor's (S&P) to—if you can believe it—*below that of France.*

Yes, France. . . .[314]

Liberals First and Scientists Second

> "Anyone who believes that there is nothing new of any importance to be discovered should understand that half of what we know—or think that we know—has been misinterpreted or exaggerated, either intentionally or unintentionally, by liberal researchers and scientists." — Dr. J. R. Fiction, Ph.D.

It is only recently that the extent to which liberal propaganda affects the sciences has actually begun to dawn on many people. Most conservatives have long been aware of liberal influence in academia but always considered science sacrosanct because, traditionally, it is based on unbiased research, facts, data, and formulae. What a laugh that idea is turning out to be. In the past, it simply never occurred to most of us that intelligent and honorable learned liberal members of the scientific community were so mentally disturbed that they would *even consider* falsifying data—and especially as a group *in unison*—for political gain. It defies everything that most of us have been led to believe about the field of science for our entire lives. I suppose it was the e-mails connected to the recent man-made global-warming fiasco that finally nudged many people in the ribs and awakened them from their obliviousness.[315] One prominent global-warming alarmist is even calling for skeptics' houses to be burned (a typical liberal solution:

---

[315] "NASA satellite data from the years 2000 through 2011 show the Earth's atmosphere is allowing far more heat to be released into space than alarmist computer models have predicted, reports a new study in the peer-reviewed science journal *Remote Sensing*" ("New NASA Data Blow Gaping Hole in Global Warming Alarmism," *Forbes,* July 27, 2011).

[316] "Now Is the Winter of Our Discontent," *The Wall Street Journal,* January 31, 2014.

decrease heat by setting more fires). But as the years go by with no need to evacuate the east coast of the United States of America and go to higher ground, or for a New Yorker named Noah to begin building another ark, it's becoming increasingly apparent that, in most cases, it's *not* global warming that liberal politicians and their bleating *Homo sheepiens* devotees are interested in; it's personal enrichment and the facade of superior—rather than suboptimal—morality, along with *global control.* (To put it bluntly, this "climate change" fiasco is nothing more than a concocted plan by liberal Democratic politicians who are trying to screw everybody out of their money.) That is why liberals so often react feverishly to the constant bombardment of decreasing temperature measurements, followed by worldwide whispers of doubt, especially after the winter of January 2014, when the city of Chicago was reported in the news to be even colder than the South Pole![316]

> "Global Energy Policy is a joke and everyone but liberals seems to know it. Maybe they just want to give billions of dollars of our tax money to their friends." —Anonymous (U.S.M.C.)

> "Are Democrats sending money to their friends in foreign countries in the name of climate change? Foreigners can't vote by mail yet, can they?" —Minnie Mouse, Home Economics Expert

Yes, it does appear that wherever liberals live and breathe, so does inaccurate and useless pseudo-information—if not outright lies.—whether in politics, education, meteorology, anthropology, or any other field of study, including—*yikes!*—basic economics. And we all know how that turned out, don't we?

Here is what the authors of *Evolutionary Psychiatry: A New Beginning* say in the final pages:

> Some politically motivated writers, such as [last name] (1992), for example, still cling to a rigidly anti-biological position, maintaining that to acknowledge the existence of social hierarchies in human populations, and to trace their evolutionary origins, is to condone them at best and to promote fascism at worst. If we are unsympathetic to such arguments, it is because we feel that authors like [last name] would have us become scientific ostriches, burying our heads in the sand of political correctness, in the pious hope that those powerful competitive propensities

that behavioural biology has revealed, will, if we refuse to acknowledge them, quietly go away. . . .

The often repeated criticism made of evolutionary psychologists by their opponents that they are ideologically motivated by a private 'right wing' political agenda is unjustified. Not only is it untrue of ourselves, but we believe it to be untrue of those evolutionary psychologists who are known to us personally. . . . In fact, as [another last name] (1995) has pointed out, it is the *critics* of evolutionary psychology who are ideologically motivated: it is *their* strong political conviction that forms the basis of their approach to social and psychological issues rather than the scientific objectivity aspired to by the evolutionists. By denying their own political motives and projecting such motives on to others, these critics seem to be displaying that incipient paranoia which typically occurs when human communities divide.

But it is not profitable to debate this issue any further: we believe the argument has been won. The evidence for a biologically determined propensity for human and non-human primates to form hierarchically structured societies, in which individual rank has important social and psychological consequences, is so overwhelming that the onus is now on those who *refuse to believe it* to prove their case.[317] [italics added]

Hierarchies are systems or organizations in which people or groups are ranked one above the other according to status or authority. This, we should all note, usually depends on wealth, which conflicts with the supposedly marvelous precepts of communism. So, any scientific acknowledgment that hierarchies are, indeed, not only man's 4.5 million-year-old genetic heritage but the natural order of things would come as an incredibly severe blow to those at the bottom of the pecking order who refuse to face reality. Clearly, no one has more peck marks on his or her noggin than a slave. Some people see communism and/or socialism as their only hope of achieving social superiority (under the guise of equality), now being marketed worldwide under the misnomer "social justice."[318] Socialism, by the way, is not about fairness; it's about control: the control of the successful and productive by the unsuccessful and nonproductive. Socialists attempt to achieve this control by essentially eliminating any possible benefit to being ambitious and industrious—i.e., eliminating private ownership and profit. *Socialism is the (plastic) flower of envy.*

---

[317] Stevens and Price, *op. cit.*, pp. 276–277.
[318] For more on communism, see "Red States and Blue Dress States," page 193.

Furthermore, here is what Nobel Prize winner James D. Watson, author of *The Double Helix,* has to say about liberal influence on science:

> Modern genetics has taken to heart the lessons of the eugenics experience. Scientists are typically careful to avoid questions with overtly political implications and even those whose potential as political fodder is less clear. We have seen, for instance, how such an obvious human trait as skin color has been neglected by geneticists. It's hard to blame them: after all, with any number of interesting questions available for investigation, why choose one that might land you in hot water with the popular press or, worse, earn you an honorable mention in white supremacist propaganda? But the aversion to controversy has an even more practical—and more insidious—political dimension. It happens that scientists, like most academics, tend to be liberal and vote Democratic. While no one can tell how much of this affiliation is principled and how much is pragmatic, it's certainly the case that Democratic administrations are assumed to be invariably more generous toward research than Republican ones.* . . . *Wrongly, it turns out. The stingiest science budget in recent history was Jimmy Carter's. . . . And so having signed on to the liberal end of the political spectrum, and finding themselves in a climate intolerant of truths that don't conform to ideology, most scientists carefully steer clear of research that might uncover such truths. The fact that they duly hew to the prevailing line of liberal orthodoxy—which seeks to honor and entitle difference while shunning any consideration of its biochemical basis—is, I think, bad for science, for a democratic society, and ultimately for human welfare.[319]

It has become increasingly clear (especially through recent exposure on the FOX News channel) that many esteemed and influential liberal university professors are confusing their scholastic accomplishments with having a superior intellect. These self-important know-it-alls, many of whom are probably dizzy from running around in circles, chasing co-eds, appear to be oblivious to the fact that an above-average vocabulary and/or communication skills, both of which are highly prized on an Ivy League campus such as Harvard,[320] Yale, or Princeton, or the University of the Ozarks, doesn't make their opinions about such things as the Afghanistan War, human embryo research, the National Debt, automobile engines, a/c repairs,

---

[319] Watson, with Berry, *op. cit.*, p. 364.
[320] Harvard Law School, President Obama's alma mater, was recently in the news, not for their exemplary staff and teaching, but for the fact that a group was permitted to hold a satanic black mass on campus (FOX News channel, May 8, 2014).

microelectronics, or northern spud crops any better than that of someone less linguistically inclined—be that person a N.A.S.A. astrophysicist or a conservative plumber from Ohio named Joey. In fact, most authoritative liberal university whizzes, with their impressive credentials, eye-catching awards, and multiple diplomas, always seem to turn out to be, as we have all now come to expect in a world full of irony, intellectually dishonest and dead wrong about practically everything.

Don't be fooled: "Upper class" and "elite" are two very different things.

You see, contrary to popular perception and frequent references by conservative pundits to the so-called "liberal elite," the roots of liberalism lie not in the Ivy League halls of academia, elegant D.N.C.-leased ballrooms, Martha's Vineyard, Hollywood, or the private cocktail parties of the rich and famous, but in the mindless, wretched dregs of human suboptimality and abject poverty --i.e., les miserables --except today, these liberal victims-in-need have free cell phones, rusted Lincoln Continentals with bald tires, and stolen color TV sets. From this place, a huge trunk sprouts, then branches throughout our culture from sea to shining sea, dropping multitudes of shady leaves, twisted twigs, and nutty poisonous seeds in all fifty (er, fifty-seven?) states --including, of course, that thoroughly enchanting liberal wonderland and vacation spot called Hawaii, a volcanic island chain located some 2500 miles out at sea --where there's no food for the brain. The place is loaded with indigenous dopey Polynesian surfers and chubby, half-naked hula girls drinking raw coconut milk, exchanging fish tails, and eating pit-roasted Hawaiian swine (pigs, not other human beings, as they once did). So who dares insinuate that our president wasn't born in the United States?

Gross suboptimality, in fact, is apparently the main reason why many liberals prefer to remain safely nestled within the confines of sprawling college campuses, insulated from the real world and surrounded by their peers (similar idiots) and lots of inexperienced young people willing to show them due respect because they're either too shy or too polite to admit that they know a fool when they see one. Also, be aware that what helps many of these silly, aged, socially retarded male professors—with haircuts like Thor, the god of thunder, or Audrey Hepburn, or one of the Monkees—achieve their most important biological imperative, *reproduction,* is their constant regurgitation of naïve liberal mush and their espousing of compassionate claptrap, thus making them

---

[321] Actually, what's going on in today's leftist Ivy League universities is even worse. Columbia University's School of Social Work, for example, has reportedly made the terrorist and cop killer Kathy Boudin, a former radical member of the Weather Underground convicted in 1984 of felony murder, an adjunct professor. After being a fugitive on the run for more than a decade, she served twenty-two years in prison for her role as the getaway driver in a botched $1.6 million Brinks armored car robbery by Black Liberation Army members in 1981. An innocent guard and two police officers, all family men, were gunned down in cold blood. Boudin also rented cars for bank robberies and for the prison escape of radical Black Nationalist and convicted cop killer Joanne Chesimard. But that's not all Boudin did. She actually schemed to plant bombs in Butler Library in 1970 that would have killed hundreds of Columbia students, faculty, and staff! The *New York Post* stated: "Boudin was personally involved in at least a dozen bombings across the country—including at the Pentagon, the U.S. Capitol and N.Y.P.D. headquarters—before the Brinks job" ("Columbia's Pet Terrorist," *New York Post,* April 3, 2013, N.Y.P. Holdings).

appear to be members of the "in" crowd. This, of course, can help maximize an adult learned dolt's popularity on campus with impressionable young men and women. The tendency of many often petty left-wing educators is to take out their mating frustrations on the grades, and thus occasionally even the careers, of clear-thinking conservative students who may be decades younger than themselves (and whom they've recognized and correctly identified as their mortal enemies) is probably enough to write a set of encyclopedias about.

So, instead, let's just keep it short. Ask yourself this: What is there to keep liberal socialist Democrat professors from playing No Child Left Behind in their classrooms in order to keep colleges and universities well stocked with *unqualified radical left-wing teachers, tutors, and pedagogues of their own kind?*

Beginning to get the Ivy League picture?[321]

The Laws of Liberal Scientists in Motion

The three laws of Liberal Scientists in Motion are the physical laws forming the basis of understanding for all of modern science. They describe the relationship between the inner and outer forces acting on an academician and his or her torso's reaction and motion because of those forces:

> First law: Always be very suspicious of any scientific book, research paper, or magazine article that contains one or more statements, references, or conclusions that will make the author wildly popular with Hollywood liberals, illegal Mexican aliens, or eighteen-year-old girls wearing "SAVE THE WHALES" T-shirts.

> Second law: The spiraling downward velocity of a failing academician's career gradually accelerates (approximately 32.174 feet/second^2) unless he or she manages to obtain government funding, which often requires the academician to "toe the liberal line."

> Third law: The opinions of experts, no matter how renowned, acclaimed, or famous in any field of study, turn out to be wrong about 50 percent of the time, so flip a coin.

(Note: The third law, which was secretly approved by former vice president Al Gore (D), is now considered by virtually all liberal academicians, educators, researchers, scribes, and scholars to be settled science.)

---

[322] The English-Kilawabo translation of this phrase is (the deep dark guttural utterance) "boo."

Human (D) Evolution

The Ancient Kilawabo: "White Man Bad"[322]

Why are liberals so prone to confuse real life with the standard plots of Hollywood movie scripts? Are they just more susceptible to fantasy and suggestion? Or is it the TV stations that they watch? Whatever the case may be, it is something that society should always be fully aware of and obviously concerned about, especially when the intentional misrepresentation of facts can result in rioting, murder, mayhem, arson, theft, and rape by ghetto dwellers yelling "Black Planet!" Although liberal propaganda is not the focus of this book, it's plainly a serious long-term problem. That problem stems primarily from the well-known underlying theme of most contemporary Hollywood films: *poor minority underdog good; rich, successful white man bad.* This, of course, is hogwash and, more often than not, the inverse of reality, but fortunately, all clear-thinking people realize it.

People who deal with the public regularly—as opposed to watching Hollywood actors regurgitate their memorized scripts—know that today's prevailing liberal storylines are ludicrous. In real life, the exact opposite is true. If you don't believe it, try pitching a tent in any "underprivileged" (i.e., ghetto) neighborhood and live in it for a week—but be sure to wear a football helmet while you're sleeping so that you don't get your head bashed in with a cement block (this actually happened to some foreign tourists in New Orleans). And if that neighborhood you've chosen happens to be located in the depths of Chicago, Illinois, you'd better just stay away. The same goes for Johannesburg, South Africa.

The perception of police officers as bad and of all idle citizens with no visible means of support as good is now so widespread that whenever an incident occurs, even intelligent conservatives subconsciously try to connect the made-for-TV-movie-plot dots. People need to stop basing their opinions on what they see on television, because it isn't real. What we see on TV is having a negative effect on race relations.

The "iced-tea and Skittles" Trayvon Martin murder case in Sanford, Florida, is just one of the latest examples.[323] The (illegitimate) liberal news media pounced on it and intentionally distorted the facts to fit a popular Hollywood plot. The "white Hispanic" man who was attacked and pummeled and justifiably defended himself with a handgun was immediately portrayed as a racist, and the African American teenager who attacked him and was killed was portrayed as an innocent and cherubic young angel, so NBC was sued.[324]

So what are we to do?

For the official liberal position on the topic of race, one need look no further than the American Anthropological Association. The following is an excerpt from the A.A.A.'s "Statement on 'Race.'"

---

[323] The defendant was found not guilty, so it wasn't actually a murder. It was self-defense.
[324] Specifically, NBC and its news executives were sued for creatively editing the 911 tape.

As they were constructing U.S. society, leaders among European-Americans fabricated the cultural/behavioral characteristics associated with each "race," linking superior traits with Europeans and negative and inferior ones to Blacks and Indians. Numerous arbitrary and fictitious beliefs about the different peoples were institutionalized and deeply embedded in American thought.[325]

(Translation: minorities good, white man bad.)

Can you believe this asininity? Are they trying to make us all laugh? "Constructing"? "Fabricated"? "Fictitious beliefs"? What in the name of Creation (or their great Pygmy god Bes) are these mental midgets talking about? Are we supposed to ignore the exhaustive detailed research of *The Bell Curve* and the innate common sense that we've all had since childhood and everything that we can clearly see happening around us with our own two eyes?[326] All you have to do is take a stroll through the nearest impoverished neighborhood, and then you can count how many examples of anthropological "arbitrary and fictitious beliefs" you see.

Apparently, the mongoloids at the American Anthropological Association (A.A.A.) would have everyone believe, including, no doubt, many amused blacks and Indians, that there really is no such thing as race at all and that race is just something that somebody made up as a rationalization for slavery—which, don't forget, has been illegal in the United States since 1865.[327] If some unidentified "leaders among European-Americans" did make everything up, who exactly were those omnipotent beings who so drastically affected today's racial attitudes? When was the big conspiratorial world meeting held, and how did they get so smart?

---

[325] American Anthropological Association, "Statement on 'Race,'" 2006. Note that this *living statement* "does not reflect a consensus of all members of the A.A.A."—probably just the ones whose last names nobody can pronounce.

[326] *The Bell Curve*, published in 1994 by psychologist Richard J. Herrnstein and political scientist Charles Murray, argues that human intelligence is substantially influenced by both inherited and environmental factors. Its title comes from the bell-shaped graph of the normal distribution of I.Q. scores in a population. The controversial book, which is considered offensive and taboo among liberal academicians, discusses racial differences in intelligence, along with the societal implications. The book also argues that the people of the United States, to their economic detriment, are in denial of the facts.

[327] Although some forensic anthropologists and other scientists continue to use the term mongoloid in some contexts, such as criminal justice, the term mongoloid is now considered derogatory.

[328] Coolies were manual laborers and slaves from Asia (China and India) during the nineteenth and twentieth centuries. Even though many were sold like animals, we rarely hear anything about them today. Not all of them were forced into bondage; some worked of their own free will. Coolies often lived in the same neighborhoods as Negroes and occasionally intermarried with them. Chinese immigration to the United States, mostly voluntary, contributed to the building of the First Transcontinental Railroad (1863–1869), which joined the eastern and western halves of the United States. It is considered one of the greatest technological feats of the nineteenth century. Probably, the greatest feat of the twenty-first century will be paying China back all of the money we owe them.

What did they do after this secret summit was over, send postcards to everyone in the United States and let them know what they should think? What do these morons imagine human beings are, anyway, mindless robots? Also, just out of curiosity, why didn't they mention any other minorities—like, say, Asian coolies—in their official statement?[328] If lockstep "leaders" were so busy fabricating everything that different groups of people think about each other, which assumedly includes the Italians, Germans, and French, then they must have also fabricated the Asian reputation for politeness, industriousness, and intelligence, along with that utterly ridiculous and laughable myth that the Japanese people manufacture high-quality electronic equipment—which, of course, they do.

Wow! Isn't it amazing what "mean" Anglo-Saxon and European-American big shots can accomplish just by having a secret clandestine meeting and making important decisions about what all of us should think hundreds of years later? Did someone also decide that Scotsmen should be considered thrifty because they pinch pennies and never throw anything away and their closets are filled with empty jars, paper bags, boxes, and string? The truth is, our ancestors led hard lives and had little tolerance for nonsense. If something looked like a duck and quacked like a duck, they called it a duck. They didn't refer to it as nature's magnificently feathered noble songbird of the lakes and streams.

Anthropologists deserve our respect, especially the ones who do all the digging, but statements like the A.A.A.'s are nothing more than the usual politically correct liberal lunch platter of bullshit, rotten grits, sugary fruit-twist salad, and snake-flavored ice cream that we've all come to expect from academics these days. Their naïve socialist opinions are concocted not only for the purpose of procuring party invitations from their partisan ponytailed peers but also to increase their chances of garnering great big government grants. Now, if anyone winced at the use of the word socialist, consider the following sentence that the A.A.A. has also included in its edict on race: "The 'racial' worldview was invented to assign some groups to perpetual low status, while others were permitted access to privilege, power, and wealth."[329] See where all of this is leading? Almost sounds like a direct quote from the president's teleprompter, doesn't it? Soon, members of the American Anthropological Association will be calling for all farmland to be divvied up evenly among the populace, based on minority status (or maybe estimated brain volume and cranial measurements).

Our liberal socialist Democrat friends are much like amateur magicians. To make us all believe that flying doves, white mice, silk scarves, and colored balls are appearing out of thin air, they attempt to distract our attention by cleverly motioning with one hand while smoothly dipping the other hand into their pocket (and then your pocket). But illusions fool the average person only temporarily.

---

[329] American Anthropological Association, *op. cit.*

After seeing the trick performed enough times, a clever audience begins to figure out what's going on. Then it's time for the long-handled wooden cane to reach out and pull the illusionist by his neck off the stage.

Indian Territory

Things sure have changed. When I was about eight years old and exploring my great-grandmother's basement, I opened up a dusty encyclopedia and found an old map of the United States. There was no state called Oklahoma—just a large blank area labeled "INDIAN TERRITORY."[330] Today, it's impossible for many of us to even imagine how difficult things really were for people back then.

Now, this may come as a complete shock to many pasty-faced liberals enchanted with the mythos of the legendary, larger-than-life, wise and noble Amer-

---

[330] It should be noted here that the *prime directive* of "progressive" liberals seems to be to ignore or discredit—or perhaps even burn—every encyclopedia, textbook, and scientific research paper published prior to the end of the Carter administration (1981), especially the ones that contain real-life human photos of grinning, pointy-headed, diagnosed imbeciles. The "progressive" attempts to hide facts from the public by editing and/or revising history are probably only a prelude to their ultimate goal, which may be to convince everyone that *history does not exist at all*. This manipulation of information is also being widely practiced by liberals involved with the Internet.

[331] *Lophophora williamsii* /loˈfɒfərə wɪlˈjæmsiaɪ/ is a small, spineless cactus with psychoactive alkaloids, particularly mescaline, which is a hallucinogenic and intoxicating compound. The Spanish common name, also used in English, is peyote (/peɪˈjoʊti/; from the Nahuatl word peyōtl [ˈpejoːt͡ɬ]). Native North American Indians are likely to have ingested peyote for "spiritual" purposes for at least 5,500 years. Peyote is native to Mexico and is well known for affecting the mind. Peyote is used worldwide as an entheogen and supplement to various transcendence practices, including meditation, psychonautics, and psychedelic psychotherapy. Peyote has a long history of use by the indigenous American Indian.

[332] Robertson, *op. cit.*, p. 202 (attributed to *The Works of Francis Parkman*, Little, Brown, Boston, 1892, vol. III, especially Chapter XVIII).

[333] The Mexican–American War (1846–1848) was an armed conflict between the United States and Mexico following the annexation of Texas, considered by Mexico to be part of its territory despite the 1836 Texas Revolution. American territorial expansion to the Pacific coast, in the spirit of Manifest Destiny, was the goal of President James K. Polk, the leader of the Democratic Party. The territories of New Mexico and California were viewed as unsettled, ungoverned, and unprotected frontier lands with tenuous ties to Mexico and under imminent threat of acquisition by the British. Prior to the war, large-scale raids by Comanche, Apache, and Navajo Indians hundreds of miles deep into Mexico for the purpose of stealing livestock had left thousands of people dead, so when American troops initially invaded northern Mexico, they found a demoralized population offering little resistance. The war, fought almost entirely with volunteers, was highly controversial in the United States and ended when an American army captured Mexico City, located about 500 miles south of the Rio Grande. The 1848 Treaty of Guadalupe Hidalgo specified the forced Mexican cession of the territories of Alta California and New Mexico to the United States in exchange for $15 million (in today's dollars, that's almost half a billion) and the assumption of $3.25 million of unpaid debt owed by the Mexican government to U.S. citizens. (In 2012, Texas threatened to secede from the union—the United States of America—because of the Democratic Party's policies. The number of Mexican Americans now living in Texas may have had something to do with that.)

ican Indian who is "at one" with nature—after, of course, ingesting some peyote[331]—but here in the United States, we have detailed descriptions from the 1800s of Indian cannibalism, along with the documented Indian habit of torturing white prisoners of both sexes.[332] That's right, burning people alive. (I guess liberals just didn't know that.) Furthermore, prior to the middle 1800s, before the Mexican-American war, hundreds of Mexican villages and unlucky-to-be-born villagers were devastated by Indian attacks.[333] Are the details really necessary?

Oh, but it doesn't end there; it gets much worse. You see, Indians also attacked children. (I guess liberals didn't know that, either.)

One handwritten genealogical record that is more than a hundred years old describes a child who was scalped by an Indian. This occurred in the 1750s during the French and Indian War. The little boy was attacked on his parents' farm near a perimeter fence while looking for his mother. Fortunately, a neighbor heard the child's screams and began shooting at the savage, so he ran off. The poor kid lived, but with part of his skull showing. (Do liberals need photos of bad things to prove it to them?)

This happened to hundreds of settlers who roamed the Wild West.

Of course, you'll never hear stories like this from dreamy-eyed liberals. In their contrived and ridiculous juvenile fantasy world, all minority members are good and the white man is bad. This attitude of virtually all liberals that minorities throughout history could do no wrong is an extension of their Hollywood-fed misbeliefs about the present. Liberal dogma dictates that red-skinned, brown-skinned, or black-skinned people, or members of any other minority, are *always* in the right, even when they riot, rape, smash windows, ransack businesses, burn down people's homes, and maim and kill innocent civilians (occasionally, members of the ruling white majority) who happen to be driving through the neighborhood and stop to have a look—having no idea what the hell is going on. Liberals would have us believe that minority members have a right to riot, and that members of the white majority have only themselves to blame. The fact that the innocent bystanders who are killed are frequently poor black liberal ghetto dwellers, along with a few poor white homeless liberals—and sometimes even stray cats and dogs—doesn't seem to faze L.S.D.ers at all.

"Here's a big puzzle: Why have there been so many *left-wing* radical bomb throwers but only one *right-wing*? Whenever the subject of domestic terrorism comes up, liberals gleefully point to Timothy McVeigh. He must have been a rare exception to the radical rule (i.e., a platypus). But maybe he wasn't really a right-winger. Maybe he was just a militaristic libertarian borderline-schizophrenic left-wing nut case on drugs. Who else would want to kill innocent people? A conservative? If he really was a right-winger, then he must have had a left-wing loon's smelly tail feathers." —John Hayberry (2008)

Revising World History

Liberals are compelled to rewrite world history because it is only through the revision of reality that their fantasies can be perpetuated. It is a formidable juggling act. What little instincts they have drive them to modify historical records, not only those of the United States but also those of other countries. Liberals have various motives, but often, their goal is simply to please *themselves,* along with special-interest groups and voting minority members. The key word is "voting." That's all L.S.D.ers are interested in, and that's why they have no desire to seek out, promote, and celebrate famous Tahitians, Pygmies, Fiji Islanders, New Zealanders, or Korowai. Liberals would have us all believe that their philosophy is rooted in compassion and altruism. Do not ever be fooled by them. Nothing could be further from the truth. It is all about liberal self-interest and political power. That is why the vast majority of liberal politicians do not waste any of their precious time worrying about others unless it is beneficial to the Democratic Party specifically and/or themselves personally.

"Progressive" liberals have been partially successful with their reinterpretations of history, as they always will be when no one is paying attention. Now, all of the things that we were taught in grade school about our forefathers and the discovery of America has been twisted into something so unrecognizable, you'd think everything good we have today was invented by Mexicans, Africans, manly liberal females, the Chinese, and homosexuals, and that every famous white man—George Washington, Thomas Jefferson, Benjamin Franklin, Thomas Edison, Alexander Graham Bell, and a long list of others—was either unimportant or a creep. (You see, with liberals, a person's communist leanings are always considered a plus.) Fortunately, the liberal rewriting of history books has been thoroughly exposed now that millions of children's schoolbooks have been corrected and reprinted. Of course, there is also the usual barely concealed liberal bias against the Republican Party, our nation's forefathers, U.S. military heroes, and Christianity.

With liberals, the rule of thumb seems to be this: If it makes the U.S.A. look bad, it is *good.* That's why it's more than likely that "progressive" liberals with Hollywood expertise have even gone so far as to negatively alter, edit, or destroy documentary filmstrips, along with archeological/anthropological samples, including fossils, in museum archives[334]—anything that may conflict in some small way with their dysgenic view of the world or their ultimate political goals. Unfortunately for us all, they have probably been doing this for decades. Today's onslaught of "progressive" liberalism is reminiscent of the old hit series about aliens from

---

[334] Including those available for viewing on the Internet.
[335] Actually, there's really no such thing as so-called Native Americans—unless you're referring to everyone who was born in this country after it was named America in 1507. Prior to that, all of the natives who lived here were called Indians.

another planet: *The Invaders.* But with "progressives," it's not their ridged necks and thumbs that stick out, it's their middle fingers. (Now, all of a sudden, suspicious-looking persons claiming to be conservatives are appearing as guests on televised news broadcasts.) So before you ever believe what any liberal scholar has to say about American history, our forefathers, or the Constitution, you may first want to check his or her opinion about Indian—or, if you prefer, Native American[335]—attacks in the 1750s, so that you can compare it to the consensus of opinion among people who witnessed those attacks and sometimes had to fight back, and to the genealogical records and writings of *people who knew!*

Nevertheless, always be very careful never to offend any anti-athletic, 0.2-percent American Indian liberal Democrat by referring to a football team as the "Washington Redskins." He might take offense and begin shaking with *apoplection.*

INTERVIEW WITH A DEMOCRAT

The following is the transcript of an exchange that took place on FOX News on April 1, 2011, but was never broadcast. It's a classic example of F.A.D. and the liberal inability to acknowledge reality. It was obtained from a reliable source who empties the office wastebaskets at 1211 6th Avenue in New York City.

BLONDE NEWSWOMAN (*pointing to a green banana*): Sir, in your opinion, what is that on top of this table?

HANDSOME SCHLEMIEL (*confidently adjusting his bow tie*): Well, there are no simple answers. As President Barack Obama has clearly explained to us . . . yada, yada . . . .

BLONDE NEWSWOMAN (*smiling politely, still pointing at the banana*): Okay, I'll ask again. What is that?

HANDSOME SCHLEMIEL (*ignoring the question and forcing a smile*): . . . and, during the horrific, disgusting, eight years of the failed Bush administration . . . yada, yada, yada . . . .

BLONDE NEWSWOMAN (*carefully picking up the banana*): With all due respect, it's a fairly simple question. What is this? Is it a green banana?

HANDSOME SCHLEMIEL (*nervous, fidgeting*): Well, er, that depends . . . on . . . what the word *a* means.

BLONDE NEWSWOMAN (*holding the banana under the interviewee's nose*): Oh, please, it's obvious to all our viewers what this object is—an elongated green and yellow wild fruit. Why can't you bring yourself to identify it?

HANDSOME SCHLEMIEL (*talking fast, eyes darting*): Er, ahem, well, we all (*cough*) know that Bush lied and kids died, Bush lied and kids died . . . lied . . . died . . . tied . . . tie-dyed . . . Mai Tai . . . (*stuttering*) t-tongue-tied-horsehide-petrified . . . .

BLONDE NEWSWOMAN (*smiling and peeling the banana suggestively*): See, it's a banana. *Ba-nan-nuh.*

HANDSOME SCHLEMIEL (*continuing*): . . . and the Republicans, as we all have seen, are the party of "negativity," "niggling," "gnats," and "no-no" . . . .

BLONDE NEWSWOMAN: *Baa-naa-nuh.* C'mon, say it, honey.

HANDSOME SCHLEMIEL: . . . and the demon Sarah Palin, the cloven-hoofed spawn of Beelzebub . . . .

BLONDE NEWSWOMAN: All right, now, repeat after me . . . *baaa* . . . *naaa* . . . *nuhh*. Why can't you say it?

HANDSOME SCHLEMIEL: . . . and Republicans are Nazis who want all Americans—young, old, and even middle-aged—to drown in rat poison . . . .

BLONDE NEWSWOMAN (*taking a big bite and chewing with her mouth open*): BAAA-NAAA-NUHHH . . . You know, what monkeys eat? (*Accidentally gags, blowing a chunk on his shirt.*)

HANDSOME SCHLEMIEL (*wide-eyed, jumping up from his chair and screaming*): RACIST!

Human (D) Evolution

Racism!

> "How come it's okay to name a group "Black Panthers" but if you name a group "White Panthers" it's considered racist?" —Anonymous

This is the subject that most people, for obvious reasons, make a point of tiptoeing around in their bare feet. Slavery has been dead now for almost 150 years here in the United States, although it still exists in various forms in Third World countries, and in 2009, Americans—who are more than 70 percent white—elected their first African American president. How's that for racism? So who keeps fomenting all of the angry talk? Why didn't liberals calm down five years ago? Why are liberal charges of racism constantly in the news? Why are so many Democratic politicians, pundits, and public figures hanging on to racism and shaking, twisting, and wringing its neck like the goose that laid the golden eggs?

It's all about power and money, sonny.

Democrats refuse to stop playing Pin the Tail on the Donkey—or, in this case, Republican elephant—and for the same reason, they'll probably never stop waving their get-out-of-jail-free race card instead of waving the American flag. Of course, everyone treats the subject of racism like a red-hot egg laid by a radioactive liberal New York chicken, tossing it back and forth with oven mitts as gingerly as a bag of plutonium waste so they don't dare break it. As most of us know, our personal feelings about others who are not members of our own race is just something that we should never, ever, ever publicly discuss (not truthfully, anyway) because if we do, we'll undoubtedly be branded by liberals as hideous racist ogres, so very few people even dare to whisper what they really think.

Now, maybe that will end.

To begin with, we should all be aware that our nation's first African American attorney general, whose ancestral roots actually lie in the tiny island of Barbados, was *wrong* when he said that the people of the United States of America are "a nation of cowards."[336] Maybe he just got the U.S.A. mixed up with the distant isolated place that some of his relatives are from.[337] You see, the U.S.A. is a nation of

---

[336] One possible explanation for this remark may be projection (refer back to page 89).

[337] On June 28, 2012, the president's handpicked attorney general, Eric Holder, the first African(?) American to ever hold that position, was accused of stonewalling the House Judiciary Committee investigation of operation "fast and furious" by refusing to provide requested documents. The president's A.G. thus became the first sitting member of the Cabinet of the United States, established some 200 years ago, to be held in contempt of Congress—a charge that normally carries a punishment of up to one year in prison. The president then decided to invoke executive privilege, which meant that his A.G. didn't have to plead the Fifth. It's a liberal legacy of which future Americans of all races, colors, and creeds can be proud.

brave and intelligent people who are currently being browbeaten into silence by a seething, fishy mass of misguided, weak-minded liberal foreign-Americans and personable smiling representatives of naïve illegal immigrants—many of whom are, to put it bluntly, a hodgepodge of gang members, ne'er-do-wells, and angry not-born-and-raised-in-the-U.S.A. misfits.

Let us examine the definition of *racism:*

> **racism:** the belief that all members of each race possess characteristics or abilities specific to that race, [especially] so as to distinguish it as inferior or superior to another race or races; prejudice or discrimination directed against someone of a different race based on such a belief[338]

So does that mean that prejudice or discrimination was directed against the Democratic candidate, Senator Barack H. Obama, who is half black, in a country that is over 70 percent white, when some sixty-five million people voted for him?[339] It doesn't? Well, then, that must mean that America *isn't* a racist country like liberals keep saying it is. America wasn't a racist country in 2008 and 2012 when it elected him to the presidency, so why do liberals keep saying that America is racist now? Do liberal politicians stand to profit financially in some way? Why is it that voters who liked Mr. Obama and elected him president were not racists then, but if they changed their minds and don't like him anymore are racists now? Why is it that people who didn't vote for him but decided to give him a chance *aren't* racists, but after getting fed up with his increasingly poor judgment, *are* racists? I'm confused (as they so often say on CNN and MSNBC). Why is it racist to be critical of anyone who is intentionally destroying our country financially? Here's another puzzle: Why are conservative men and women who despise white liberal Democratic politicians *not* racist, but if those same conservative men and women don't like black liberal Democratic politicians, either, they *are* racist? It's all so very difficult to understand. Maybe if hardworking taxpayers—men, women, and children—

---

[338] The *Oxford American College Dictionary.*
[339] According to the 2012 U.S. Census, 77.9 percent of the U.S. population (that means .779 x 320 million people) identified themselves as white. After the 2008 presidential election (in which about 69,500,000 people voted for Obama) and the 2012 presidential election (in which about 66,700,000 voted for Obama), it became very clear that the Democratic Party had a lock on the *ignorance vote* (i.e., politically uninformed voters). That group includes well over fifty percent of liberals, along with some seventy-five percent of the African American community, and a throng of multicultural college kids who must have believed everything that the liberal media was telling them. Another advantage that candidate Barack Entertainment had was a very tricky campaign manager.

just reach into their pockets and give these liberals mo' money, they'll shut up and leave us all alone.

Now, please note that, according to the strict definition above, the word racism means *prejudice or discrimination* against someone based on his or her particular race. Racism does not mean the dislike of someone because he is not trustworthy, or because he is a liar, or foolish, or anti-American, or because his ideas stink like a three-day-old dead catfish. No, racism is clearly something different altogether. So why are liberal socialist Democrats so quick to scream *"Racism!"* every time a conservative criticizes "the Man Who Shot Osama bin Laden" for his seemingly endless string of dropped balls and long line of mistakes?[340]

Remember the time when a preeminent Republican former Speaker of the House remarked that President Obama spends too much time playing basketball?[341] Suddenly, that observation became the most hotly debated new "racism" topic on the national news.

> "Why do the Democrats keep saying that people don't like President Barack Insane Obama because of his skin color? If that were true, then why do most people like black orcas a whole lot better than white sharks?" —Anonymous Contributor

> "Yeah, sure, sure, I know, I know. Democrats are good and Republicans are baaad." —Yosemite Sam and His Six-Shooter

Undoubtedly, charges of racism help keep lots of money flowing from concerned supporters' pockets into liberal socialist Democrat politicians' wiggling fingers. That is why they like racism so much. There's another reason, too, and it's this: Accusing innocent people of racism also makes childlike liberals feel moral, principled, and decent—and "good" about themselves. See, it's all a fraud.

Some people remember the old *Saturday Night Live* skit in which New York Mets All-Star second baseman Chico Escuela keeps saying, "Base-ball . . . been berry, berry good to me." Well, racism has been very, very good to Dems—and so has prejudice. It keeps their jobs secure and their pockets lined with cash. Let us

---

[340] Rumor has it that Osama bin Laden didn't go near any electronic equipment because everything has some kind of an electronic chip inside of it that collects a little information and then sends it to the Internet, just like a wireless printer does. That way, anyone who doesn't believe in God will behave as though they do. (So all of our liberal friends and enemies should probably cover their TV sets with beach towels.)

[341] He reportedly missed twenty out of twenty-two free throws in a televised public performance.

begin our discussion of *prejudice*, as we did with racism, by examining the official dictionary definition of that word.

> **prejudice:** preconceived opinion not based on reason or experience; [and] dislike, hostility, or unjust behavior formed on such a basis: *racial prejudice*[342]

If prejudice is a "preconceived opinion not based on reason or experience," that means that a person who is prejudiced has a

preconceived opinion (i.e., a false premise)
not based on reason (i.e., illogical)
or experience (i.e., naïve).

A false premise? Illogical? Naïve? Who does that remind you of? (Hint: *liberals.*)

There was a time years ago when most Democrats were patriotic, hardworking, family-oriented blue-collar types and Republicans were mostly rich guys who smoked cigars and wore three-piece suits, but after the 1964 Civil Rights Act, that all changed. Many Democrats began to register as A.O.T.D.s—Anything Other Than Democrats (which included the smaller Republican Party)—and then the leftover space in the Democratic Party began to fill with (1) African Americans, (2) multicultural immigrants, and (3) the growing "L.G.B.T. (lesbian, gay, bisexual, transsexual[343]) community." Of course, this all began to occur after the Voting Rights Act of 1965 and before most African Americans had any money of their own to donate to political candidates.[344] Suddenly, faster than you can say, "Jim Crow," Democratic politicians began rehearsing and performing a new liberal "theatrical play" called *Compassion for the Poor*, which was a big hit! Liberals are such fine actors. No wonder they've taken over Hollywood.

Now, let's take a close look at *bigotry*—another one of the L.S.D.ers' favorite words.

---

[342] The *Oxford American College Dictionary*.
[343] Medical definition: A transsexual is a person who psychologically identifies with the opposite sex and who may choose to undergo plastic surgery to change his/her external sex organs.
[344] The Voting Rights Act of 1965 outlawed discriminatory voting practices such as poll taxes and literacy tests that had been used to keep African Americans (and also Hispanic Americans) from registering to vote, and it's widely considered a landmark in civil-rights legislation, which may be not only the proudest but also the most costly event in our nation's history.

bigotry: bigoted attitudes; intolerance toward those who hold different opinions from oneself[345]

Try to remember this definition next time a liberal mob physically attacks a public speaker.

The big question is this: Why are words like *racism, prejudice,* and *bigotry* generally associated with conservative Republicans rather than with the problematical liberal Democrats? One reason may be that a *bigot* is often defined as anyone who wins an argument with a liberal. But why is it that conservatives are always made out to be the bad guys? Want to take a wild guess? *The liberal media,* that's why—television, books, magazines, newspapers, Internet Web sites, and such.

Liberal Democrats, however, have always been their own worst enemies. (Just look at the political fallout from the Obamacare debacle.) One day, the greatest propaganda tool the world has ever known—liberal television stations—is going to stop working for our liberal friends and enemies, and when it does, the vast majority of the public (and even many liberals, for that matter) will finally realize to their surprise that it has never been *skin* color that conservatives dislike. It's *brain* color: (1) communist red, (2) chicken yellow, (3) bullshit brown, (4) promiscuous purple, and (5) know-nothing green.

Some Vegan Food for Thought: If a large-brained, highly intelligent, mind-reading alien genius from another galaxy happened to land on planet Earth and had never seen a made-for-TV Hollywood movie, who would he (or it) conclude are inexplicably foolish, racist, and out of control: liberals or conservatives? The answer is obvious: the human *left-wing species.*

---

[345] The *Oxford American College Dictionary.*

Chapter 12

Are They Really Our Friends?

The Vietnam War: Liberal Privates Exposed

Those of us who have had the unique experience of growing up in the '60s remember how much people hated each other back then. It was during the Vietnam War (our military involvement was 1964–1975), and America eventually pulled out because Washington politicians, influenced and intimidated by an overwhelming media-driven culture of liberal propaganda, did not allow our military to win, and *everyone* had strong opinions about it. In 1963, Democrat Lyndon Baines Johnson, our thirty-sixth president, began serving in that office before most teenagers even knew what the words disingenuous, duplicitous, and conniving—and *liberal*—meant. This deceitful cowpoke was not fit to represent the United States of America, and yet, here he was. Even the Kennedys disliked him—probably, for one reason, because of the way he pronounced the word Negro: "niggrah." Did you know, for example, that L. B. J.'s rise in politics was made possible by the votes of deceased (i.e., dead as a doornail) Mexican Americans whose ghosts apparently showed up and voted at Texas polling booths?[346] Yup, the more things change, the more they stay the same.

---

[346] Robertson, *op. cit.,* p. 415. Furthermore, what's the problem with being required to show your I.D. before voting? All a person has to do is reach in his or her wallet and flick a B.I.C. (Benefit Identification Card).

"Three questions. One, why are Democrats so beholding to unions? Two, why are unions allowed to break the laws of these United States of America? Three, are unions involved in massive—I mean, massive—electoral fraud? Maybe someone would be willing to stake a $1 million dollar bet on it!" —Name Withheld, Pending An Investigation

Yes, L. B. J., a paregoric politician of questionable integrity, was the lucky inheritor of an assassinated president's seat and was the jolly mental giant who signed the 1965 Johnson Act, purportedly to end liberal-loathed racial immigration quotas. (There were too few potential Democratic-voting minority members being allowed to come to America.) This had the radical effect of favoring nonwhite over white immigration, which guarantees a steady stream of liberal socialist Democratic voters pouring into this country, as was its purpose. In other words, unskilled foreigners with below-average intelligence quotients from countries with long and colorful histories of lawlessness and unsuccessful self-governance (i.e., complete failure in this regard) were allowed to begin populating the United States in hordes, bringing their marvelous genetic predispositions with them. For liberals, it has been a gold mine. They have accidentally stumbled onto the only way to get marijuana legalized in the United States: by letting millions of people who grow, smoke, buy, and sell the stuff come live here. Further exacerbating the problem is that when foreigners become United States citizens, they are guaranteed government support, which helps them propagate. The result of this is an overcrowded prison system requiring an extravagant amount of money to maintain. Isn't it nice to know that liberals have only America's best interests, *including the safety of our children* and the financial well-being of future generations, in mind?[347]

---

[347] Note that the P.E.T.S. hypothesis predicts this previously inexplicable quirk of liberal behavior. Enslaved populations that own little or nothing—including their own freedom—have little or nothing to invest in kin; therefore, instincts pertaining to kin investment serve no purpose and have no effect on gene survivability. Perpetually powerless individuals would understandably be concerned primarily with their own welfare, and even poor enslaved children would be looked upon as helpless equals. Obviously, the welfare of future generations is going to be the farthest thing from any enslaved individual's mind. He or she would understandably be concerned only with the here and now. Saving one's own skin would be of primary importance, so it follows that if a slave gene does indeed exist and those who have it in their makeup are put in charge of making policy decisions for our country, the decisions made will depend entirely on what the policymakers think is best for themselves—despite all the proud and noble rhetoric. That's why politicians of the liberal persuasion so often vote enthusiastically in favor of legislation when it's good for them to do so and then later turn vehemently against it. The actual merits of the legislation are given little, if any, consideration. The passage of Obamacare, for example, was perceived as good for all Democratic Party politicians in 2010, so they "horse fed" it to us all. But many of those same politicians now seem to perceive correctly that it's bad for them, so—billions of wasted dollars later—they call it a train wreck and try to pretend that they had nothing to do with it. It's government gone insane.

"Democratic politicians like foreigners because they can be easily persuaded, coerced, tricked, or paid to vote for them—so, the more foreigners, the better. *Comprendé? Visto bueno? Dong? Mingbai? Bamba rada? Gutu? Say wha', man?"* —Anonymous Political Analyst

It is because of immigration policies and the way liberals were portrayed as brave and heroic conscientious objectors during the Vietnam War that liberalism enjoys the media-protected legitimacy that it does today. Liberals, who, prior to the war, had been viewed as a scattering of weirdoes, deadbeats, antisocial loners, and weak-minded underdogs, were now being portrayed by the media as a good and just class of angry, organized protestors, an admirable grassroots movement with a legitimate gripe. (Secret: It makes a better movie plot.) Those of us who were around back then will never forget the rage and chaos. The war was very unpopular—at least, according to most media reports. The young hated the old, and vice versa; liberals hated conservatives, and vice versa; and long-haired males despised any guy who had a short (military) haircut. The liberal point of view drowned out that of the conservatives; it was everywhere—books, magazines, movies, television—and there was an unmistakable undertone of communist sympathy. This was, of course, long before the collapse of the Soviet Union. Today, the idea of communism as superior to capitalism is no longer taken seriously by anyone with even a modicum of common sense. Unfortunately, those who fall into this category are far too few. Those who do not may number in the millions.

Notable Liberal Quote

"No member of our generation who wasn't a communist or a dropout in the thirties is worth a damn." —President Lyndon B. Johnson[348]

Yes, a Democratic President of the United States of America *actually said that.* Believe it or not.

The prevailing storyline of the "unbiased" media back then was that conservatives were "angry" and "stupid" and "mean," and liberals could do no wrong—instead of *no right.* Every low-quality, unwashed, pot-smoking, wine-gulping, flea-bitten ne'er-do-well was given instant stature as a war protester, and every naïve

---

[348] This moron served as president of the United States of America from 1963 to 1969, and his legacy still lives on.

and promiscuous shoplifting runaway piece of white trash with braless breasts flopping around in a dirty undershirt was labeled and ennobled by the liberal media as a wonderful flower child.[349] Today, that media myth still persists, along with the perception of hippies as romantic revolutionaries fighting for freedom—rather than fighting for shelter, drugs, money, and food, and for eating scraps of wings and legs at night from Chicken Little dumpsters. (It's probably just a coincidence, but have you ever noticed that men with long, flowing locks are always pictured on the covers of *fantasy* novels?)

You should meet some of these people in person!

Those of us who were youngsters at that time didn't know for sure what was going on. Liberals exposed themselves—literally—during the Vietnam War.[350] Those were the days when wide-eyed little boys were likely to catch a glimpse of a trashy braless woman's nipples at a grocery store or a gas station when their parents stopped to fuel their car. Those were the days when wounded soldiers back home from the jungle or the Mekong Delta could be seen drinking at neighborhood bars in wheelchairs.[351] And believe it or not, when some of them returned home, they were scorned. Those were the days when the Doors musician Jim Morrison was arrested at a concert for whipping out his you-know-what (five-star genitals) on

---

[349] "Luckily, Moses, one of the chosen people, climbed to the top of Mount Sinai and then handed us two stone tablets, upon which were inscribed by God, with a hammer and chisel, the Ten Commandments. 'The chosen people' is the chosen religious name of today's Jewry (people whose ancient ancestors didn't later become Christians). The Ten Commandments helped curtail trashy behavior and, in some cases, bring it to a screeching halt. But now it's back again, and it's worse than ever!" —Angela Z.

[350] Prior to the 1960s, very few Americans knew much or even cared much about liberalism. Most people didn't even know what a liberal was. Apparently, nobody was paying much attention to the conglomeration of human weaknesses (*naiveté, greediness, narcissism*, etc.) and the resulting judgmental unsoundness that had been steadily growing since the early 1900s. How could they possibly know that it would eventually metamorphose into an organized political force that is virtually impossible to deal with? Liberals began to appear on the political scene around 1920, the same year women earned the right to vote after their suffering and efforts during World War I (1914–1918). This right was granted with the passage of the Nineteenth Amendment to the Constitution, which provided this: "The right of citizens of the United States to vote shall not be denied or abridged by the United States or by any State on account of sex." But things have changed drastically since the 1920s. Now, Washington, D.C., is visibly populated with a multitude of naïve multicultural liberal socialist Democrats who are constantly making excuses for their childish behavior and mistakes. Why? Because male and female political candidates who resemble children instinctively appeal to the vast majority of American females. Undoubtedly, many housewives will vote for a man who resembles the type of overly friendly male sissy who appears on daytime children's television shows. But why are women so easily fooled by political candidates who look and act like dodos? *It is genetic:* Women tend to be swayed by a candidate's physical appearance, whereas men tend to be more analytical. Throughout history, men have had to follow leaders into war and risk their lives, so men instinctively choose only those leaders whose judgment they trust—so they won't be killed. Only a political puppet would do otherwise.

[351] Any wounded veteran who thinks that he fought in a war against the enemies of the United States of America for nothing needs to realize that he helped eliminate plenty of bad actors from the human gene pool, so his efforts were not in vain. In the larger scheme of things, he made a big difference.

stage in front of a cheering crowd.[352] Those were the days when it wasn't unusual to be woken up in the middle of the night by a screaming teenage girl on LSD wandering down the street, stark naked, staring up at the moon. Unsuspected by anyone, most of the television news media was liberal and they were in control of public perception. Ignorant and uncivilized behavior, including murder, mayhem, bank robbery, and bomb throwing, was presented to society as a form of government protest that might possibly be justifiable and even worthy of respect. The image of radicals as cop-killing heroes persists in many quarters even to this day.

Back in the '60s, many newspaper editors (at least, those who were liberal socialist Democrats), began to stop reporting that "a black man raped a white woman" in order to discourage racial animosity. They insisted that all writers and reporters leave out the words "black" and "white," so that members of the newly named *African-American community*, including their leaders and their organizers, would not be offended.

It was also at about this same time that discussions on television about illegal drug use began to become acceptable. Prior to that, such discussions would have been considered repugnant. Soon, comedians using the word "LSD" in the punchline of a joke began to elicit uneasy kneejerk laughter, despite the very real danger of future flashbacks. Also, using the words "pot," "weed," and "grass"—instead of the illegal plant's real name, *marijuana*—was considered "hip" and "cool" by liberal male and female know-little-or-nothing college campus intellectuals.[353]

Most conservative-leaning teenagers—and probably many adults, as well—having no idea that they were being overwhelmed with subtle anti-conservative liberal propaganda, began to question their own opinions and felt awkward, unsure, and out of place. How could a teenager have confidence in his or her own views and beliefs when all of the news anchors—people like Walter Cronkite, who was universally liked and respected—always seemed to have opinions that were contrary to his or her own? We kids didn't understand and wouldn't until decades later.

It was also in the 1960s that the liberal celebration of human abnormality began to rear its ugly head. Liberals, backed by other liberals throughout the media and by ever-increasing numbers of liberals against the war, were encouraged to seize upon the opportunity to actually begin ridiculing ordinary, law-abiding citizens

---

[352] To be fair, some teenagers present at the Doors concert said that nothing bad really happened that night. Who knows? Morrison's antics may have been nothing more than the germination of today's offensive African American (hip-hop) salute: the habitual crotch grab that even grade school kids often do in public these days. It happened a long time ago, so who can say for sure?

[353] Through the use of films and television, the liberal media-enhanced 1960s drug culture and other social anomalies have now been established as normal, thus creating an open gateway to more deviant human behavior. Hopefully, this book will help close the unknown liberal Hollywood other-dimensional portal.

(i.e., conservatives), and it was even the subject of derogatory liberal song: *"Hey, there, Mr. Normal..."*—or some such rot. Any conservative who was around back then probably hasn't forgotten and probably never will. So what kind of people would ridicule normality? Why, the abnormal, of course:

> P.E.T.S. with mouths full of bullshit, ears full of cotton, and heads full of F.A.D. *(fantasy addiction disorder).*

Today, liberals are still trying to promote and mainstream abnormality and have had some limited temporary success. The current fad seems to be to help and encourage transsexuals, lesbians, the mentally retarded, and midgets to marry and even bear offspring, which is now scientifically possible in all cases. Even three people—*of any sexual orientation*—can now create a child if they want. The long-term effect of this on the human genetic pool is deplorable. Not only does the likelihood of more abnormal births increase, but also the likelihood of abnormalities and combinations of abnormalities that we've never even seen before. (But the good news is, it'll increase Democratic voter rolls!)

One benefit of our experience with liberals in the '60s and early '70s is that it has helped give many conservatives the confidence and strength of conviction that we have today. Out of the fire comes hardened steel. Now we know how liberals operate. There is little, if anything, that they can pull over on us. We know them from the past. We've seen all their faces and antics before. We can identify many of today's aging former pill-poppers, pinkos, and marijuana/LSD worshippers instantly, often without even having to give them a second glance.

Back in the '60s, if films made about places such as Cuba or Venezuela had been like those made today by rebellious Hollywood liberals—with the obligatory adulation of them by liberal critics—it would have caused many conservatives to reconsider their opinions and to question their own beliefs. Why? Simply because they did not know for sure what was really going on in the world, but now things have changed. Today, most of us instantly dismiss such nonsense despite the multitude of media supporters. We've already had a taste of that liberal tripe. It should also be noted that liberal propaganda only qualifies as such if somebody other than liberals believes it. Now that conservatives are fully aware of how liberals think and behave—and sometimes even know what's going on behind closed doors—we frequently know what our liberal friends are planning to do, probably even before they do. The problem is, we're not doing anything about it. Confidence in the superiority of our beliefs and opinions over those of liberalism has caused complacency.

It's time to fight back. First, find out what your representatives are doing in government.

The Vietnam War was a military quagmire of needlessly prolonged death and destruction that ended with a victory by the enemy. After the United States of America withdrew, more than a million South Vietnamese were slaughtered by various means including decapitation, evisceration, drowning, and live burial, but interestingly enough, "compassionate" liberals—to this very day—still act like they couldn't care less. Ask any of them about it and they will probably just smile, change the subject, or simply ignore you. This loss was the result of political indecisiveness and moral weakness in Washington, D.C., caused by a shrieking cyclone of venomous liberal propaganda. The Vietnam War was the ultimate antithesis of the liberal fantasy world. Why, they were even being drafted to fight! That is why liberals went berserk, but in doing so, they exposed themselves to us completely. America's "military defeat" (it was actually a withdrawal) in Vietnam is just one of liberalism's many sad legacies, and sometimes it still seems to be in force. The morale of our military continues to be weakened by social experiments. That's not how wars are won; that's how wars are lost.

Thank you, good people, for all your fine help. Now we know you have F.A.D.

What Happened to the Sad Songs?

Here's a funny thing: Have you ever noticed how most of the antiwar protestors suddenly disappear when a Democrat is elected president—even when a war is still going on? But why? Does somebody stop paying them to scream at Republicans, or something? This reoccurring disappearance of protestors is especially remarkable, considering the increasing number of soldiers who were reportedly losing their lives in Afghanistan during the years of President Obama's first term. Aren't *casualties* what liberals care about most? Why did Hollywood actors suddenly stop throwing themselves around and purposely getting themselves arrested for the publicity? Why did liberals who want attention stop sitting on railroad tracks? More importantly, what happened to all of the sad songs? Did the famous George Soros stop mailing everyone paychecks?[354] Or did the liberal media just stop reporting

---

[354] George Soros (/ s ro s/ or / s r s/) is a U.S. immigrant who was born to a Jewish family in Budapest, Hungary, on August 12, 1930. His real name is Schwartz György. He is known as the man who broke the Bank of England because of his $1 billion in investment profits during the 1992 Black Wednesday currency crisis in the United Kingdom. France convicted him of insider trading in 2005. He is a well-known supporter of "progressive" liberal political causes. But why? Did he figure out that if you destroy a country's economy—along with the standard of living of millions of people—the value of gold will skyrocket? (A tricky investor could make a fortune.)

anything that throws a bad light on the president? What will it take for all of the players and actors to come out of the woodwork again—another Republican in the White House? It kind of makes you wonder what their complaint really is, doesn't it? Maybe it's not the body bags that bother liberals so much. Maybe all they really care about is improving their poll numbers. (If you're skeptical, don't forget what liberals are all about: self-interest and delusion—and *illusion*.) If so, they are a clear and present danger to all men, women, and children in any civilized society.

> "Why do so many Democrats consider a president's military decisions, when made for personal political reasons, to be okay? Don't they realize that when American men and women in uniform are unknowingly sacrificed just to further some smooth-talking politician's career, it's criminal?" —Walter W., "Wag The Dog," Geopolitical Analyst

A Few Notes on a Previous War

As the old put-down goes, "We sure could have used *you* back in World War II." Of course, plenty of liberals *did* fight in World War II, but they were a far different breed. For one thing, their opinions were more rooted in reality, and for another thing—coincidentally enough—their lives didn't revolve around illegal drug use. (For example, just watch some old reruns of "The Lawrence Welk Show." At least twenty percent of them would be the liberals of today. You make the comparison.) Back then, illegal drugs were not readily available. But today, they are. The problem is that many liberals don't just use drugs, they *feed* on drugs—regularly. For these people, staying high is a big part of life. As might be expected, constant drug use can make a big difference in a person's state of mind, not to mention his or her physical appearance. Illegal drug use can affect some people's minds permanently.

I once had a job where many of my coworkers were amiable old leather-skinned World War II veterans, along with a couple of Korean War vets. Some of them had fought the Japanese on remote islands in the Pacific and the Germans in France. Soldiers who have been to the edge of hell and back see the world much differently than people who have not. They often understand things that others do not. They view life as a gift, not as a right. For seven years, I listened to their tales and war stories. One of them told me about the barn his squad discovered full of dead German soldiers. The Germans had obviously been rounded up before being executed with pistols/rifles—despite the protocols of the Geneva Convention. The Germans, of course, did the same thing. In World War II, it was not unusual for prisoners to be taken out of sight, questioned, and then shot. Just because civilians did not hear about it does not mean that it did not happen. That's because war is serious business. It's not a game played with any thought of losing. When soldiers' lives are on the line, they do whatever it takes to get the job done. Today's liberal socialist Democrats probably do not even comprehend—or want to believe—a single word of this.

I also heard a story from these men about all of the starving women in liberal France after the Nazi occupation and their frantic offers to have sex with soldiers in exchange for food, drink, or just small pieces of chocolate bars. Sometimes, long lines of men formed, so you can be sure that there were no puffed-up, self-important liberal females admonishing Army generals for calling them ma'am. Some readers may also be surprised to learn that criminal activity takes place in the military just as it does in the rest of society, and it is not unheard of for a soldier to have his wallet stolen at gunpoint by another. The criminal element is everywhere, and crime is on the increase. As a society downgrades, so does its military. The two do not exist separately. They depend on one another. Liberalism's degenerative influence is not restricted to our television sets and public schools. It has far-reaching consequences. As we have already seen, it can affect the outcome of a war.

Those who've experienced war firsthand and have had to live in mud holes or in the sand or behind rocks in the middle of nowhere, or who have spent days on end sweating inside armored tanks know real life far better than those who learn about it from reading liberal-authored fiction and/or politically correct college textbooks. So all of us should pay close attention to what our war veterans have to say. Men and women who risk their lives defending this country deserve our respect, admiration, and gratitude, not apathetic left-wing smirks, scorn, ridicule, and liberal spit.[355]

Why don't liberals like the military? The U.S. military protects their right to breed.

---

[355] What other group of U.S. citizens beside liberals would make fun of severely injured American soldiers, including military women, under the guise of doing charity work? It's a disgrace—*a national disgrace*—and yet they are allowed to continue to do it with apparent glee on television unchecked. Think about how the wounded soldiers who see it must feel. The liberals' objective here is clear: to hurt their political opponents by making fun of the U.S. military and lowering their morale. No wonder foreign countries look upon America with such scorn. We must appear to be fools of the highest order.

Human (D) Evolution

Red States and Blue Dress States

Red states, Blue states—do you ever have difficulty remembering the difference?[356] Which vote Republican? Which vote Democratic? Here's a little info to help keep you from forgetting. During the 2000 presidential election, Democrats intentionally tagged the Republicans with red (as in "communist red") because they were afraid of their own party being associated with this color. Republicans didn't worry about it because everyone knows they're anti-communist, so there has never been a problem.

Many L.S.D.ers, in contrast, have well-known leanings toward socialism and communism. In some cases, this has been publicly acknowledged. That's why the color red is simply *too appropriate* for the Democratic Party. They prefer that the public think of them differently—which requires lots of smoke and mirrors.[357] That's why the D.N.C. abhors the implication of certain colors of their Rainbow Coalition. Yellow is another one, for obvious reasons. Be assured that many Democrats running for public office no more want to be associated with Chinese communists than a town drunk who has been arrested multiple times wants to be seen drinking a quart of Jeremiah Weed.

Why are liberals in D.C. and Hollywood always glad-handing socialists, communists, union thugs, and dictators? Is it because all of the world's infamous tyrants are and were really nothing more than brutal iron-fisted liberals—with screws loose? Years ago, prior to the 1988 Lockerbie bombing, in which 259 airplane passengers and crew were killed, pictures of Libyan leader Muammar Gaddafi with the caption "BROTHER KHADAFFY IS RIGHT!" could be seen taped to street signs and tacked on telephone poles in ghetto neighborhoods all across the South. It's puzzling. If people born and raised in the United States of America consider a mental defective like "Brother Khadaffy" to be right, then whom do they believe is wrong? The United States? The U.S. military? The list of Libyans who

---

[356] Blue states are sometimes referred to as "blue dress states" because of Monica Lewinsky's famous blue dress with a U.S. president's stain on it. In 1995, President Bill Clinton, full of liberal joy, had sex with Lewinsky, a young intern, in the Oval Office. It was a national disgrace. It's the legacy of eight years (1993 to 2001) of the Clinton White House—that and the North Atlantic Free Trade Agreement (N.A.F.T.A.), which had the ultimate effect of putting millions of Americans out of work, and thus forcing people dependent on the Democratic Party to support Democratic candidates. Can the United States of America absorb another eight more years of Bill and his wife Hillary's leadership and unusual relationship? Their photos can be found in fifteen-year-old dictionaries.

[357] The same goes for "the Recovery." Everything that the Democrats do is smoke and mirrors. Nothing has changed for the better since Obama took office. Just listen to the National Debt Clock. It's still ticking—louder and louder, like a time bomb ready to explode! The ballooning National Debt has lowered every American's standard of living. It may take a hundred years for the United States of America to recover from what liberal socialist Democrats have done.

219

were beaten and tortured in prison cells? For most of us who live in the civilized world, it's difficult to even imagine the kind of diseased thinking that would support a person like Gaddafi—although in the Middle East, Islamic leaders like him are not unusual at all. He was a close supporter of Ugandan president Idi Amin (another handsome guy), who was also a supporter of world terrorism.[358] Who in his or her right mind admires such psychotic creeps? The same sort who admire communist prison camps? Or who prefer Islam over the United States? Is this communism, Islamism, or just ignorantism?

> "Why don't we just deport all foreign-Americans who refuse to condemn radical Islam? What's the F.B.I. supposed to do, follow them around everywhere to make sure they don't take photos of office buildings?" —Anonymous Analyst

Probably, in this particular case, it's all three combined. So what exactly is communism, anyway? Communism is a political theory introduced by Karl Marx that advocates class war (that's right, class warfare—sound familiar?). This leads to a society in which all property is publicly owned and each person works and is paid by the government according to his or her abilities and needs. Socialism, in Marxist theory, is a transitional social state that occurs between the overthrow of capitalism and the ultimate takeover of communism. In other words, socialism is just communism lite.

It was only fifty years ago that communism was taken very seriously in the United States of America and was considered to be the number-one threat to our country and our way of life. (Now, *liberalism* has taken over that spot.) Everyone was constantly on guard for any indication of communist influence and was very suspicious of anything new that came along that they did not completely understand. Even the fluoridation of public water was widely suspected to be a communist plot. It might surprise you to know that, at that time, communists were considered much worse than racists, and a person's reputation and career could be destroyed if an investigation determined that he or she was a Soviet sympathizer. But, inevitably, things change, and today, we don't worry too much about communism. The idea that communists could take over and destroy the United States seems about as likely as black stovetop hats coming back into style—but if the public's tastes change, maybe they could.

---

[358] Idi Amin's notorious dictatorial rule of Uganda was characterized by gross human-rights abuse, corruption, and economic mismanagement, under which the real value of salaries and wages collapsed by 90 percent. During his eight years in power, thousands of people simply disappeared. The number of Ugandans killed and tortured by his Islamic regime has been estimated by international observers and human-rights groups to be as high as half a million.

These days, communists, like homosexuals, will often admit to their proclivity. Some liberals do not even try to hide the fact that they are avowed; some even seem to be proud of it. Others, less bold, declare themselves merely socialists. Nevertheless, the rhetoric of liberals makes them all highly suspect, so it is probably safe to assume that many of them just haven't come out of the Red Chinese political closet yet, and we should probably try to coax them. After all, it's easily understandable why that *wonderful* foreign system of government that we refer to as communism—so popular with our Chinese and Russian "friends"—is often preferred by liberals living among us. Apparently, those who espouse communism, through no fault of their own, are too terribly ignorant, lethargic, or slothful to compete successfully in the public sector alongside their fellow man.[359] Communal sharing of all (yes, all) wealth—tasteless food, used clothing, concrete shelters, homemade toothbrushes, bread crumbs, toilet tissue squares, and dog-chewed scraps of bologna sandwiches—would appear on its utterly charming surface to help guarantee an aspiring but limpsy, socially underdeveloped subcompetent's life to be much, much better, ensuring his or her survivability and financial equality with people of higher principles and superior moral sophistication. This, of course, would allow more free time for recreational crack smoking and vodka binges behind the gorgeous dying trees and shriveled brown shrubbery in the darkness of the woods in a creepy neighborhood park. My, oh my, look at the pretty little birdy singing, "Tweet, tweet, tweet!"

Nature's wonderful wild beasts have no such safeguards against the unpredictable and dire forces of man and the elements. If a large, hairy black Russian bear, for example, is too sluggish or dull-witted, it may be unable to locate food and may thus starve, or, while crossing an interstate highway, may be hit by a speeding eighteen-wheeler and be splattered all over the place. Yet even those who are intelligent, thinking members of free Western society rarely contemplate the possibility of two pieces of future human roadkill breeding. Or emboldened nitwits gathering together to carefully falsify their names on I.D. cards and voter registration rolls so they can elect whomever they want. Or a meat-headed dolt hiding inside a Porta-Potty and inhaling a tube of superglue—or maybe two tubes: one in each nostril (which would probably be the best thing for his future ex-wife and kids).

Yes, "Ignorance"—and liberal absurdity—"is the womb of monsters."

---

[359] Don't misunderstand: A lower I.Q. is not what determines a person's affinity for communism. Even Albert Einstein (1879–1955) subscribed to communism's precepts. The stated desire for a system that ensures through force that everyone is equal by all measures—including moral stature—appears to originate in the minds of those having diminished standards and who are suboptimal in both spirit and principle. Liberals clearly desire to rise somehow above those who are superior to themselves morally. (Don't be fooled: Equality has never been their goal.) How? By dragging those with better judgment down by their white collars, blue collars, and khaki military collars and limiting their ability to excel.

John Hayberry

All the News That's Print to Fit[360]

The liberal socialist Democratic Party's policies have allowed mentally underdeveloped Third World anti-Americans to flood into our country by the hundreds of thousands. As a result, there are now people actually living here in the United States of America who think it's "cool" to be an Islamic terrorist. Approximately 15,000 foreign immigrants are even on the U.S. government's terror watch list! So what do we do now? Panic? Here's an idea: How about sending them back where they came from on the next available flight whether they like it or not. How many Boston Marathon bombings is it going to take before we all get smart? Are we going to continue to allow missing human limbs to be the liberal legislative legacy? Why is the federal government operating like a bunch of human family tree leaves "blowin' in the wind"? We Americans have a right to choose who lives in our country—and nobody has that right but us. Not Kersigkstan, or the president of Mexico, or the A.C.L.U., or C.A.I.R.[361] The litany of multicultural problems that we now face is, for the most part, the direct result of both political correctness by Republican politicians who seek to be reelected and by liberal socialist Democrats who have diminished instincts, more specifically, a decreased ability to mentalize (i.e., understand what other people are thinking).

Unfortunately, the illegitimate liberal news media will do practically anything to increase its popularity with virtually *any* liberal politician, minority group, or Democratic organization as long as a common goal exists: that of opposing conservative ideals, traditions, values, and policies. Why? Because that is what is needed to transform our country, the United States of America, into something "progressive," European-like, militarily weak, and unrecognizable. The liberal media has apparently decided that the best way to advance their cause is through appeasement and by protecting any liberal politician, union, alliance, coalition, or

---

[360] "All the News That's Fit to Print" is the slogan of the *New York Times*.
[361] "C.A.I.R. [the Council on American-Islamic Relations] has more influence on the media than any other group" (Glenn Beck, *The Glenn Beck Radio Program*, April 18, 2013). "CAIR is a powerful front organization, and they hold power in all of the networks and the news outlets, and the government [by determining what words our media can and cannot use in describing Islam]" (GlennBeck.com, "Responding to the Tragedy in Boston: Build up His Kingdom," April 16, 2013). "CAIR is growing in influence. CAIR has infiltrated all of our media, CAIR has infiltrated our government, our Pentagon. CAIR is a front group for the Muslim Brotherhood. I'm convinced of it. They have unindicted co-conspirators. That's not me saying that. That's a federal judge in the Holy Land trial. They are not friends of the United States, but they are friends of this [Obama] administration. This administration is putting Muslim Brotherhood members into our own Department of Defense, into our Homeland Security, into the TSA" (GlennBeck.com, "Are Muslims the Most Oppressed Group in the Country?" May 16, 2012). "CAIR is a danger to this country" (Glenn Beck, *The Glenn Beck Radio Program*, April 19, 2013). Media personality Glenn Beck is the founder and C.E.O. of Mercury Radio Arts, a multimedia production company through which he produces content for radio, television, publishing, the stage, and the Internet. His news Web site is TheBlaze.com.

association, so they manipulate public perception by *never saying anything negative about L.S.D.ers.*

> "There was a time in America's history when subversives, deserters, and traitors were shot. But now, they're often treated like celebrities by liberal politicians and the television news media, as though they are worthy of praise and might even qualify for a job in Washington, D.C.—maybe even at the White House!" —Don F.

That's why those in the media always use language designed to put liberal persons, policies, and D.N.C. support groups and donors in the most positive light possible (e.g., refusing to use the term "Islamic extremist" even when it is clearly applicable).[362] It is time to put a lid on suboptimal foreign influence in American politics.

Liberal and Conservative Opinions Are *Not* Equally Valid.

Should the opinions of liberals and conservatives be given equal weight? If you don't already know the answer to this question, you should probably review what you've read so far. One reason that liberal opinion differs so sharply from that of conservatives is that most liberals, as they will readily admit, base their decisions on personal *feelings*. Conservatives, in contrast, generally try to ignore their feelings and base their decisions on a logical analysis of the *facts*. As many of us have

---

[362] Apparently, FOX News was the only channel willing to use the term "Islamic extremist" following the Boston Marathon bombing in which four people were killed and over a hundred injured. The surviving bomber, Dzhokhar Tsarnaev, described as an ethnic Chechnyan Islamic pothead, was visibly malevolent and dead inside. His older brother, described by those who knew him as a *devout Muslim* and by his uncle as a loser, was reportedly receiving liberal welfare checks. In the end, he was peppered with bullets and killed, either by himself with an explosive device or by the advancing swarm of police. Shortly after the bombing, even before the chaos had ended and the perpetrators were apprehended, homemade peace signs began appearing in the Boston Public Gardens. Incredibly, some Democratic officials and pundits appearing on camera in the days that followed seemed overly unconcerned, almost amused, about the whole affair—as though nothing of any importance had really happened.

learned, however, the quality of *reverse veracity* can give liberal opinion a certain intrinsic value. For example, if a person has little or no knowledge about a particular subject, he or she can usually count on what a liberal says to be patently untrue. (E.g., "Waterboarding doesn't work," "Mandatory health insurance will save money," "The economy has turned around," "Global warming is going to cause massive flooding,"[363] "You can keep your doctor," and "I did not have sexual relations with that woman.") It's uncanny. When liberals say they like something, you can usually bet your bottom dollar that it's an awful idea. If liberals say they don't like something, then, almost without exception, you can count on the fact that it's the right thing to do. Also, when liberals "take umbrage" or profess outrage, this is a sure indication that an important truth of some kind has been told. Yes, when liberals become upset and begin protesting, it generally means that something good and positive for society has occurred, so we can kick off our shoes, sit back, and relax.

Make no mistake about it; the liberal reverse-veracity indicator is a valuable tool. (Example: No matter what your views may be about same-sex marriage—whether you're for it or against it or still weighing the facts and haven't quite made up your mind yet—when someone like Vice President Joe Biden says he's "absolutely comfortable" with the idea, the hair should immediately stand up on the back of your neck.)

Now, for anyone who still believes that liberalism and conservatism are nothing more than two opposing points of view, each having equal legitimacy, consider the following comparison.

Conservatives most often claim that liberals

- are illogical,
- ignore facts,
- ignore history,
- are naïve, and
- are disingenuous.

---

[363] "According to calculations made by one conservative think tank, the United States could decrease so-called global warming by at least 10 percent if liberals would just stop smoking marijuana, burning American flags, and producing methane gas after eating tofu." —Mighty Mouse, contributing editor

Human (D) Evolution

Liberals most commonly claim that conservatives

- are mean,
- are racist,
- are uncaring,
- are greedy, and
- are very, very bad people.

Notice the difference between the way liberals and conservatives describe one another. Now ask yourself which group most closely resembles an adult at odds with a child and which most resembles a child at odds with an adult. More importantly, note that liberals rarely claim that conservatives are illogical or ignore facts. Instead, liberals bob and weave and obfuscate. That detail alone would cause most objective observers to instantly conclude that the conservative viewpoint is by far the more worthy. Believing that a liberal's views are simply the opposite of those held by a conservative but are just as valid is kind of like believing that vomit is the opposite of food but is just as good to eat.

Furthermore, there is really no such thing as a conservative, per se, because the word *conservatism* (a noun) is nothing more than a synonym for *normality*, so it's like calling someone "a normal." It's kind of like making doctors and nurses in a psychiatric hospital fill out medical charts on themselves even though they're not sick in the head and then making them wear identification bracelets, as though they are mental patients. Because today we label normality as conservatism, many uninformed persons (i.e., 95 percent of registered voters) now mistake the belief system of conservatives and liberals as being two equally sound choices, both rational in nature. It's nonsense. Society has been led to believe this for so long, it is now virtually impossible for most of us to conceive of the truth.

A Famous Liberal Quote

Let us never forget the immortal words of our legendary liberal Democratic President John F. Kennedy: "And so, my fellow Americans, ask not what your country can do for you; ask what you can do for your country." This wise-and-noble-sounding blather, commonly believed by 99.9 percent of the liberal Democrat community to be one of the greatest quotes of all time (other than, perhaps, those of Chairman Mao) was read in a televised speech aimed at millions of screaming fans, some of whom desperately sought Kennedy's autograph, a saintly lock of his reddish hair, or a piece of his zipper.

It was a *stupid* question. The real question we should be asking instead is this: What the heck kind of pathetic boob would be standing around in the first place, whining, "What can my country do for me?" (Here is the secret liberal translation: "I'm stupid and lazy and sleep sixteen hours a day, so what can my tax-paying neighbors gimme outta their wallets?")

It's really not a puzzle at all why Kennedy chose to address such an ignorant question. In fact, it's crystal clear. He did it in response to drunken shouts from naïve cretins, dead heads, and smarmy liberal campaign contributors in the pushing, shoving, and elbowing crowd. You see, the truth is, such a question would not even cross a normal person's mind. Why should it? Who is it that gets out of bed in the morning wondering what all of his neighbors—including complete and total strangers: men, women, and children—are going to do for him today? He would have to be a borderline mental invalid.

As far as "what you can do for your country" goes, that's a no-brainer: Just file a federal income tax return and *pay what you owe*—you know, like all well-known and prestigious Democrats (e.g., our good friends T. D., C. W., and T. G.) do.

Frogs in a Pond

Imagine two groups of frogs in a small body of water. One group is composed of normal, healthy frogs, and the other group is mostly abnormal (six-legged, four-eyed, two-tongued). Now, suppose we refer to one group as "mjkwxzp" and to the other as "wtypzqt," rather than as normal and abnormal. Anyone not familiar with this terminology would assume that the groups of swimming, hopping, and croaking amphibians were simply two different types with generally equal capabilities. What person would suspect without being told any specific details that one group of frogs is normal and the other group requires constant hand feeding by little children to stay alive?

That is why so-called *bipartisan compromise* (i.e., a partially evil agreement) between Republicans and Democrats is not as good as it is popularly portrayed. It's not a bargain between conservatives and liberals, between rich and poor, between successful and unsuccessful, or between the happy and the sad; it's a covenant between good and evil.[364] As such, it will always—without exception—result in

---

[364] "Biblical scholars refer to this as the 'Mystery of Inequity,' predicted to occur in the 'Last Days.'"
—D. Falcon, editor

unnecessary pain and suffering, if not death. This has been proven repeatedly throughout man's history.

Liberal White Lies

Liberal propaganda knows no bounds. You'll be interested to know, for example, that during the War Between the States (1861–1865), the word *miscegenation* was coined in an anonymous pamphlet entitled "Miscegenation: The Theory of the Blending of the Races, Applied to the American White Man and Negro." It was published in New York City in December of 1863. It purportedly advocated, as a cultural goal, the intermarriage of whites and blacks until they were indistinguishably mixed. The pamphlet further asserted that this was the objective of the mean and angry Republican Party: that white people have sexual intercourse with blacks. What the American people didn't know at the time was that this little pamphlet, which more than likely helped fuel numerous physical attacks on blacks—including lynching—was actually *a hoax concocted by liberal Democrats* to discredit innocent Republicans by attributing to them radical views that offended the vast majority of Americans, including most Democrats themselves.

So who were the ones doing all the lynching? Other liberal Democrats? It certainly seems likely, but we will never know for sure. But in this new computer-information age, it has become increasingly clear that the new liberal Democratic Party is the party of people who think it's okay and sometimes even funny to physically attack others with whom they disagree and don't like—no matter who, or what sex, or what color they are!

Just take a look at the loony Occupy Wall Street (OWS) protestor/rioter types (sometimes referred to as "scabies farmers gone wild"). Do you really believe that jobless liberals like that are beyond lynching well-groomed, content African American men just minding their own business and walking on the sidewalk? Anyone who doesn't believe that they *are* should probably try to get out more often and meet a greater variety of *low-class people*. Clearly, many liberal teenagers, when they gather in a mob, have a Lord of the Fleas—excuse me, I mean, Lord of the *Flies*—mentality. Today, the American people have even begun to figure out the reason that L.S.D.ers (liberal socialist Democrats) are so pigheadedly in favor of gun-control laws and against *Stand Your Ground* is that they want to be able to beat innocent people up without being *legally shot* in defense!

Attention all African Americans: *Beware of teenage liberal Democrats.*

Is there really *anyone* still alive in the United States of America today who believes that the likes of the OWS crowd are *morally incapable* of rape and murder? If so, he or she should take a closer look at some of these drugged-out liberals' mug shots.

The miscegenation pamphlet and variations of it were reprinted widely in both the North and South and likely added to the uncounted number of blacks murdered on the streets around the time of the New York Draft Riots—the largest civil insurrection in U.S. history other than the Civil War itself. Only a year later, in November 1864, was the pamphlet exposed as a hoax written by David Goodman Croly, managing editor of the *New York World* (a Democratic Party paper), and George Wakeman, a *World* reporter. That same year, the *New York World* was shut down for three days after it published forged documents from Abraham Lincoln (a Republican, by the way), and its circulation battles with competitors in later years gave rise to the term "yellow journalism."

How does that saying go? The more things change, the more they stay the same? No wonder Democrats are so big on revisionist history. After all, they can't very well pass themselves off as the devoted lifelong champions of Negroes when hundreds of state and federal government records, reports, and documents indicate that the *exact opposite is true.*

Frequently Asked Questions

Q: Why is there a double standard with regard to the way liberals and conservatives are treated by the media?
A: The obvious reason is that media outlets are staffed mostly with liberals. From a psychiatric point of view, however, the double standard may be justified. You see, conservative Republicans and liberal Democrats probably *should* be held to two different standards for the same reason that adults are held to higher standards than are children. That's also why grown-ups and kids have similar but different rights and responsibilities.

Human (D) Evolution

Q: Why do liberal Democrats always appear uneasy even after one of their candidates wins an election?
A: Probably because suboptimality will never be the equivalent of optimality, no matter who wins any election. Even liberals with full-blown F.A.D. subconsciously realize this. A suboptimal person serving in a position of power over an independent and capable populace is not the natural order of things, and it never will be. That is why such a situation is predicted to end so badly.[365]

Q: Why do liberals in our state and federal governments make so many decisions that conservatives instinctively and immediately know are mistakes and that later prove to be?
A: Because liberals do not have the same genetic instincts as conservatives. Consider, for example, the difference between a husky timber wolf and a little toy poodle, or a six-foot barracuda and a tiny goldfish, or a wild mustang and a Shetland pony at the petting zoo.

Q: Why are there so many liberals in the news media, the teaching profession, and the arts?
A: It's certainly not because they're smarter. Liberals seem to be attracted to those professions in which incorrect facts, flawed logic, and nonsensical ideas just do not make any difference. Not all professions are so forgiving. For example, certified automobile mechanics must be able to figure out the correct solutions to various problems. If the air conditioner doesn't work on a pickup truck, it may need a new compressor, or a fan motor, or some Freon. A mechanic can't just automatically throw up his hands in anger, then begin crying and blame everything on fossil fuels.

Q: Why are liberal comedians often funnier than conservative comedians?
A: For the same reason that it's more entertaining to watch someone try to put a round peg in a square hole than it is to watch someone put a square peg in a square hole: The recognition of our own naïve childhood ignorance in others is what makes us all laugh. They're also funnier looking.

---

[365] On February 18, 2014, FOX News reported that there is $1 trillion outstanding in student loans. Unfortunately, many college students who were registered to vote believed everything that candidate Barack Hussein Obama told them, so after he was elected president, they ended up in financial straits. Now, it's difficult for them to find a job to pay the money back. Maybe the Republican Party can do something about it.

Q: Is there any scientific way to determine whether someone is a liberal?
A: Yes, by counting the number of pot-seed burns on his automobile upholstery, T-shirt, and loafers.

Q: What's the best-kept secret of the Democratic Party?
A: Probably, the I.Q. of Nancy Pelosi.

Part Three

The Origin of Our Left-wing Species

Chapter 13

Why Aren't They Nice To People?

The Descent of Liberal Man

Unlike the origin of all other groups, such as the Irish, Italians, Germans, Poles, Africans[366], Mexicans, Puerto Ricans, and numerous additional ethnicities—including escaped circus animals—that make up our widely diverse population, the origin of liberals is not confined to any specific region of the globe. Liberalism exists in all ethnic groups, for liberals are *the fruit of all worldwide humanitarian efforts* in the form of mercy, charity, and aid. That is why here in the United States of America, our already multicultural population includes a growing number of Mercy Americans, Charity Americans, and Aid Americans, who, like other ethnicities, are often identifiable by their unique appearance, speech pattern, vocabulary, or behavior. Imported from 193 countries worldwide, today's high-and-mighty fire-breathing liberals are, to put it bluntly, the ungrateful genetic descendants of surviving traitors, fools, pacifists,[367] and cowards (with all due respect, of course)

---

[366] The continent of Africa is made up of fifty-four different countries, some of which are still being named by foreign explorers. Here are just a few of them: Angola, Rwanda, Chad, Botswana, Democratic Republic of Congo (formerly "the Congo"), Equatorial Guinea, Ghana, Gabon, Ivory Coast, Mali, Kenya, Ethiopia, Tanzania, the Island of Madagascar, Liberia, Libya, Mozambique (sometimes pronounced "Mozam-B-Que" because it was once inhabited by cannibals who cooked their victims), Nigeria, Somalia (also known as the "Horn of Africa"), Sudan, Swaziland, Uganda, Zimbabwe, Togo, Niger, etc.

[367] If a person is allergic to milk, that means his or her ancestors were probably hunters, not farmers, and did not drink any milk. If a person is allergic to shellfish, that means his or her ancestors probably lived inland, rather than near the sea, and did not eat any shellfish. If a person is allergic to war, that means his or her ancestors were probably pacifists, not warriors or soldiers, and refused to fight any wars. Instead, they became victims of tyranny, oppression, and enslavement.

and generally have the fierce fighting instincts of helpless domestic servants. That is why the unfathomable lack of logic of some contemporary L.S.D.er politicians and pundits can be so breathtaking.[368] The liberal lineage is primarily—but, of course, not entirely—seen standing in line at soup kitchens, sitting cross-legged on the ground at bus stops, and wandering aimlessly around church projects wearing clothing purchased at the Salvation Army (or orange prison garb) and stolen shoes—or perhaps, in drug-induced nakedness, nothing at all—and holding a government check in one hand and a bag of free cell phones in the other. Liberals are the colorful produce of family trees forever watered by compassionate, mostly conservative, human gardeners. Liberals are the not-so-surprising yet still unanticipated product of Good Samaritanism. As with most marketplace baskets of fruits, nuts, and vegetables, the very best and most attractive ones—the movie stars, media figures, and handsome politicians—appear on the very top, concealing all of the defective refuse below that are visibly rotten at a glance and so must be hidden from everyone's sight (like the teeth and toenails of methamphetamine addicts) in order for liberalism to be able to sell its bill of goods to the public. People with few, if any, morals tend to do things that *benefit themselves only*, with little or no regard for the effect that it has on other people's lives. For that reason, such people can be accurately labeled as walking talking human trash.[369] However, we must all face the fact that none of our ancestors lived in a vacuum, and so there is undoubtedly at least a smidgen of liberal in all of us—*without exception*—not to mention the inarguable presence of liberal DNA in the skeletal remains of Adolph Hitler.[370]

In other words, absolutely no one is exempt.

> "Apparently, some liberals heard about Darwin's theory that man evolved from the apes, so they figured that since human beings are just animals, it's okay to do anything an animal does." —Anonymous

---

[368] Did the president, for example, decline to order any response team deployed when our diplomatic mission compound in Benghazi, Libya, was attacked? The next day, despite the murder of Ambassador Chris Stevens—the first U.S. ambassador killed by terrorists in more than thirty years—along with three other brave Americans, it was White House business as usual: Commander in Chief Obama flew to Las Vegas to engage in campaign fundraising.

[369] This term is just one of the reasons why liberals try so hard to manipulate and control everyone's use of language. They seek to eliminate any possibility of a return to the common language of a prior era, when everything, including liberals, was clearly defined with confidence and accuracy.

[370] A few quotes by Adolph Hitler: (1) "Society's needs come before the individual's needs," (2) "We are Socialists, we are enemies of today's capitalistic economic system for the exploitation of the economically weak, with its unfair salaries, with its unseemly evaluation of a human being according to wealth and property instead of responsibility and performance, and we are determined to destroy this system under all conditions," and (3) "National Socialism will use its own revolution for establishing a new world order" (Liberty-Tree.ca., "Adolph Hitler Quotes," n.d.).

"Liberal human genes will probably always be with us, but our liberal behavior can be controlled. Some religion may be required." —C. G. (2014)

A Timeline of the History of Slavery

Slavery is undoubtedly as old as prostitution. It's an ancient practice in which laborers who work for minimal compensation—sometimes only food and water—are treated as property to be bought and sold. In the distant past, the institution of slavery was acknowledged and endorsed by Christianity, Judaism, and Islam, as well as other religions. The Islamic Qur'an, for example, not only condones the slavery of any non-Muslim but also discusses it in detail.[371] Slavery has been illegal in the United States for almost 150 years, even though liberals act like it's only been a couple of months, so there's no one living today who was alive back then. Historically, slavery has been accepted by societies all over the world—which, by the way, includes Martha's Vineyard (no, I'm not joking). In more recent times, however, the criminal practice of enslaving people has been declared illegal, but conditions tantamount to slavery continue to exist in the dreadful forms of human trafficking, serfdom, debt bondage, indentured servitude, domestic servants kept in captivity, child soldiers, forced marriage, involuntary prostitution, and adoption of fatherless and motherless children who are put to work as slaves.

Slavery, which undoubtedly predates historical records, has existed, in one form or another, in virtually all cultures. Surprisingly, the overall number of slaves in the world today is said to be higher than at any other point in recorded history. Over the past couple of hundred years, the term slavery has erroneously begun to be associated with the enslavement of Negroes by white Anglo-Saxon Protestants, but historically, there were no racial associations. It is also known that for the past 5,000 years, the enslavement of various groups of people, typically prisoners of war—or captured liberal "fellas," "dudes," and "blokes"—has been commonplace. No known form of slavery exists in the animal world; the practice is uniquely human.

---

[371] Wikipedia, "Islamic Views on Slavery," March 7, 2013. As in many other cultures, eunuchs, women-haters, and effeminate males were preferred as slaves because they could be trusted not to mate with the females.

Human (D) Evolution

A brief historical timeline follows.

4.5 million B.C. The dawn of man. . . . When did human slavery begin? No one knows.

2100 B.C. Records treat slavery as an established institution, not a new practice. The Sumerian Code of Ur-Nammu (circa 2100 B.C.–2050 B.C.) is the oldest known tablet containing laws regarding all male and female slaves.[372]

1760 B.C. The Babylonian Code of Hammurabi (circa 1700 B.C.) refers to slavery as an established institution and makes distinctions between the freeborn, freed, and slave.[373]

3rd century B.C. Emperor Ashoka abolishes the slave trade and encourages people to treat male and female slaves well but does not abolish slavery itself in the Maurya Empire, covering the majority of India, which is under his rule.[374]

168 B.C. After the battle of Pydna, Macedonians are sold as slaves in Rome. Most prices vary from the equivalent of $50 to $75. Prices for female slaves are as high as $1000.[375]

71 B.C. The revolt of male slaves and gladiators led by Spartacus and others against the Roman republic is crushed by consuls Pompey and Crassus.[376]

1300 A.D. The lucrative European slave trade temporarily ends.[377]

1441 Portuguese navigators find and capture Negroes near Cape Blanc, western Africa, so they restart the slave trade.[378]

---

[372] Encyclopædia Britannica, "History of Mesopotamia," 2013. The content of the Code of Ur-Nammu is not yet completely known.
[373] "Code of Hammurabi, c. 1780 BCE," Fordham University, Ancient History Sourcebook, 1998. A slave bore an identification mark that could be removed only by a surgical operation, and it later consisted of his owner's name tattooed or branded on his arm.
[374] Wikipedia, "Abolition of Slavery Timeline," March 17, 2013.
[375] Bernard Grun, *The Timetables of History*, based upon Werner Stein's *Kulturfahrplan,* 1963, F.A. Herbig Verlagsbuchhandlung, Simon & Schuster, New York, N.Y., p. 21.
[376] Ibid., p. 22.
[377] Ibid., p. 183.
[378] Ibid., p. 207.

1509 Bartolomé de Las Casas, Roman Catholic bishop of Chiapas, proposes that each Spanish settler should bring a certain number of working slaves to the New World.[379]

1511 Friar Antonio de Montesinos preaches in Hispaniola against the incarceration and enslavement of innocent Indians.[380]

1517 Las Casas, the first priest ordained in the New World, protests the seizure and enslavement of (guilty) Indians.[381]

1518 A license to import 4,000 African slaves to the Spanish American colonies is granted to Lorens de Gominot.[382]

1555 John Lok, a successful London trader and the first Englishman ever recorded to have shipped Negro slaves from Africa, brings five of them from Guinea to his home in England.[383]

1562 Admiral Sir John Hawkins, an English shipbuilder, makes his very first journey to the New World and thus begins a profitable slave trade between Guinea and the West Indies.[384]

1619 The first surviving Negro slaves in North America arrive on the pristine shores of Virginia.[385]

1702 The Asiento Guinea Company is founded for the now-blossoming human slave trade between the dark continent of Africa and early colonial America.[386]

1712 Bloody slave revolts occur in New York City.[387]

---

[379] Ibid., p. 227.
[380] Digital History, "Antonio de Montesinos (1511)," March 24, 2013.
[381] Wikipedia, "Bartolomé de las Casas," March 24, 2013.
[382] Grun, *op. cit.*, p. 231.
[383] Wikipedia, "Slavery in the Colonial United States," March 3, 2013. The slaves reportedly came to England voluntarily.
[384] Grun, *op. cit.,* p. 249.
[385] Ibid., p. 279.
[386] Ibid., p. 321.
[387] Wikipedia, "New York Slave Revolt of 1712," March 16, 2013. Any slave caught handling a firearm received twenty lashes.

Human (D) Evolution

1730 A small reduction in the number of Chinese, Japanese, Korean, and other foreign and domestic slaves begins in China under (an increasingly unpopular) Emperor Yung Cheng.[388]

1778 An (arguably illegal) act of Congress strictly prohibits the import of females of any ethnicity into the continental United States for purposes of slavery.[389]

1792 Denmark is the very first nation to decide to abolish the international slave trade.[390]

1793 A U.S. law compels escaped human slaves—both male and female—to return to their owners.[391]

1794 The king of liberal France supposedly abolishes slavery of any kind in all of the French colonies.[392]

1807 England prohibits the growing multicultural human slave-trafficking business.[393]

1808 The United States government prohibits in no uncertain terms the importation of any more slaves from financially strapped Third World African countries.[394]

1831 Another bloody slave revolt occurs, this time in Virginia. Fifty-five innocent white men, women, and children are killed by Negroes who are quickly recaptured, put on trial, and executed by hanging.[395]

1833 Human slavery, a multicultural institution, is abolished in the British (formerly Roman) Empire.[396]

---

[388] Grun, *op. cit.,* p. 337.
[389] Ibid., p. 361.
[390] Ibid., p. 368.
[391] Ibid., p. 369.
[392] Ibid., p. 371.
[393] Ibid., p. 379.
[394] Ibid., p. 378.
[395] Ibid., p. 394.
[396] Ibid., p. 399.

1842 The British Consul General in Morocco, as part of his endeavor to bring about the abolition of slavery, asks the sultan of that Islamic country what measures, if any, he has taken to accomplish this goal. The astonished sultan replies in a letter: "The traffic in slaves is a matter on which all sects and nations have agreed from the time of the sons of Adam . . . up to this day."[397]

1848 Abolished in liberal France in 1794, slavery finally ends in France fifty-four years later.[398]

1865 The American War Between the States (the Civil War) ends, and the Thirteenth Amendment to the Constitution is passed, abolishing the captivity and forced labor of human beings once and for all.[399]

1866 The Cherokee nation abolishes the practice of African slavery in exchange for some beads and trinkets and in accordance with a treaty made with the United States government.[400]

1873 Slave markets and slave exports end on the beautiful African island of Zanzibar.[401]

1886 Cuba is the last country in the Americas to abolish human slavery.[402]

1897 After giving it much thought, the Sultan of Zanzibar decides to abolish slavery, too.[403]

1910 China says that it is also abolishing human slavery.[404]

1944 A white Russian slave labor camp in Magadan, Siberia, is part of a complex in which the death rate among lucky prisoners is only about 30 percent per annum.

---

[397] Bernard Lewis, "Race and Slavery in the Middle East," Fordham University, 1994, Oxford University, chap 1, para 1.
[398] France in the United Kingdom, French Embassy, June 12, 2006.
[399] Grun, *op. cit.*, p. 428.
[400] Wikipedia, "Cherokee Freedmen Controversy," February 21, 2013.
[401] Grun, *op. cit.*, p. 434.
[402] J. A. Sierra, "End of Slavery in Cuba," n.d.
[403] Grun, *op. cit.*, p. 451.
[404] Wikipedia, "Slavery," March 22, 2013. The practice of slavery continues unofficially in some regions of China. In June and July 2007, some 550 Asians who had been enslaved by brick manufacturers in Shanxi and Henan were freed by the Chinese government.

Outside work is compulsory until the temperature reaches –50°C, and the food ration of prisoners is reduced to the starvation level if they do not fulfill norms. It is difficult for prisoners to live on the camp rations for more than a couple of years, so the fate of most inmates follows a lovely pattern of "sickness, self-mutilation, suicide."[405]

Post 1950 During the last active years of the communist-socialist (i.e., liberal) Russian dictator Stalin, the white slave labor camp population numbers at least 10 million.[406]

1963 The Reverend Dr. Martin Luther King Jr. delivers his famous "I Had a Dream" speech.[407]

1966 Some slick Arab traders continue doing a flourishing business in black-skinned male and female slaves; observers estimate that as many as 125,000 blacks a year are still being sold on the slave block.[408]

1999 According to Kevin Bales of Free the Slaves (F.T.S.), an advocacy group linked with Anti-Slavery International, there are 27 million people still in slavery all over the world.[409]

2014 Despite being illegal (or at least declared so by the West), slavery continues to thrive in parts of Africa and the rest of the world, notably in Islamic countries such as Iran, Kuwait, Saudi Arabia, and Syria. Forced labor in the sub-Saharan

---

[405] Robertson, *op. cit.*, p. 462.
[406] Ibid., p. 461. Stalin has been said to have had a *mental illness*.
[407] Dr. Martin Luther King was a prominent African American activist leader of the 1960s civil rights movement. His detractors point out that he was suspected of serial adultery—an offense sometimes punishable by death in certain parts of the Middle East. He may not have even graduated from high school. There is a report of plagiarism in college. Once, in an interview with *Playboy*, he announced his idea that all African Americans should be compensated with taxpayer money for historical wrongs. He proposed the establishment of a government program to dole out a $50 billion settlement to all black people living in the United States. According to *The Smoking Gun*, Dr. King was once stabbed in the chest by a black woman with a 7-inch letter opener—with such force that it pierced his sternum. (It happened after she watched a Tarzan movie.) In 2009, liberal socialist Democrats, in an attempt to garner more votes from the "chocolate community," spent $120 million at the height of America's economic crisis to erect a thirty-foot-high memorial statue of Dr. King on a four-acre site in Washington, D.C. The liberal-designed statue, which is now being maintained by the National Park Service, was carved by the communist Chinese out of huge blocks of *white* granite. Unfortunately, it doesn't look like Mr. King, a black man, at all. It's a cacodaemonical left-wing *horror!*
[408] Robertson, *op. cit.*, p. 501. According to a report made to a meeting of the International Council of Women in Tehran, Iran (1966).
[409] *Disposable People: New Slavery in the Global Economy*, 1999, University of California Press, Berkeley/Los Angeles, p. 9. The book is available at Amazon.com.

region, for example, where there is an increasing Islamic political, religious, and economic influence, is estimated at about 660,000 people. That is approximately 5 percent of the population.[410] The once-thriving slave trade routes across West Africa have been revived after a lapse of some twenty-five years. Slavers carrying mobile telephones have reappeared with trucks, Jeeps, modern four-wheel-drive vehicles, and, on occasion, aircraft, which have replaced slow-moving camels. Poor unsuspecting children are kidnapped or purchased for $20 to $70 each by slavers in poorer states, such as Benin and Togo, and are sold into slavery in sex dens or as unpaid domestic servants for $350 each in wealthier oil-rich states, such as Nigeria and Gabon.[411] Enslavement of the genetically unwary is also prevalent in South Asia.

Slavery has existed in one form or another since the beginning of man, and it will continue to exist, but it seems probable that this widely accepted historical practice did not actually begin to take hold as an institution until the end of the Neolithic period. Archaeological data indicate that various forms of domestication of plants and animals arose independently in six separate locales worldwide, circa 8000 B.C.–5000 B.C. The advent of organized liberal enslavement most likely coincided with the end of man's nomadic hunter-gatherer existence and the beginning of sedentary societies involved in agriculture and animal husbandry. The earliest known evidence of farming has been found throughout the tropical and subtropical areas of southwestern and southern Asia, in northern and central Africa, in Central America, and in its first full-blown appearance in the Middle Eastern Sumerian cities, circa 3500 B.C. Other than women in a harem, slaves for nomadic tribes would probably have been more trouble than they were worth because it would have been difficult to keep an eye on someone who wanted to escape while the tribe was constantly on the move and preoccupied with hunting. Slaves, of course, must also be fed. Only in stationary settlements where food was plentiful would enslavement of liberals seem to offer any benefit to a slave owner. It is therefore likely that slavery as an established institution did not begin to occur until farming and permanent settlements began to appear about ten thousand years ago. Male and female slaves can help harvest crops, but they can't very well hunt game unless they are given weapons.

Whatever the case may be, it seems safe to conclude that large-scale liberal enslavement has probably existed for at least 10,000 years and has *never known racial boundaries*. The visually dramatic and all-too-common *Anglo-Saxon vs. African*-type Hollywood scenario just seems to get more attention and to sell the

---

[410] Wikipedia, "Slavery in Contemporary Africa," February 28, 2013.
[411] Anti-Slavery Society, "The Modern West African Slave Trade," 2003. The material in this report is based on a mission to West Africa by the society's secretary-general, supplemented by material from Cleophas Mally of W.A.O.-Afrique.

most tickets. Anyone captured and not executed in war would have been a likely candidate for slavery or as a domestic servant of some kind. Captives were also released after some time had passed, and they became members of a thoroughly oppressed and frightened populace, so it's likely that untold millions of our distant ancestors were enslaved for at least part of their difficult and miserable lives. This conclusion, combined with the fact that if we go back far enough in time, all human beings are ultimately related, making it highly improbable that any person alive today doesn't have at least one ancestor who was a slave.[412]

The #1 Jackass Political Tactic

It has come to the general public's attention by way of recent news reports that Democratic politicians in Washington, D.C., apparently enjoy retreating to back rooms, carefully double-locking the doors, drawing the curtains closed, and sitting hunched like flamingos and African vultures around a table, quietly discussing what nonsensical and demeaning new names they can begin calling Republicans in unison—"obstructionists," "extremists," "racists," or (most popular of all) "horrible, shameful, grandmother-killing Nazi monsters"—often for no other reason than to draw the American people's attention away from themselves in light of some new and inexplicable liberal socialist Democratic scandal or blunder. (Note that adding "-ist" to the ends of uncomplimentary words and then using those same words to describe conservative Republicans is the usual sly old liberal Democratic response to the now-proven longstanding charge that most liberals are basically socialists and communists.) This tactic, of course, fools only the remarkably ill-informed and grossly ignorant, but all Democratic politicians are well aware that the overwhelming majority of their constituency is exactly that. How important, wise, and clever that must make these crafty old experienced and seasoned—and by all appearances, socially underdeveloped and buffoonish—political devils feel!

Branding Republicans as racist was the liberal news media's frontline tactic in 2012 as it strove with all of its God-given might to help its increasingly unpopular presidential pick, Barack Hussein Obama, be reelected. As you can see, charges of racism work. But my sincere advice to all donkeyist politicians, burroist operatives, jackassist consultants, and muleist media hacks is that they should be very, very careful about making unfounded insinuations and calling respectable

---

[412] Calculations based on mitochondrial DNA studies show that even the most distantly related humans living today share a common ancestor as recently as 150,000 years ago (*DNA: The Secret of Life*, 2003, Knopf, New York, N.Y., p. 239).

local people ugly, undeserved names. If liberals persist in labeling as racist every single conservative American who fails to watch his tongue or who makes the colossal social blunder of criticizing the radical left-wing policies of a liberal half-African Democrat commander in chief, then, if the liberal name-caller is correct and the conservative is truly a racist, liberals open themselves up to an unavoidable conclusion, and that conclusion is this: "Thoroughbred" Anglo-Saxon-mongrel liberal types (e.g., an adult father and teenage son with matching ponytails and "BUCK FUSH" T-shirts), who are discernible as bird-brained liberals at a single glance, even before they open their silly mouths to speak, and no matter what their skin color—be it white, black, red, yellow, brown, or various shades of green in the bright sunlight—are . . . (drum roll and cymbals, please) . . . a *subspecies!*

Let the screaming begin.

This statement begs further explanation, of course, so here it is: Race is defined as "each of the major divisions of humankind, having distinct physical characteristics," and in biology, race refers to "a population within a species that is distinct in some way, esp. a subspecies." The perceptive person can, in all likelihood, make a successful argument that liberal males and females (perhaps we should refer to them as *Homo sapiens neanderthalensis lite*) are often inherently weak-minded and visually distinguishable for various reasons from the rest of the populace and are therefore identifiable, not only by others but also by their own ilk, with something akin to about 75 percent accuracy, and often simply by a small medium-quality black-and-white two-by-two-inch snapshot of the complete anterior part of the head between the chin and the eyebrows (i.e., the face). Radical liberal females, in particular, have a characteristic petulant and/or angry disappointment-with-humanity-and-concern-for-the-world facial expression that can easily be spotted a mile away.[413]

---

[413] Some people believe, erroneously, that liberals evolved from reptiles. They did not. Liberals evolved from apes, just like the rest of us. Nevertheless, always be wary of an odd-looking, multicolored Democrat with peculiar body language, a silly smile or speech impediment, and a "reptilian-like" glare, indicating that he or she does not want or need to be friends with anybody. This also goes for anyone claiming to be a Republican. You see, nine times out of ten, anyone who fits this description was a registered Democrat before he or she suddenly changed into a "Republican" overnight. L.S.D.ers do this so that they can be perceived as normal, run for political office, and have any chance of winning—and we all know what happens when they win an election, don't we? Also beware of liberals trying to infiltrate the Tea Party. What they will do is pretend to have conservative views until they are elected to office, then they'll do whatever the Democratic Party wants, even if it's unconstitutional. Be wary, too, of liberals in the television news media. Some of them have suddenly begun acting like mainstream conservatives now that their presidential pick, Barack Hussein Obama, is perceived by the public as unpopular. Don't be fooled by their rhetoric. It's a ruse to increase their ratings. The same liberal experts and media clowns that used to be on television acting as though Barack Obama could do no wrong are now on television acting as though Barack Obama can do no right. And you can bet your bottom dollar that when the next presidential election rolls around, those same *pseudo conservative mainstream* news people will work as hard as they possibly can to get a Democrat—no matter who he or she is—elected, and *no matter what the consequences*. They will do everything humanly possible to make Republicans look bad. That's how they got their last candidate, Barack Hussein Obama, elected. Liberal domination of the airways ought to be illegal.

It's not unusual, either, for the voices of many liberal males and females to have a unique and recognizable tone and tenor (not to mention the cheesy vocabulary). This is especially apparent in certain agenda-driven public speakers, D.N.C. mouthpieces, and popular female vocalists from the '60s, who almost seem to have been born with a dislike for their betters (i.e., the rest of the human race). This familiar sound of some liberals' voices makes their characteristic self-concerned political and societal views easily discernable and irritatingly predictable no matter what particular subject they may be talking about (how wonderful President Entertainment's economic policies are, for example). These half-smiling, pathologically angry and accusatory, lifelong-mistreated human underdogs evidently think that the world owes them something—even if they already have a million bucks. Weedy physical mannerisms, vulnerable postures, quizzical childlike facial expressions, unusual clothing (or lack of clothing), South American/African body ornaments, wacky hairstyles, and certain combinations of various mouth, tooth, and ocular features all play a part.

A conservative individual who, for whatever reason—say, the depleted value of dollar bills in his soon-to-be-worthless 401(k) retirement account—happens to *dislike* our liberal friends could therefore, by current Washington, D.C., standards, be labeled a hideous racist. Why? Because liberals, in this sense and by definition, can clearly be categorized as a separate human family tree branch, race, or ethnicity. So I would suggest that liberal Democrats cease the orchestrated name-calling. Everyone knows what's going on now, even those liberals with only half a mind.

> "Sometimes, when a sleazy person outside of politics is arrested, TV liberals like to announce that the person is a 'Republican,' when nobody knows for sure. They do this just to harm their opposition and to try to make them look bad." —Anonymous Conservative Political Analyst

> "The biggest mistake that congressional Republicans make is in thinking that liberal socialist Democrats are respectable normal people who think like they do. They don't. They're fruitcakes." —Donald Duck

> "Actually, the #1 Jackass Political Tactic is treating liberal news organizations as though they are D.N.C. front groups. After a while, they are." —John Hayberry

John Hayberry

The Little-Known U.S. Presidential "Legacies"

Our twenty-eighth president, Woodrow Wilson (1913–1921): a Democrat who was rumored to have cheated on his wife. He got the United States of America involved in World War I.

Our thirty-second president, Franklin Delano Roosevelt (1933–1945): a Democrat who is known to have cheated on his wife. He got the United States of America involved in World War II.

Our thirty-third president, Harry S. Truman (1945–1953): a Democrat who got the United States of America involved in the Cold War with the Soviet Union. He also got us involved in the Korean War.

Our thirty-fifth president, John F. Kennedy (1961–1963): a Democrat who cheated on his wife every chance he got. He ordered the Bay of Pigs Invasion, then changed his liberal mind and called it off, leaving everyone to fend for themselves. It was considered a *major embarrassment* for U.S. foreign policy.

Our thirty-six president, Lyndon Baines Johnson (1963–1969): a Democrat who was rumored to have cheated on his wife. He got the United States of America into the Vietnam War.

Our thirty-ninth president, Jimmy Carter (1977–1981): He stated, in an interview with *Playboy* magazine (if you can believe it) that he had lusted after women while he was married but never did anything about it. Up until recently, he had been considered by most Americans to be the worst U.S. president in modern history—even though he didn't get America involved in any wars that we know of.

Our forty-second president, Bill Clinton[414] (1993–2001): He cheated on his wife, and he signed a piece of legislation that is the major cause of our nation's economic woes: the North American Free Trade Agreement (N.A.F.T.A.).[415]

---

[414] "Bill (I Didn't Inhale) Clinton was our 'first black president,' but Barack (I Used Drugs) Obama is blacker in skin color and also in temperament. The actual quote from the book *Dreams from My Father*, is this: "I had learned not to care. I blew a few smoke rings [with cigarettes], remembering those years. Pot [marijuana] had helped, and booze [alcohol]; maybe a little blow [cocaine] when you could afford it. Not smack [heroin], though." In other words, he was a drug addict. Now, imagine what would happen if the United States of America had a full-blooded black African president. The illegal drug problems and number of people with A.I.D.S. would probably triple overnight, along with the National Debt and number of autochthonous grass-roofed mud huts." —Archie B., Jr. (think about it)

[415] President Clinton signed it into law on December 8, 1993, and Mexicans cheered.

Our forty-fourth president, Barack Hussein Obama (2009–present): It looks as if his three major accomplishments by the time he leaves office will be (1) almost doubling the National Debt, (2) the (Un)Affordable Care Act, and (3) not approving an eyesore oil pipeline. He has proved, as predicted, to be an "unmitigated disaster."[416]

Notable Liberal Female Quote:

"So who the goddamn hell do you want to be our next president, you S.O.B.? A Republican male chauvinist pig? You better watch what the hell you say about Democrats or I'll get somebody to f*** you up really good! I voted for Barack Obama twice and I'm damn proud of it!" —Name withheld[417]

Trojan Donkeys

Why do so many people think that there's no difference between the two major political parties? Here's why: It's because the Republican Party is riddled with liberals (i.e., Democrats) pretending to be Republicans. It is the only way that they can win an election. That is why so many of our politicians, some of whom may become candidates for president, act as if they couldn't care less about the *future* of the United States of America.[418] Their own personal lives and political ambitions are much more important to them. They are referred to as R.I.N.O.s (Republicans in name only), and there are a lot more of them than most people think. Liberals are far more prone than are conservatives to dole out taxpayer money to any person or group—even furtive foreigners—if they think it will help them win the next election. Question: Are politically smart (Jewish) puppeteers helping the D.N.C. to infiltrate the Republican Party and/or the Tea Party with personable trained political puppets who once served in

---

[416] He has reportedly also started another "Cold War" with Russia.
[417] These words were written and signed in blood with a buzzard's feather on a piece of sulfur-scented stationery. Perhaps, the sender of the letter was an Internal Revenue Service (I.R.S.) office manager. Who knows?
[418] *Re: Presidential Candidates:* "The biggest problem with the United States of America is that we are not electing presidents that are related by blood to those who fought for our country in the American Revolution. Instead, we elect bastards. That's why we keep having the same problems over and over again." —Sons of the Revolution

the military? If so, that could eventually result in two liberal candidates, one a Democrat and the other a Republican, running against one other in 2016 for the office of president of the United States of America. It's the stuff of nightmares.

Here are a few ways to detect a Trojan Donkey—or, if you prefer, a "Pinocchio" R.I.N.O.—before voting. Simply ask yourself the following questions.

1. Does the candidate look like he (or she) is only interested in being elected, rather than doing what is right for the United States of America?

2. Does he (or she) answer questions by speaking in platitudes—i.e., generalities that we've all heard over and over again before?

3. If he (or she) were standing in front of you right now, rather than on appearing on your TV set, do you think that he (or she) would really like you or be interested in being your friend?

4. Does the candidate provide photos of himself (or herself) to prove that he (or she) served in the military but still seem wishy-washy and/or dispassionate about major problems that may drastically affect us all?

5. Does he (or she) discuss things such as *military casualties* objectively, like an attorney—i.e., emotionless, politely caring, or rehearsed, as though defending a client—without offering any honest opinions or obvious solutions?

6. Does the candidate always seem in good cheer, even when discussing topics such as the National Debt or other things that negatively affect the people of the United States of America?

7. Is the candidate always smiling, relaxed, and pleasant when appearing before TV news cameras, as though there's really nothing for anyone to worry about, as long as all U.S. congressmen, U.S. senators, and Wall Street fat cats are making lots of money?

8. When discussing any subject that has serious security implications for citizens of the United States of America and for those serving in the U.S. military, is the candidate really concerned about it, or does he (or she) just seem to be putting on an act?

9. Does the candidate appear to be someone who is easily influenced by others, or does he (or she) seem to have a mind of his (or her) own? In other words, is the candidate a potential political puppet—who can be played like a piano—or is he (or she) going to do what's right and *in the best interest* of the United States of America? If not, why not?

10. Did the candidate actually write a book about himself (or herself), or did he (or she) pay someone the going rate of about $20,000 to do it—in order to make himself (or herself) look good?[419]

11. Does the candidate state clearly what he (or she) thinks is *right* and *wrong* when it comes to subjects such as abortion, or does he (or she) hem and haw like a jackass in an attempt to appeal to "both sides of the aisle"?

12. Does the candidate blink excessively when talking? This may be a sign of lying, nervousness, bright lights, or avoiding reality—or because his (or her) political puppet eyelid strings snapped.

13. However, the most important question to ask yourself is this: *Would that candidate be willing to pass legislation to allow a third term for President Barack Hussein Obama?*

Undoubtedly, there are some *conservative liberals* and *liberal conservatives* out there who are so confused by what they see on their television sets that they simply "don't know what to think" about anything. Maybe after reading this book they'll be better able to make up their minds. Too much legislative time and a

---

[419] That's what politicians do. John F. Kennedy and Barack Obama may have done the same thing. It's in the official D.N.C. playbook.

mountain of taxpayer money is being wasted every day all over the country by assorted (multicultural) Democratic and Republican lawyers and politicians vehemently arguing and suing one another over trivial matters. Hopefully, everyone who reads this book will understand why, so we can all be friends again.

A Human Slave (or "Puppet") Gene?

Human chromosomes contain DNA in a double-helix structure. The DNA houses thousands of genes along the strand. Genes, the fundamental units of inheritance, are a stretch of sequence in a specific position on the DNA strand. There are genes for everything: fat genes, math genes, linguistic genes, homosexual genes, and liberal nincompoop genes. Today, biologists mapping the human genome are literally on the verge of identifying persons who, for various reasons, will require governmental assistance (i.e., access to all taxpaying people's wallets, purses, and piggybanks). It is a fact that each person's own genome is at least 99.9 percent identical to anyone else's on the planet Earth. Compared to someone closely related to you, that figure is even higher. A difference of 0.1 percent might not seem like much, but it translates to about three million differences embedded in our own genetic code.[420] Some of these differences influence one's appearance, behavior, vulnerability to disease, and response to medication. Some differences have no identified effect as of yet. The question is, do locatable regions of genomic sequence exist that can be directly attributable to the long-term enslavement or domestication of a human or animal population (e.g., cattle): a *slave gene*, if you will?

In my opinion, a human slave gene does exist; that is what defines liberals, and thus liberalism.

A future population of slave-like human cattle was first described by H. G. Wells in *The Time Machine* (1895). In this story, a devolved race of weak and fragile, naïve and childlike, almost mindless men, women, and children, the Eloi, live in a beautiful and peaceful world with no violence and are controlled by another race: the Morlocks, who are filthy, ugly, ignorant, cannibalistic human troglodytes who reside in caverns underground and come out only at dark to herd the Eloi and feast on their flesh. In the movie, at least, the Eloi were walking to their potential

---

[420] *The Human Genome*, 2001, Nature Publishing Group, Palgrave, New York, N.Y., p. 9.

deaths like puppets in a trance. (Apparently, all of this occurred after hardworking conservatives deserted the planet Earth, leaving liberals by themselves with no food stamps.)[421]

Does a slave gene—i.e., a gene that is the result of generations of human or animal enslavement—actually exist? If it does, it would help explain the liberal neurosis that is so apparent with regard to their attitude toward free-market capitalism, independent human beings, and the Western concept of liberty and freedom. However, you can be sure that if a human or animal slave gene is ever correctly identified (it may already have been) and that fact is ever made public, then liberal Democrats, who already try to pretend that there are really no such things as racial dissimilarities, will try to pretend something equally as silly. They will pretend that visible differences of any significance do not really exist between human DNA-sequencing photographs. It's also a given that Democratic operatives will do their very best to put the kibosh on any such slave gene findings by arguing about it in circles for, say, six to twelve months and then pronouncing that everything—be it sober opinion or disquieting fact—has been "refuted," "discredited," and "debunked," even if the findings clearly have not. This is, of course, exactly how they reacted to the extensive commonsense data of *The Bell Curve*, which everyone seems to have forgotten about, as though it does not matter.

You can be sure that any suggestion by members of the scientific community that liberals, as a group, are clearly identifiable by the details in color photos of their DNA sequencing will be met not only with the usual left-wing hysteria that results when anyone tells the truth, but also with a sulfuric wailing and gnashing of teeth never before seen outside the gnawed iron gates of Hades.

(Note: It may be necessary at this point for some readers to try diligently to overcome the effects of a life of being subjected to liberal propaganda. That is going to take some time and will not occur immediately after you have read this book. For decades now, everyone has been exposed to films that portray Hollywood liberals as tough-talking World War II heroes, daring spies, clever Scotland Yard detectives, fearless medieval warriors, or brilliant scientists who battle aliens from another planet and save the Earth. We've listened to political rhetoric by liberals characterizing themselves as people of great empathy and compassion; we've read liberal-authored novels celebrated by the liberal establishment telling us what everyone's attitudes should be and how everyone should think; we've read newspapers daily for most of our lives that provide cherry-picked data and information from the liberal perspective. No matter how intelligent, wary, and

---

[421] According to *The Wall Street Journal*, the state of Mississippi reports the largest share of food stamp usage: over 21 percent *(WSJ*, "Some 15% of U.S. Uses Food Stamps," November 1, 2011). Actually, our nation's capital, Washington, D.C., surpasses Mississippi; it's playing in the neighborhood of some 22 percent.

astute a person may be, all of these things that he or she has been exposed to since childhood have had a profound effect, and that effect will be difficult—but not impossible—to overcome. It may actually take from six to twelve months or longer for most readers to understand the significance of the facts in this book.)

Before proceeding any further, please bear in mind the liberal's three main characteristics: (1) diminished capacity, (2) addiction to pleasure, and (3) monetary self-interest. Suboptimality, borderline hedonism, and greed define liberals.[422] Nothing else—no book, no movie, no television news report, no magazine article, no performance by any Hollywood actor reading a script, no teleprompter speech given by any politician. Try to forget—no, *erase*—all of the fashionable liberal "moral" opinions that you may have erroneously learned, along with the faddish multicultural social nonsense that most people have been taught to believe ever since they were born. Instead, rediscover and trust your own instincts. If you look deep into your heart, you will find that for which you are searching. Also be aware that it is not unusual for any person with liberal views to know little or nothing about politics, nor even know what the word *liberal* truly means. Many impoverished young people do not actually discover what they really are (liberals) until our federal government loans them money to go to college. Then they take courses and learn what all the big words mean.

Please note once more that the term liberal is best understood as a *defective human gene* or combination of genes rather than as a *type of person*.[423] Being a liberal has nothing to do with aptitude, social standing, or intellect. A liberal may be talented, smart, and wealthy, or unskilled, stupid, and poor. A liberal gene can exist in a skinny runt of a man, or it can exist in a hulking football coach—say, someone like Jerry Sandusky (see the Internet photos). We've all become so conditioned to believe certain things pertaining to liberalism, as a result of years—no, decades—of the liberal media mischaracterizing themselves, that a substantial period of time for thought and personal reflection is required for most readers to finally *absorb and comprehend* the fact that virtually none of what any of us have been led to believe by and about the growing liberal-American community is true.

For one thing, the specific types of characters being portrayed by liberal Hollywood male and female actors—including their attitudes, behavior, popularity,

---

[422] Note that *hedonism*, or pleasure seeking—which often includes the use of illegal drugs—is very expensive, so a suboptimal person devoted to that endeavor 24/7 would have to be *greedy* to pay for it. That is one reason why so many people today think only about themselves. They are called the "Me Generation." Unfortunately, greed has been glamorized, so white-collar crooks' hands are only slapped. This has had the expected evolutionary consequences: the increased growth of liberalism.

[423] What everyone needs to understand, however, is that liberalism comprises the *criminal element* in society. That is why the liberal socialist Democratic Party wants all convicted felons—including the illegal alien gang members—to be able to register to vote. Some Democrats even want to release prisoners from jail early so they can do so. It is absolute madness.

intelligence, and achievements—simply do not exist.[424] The extent to which the media, as a whole, continues to be complicit in drumming erroneous African American and Anglo-Saxon racial caricatures and prefabricated mythical storylines into television viewers' heads is now only just beginning to be perceived by the public.[425] That's one fortunate advantage to having cable TV and a laptop in this new computer-information age. Now people have the opportunity to ascertain instantly whether what they are being told is true or false. Prior to the instant availability of facts and information on the Internet, much of what people thought they knew was based strictly on hearsay evidence and stated "facts" from liberal sources that no one could confirm, and so viewers' minds were continually filled with mush. As the world's knowledge grows, however, it becomes increasingly clear that much of what is considered today to be standard Western thought is based on high liberal nonsense and coordinated group fantasy. It is rooted in the liberal desire for social and moral—and *monetary*—equality with those whom they secretly and sometimes not so secretly despise for their conservative confidence, independence, and success. Do liberals love their fellow man, or hate him? That is the question. Do liberals really care at all about anyone other than themselves? The answer lies not in what liberals say or do (or fail to do) but in the *observable consequences* of virtually everything they touch: It always turns into dog shit.[426]

Now, back to the discussion of the possibility of a human/animal domestication gene—or slave gene. In the field of genetics, where it is now possible to study genes and DNA, the chemical blueprint of life, scientists are now able to locate the precise position of a gene and determine what it is responsible for doing. Estimates vary, but in humans, there appear to be about 25,000 genes. The slave gene, if it exists, works in the brain by influencing behavior. If so, it would be the source of certain well-known liberal traits, including, but certainly not limited to, the following.

Trait #1: Immature Thinking. Slave owners clearly prefer certain features and characteristics in their human chattel. People having childlike qualities are easier to control. Strong-willed individuals do not make good slaves. Anyone with the adult

---

[424] Nevertheless, these actors and those who resemble them become "the cat's meow." (For more, refer back to "Hollywood, California, Brainwashing Techniques," page 233.
[425] The invention of the television set is what enabled liberals to build a fictitious world of make-believe about themselves and their true agendas in the eyes of all Americans. For anyone who has trouble understanding this, try unplugging your television set for a couple of years and working on a research submarine, or on a farm, or read some books or something. Then plug it back in and see what you think. Most of the programs are utter nonsense.
[426] A few examples follow: (1) the U.S. economy, (2) the jobs market, (3) the National Debt, (4) the health care system, (5) General Motors, (6) Detroit, Michigan, (7) when liberals were in charge of protecting the U.S. ambassador in Benghazi, Libya. The ambassador and three others were killed, and the diplomatic compound building was destroyed.

drive to be independent would turn out to be defiant and disobedient. In situations where guards are needed for women, such as a harem—and they must be left alone with them—unattractive, effeminate male slaves are preferred. However, intelligent slaves with a sense of humor are favored, too. So, over time, no "dumbing down" normally occurs in any given population of slaves. In fact, the institution of slavery, which may include involuntary breeding, actually promotes something of an increase in I.Q. among slaves.[427] If anyone doubts this, they should consider the effect that canine (K9) ownership and breeding has had on the intelligence of today's dog breeds.[428] Qualities such as courage and bravery are admired but not preferred, unless the plan is that the slave wrestle a lion or bear to the death for some narcissistic liberal king's sick entertainment. No doubt, in the past, some slaves were even told to put on a show for everyone's amusement in exchange for being left alone—or perhaps even in exchange for their very lives—and the ones who made people laugh survived. Many slaves were employed as domestic servants. Not all of them were sweating, muscle-bound laborers toiling in fields, digging holes, and breaking stone. Their masters probably valued obedience, acquiescence, naïveté, childlike thinking, and docility in those whom they sometimes worked unmercifully.

Trait #2: Herd Mentality. The term *herd mentality* (suggesting a "group of animals") means a certain frame of mind in a group. Herd mentality is different from herd behavior, which refers to stampeding and panicking—for example, when the *"Air Jordan 3 Black Flip are on sale!"* Herd mentality describes how people are influenced by their peers to adopt certain behaviors, attitudes, and ideas. Group intelligence, crowd wisdom, and decentralized decision-making are topics of interest to social psychologists. Psychologists report that people who are easily influenced look to others to see how to behave. Herd mentality is a reaction to peer pressure, which can make individuals act mindlessly to gain friendship. The idea of group mind and mob behavior was first put forth by nineteenth-century French social psychologists, who, after the French Revolution of 1764, of course, should know.

---

[427] *Re: Involuntary Breeding.* Forced breeding among enslaved populations has also been known to occur. For example, prior to the Civil War, there are known instances of white prostitutes being forced to have sex with Negro slaves. In prehistoric times, enslaved women were probably also forced to have sex with Neanderthals and the mentally retarded—which may have included their masters. The evolutionary moral of the story is this: Forcing anyone to do anything that he or she does not want to do can alter the natural course of human development. Believe it or don't believe it. The choice is yours.
[428] Dogs, known as "man's best friend," are descended from wolves, which were first domesticated in East Asia about 15,000 years ago. Cows were domesticated in Western Asia and the Near East by 8,000 years ago. The Egyptian ass was domesticated about 5,000 years ago. Many southern Europeans are domesticated animals, too. Butt be careful. Always heed the old warning, "If there's a Greek nearby, don't bend over."

Human (D) Evolution

It's easy to see how a group of people who are enslaved and treated like animals, rather than as individual human beings, would begin to lose their sense of personal identity. They would be forced to depend on their enslaved peers for support against a much more powerful authority figure, such as a master. There's value in having strength in numbers among like-minded individuals who react in unison to achieve a particular goal, but unfortunately, strength in numbers is also available to the weak, ignorant, and unthinking—i.e., those who lack a decent and properly functioning moral compass. So they achieve their strength by joining and following a crowd—that often does evil—for the *feeling* of (1) belonging, (2) security, and (3) power.

Trait #3: Government Dependency. Inarguably, long-term male and female slavery/domestication has the same effect on human beings as it has on any other animal on earth. Domestication, or animal husbandry, is defined as the taming of an animal kept as a pet or for produce—whether that produce be food, such as eggs or milk, or more animals of the same species. Animal husbandry, the science of caring for and breeding farm animals, includes the raising of animals for warfare and as mounts for soldiers and as pack animals for carrying their supplies. Human slaves, like domesticated animals, rely on their owners not only for food and shelter but also for protection from environmental dangers, especially predators, which is a substantial reward, so along with the misery of working come benefits. Over time, dependency inevitably develops, which means slaves then rely on either a master or a governing authority for health and security, rather than on themselves. People born in captivity in an isolated society have little contact with the outside world and consider their lives as slaves to be normal. Any slave who gets the idea that his or her life is not normal and who rebels will suffer the usual consequences, which might include a grave with no headstone.

The big question is this: How many generations does it take for the effects of slavery to become apparent in an enslaved population's offspring? Two or three? Five or six? Ten? Twenty? Thirty? We should all realize that, even if it took as many as fifty generations (a period of about 500 years in a very primitive society), stark genetic differences could easily occur. So, as you can see, this is a mere snap of the fingers in the evolutionary scheme of things. It was only a little more than 500 years ago that Christopher Columbus discovered America: 1492.[429]

Fossil evidence indicates that the species *Homo sapiens sapiens* began evolving about 200,000 years ago. Did the mentally abnormal "first liberal" evolve prior

---

[429] Actually, Christopher Columbus discovered the Bahamas. The place was deserted. That was prior to the African slave trade by British explorers and sea merchants, who often paid for their human cargo with colorful scarves, beads, and trinkets.

to that? Even more importantly, we should ask ourselves exactly how long it would take for an enslaved population of, say, 300 million to become thoroughly domesticated—i.e., to lose their instinctive desire for independence and to instead prefer an all-powerful controlling authority to care for them literally from cradle to grave. *Social dependency is the inevitable result of charitable government feeding, whether those who receive the sustenance are people or wild animals.*

Trait #4: Inability to Understand Other People. (This subject was mentioned previously.) Clearly, the enslavement of any population over a long period has a detrimental effect on all of the natural instincts and abilities needed for self-reliance and independent survival. Any person with a diminished capacity to figure out what others are thinking is more likely to be captured and enslaved in the first place, so such people are prevalent in any enslaved group. The ability to mentalize is of no use to a slave because slaves must do as they are told regardless of whether they understand what other people are thinking, so this capability, at any level, has little effect on a slave's social status, level of comfort, or survivability quotient. Because slaves are, by definition, under the control of others, what happens to each slave is still going to happen to him or her whether he or she knows what other people are thinking, or not.

When an enslaved person's life is put in a master's hands, any special talents or abilities the dependent slave may have become irrelevant because the slave is not allowed to benefit from them. That is why, over time, among any enslaved population, the ability to mentalize eventually atrophies, disappearing altogether. You see, with slaves, the power to mentalize simply ceases to exist because it serves no useful purpose. What good does it do to understand what other people are thinking if you are not allowed to make personal decisions based on your understanding and feelings? For a subjugated individual, the only possible advantage in being able to mentalize and to know what your captor or captors are thinking is to *aid in your escape*. (Please note that, if such did occur, that person would then be free—*an escaped slave*—so he or she would inarguably and by definition be a normal, clear-thinking conservative and thus have no relevance in this discussion.)

Trait #5: Inherent Promiscuity. It is easy to understand why people who are treated like animals will eventually begin behaving exactly like animals. Lack of even a smidgen of morality may become prevalent under exceptionally harsh conditions of enslavement because male and female breeding opportunities would likely be rare. In fact, sexual intercourse with a master and/or other people in charge might even be necessary for one's survival. Adultery, incest, homosexuality, bisexuality, and pedophilia are shunned in all civilized societies because such behavior results in fits of rage—and, frequently, murder—among normal persons. Sexual misconduct even warrants the death penalty in some cultures because it is not conducive to maintaining an orderly conservative society.430

You see, conservatism evolved as a way for all human beings to live in a peaceful, law-abiding, and organized fashion, whereas liberalism evolved as a way for slaves to survive in captivity. Peace and tranquility in the *real world*—which includes life, liberty, and the free pursuit of happiness—can exist only if everyone involved has respect for everyone else's property, which includes all other men's wives and daughters. Under conditions of enslavement, however, in which the slaves *do not actually own anything*, these conservative ideals serve no purpose. That's because an individual cannot lose what he or she does not possess in the first place and so cannot lose control of what he or she has no power over. A human slave's "rights" are in an *unnatural* state of limbo.

Trait #6: Lack of Moral Character. Why are liberals so often said to have no core beliefs? As might be expected, it's in their genes. Any enslaved person too principled to do certain things requested by his or her master(s) would have been beaten and/or killed, whereas those who were willing to comply and do whatever was asked of them would have been allowed to live. They might possibly have even been set free.

Moral character is what really defines the difference between liberals and conservatives more than anything else does.431 You see, conservatism is a positive human instinct—an inherent lifestyle, if you will—that evolved with the species *Homo sapiens sapiens* because adhering to it increases the person's likelihood of survival. Animal species have not yet been so evolutionarily blessed. (Nor have some liberals, who appear to be, according to every single bit of objective information, evolutionarily damned.) Furthermore, liberalism, because it is a human adaptation to tyranny and/or slavery, has new features that have developed, which are similar to those found only in the *domesticated* animal kingdom. The truth of the slave gene postulate is even more difficult to dispute in light of the fact that it clearly explains the liberal's next trait, number seven.

---

430 The names of and number of prominent, well-known, highly influential liberal politicians, pundits, and television personalities who've admitted to having had adulterous interracial heterosexual or homosexual liaisons, many of which undoubtedly resulted in secret abortions, is shocking, to say the least. The devil is in the details. (Who knows, maybe *Rosemary's Baby* was based on a true story! It happened in New York City, didn't it?)

431 *Re: Lack of Moral Character.* Another reason that liberal socialist Democrats so often engage in unethical political conduct, such as voter fraud, bribery, a variety of unconstitutional acts, serial bald-faced lying to the American people, and so forth—with seemingly no hesitation, guilt, or remorse—is that liberals have a severely diminished capacity. In other words, liberals are at a distinct disadvantage, and most of them seem to know it. So they probably feel justified behaving unethically.

Trait #7: Fondness for Communism. Respect for another person's property is one of the most basic and important tenets of conservatism, but it is frequently not shared by today's liberals. The often-stated liberal Democratic politician's dream to "spread the wealth," which is simply code for *buying poor people's votes,* is nothing more than the act of confiscating money from taxpayers who've earned it and giving it to nonworking people who haven't earned anything—i.e., liberal Democratic political supporters.[432] We should also note that in poor neighborhoods, constant use of the phrase "spread the wealth" results in much levity, big grins, boisterous laughter, high fives, and fist bumps. This poor liberal attitude toward the property of others is easily understandable, considering the fact that enslaved persons have no property that they can truly call their own. Slaves are, in reality, property themselves. Unfortunately, slaves own nothing—*not even their own lives*—so it stands to reason that any respect slaves may have for what other people own is going to be minimal, at best. That is why passing any legislation that increases the security of other people, their money, and their possessions is pretty much going to be way down at the bottom of any liberal politician's to-do list.

We all know how communism and socialism (i.e., communism lite) work. They don't. Whenever these systems have been tried, they always begin to fail—unless you consider mass corruption and state-sponsored murder a success—but apparently, this does not dissuade liberals at all. It's almost as though they relish failure, because they instinctively gravitate toward various forms of 1929 Slavic governance as predictably as cast-iron flakes keep hopping back on a magnet.

Years ago, anyone would have reacted with shock and anger at the suggestion that he or she was a communist/socialist and would have protested vehemently, but today, more and more liberals, even those in the highest positions of government, not only fail to deny such charges but will casually admit it with a smile. Incredible as it may seem, it has even become fashionable in certain liberal circles to be perceived as an enemy of the United States. Many people over the age of fifty-five still remember being taught how to squat beneath their school desks, with both hands on their heads, in case of an enemy attack with an atomic bomb. Some of us may even remember seeing the metal air vents for underground bomb shelters sticking up out of our neighbors' front lawns or backyards. We also remember watching cartoons on Saturday mornings and having our television screens go blank for sixty seconds during tests of the Emergency Broadcast System. That's why some of us have such a difficult time understanding today's shameless unrepentant liberals who brazenly favor anti-American foreign leaders of all races and their tyrannical dictatorial systems of government. To some of us, it's almost like hearing a close friend, neighbor, or relative

---

[432] Men's upper-body strength (i.e., bicep size) predicts their political opinions on wealth redistribution, according to new research published in the journal *Psychological Science*. No such link was found among women (Association for Psychological Science, "Political Motivations May Have Evolutionary Links to Physical Strength," press release, May 15, 2013). .

calmly admit that he or she is a traitor and, perhaps, is secretly employed as a foreign spy.

Trait #8: Fantasy Addition Disorder (F.A.D.). We've all heard the *sage* advice "Don't worry, be happy," but this is not really a very bright thing to do. It is the mantra of a liberal slave. "Don't worry" is what a tortured soul with little or no power over his or her life would say to cheer up, and "be happy" is the advice of a fool. Some people, of course, are much more capable of not worrying about things than are others. Irresponsibility, in fact, is their way of life. However, as one would expect, those who tend not to worry about anything at all are historically the ones most likely to have lots of things to worry about—such as being conquered and enslaved. A dillydallying person who simply cannot be bothered with taking precautions is usually one of the first to lose everything he or she has—including his or her life. For that very reason, slave populations are well stocked with the naïve and foolish, and their gene pools runneth over with F.A.D. Different forms of slavery exist, of course, and some are worse than are others. Feudalism, for example, the dominant social system in medieval Europe, may have helped contribute to the development of fantasy addiction disorder in many oppressed peasants' family trees.

It is also clear that, over time, F.A.D. propagates under conditions of enslavement, eventually becoming a well-established trait. Slavery is only one example, however, of an environmental factor capable of propagating F.A.D. Tyrannical dictatorial oppression of a populace has the potential to do it, too. For that very reason, the tropical island of Cuba has become an excellent example of a liberal-production facility. The way it works is this: Anyone in Cuba who isn't submissive and who demands his or her freedom and is caught trying to escape by boat is promptly imprisoned, tortured, and killed, yet those who remain acquiescent are allowed to continue breeding. So, today, the Cuban gene pool is affected accordingly, and so is the Cuban way of life. Content, F.A.D.-riddled Cubans who can tolerate tyranny remain on the island indefinitely and propagate, so the lives of Cubans revolve around crumbling, roach-infested hospitals, dilapidated fifty-year-old automobiles, slashed tires, epidemics, child prostitution, and very few modern conveniences, such as food. Cuba, you see, is a communist country that believes all citizens should live their lives for the state. In other words, the Cuban government thinks that it should "spread the wealth" until there is no bread and butter (or wealth) left to spread.[433] Sound familiar?

---

[433] Ironically, "spreading the wealth" increases the number of liberal suicides. That's because some of the money ultimately comes from liberals, who tend to live on the edge. Unfortunately, cash doesn't grow on trees (but sometimes ropes and nooses do).

A Brief Note on Sympatric Speciation

In a series of highly influential books, geneticist Theodosius Dobzhansky, ornithologist Ernst Mayr, and paleontologist George Simpson expressed their satisfaction with the idea that virtually all evolutionary phenomena are the result of long-term changes in the genetic makeup of populations under the guiding hand of natural—as opposed to artificial—selection. Mayr himself was a leading advocate of the concept of *allopatric speciation*—the formation of new and distinct species occurring in separate, nonoverlapping geographical areas. However, there's another way for different species to develop: *sympatric speciation,* which means the formation of new species occurring without geographical separation but rather as a result of the development of isolating mechanisms within the population itself—bamboo cages, for example. If this human slave (or "puppet") gene model is true, then it will stand the test of time and research.

Chapter 14

Why Do They Look So Funny?

The Neanderthal Enigma

"Neanderthals were nothing but a bunch of lazy, dumb ugly people. Some had ruddy white skin, some had brown skin, and some had black skin. Some had reddish hair, some had black or brownish hair, and a few had dirty-blond hair. Some were short and some were tall. There was nothing special about them except that they had thick eyebrows, noses that were about three inches wide, and primitive skulls—like human apes—that were as hard as petrified wood. So they could probably take dozens of punches to the head without ever being fazed, just like Cassius Clay (after his conversion to Islam, Muhammad Ali), former heavyweight boxing champion of the world. Early Neanderthals walked with a sideways swagger much as chimpanzees do. Some people today even fit their description. All you have to do is watch how some lumberyard workers in South Miami (or, perhaps, permanent residents of the Bronx Zoo) cross over a loose pile of two-by-fours. A hundred thousand years ago, Neanderthals had an untold number of tribes that battled each other and ate all of the dead. Neanderthals

> were spread all over the continent we call Eurasia. Anatomically modern man couldn't stand the Neanderthals because they were dangerous and as dumb as animals, so he killed them whenever he could. But some unwary or mentally retarded modern men and women were probably attacked and captured by Neanderthals, so miscegenation occurred anyway. As a result, there were a lot of half-breeds running around. Those half-breeds are the direct ancestors of today's human trash. You see, they were the First Liberals." —John Hayberry (2010)

Today's liberals are undoubtedly the result of ancient miscegenation with Neanderthals, prehistoric human trash. It's likely that most of them were (in liberal lingo) "pussies." Anyone who thinks that this theory is shaky should remember that *it's all about stupidity and the human ability to help it thrive.* Just look at liberals' faces closely and compare them to those of your own family. See the difference? Liberal Internet bloggers keep saying that whites evolved from blacks. Well, guess what? Maybe they're actually right about something! They did. The continent of Africa is called the "birthplace of man," and who ever heard of an isolated group of *albino anything* surviving in Africa? So were the now supposedly extinct Neanderthals (*Homo sapiens neanderthalensis*) black in skin color? Yes, probably, the early five-foot-three-inch-tall ones were as black as the ace of spades, despite the illustrations in many college textbooks. Were modern men (*Homo sapiens sapiens*) white in skin color? Yes, they were. Like today, they were white and various shades of brown.

According to the fossil evidence found at various sites, these two groups, Neanderthals and modern man, lived side by side only 20,000 years ago, at the peak of the last ice age.[434] But what everyone needs to realize is that both modern man and the liberal Neanderthal were also *multiracial.*

Were the Neanderthals savage, knuckle-dragging brutes, as so popularly portrayed in books and movies, or were they relatively short (by modern standards), lazy, dumpy, pear-shaped, human cave potatoes? Of course, there's no way to know for sure, but they were probably quick and strong-smelling and, when agitated, jumped around like monkeys all over the place. Most liberal archaeologists and geneticists have insisted for decades that "modern man" did not descend from the

---

[434] There have been several ice ages throughout history, and, undoubtedly, there will be more.

Neanderthals and that they are not really members of our human family tree.[435] However, a recent detailed research article written by some German researchers in *Science* magazine concludes:

> It is important to note that although we detect a signal compatible with gene flow from Neandertals into ancestors of present-day humans outside Africa, this does not show that other forms of gene flow did not occur. For example, we detect gene flow from Neandertals into modern humans but no reciprocal gene flow from modern humans into Neandertals. . . . Thus, the actual amount of interbreeding between Neandertals and modern humans may have been very limited, given that it contributed only 1 to 4% of the genome of present-day non-Africans.[436]

Some experts have suggested that *miscegenation* occurred based on an analysis of all available data.[437] And, of course, it did—just as it still does today. Other experts believe that the Neanderthal could not tolerate cold weather and eventually dropped dead of starvation. Many probably did. Still others believe that the Neanderthals were hunted by modern man and killed. That probably happened a lot, too. However, the real reason for the disappearance of the liberal Neanderthals may be that they were simply a suboptimal human species that disappeared for hundreds of different reasons as they were slowly bred out of existence. In other

---

[435] Anthropology, along with its various fields of study, is not an exact science. In fact, anthropology is not a science at all. It's just an interesting ongoing investigation. Everyone has their own opinion about prehistoric man, but here's the truth: Early mankind, like today, was just a bunch of different people of various sizes, shapes, and colors running around like upright baboons all over the land mass that today we call Eurasia. (Neanderthals didn't call it anything.) There's no way to figure out exactly what was going on, and it doesn't matter, anyway. It'd be like trying to figure out what happened at the Biloxi, Mississippi, seafood festival of 1936 a hundred thousand years later.

[436] "A Draft Sequence of the Neandertal Genome," *Science*, May 7, 2010, vol. 328, pp. 710–722. But what kind of gobbledygook is that? How can there be gene flow one way but not the other? What happened, did all of the "Neandertal" half-breeds disappear? If what the Germans say is true, then Neanderthals *are* part of modern man's family tree. That means that *miscegenation* between modern men and, presumably, black Neanderthals did occur—as it would be expected to occur among certain populations and under certain primitive circumstances over the course of many, many thousands of years. Since gene flow works both ways—assuming that Neanderthal women were able to give birth to half-breeds—that means that modern men are also part of the extinct Neanderthal's family tree. In other words, Neanderthals were half-breeds, either by the father or by the mother—that's the way it works. But since they're all gone now, there's no way to know for sure. They supposedly disappeared about 20,000 years ago, during the last ice age, probably after a cannibalistic simian-like free-for-all.

[437] Liberal anthropologists prefer to use the term *hybridization*, instead of miscegenation, to show due respect to all of our world's admirable past and present human races.

words, before Neanderthals completely vanished as a species, there were thousands of half-breeds (half Neanderthal, half modern man/woman) running around. Until more fossils are uncovered and more data is gathered, who can say for sure?

The prevailing theory now is that some modern humans and Neanderthals interbred over 20,000 years ago. But of course they did, and it occurred over a period of over a hundred thousand years. Because there were many more modern humans than Neanderthals, modern human genes dominated over generations. The two groups competed for food and sporadically attacked one another's females. The controversial data that exists from independent studies of the human genome show incontrovertible evidence that humans and Neanderthals interbred. Undoubtedly, rape occurred, and it's more than likely that the Neanderthals did most of it.

It's also true that (some) "white people evolved from black people," as many liberals have said with malicious glee in their Internet blogs, which are designed to get on conservative anthropologists' nerves.[438] However, what liberals do not seem to realize is that it was *white liberals*, not conservatives, who evolved from black Neanderthals. How do we know? Because of their physiognomy, stature, personal habits, behavior, and I.Q. Therefore, today's liberals must be the ones who are by far the most closely related to our prehistoric "friend," the Neanderthal.

Are today's liberals the "rear-end" product of over 4.5 million years of miscegenation opportunities—i.e., multiracial crossbreeding? If so, then today's liberals must be "evolutionarily bleached" Afro-Eurasian Neanderthals. Seemingly irrefutable proof of this can be found in the fact that *Neanderthalism* would also explain the puzzling habit of some modern liberals to cherry-pick what they believe they should think from the collected wisdom of Confucius—a kind of modern Eurasian—and also espouse communism, the historical political preference of aboriginal Sinodonts and Red Chinese Mongoloids.[439]

(Maybe we should ask our congressional representatives where they stand on this.)

Here's something else to wonder about: Was Neanderthal man a normal member of the genus *Homo*, or was he somewhat mentally retarded? Did he sling animal pelts over his shoulder like an American Indian and stand around looking proud and noble, as he is so popularly portrayed in many textbooks? Or was he a perpetually naked "human hyena" covered with animal dung and mosquito bites and large prehistoric insects—ants, ticks, gnats, lice, and no-see-ums?

---

[438] Modern man evolved from albino primates, whose black parentage, of course, had very similar physical characteristics. The white siblings were probably either attacked and killed, or chased right out of the jungle, much as albinos are treated today in Africa by ignorant witch doctors. Only the smartest victims manage to survive.

[439] But, of course, I could be wrong.

Human (D) Evolution

"Undoubtedly, the first liberals experimented with smoking prehistoric animal dung to get 'high'—and in some cases, they died. Hopefully, they didn't try eating it too." —Anonymous Paleontologist

Was the liberal Neanderthal fearless or a chicken? In other words, did he (and she) hunt large, dangerous animals, such as the woolly mammoth, with nothing more than a thick, clumsy-looking spear that was good for nothing other than jabbing big catfish—and other Neanderthals—or did he prefer hunting smaller animals, such as mice and baby turtles? Maybe he didn't want to bother hunting at all and instead survived on a diet of prehistoric gnats, wild nuts, and berries. Or maybe he chose to eat the rotten, vulture-pecked kills of more successful predators—e.g., saber-toothed tigers and his nemesis, "modern man." Did he eat everyone's leftovers? Who knows? Maybe he was the first "food stamp" recipient.

But more importantly, were Neanderthals *anthropophagus*—i.e., drooling cannibals? The answer is, yes, they were. Piles of chewed human bones have been found to prove it.

Did the Neanderthal daily roam the savannas? Or did he wait for friendly *Homo sapiens sapiens* to hand-feed him? Possibly. Was the Neanderthal as dimwitted as commonly believed? Or was he intelligent and able to count to three?[440] Hopefully, he could use his toes and had a rudimentary concept of arithmetic. Was he trustworthy? Or did he frequently grab his neighbor's food like a monkey and run? Was he honest or a thief? Was he kind to his fellow Neanderthals, or was he pron to murder? Probably both. Did he behave more like a human being or an animal? That's difficult to say for sure. Paleoanthropological experts will probably never be certain, but we all have our suspicions. (Hint: His brain was located in his foot.)

We can only conclude that primitive liberal Neanderthals were all of the above because no two were alike. Although many probably had identical skin pigmentation, no two had exactly the same weight and height or exactly the same personality. Neanderthals were all different, just as human beings have always been and always will be. We should also bear that in mind when trying to categorize the Neanderthal or any other early human species. Neanderthals were all just a bunch of human apes with sticks and stones and half an ounce of intelligence climbing trees and jumping all over everything. If the original Neanderthal still lived today, he'd be considered stupid human-animal trash.

---

[440] Albinism occurs in all (dumber) animal species on a limited basis, so maybe an isolated colony of lighter-skinned Neanderthals somehow managed to survive the early snowflakes and lived in a frozen tundra that is now called Poland.

Let's examine the fossil evidence. Paleoanthropologists sometimes use human and/or animal tooth shape to distinguish between vegetarians and carnivores, which can help determine the diet of early hominids. Large incisors, for example, are characteristic of New World monkeys, which have a diet that includes insects, fruits, flowers, and tree leaves. But very large shovel-shaped incisors are characteristic of the Neanderthal. Some experts believe that heavy wear on most Neanderthal incisors suggests that male and female Neanderthals used their teeth to not only devour tough dried-up fruit and sun-hardened vegetables but also as a clamp to keep animal hides taut with their head and neck muscles while scraping, cutting, and butchering with sharpened stone "tools."

Of course, it's also possible that some later captured Neanderthals had to use their teeth to chew through heavy vines made by their masters to bind their hands and feet. Tightly bound, arm-and-foot-dragging Neanderthals may have also tried nibbling on indigestible foods, such as their own toenails or any accessible rocks.[441]

The average height of a Neanderthal was only about five feet, three inches (about twice the height of a dwarf). Not surprisingly, liberal Neanderthal men, because of their close association with a variety of gorillas and large prehistoric monkeys, appear to have been overly muscular, as were the low-browed, not-so-dainty females—whom they constantly chased with their things hanging out, howling at the moon.

"Mommy, was a black Neanderthal man named Cheetah?" —Anonymous Six Year Old

The Neanderthal inhabited much of Europe and the Mediterranean lands during the late Pleistocene Epoch, which was about 100,000 to 30,000 years ago. Neanderthal remains have also been found in the Middle East, North Africa, and Central Asia. The chest was broad, and the limbs were heavy, with large feet and hands. The Neanderthals appear to have walked in a more irregular, side-to-side fashion than do modern humans. Research has proven that for tens of thousands

---

[441] Even though the adult male buckteeth of many well-known liberals—e.g., Eleanor Roosevelt (MF1, FF5, JF2, LF4, HF2, NF2, EF?), 75 percent of the British, and Alfred E. Newman before he lost one—have been noted for years by humorists, we should not assume that any dental abnormality is proof of strictly vegetarian ancestry. It is also unlikely that any visible similarity between a person's two front teeth and the large incisors of New World monkeys has little or anything at all to do with that person's political persuasion. In fact, this oral oddity in many liberal males and females may be nothing more than a deformed lip illusion caused by frequent use of the F word.

of years, scattered groups of Neanderthals occupied the tundra and forests of western Eurasia. (It must have been similar to the suburbs of Detroit.)

The question is, how did these primitive early humans manage to spread across such a vast region so *liberally?* Were liberal Neanderthals adventurous explorers curious about the world in which they lived? Or were they droopy schlubs weighted down with body fat who jumped at the sight or sound of moving bushes and tree shadows?

Undoubtedly, there were constant battles between different groups. Then cannibalism ensued. Most paleoanthropologists believe that any Neanderthals who managed to stay alive eventually succumbed to the Ice Age.[442] The Neanderthal likely played a larger role in the evolution of "modern man" and today's human races than we would like to think. Liberals, of course, refuse to admit publicly that such a politically incorrect thing as so-called "human races" even exists. Maybe the lyrics have to be sung to the tune of a John Lennon song.

Paleoanthropologists have hypothesized that if an indolent human population simply increases its territory by a mile or two each generation, it will be all over the place in a few thousand years. But what would make an ancient do-nothing hominid bother to increase his or her territory at all? Overpopulation? Lack of food? Noisy screeching and howling neighbors? Whatever the reason, the Neanderthal slowly spread across the continent that we now refer to as Eurasia and kept spreading north to colder climates and also to the sometimes difficult to reach shelter and protection of mountain caves.[443]

If the Neanderthal was so big and strong compared to "modern man," then why did he become extinct? The distinguished Professor Hiram Q. Kneebish, a marijuana-smoking fossil scientist and a receiver of large unnecessary federal grants, is constantly posing new and thoughtful questions, such as "Did Neanderthals know how to belch?"[444]

Liberal science marches on.

Although Neanderthal man's "complete disappearance from the face of the earth" remains a mystery to this day, it's generally believed that somehow or other, our own conservative species, *Homo sapiens sapiens,* gained some kind of secret

---

[442] "Ice Age" refers to the most recent glacial period. At least five major ice ages have occurred in the earth's past—perhaps several more. Global warming, of course, occurred between each one of them.
[443] The Neanderthal, as most humans and animals instinctively do, sought surroundings with coloration in which they could blend, so they began to move away from the snow and ice into dark, difficult-to-reach caves. One theory has it that some of them got lost in underground caverns, where they lived for a while, then reemerged many thousands of years later as Europeans. However, the Neanderthals' place in our human family tree and their relation to modern Europeans and Africans continues to be hotly debated among rocket scientists and liberal anthropological professors (and in certain subterranean circles).
[444] Virtually all liberals seem to gravitate toward endeavors and fields of study that are conducive to the smoking of marijuana cigarettes on the job without fear of being discovered.

advantage, maybe technological (e.g., advanced spear-chucking techniques), or maybe cultural (like not eating dirt).

Whatever the cause, Neanderthals were unable to compete, and they are believed to have died out about 20,000 to 35,000 years ago. Who knows? Maybe fossils that are more recent just haven't been found yet, because there are so few of them. Did our ancient ancestors eradicate the Neanderthal? Was he hunted to extinction? That's a distinct possibility, but difficult to imagine because Eurasia is pretty big. (Maybe they all died from sickle cell anemia.)

Did "modern man" consider thickheaded Neanderthals to be friends or his enemies? The latter is almost certainly the case. Why? Because the Neanderthal evidently had breath so bad, he could make a dead wooly goat do a backflip. Or did the Neanderthal's habit of cannibalism maybe have something to do with it? Either way, it doesn't make any difference now. Liberal Neanderthals were systematically killed by "modern man." But they eventually all died off because they just could not take care of themselves.

Yes, the "First Liberal," *Homo sapiens neanderthalensis* is quite the anthropological enigma.[445] If he existed today, what would liberal socialist Democrats call him? A preeminent prehistoric person of prosimian heritage? A highly valued and respected constituent? How about a cross between a common chimpanzee and a Congolese Pygmy on steroids?[446]

Was the liberal Neanderthal religious? It is suspected that he was. But the once popular belief that Neanderthals worshipped cave bears (as presented in the 1986 movie *The Clan of the Cave Bear*, starring Daryl Hannah as a sexy Cro-Magnon) now has few serious supporters among the (conservative) scientific community, for it appears that the idea was probably based on faulty liberal interpretation of fossil evidence.[447] Big surprise. It turns out that, instead of worshipping cave bears, liberal Neanderthal man was more than likely *a staple in the diet of cave bears.*

---

[445] For years, important scientists have debated whether Neanderthals should be classified as *Homo neanderthalensis* (a separate species from *Homo sapiens*) or *Homo sapiens neanderthalensis* (a subspecies of *Homo sapiens*). Some morphological studies support the Neanderthal as a separate species, while others support him as a subspecies, but because of strong evidence of interbreeding that appears to have resulted in fertile offspring, scientists are increasingly inclined to reclassify the Neanderthal as a subspecies of *H. sapiens*—for, by biological definition, two *different* species cannot produce fertile offspring. If this is true, the Neanderthal's correct classification is *Homo sapiens neanderthalensis*.

[446] Odd, forest-dwelling Pygmies inhabit various parts of central Africa. A Pygmy is short, with a small head, long arms, short legs, dark yellowish- to reddish-brown skin and somewhat heavy body hair, a wide nose with a low bridge, prognathous jaws, and a receding chin.

[447] Coincidentally, *The Clan of the Cave Bear*, despite a few scientific inaccuracies (Hollywood's specialty) is well worth viewing by any adult—but no children, please—who wishes to briefly experience *escapism,* a feeling that may be akin to what many liberals delight in daily while immersed in their mind-made illusoriness.

Could liberal Neanderthal man talk? In the book *The First Humans,* one dedicated researcher states, "There is also some (controversial) evidence, derived from studies of the lower parts of skulls, that Neanderthals could not have been able to make all the complex sounds we can make."[448] (Apparently, all he could do was ask the question "Whodat?")

What about primitive liberal Neanderthal woman? Was she a proud, noble, and courageous hunter-gatherer who braved the elements to feed herself and her family? Was she a mother fiercely protective of her brood? Or was she a petty, rude, and uncouth odoriferous slob—buzzing with flies—who ignored her screaming litter all day long while idly squatting in a communal circle, sharing chewed food and fermented grapes, while eating insects out of other tribe members' filthy hair?

What if a few liberal Neanderthal men and women had managed to survive and still existed today? What would they be doing? Teaching numb-tongue English at Ivy League schools?[449] Using tree branches to sweep offices at the Pentagon? Loitering around the dumpsters at 7-Elevens? Breaking open the back doors of Burger Kings? Climbing through the roofs of adult XXX peep shows? Getting strung out on crack cocaine? Refusing to earn a living? Failing to support their illegitimate children? Not paying federal income taxes? Maybe even fraudulently registering to vote? Who can say for sure? We'll probably never know. Sadly, this huge potentially Democratic voting block is no longer with us. Or maybe it is.

Conclusion: Mankind's *ancient aboriginal European ancestors,* the primitive half-breed Neanderthals, were short, dark, stocky, and dim-witted. Some were slaves, some were murderers. They are now "extinct." These early human/animals are our closest-known relatives to the primeval "Africans," who would have done anything under the sun to achieve their biological imperatives—e.g., sexual reproduction, eating fermented grapes, or smoking herbs, and eating mass quantities of food. Neanderthals were the *first liberals.*

---

[448] "Genes, Languages, and Archaeology," *The First Humans: Human Origins and History to 10,000 B.C.,* ed. Göran Burenhult, 1993, Weldon Owen Pty. Limited/Bra Böcker AB, HarperSanFrancisco, New York, N.Y., p. 145.
[449] Why has the popular American English vocabulary degenerated into words that can be easily pronounced without moving one's lips? Examples include (1) "folk" instead of *people,* (2) "notion" instead of *belief,* and (3) "king" instead of *president.*

JOHN HAYBERRY

The Descent of the (Liberal?) Neanderthal[450]

The Neanderthals *(Homo sapiens neanderthalensis)*, who lived for several hundred thousand years much like some remote twentieth-century African tribes, went "extinct" primarily because they were odiferous and clumsy and had an I.Q. of about 25. For that reason, they were very rarely able to outsmart wild animals, so they were often killed and eaten. Sometimes, Neanderthals ate one another. According to an old paleontologist friend of mine who has traveled to all seven continents in a Volkswagen boat-mobile, "This dude's gnawed bones are all over the place!" Many of them depended on help from "modern man" *(Homo sapiens sapiens)*. When there was no one around to give them food, they got angry and tried to kill modern man and rape his women, so miscegenation occurred. Some unwary Neanderthals were captured by "modern man," who was also little more than a savage. Modern man brought his captives back and kept them as slaves and/or big pets for entertainment. They were paraded around, teased, and tormented.[451] Some Neanderthals were released back into the wild, while others escaped and ran away naked. "Modern man" is white-skinned and brown-skinned. The earliest Neanderthals were black-skinned. Maybe it's just not considered politically correct for anthropologists to say such things—especially when government grants from liberal administrations are involved. Neanderthal man is inarguably a member of our human family tree. Another member of our human family tree that no one ever talks about is the indigenous Australian Aboriginal. That's probably because, if the statistics are to be believed, the aborigines have a genetic proclivity for drug and alcohol abuse that includes kava, cannabis, petrol sniffing, methamphetamines, and heroin and other injected drugs. This has reportedly resulted in a fivefold increase in mental disorders among the aborigine population. In many cases, the diagnosis is *schizophrenia*.

Maybe liberals just don't want us to know.

(To be continued.)

---

[450] Today's liberals, by definition (and in all likelihood), have a much higher Neanderthal factor (NF) than do the rest of us, so why do liberals keep denying the fact that they are neanderthalic? Why do they insist that their ancient heritage is utterly *impossible?*

[451] "Maybe the actual origin of our left-wing species are puppet-brained evolutionarily retarded females (and some males) who were being used as prehistoric sex toys." —Anonymous Woman, editor

Chapter 15

Why Don't They Tell Their Own Children The Truth?

Hollywood, California, Brainwashing Techniques

As most everybody knows, Hollywood's specialty is fantasy, not reality. Liberal adults and children especially enjoy watching movies about imaginary characters brought to life with special effects. It's all about money, and *make-believe* entertainment sells lots of theater tickets. The popularity of fantasy is probably the main reason that both liberals and conservatives are so often portrayed with gross inaccuracy in books and movies, and on television. More often than not, liberal Democrat types are made to look good, and conservative Republican types are made to look bad. You may have noticed that, in advertising, business signs that are positioned upside down or have obvious spelling mistakes tend to get people's attention. That is why in movies, liberals are usually portrayed as the good guys, and conservatives, the bad guys. But here's something important that you may not realize: The strong, brave, admirable, independent, self-sacrificing, righteous, smarter-than-anybody-else, underdog-against-the-world-who-is-fighting-for-what's-right-to-save-mankind liberal characters in films simply do not exist. I repeat: *Such people do not exist.* Only a lifetime of liberal media brainwashing has convinced us that they do exist, so I will repeat it once again with emphasis (because it may be virtually impossible for many moviegoers to believe it):

Such people do not exist at all.

Today's liberals are the evolutionary result of P.E.T.S. (people enabled to survive).

No, there are no liberals alive who are braver than military generals, consistently smarter at every turn than all world scientists, more clever than an F.B.I. agent, or more ethical than members of the Religious Right. On the contrary, the detailed information in this book describes liberals as they really are—even though this may be extremely difficult to comprehend for anyone who watches too much television and doesn't get out much. However, to be fair, some of the depictions in Hollywood movies of the old friendly, goofy-looking, childlike, *humanitarian* liberal types who reek of medicine and mothballs do appear, in fact, to be accurate.

Of course, there's no way of knowing anything for sure about a liberal's actual charitable donations to others, which may include political payoffs—or losing $20 bills when pulling coupons out of their pants pockets—but I think it's safe to assume that most liberals wouldn't withhold payment from a friendly conservative teenager who washed his or her cat or dog. Also, to be fair, the habit of casting liberals in the role of tough guys, such as cops, or secret agents, or patriots, or war heroes, is probably not always intentional Hollywood propaganda. You see, there are only so many good actors (i.e., people who enjoy fantasizing by pretending to be something they're not) to choose from, and liberals—especially those in politics—are often very good actors. But readers should be aware that nothing grabs an audience's attention better than *antithetical juxtaposition,* a literary device used by comedy writers and poets that's been adapted to the screen.[452]

The glut of films that include gun-toting female martial-arts experts who can take on three men at a time, or dozens of men in prolonged multiple fights; or male F.B.I. agents who wear earrings; or wise little old children telling silly, confused liberal adults what they should do; and the obligatory casting of women and minority members in roles as bosses, judges, generals, and presidents is done for a very specific reason. You see, it's the joke-writing equivalent of using oxymoronic phrases such as "enormous ant," "dangerous midget," or "evil nun," just to name a few examples. Another example would be the phrase that all liberals seem to find so humorous: military intelligence. Unfortunately, the effect of such filmmaking

---

[452] Antithetical juxtaposition accounts in part for the huge success of the hit comedy series *Seinfeld* (funny-looking nitwits dating good-looking women). The writer, whose net worth has been estimated to be about $800 million, reportedly donated money in the 2000 U.S. presidential race to both opposing candidates: the Democrat, Al Gore, and the Republican, George W. Bush (who was soon to be the winner). Seinfeld "subsequently made four contributions to Democratic Party primary candidates in 2000 and 2004" (Wikipedia, "Jerry Seinfeld," February 18, 2014). But why? Who would do that? Would you do that?

monkeyshines for the sake of entertainment (and, of course, moolah) is that the public eventually begins to consider the atypical to be typical, and the abnormal to be normal—which they are not, but the bottom line is this: *Deviation from social orthodoxy sells tickets.*

The unfortunate thing here is that so-called liberal art is not only a reflection of life; it can also be used to *affect* life by temporarily altering instinctual societal attitudes and remaking reality into someone else's image.[453] Can you guess whose? A liberal's.

The biggest problem is that many children, most likely under the age of eight, can barely distinguish the difference between what they see on television and what they see in real life, especially when they become engrossed in two- or three-hour movies. To adults who know the difference, it's all harmless nonsense, but not to children, who often believe that the contents of the film actually happened. A child may subconsciously remember something that can affect him or her, perhaps negatively, later in life. The experience is real for the child. A mother or father may see no indication of a problem until decades have passed.

It may seem like nothing for any of us to really worry about, but don't wait to hear your son or daughter say, *"Guess Who's Coming to Dinner."*[454]

The problem, as many unsuspecting parents have already found out, is real.[455]

"Why are all of the Hollywood movie stars so ugly these days, with their odd-looking multicultural faces and disproportionate testosterone? What happened to all of the good-looking actors and actresses like Greta Garbo, Marilyn Monroe, Clark Gable, Elizabeth Taylor, James Garner, Humphrey Bogart, Burt Lancaster, Ann Margaret, and Elvis Presley? Are fat, unpleasant, sex-starved, hook-nosed, cigar-smoking, liberal big shots (both male and female) trying to get people to marry their own kind . . . on a casting couch? Or are they trying to help us choose the next president of the United States? (Maybe they already have.)" —John Hayberry (2014)

---

[453] All Hollywood film directors should be required by both the state of California and federal law to include short film clips of the actual persons upon which their movies are based. That way, impressionable young males and females in the audience won't be misled and will be able to clearly see for themselves the real differences that exist between, say, for example, those brave American soldiers who fought in the Vietnam War and the self-absorbed, somewhat odd-looking and wimpy liberal actors who portray them. Inarguably, honesty—and accuracy—is the best policy.

[454] This 1967 movie starred a beaming young African American male, Sidney Portiere.

[455] Remember what you read previously about normalcy bias? (See page 132.)

What we are talking about here are self-serving liberal attempts at *mind control*. Sorry, guys, it's not going to work anymore. Have a nice day.

The Boob Tube: How Liberal Propaganda Works

Television is the most insidious weapon that L.S.D.ers have in their arsenal and they use it relentlessly to attack the rest of us. You see, society has become so conditioned to believe certain things about liberalism as a result of decades of incessant liberal propaganda in books, magazines, newspapers, movies, and television that readers will undoubtedly require some reflection and personal observation to grasp the following fact: Virtually *none* of what we've been led to believe by these elite media clowns, fishy cluster huggers, and starry-eyed rainbow lovers is true. It's all high liberal nonsense and coordinated group fantasy rooted in a desire for social, moral, and monetary equality with those whom they secretly—and not so secretly—disagree with categorically, and whom they often despise.

Before discussing the consequences of their propaganda, however, we must first reiterate and always bear in mind a liberal's three main characteristics: (1) diminished capacity, (2) self-interest, and (3) desire to feel good. Also be aware that it's not unusual for a person with liberal views to know nothing of politics or even what the word liberal means. Furthermore, readers should remember that the term liberal is not so much a description of any particular type of person as it is a defective human gene or genes. But as mentioned previously, it may actually take a substantial period of time—from six to twelve months or longer—for most readers to even begin to fully comprehend the significance of all this.[456] (It took me three years.)

Mind control, also known as brainwashing, coercive persuasion, mind abuse, thought control, or thought reform, refers to a process in which an individual or a group systematically uses unethical, manipulative methods to persuade others to conform to the wishes of the manipulator(s). This is, of course, detrimental to whoever is being manipulated. The term *brainwashing* applies to any tactic, psychological or otherwise, that can be seen as subverting an individual's sense of control over his or her own thinking, behavior, emotions, or decision making.

---

[456] People who only watch TV movies have more difficulty distinguishing between fantasy and reality than those who don't.

Human (D) Evolution

Brainwashing and mind-control theories were originally developed to explain how totalitarian regimes appeared to succeed in systematically indoctrinating prisoners of war through propaganda and torture techniques.

Can newspapers, books, magazines, television, and movies really be used successfully to manipulate people's minds? Yes, it can. It seems farfetched, doesn't it? After all, how can intelligent, educated people who are well aware of the meaning of the word "propaganda" ever be susceptible to it? How can simply *watching* television have any actual permanent effect on anyone?

Well, it does.

Here's a firsthand account from a personal friend of ours named Bob. He's a claims investigator. It happened many years ago, and it's true.

> Years ago, I worked in an office building with a gorgeous tomato who could've won a beauty contest. I would've asked her out to lunch, but, unfortunately, she just wasn't my type—too young, too pretty, and way too stuck up. (Barefoot Southern belles are more my style. Ya know, tall, blonde, big-eared, pimple-faced country gals in tattered straw hats with hair down to their knees who ride broken-down nags and eat pickled pigs' knuckles.) But I was captivated by this shapely female, in part, because I thought that she resembled someone I knew, a close friend or relative. I just couldn't figure out for the life of me *who*. She didn't look like my mother, my sister, my aunt, or my cousin. She didn't look like anyone I knew. So I was puzzled. I didn't know where I had seen her face before. I kept trying to remember, but then, after a while, I finally gave up. Time passed and I moved on. Eventually, I forgot all about her. Then one day, I was sitting in a hotel room watching TV and happened to click on an old black-and-white movie called *Guys and Dolls*. It's a 1955 'musical comedy' starring Marlon Brando. He's a gambler who chases after a church lady and marries her in the end. Suddenly something dawned on me. The church lady in the movie is the spittin' image of the woman who worked in the same office building as me. Mystery solved! Ya see, when I was just a tyke, I thought of Marlon Brando as my uncle because he looks and acts like my deadbeat uncle Bill so much. That's the reason the woman Marlon Brando married in the movie looks like she's a relative of mine—*to me*. Amazing, ain't it? Just because I watched a two-and-a-half-hour movie over fifty years ago, I still to this day want to hop into bed with that shapely young tomato even though she's definitely not my type and told me no, then slapped my face. But it's probably for the best. She wouldn't

even be able to stand the sight of me now 'cause I wear an old felt fedora, smoke Havana cigars, and shoot craps. Luckily, the woman Brando married (in the movie) wasn't a Papuan cannibal, or a *Brokeback Mountain* cowgirl, or a sheepdog—or Frank Sinatra. Who knows? I might have tried to kiss one of them, too. *Yuck! Ptooey!*

So don't even bother to read all of research available on the subject of brainwashing. Just remember that story. It's true: Children can be brainwashed.[457] So all that anyone needs to understand is this: Films are a dramatic portrayal of life, so when young children (and probably even infants) watch television, they can become so engrossed with what they see, that they can barely—if at all—*separate what they are watching from real life.* That's why a Hollywood movie can have such a drastic effect on impressionable people. Watching many movies with the same theme would obviously be even worse.[458] Television can shape and solidify what children believe just as permanently as real-life experiences. It can cause them to have anti-instinctual attitudes and feelings about people, animals, food, the opposite sex, and many other things that will forever be unalterable. If an individual is brainwashed as a child, trying to change that person's views later on in life may be as impossible a task to perform as trying to negate an offspring's bond with his or her own mother—and all a tot has to do is watch *one* hour-long Hollywood movie.[459]

"The big problem with television isthat if you watch everything on it, you begin to believe that anything goes and literally,everything is normal. Kids grow up seeing good-looking girls

---

[457] The British Secret Intelligence Service, Russian Sluzhba Vneshney Razvedki, and Chinese secret service all take the subject of brainwashing very seriously. (So does the C.I.A.)

[458] Consider the recent Ferguson, Missouri, riots. The same thing happens every time a white police officer shoots a black man, for whatever reason. The overwhelming number of made-for-TV movie scripts read like this: [Black man good, white man bad.] That's why so many African Americans feel justified in attacking white people for the slightest perceived verbal slight or provocation.

[459] Some movies about Jesus Christ are the best examples. Unawares, little children often watch a "charismatic" grinning, long-haired Hollywood actor playing in the role of Jesus, who, to those of us who've been around, looks like just another common liberal marijuana enthusiast. Another problem with this situation is that a child may see someone else in the movie who may resemble a close relative of his or hers. If that "relative" in the movie *likes* the actor, *worships* the actor, or *interacts* with the actor, especially in some sexual manner, then the child may be affected permanently. He or she may look upon the actor as either (1) someone to be loved, or (2) a special friend, or even (3) a likeable "relative by marriage." A problem may arise when the child grows up and reaches sexual maturity: If he or she happens to meet by chance anyone *resembling the actor* in that film, he or she will be especially attracted to that person because he or she feels *more comfortable*—even if that person happens to be of a *different race or ethnic group.* As we all know, feeling comfortable around an attractive person of the opposite sex is conducive to mating.

French kissing, so theythink it's normal, or funny --instead of creepy." --Anonymous parent (and former teenager)

"Television has changed everything. It allows those who control it to manipulate the opinions and attitudes of millions of viewers. Now, people are so used to seeing smiling creeps—and creepy stuff—on TV that everyone is beginning to think creepiness is normal." —Sponge Bob

"Liberals have inundated the cable TV channels with so many people of no quality that everyone has become used to their faces and behavior, so trashy people are thought of as normal." —Anonymous

"Liberal men are on every TV channel, telling us what's cool and uncool, what's good and bad, what's smart and dumb, what's okay to say about people and what's not okay. Why? To make themselves look good to the opposite sex?" —Angela

"Why do we have men on television talking about cheating on their spouses and then laughing, as though it's something funny to do?" —Angela

"Things have gotten so bad on television shows that it is starting to bleed over into children's cartoons. Remember when cartoons always showed the difference between good and evil? Now, everything is mixed together. Good is evil, and evil is good." —N. J.

"With the advent of television, some Jewish entrepreneurs probably realized that if a minority were able to control it, they could not only manipulate public opinion but give the appearance of being even larger in number than they really are. They could promote themselves, their beliefs, their goals, and their presidential candidates. They could even "brainwash" everyone to a limited extent and make them think like they do. That's why so many conservative TV personalities are painfully careful and

self-conscious when it comes to saying what they really think."
—Anonymous Analyst

"People should stop watching TV, read some books, and educate themselves. With the exception of FOX News, television is just a politically correct fantasy world." —Shirley

"The biggest problem with our federal government is television cameras. They encourage people who serve in government to think of themselves as movie stars, and they either become darlings or become enemies of the press. Instead of doing their jobs, politicians now spend all of their time preparing themselves with cosmetics to look good, so they can entertain television viewers and pick up women. Another problem with appearing on television—and it's one reason why there are so few 100% conservatives involved in politics—is that it can make people easily recognizable, so they and their families may be targeted by whackos. Generally speaking, *only liberals are tempted to do such a thing.*" —John Hayberry (2010)

"The thing about television is that when any minority group controls it, they can make themselves look bigger and more formidable than they really are and manipulate and sway public opinion. . . . That's what Progressives are doing." —Don B.

"They [liberals] go on television. They look normal. They talk very carefully and say what everybody wants to hear. They act like they're mainstream. But then, when they're elected, horns grow out of their heads!" —T. N. T.

"It did not take long for politicians to see the tremendous potential of television. . . . After the election, [John F.] Kennedy said of television: 'We wouldn't have had a prayer without that gadget.'" —*Awake!*, May 22, 1991

"The best way to show television viewers what kind of people liberals really are is to take away their skits and monologues and put them in a social setting in close proximity with normal conservative men and women. That way, viewers can clearly see how everyone interacts, especially with the waitress in a singles bar. If that's not proof enough, arrange for a liberal and a conservative to get on a tour bus full of athletes from the Special Olympics and drive them to a cave in the Rocky Mountains. Then, inside the cave, have them all gather around a campfire with pitchforks while chanting in tongues and drinking cups of ancient mull. (Hint: The conservative won't show up.)" —Chester "The Jester," the *Morning Brilliance,* March 7, 1999

"Some have called television the world's "third superpower." It calms us when we should be alarmed, and it alarms us when we should be calm. Those who control it are the greatest puppeteers of all time." —John Hayberry

Mindless Art and Music

Mindless "Art"

Most people who work long hard hours to provide for their family just don't have the time it takes to visit an art museum. Nevertheless, we should all try to take the time to do so. It can be quite a learning experience. If, as they say, the eyes are the windows to the mind, then art is a reflection of the artist's soul. Today, one of the *basic assumptions* of Western thought is that liberalism is the sophisticated political ideology that generates the most art. But is that really true? Or is it just more of the same rubbish that we've all been exposed to for decades? Are liberals the most artistic among us? Or are they just the ones who are the most publicly applauded *by other liberals* who hand out awards—and rewards? Maybe liberals are just the ones with more free time on their hands because most of them don't have full-time jobs. Whatever the case, one thing is for sure: Modern art is a reflection of the liberal psyche. That, we are now only just beginning to understand.

JOHN HAYBERRY

The following is from *The Dispossessed Majority,* Part V: "The Atomization of Art":

> Members of the once dominant population group mix with the newcomers and in order to compete are forced to adopt many of their attitudes and habits. Art becomes multiracial, multinational, multi-directional, and multifarious.
>
> Much of western art, particularly in the United States, is now in such a stage of atomization. The surrealist painters, atonal jazz musicologists, prosaic poets, emetic novelists, crypto pornographers and *revanchist* pamphleteers say they are searching for new forms because the old forms are exhausted. Actually, they are exhuming the most ancient forms of all—simple geometric shapes, color blobs, drum beats, genitalia, four-letter words and four-word sentences. The old forms are not exhausted. The minority artist simply has no feeling for them because they are not his forms. Since style is not a commodity that can be bought or invented, the avant-garde, having no style of its own, can only retreat to a styleless primitivism.
>
> The atomization of art is characterized by the emergence of the fake artist—the man without talent and training who becomes an artist by self-proclamation. . . . The fake artist is not unrelated to the anti-artist—the type of individual who blew up *The Thinker* outside the Cleveland Museum in the spring of 1970. It was one of the eleven castings made under the personal supervision of Rodin.[460]

Today, so-called *Piss Christ* (circa 1987), a photograph of Jesus on a cross—the Christian crucifix—in urine, is undoubtedly the most controversial example of modern art in recent history.[461] (There is just no accounting for tastelessness.) Who else but a liberal would display a pint of his own pee and other bodily fluids to the public? But this particular artist, a national treasure, who some believe may be the reincarnation of Norman Rockwell's favorite dog, has created far worse. So much worse, in fact, that it shouldn't be described to anyone who has no

---

[460] Robertson, *op. cit.* (last paragraph attributed to the *New York Times,* July 17, 1970), p. 232.
[461] Ten years later, another artist craving attention splattered elephant dung on a painting of the Virgin Mary. New York's mayor at the time described the canvas as "sick," and the National Gallery of Australia in Canberra refused to show it. (Rumor has it that some investors at D.N.C. headquarters in Washington ordered 25,000 prints.)

access to a plastic vomit bag, or a bucket. Not surprisingly, many of this artiste's fine works have been vandalized by angry protestors (i.e., men and women of good taste and breeding who know to flush a toilet). Still, Norman Rockwell likely had the same problem—you know, death threats and stuff. (Although, come to think of it, no, he didn't.) And then, of course, there are the famous Andy Warhol "pop art" Campbell's soup can paintings. Who in their right mind would have wasted their time painting such a thing? Hmm. Maybe it was just a *commercial advertisement*. (Ya' think?) If so, it must have worked, because one silk-screened painting is still hanging on a wall at the Museum of Modern Art in New York City. Tourists from all over the world can go to look at photocopies of the printed label on an ordinary large can of *tomato paste* that's been available for about a dollar on the shelves of grocery stores since 1962. [462]

Ah, liberals can be so tricky, and so entertaining, but such absolute fools.

> "This is the reason I speak to them in figures, because they see and yet cannot perceive; and they hear and yet do not listen, nor do they understand." —St. Matthew 13:13, *Holy Bible* from the ancient Eastern text, Lamsa's translation from the Aramaic of the Peshitta

Mindless "Music"

As far as today's popular music goes, we should be careful about criticizing what some teenagers listen to—even so-called gangsta rap, which celebrates such things as "Allah" (as in Allah's army), "crack" (as in crack cocaine), and "acting like an animal" (as in gang rape)—because we should all remember how adults used to criticize us when we were kids for listening to music such as "Jungle Bunny"—excuse me, I mean *"Jungle Fever."* However, there's one big difference: Adults complained about our music

---

[462] Advertising agencies often arrange for things that will get their clients more exposure, so sometimes they create ads that they know will be reported on the evening news. For example, in early 2014, much to everyone's surprise, the Campbell's company was suddenly in the news again after televising a "mixed-race family" soup commercial.

[463] National Security is the primary duty of our federal government. Its first and most important job is to protect all American citizens. So why is the Obama White House spending so much of its time campaigning for Democratic political candidates and using our tax dollars to fund and grow its support base instead of using the money to insure U.S. military superiority? (Maybe they only discover problems when they *read about it* in the newspaper.)

for the same reason that adults have complained about young people's music for decades, if not centuries: It's way too sexually suggestive. But now, here in our own country, the United States of America, it's not just sexual innuendoes that are the problem; it's National Security.[463] What kids are listening to these days is the loud, syncopated, get-in-everybody's-face-that-you-can, THUMP, THUMP, THUMP, THUMP, THUMP, THUMP, THUMP! of *"I mad, I bad, I gonna kill somebody dead!"*-type music that is inarguably mentally retarded, as are the occasional drive-by shootings by paid murderers of the big-lip-flapping "arteeests" singing such crap. That's why, so often, when we hear monkeyshit such as this: *"I mad! I bad! BOOM, BOOM, BOOM! I mad! I bad! BOOM, BOOM, BOOM!"* it's sometimes followed by the sound of pistol shots.

Human and Animal Kin Selection

In 1964, British evolutionary biologist W. D. Hamilton published two papers entitled "The Genetical Evolution of Social Behaviour" (I and II), which contained his Inclusive Fitness Theory, explaining *kin selection*. This theory accounts for the preferential investment and altruistic behavior of both man and animal toward relatives. Kin selection is a process that exists at the very core of evolution, and much of what occurs in the development of a species is dependent on it. Kin selection is an instinctual method by which individual humans and animals ensure the continuation of their genes, because increasing the number of one's genes in subsequent generations is not restricted to having offspring.

Non-offspring kin share a percentage of genes by direct descent from a common ancestor. That is one reason why most people have an instinctual interest in the survival and success of their close relatives, as opposed to the relatives of people very dissimilar to themselves (say, for example, the New Black Panthers, Neville Chamberlain, or an Armenian). Kin investment includes protecting kin from attack. It can also include a costly expenditure of time, energy, and resources, but one's genetic replication is the benefit. Increasing the possibility of genetic replication is one reason that chimpanzees, for example, invest in their offspring and collateral kin. Because parents share more genes with their offspring than with the offspring of collateral kin, parents invest more in their own offspring than in more distant kin. It is a basic instinct that can exist even in insects, like the cockroach.

This is easy to understand. Investment by parents in their offspring sharply increases the offspring's chances of survival and hence the chances of reproducing. As mentioned previously, paternity certainty is one factor that influences investment. A maternal grandmother is certain of her genetic relatedness to her daughters' children, but less so with her sons' children, and a paternal grandfather is even less certain of his grand-offspring's relatedness. Grandmothers can therefore be expected to invest more in their daughters' children than in their sons' children, and grandfathers can be expected to invest proportionately less in both instances and then take a nap.

Curiously enough, male apes do not contribute much to the care of their offspring, but whether parental uncertainty plays a part in this is unknown. Kin investment would also seem to explain why—or at least one reason why—men are generally more sexually jealous: Men face the problem of uncertain paternity, which may cost them a lot of time and money, whereas women are always 100 percent sure that they are the mothers of their children. (If not, something is drastically wrong.)

Humans, as we know, are inclined to behave more altruistically toward kin and toward those with genetic similarity to themselves than toward obviously unrelated individuals. Liberals, of course, consider generosity by conservatives toward people the conservatives like, rather than to needy liberals, to be a very, very bad thing—possibly even *racist*. Most people choose to live near their relatives (although some make a point to live as far away as possible). Relatives share food, exchange sizeable gifts, and favor each other in wills in proportion to their relatedness.

"Progressive" Liberal or Homosexual Kin Investment

"Progressive" liberals, of course, want to eliminate the evil of normal kin investment because it's in their best interest to do so. One way they do this is through the "death tax." That's because they need other people's (i.e., taxpaying conservatives') money to continue to survive and thus successfully breed. You see, homosexual persons have a tendency to leave their estates to nieces and nephews, rather than to lifelong partners. Apparently, the average "gay" relationship is *not quite what it seems to be,* despite all of the liberal media hoopla to the contrary.

Consider the Eternal Rule of Opposable Thumb:

Behaving abnormally is not conducive to survival.

And neither is kin investment in someone who behaves unnaturally.

Furthermore, the current push to legalize same-sex marriage seems to be just another attempt by regressive "progressives" to mainstream abnormality.[464] Any argument for same-sex marriage that's based strictly on such things as *inheritance tax laws* is not a valid one because it's the assessment of the taxes that needs to be addressed, not laws that pertain to marriage. Homosexual men and woman can *already get married* if they want to. They can hold a wedding ceremony any time they want. They can buy a cake. They can arrange for catering and invite all of their friends. They can exchange vows and put rings on each other's fingers. Then they can hug, kiss, and even go on a honeymoon. Later, they can buy a house together and live "happily ever after." Nobody is stopping them from getting married. Common-law marriages have worked for untold thousands of years—without any government record keeping. So what's the problem? The problem is this: "Progressives" appear to want all sexual behavior—no matter how outlandish—to be considered normal, so they're trying their best, step by step, to achieve *legislated social acceptance of virtually all human abnormality*.[465] It also appears that "progressive" liberals use some members of the homosexual community as *political puppets*.

Kin investment can also pertain to *groups*. Kinship groups generally share the same customs, values, rules, and attitudes. They often share the same religion, too. Kin selection forms much of the conceptual basis of the theory of social evolution. There is even some evidence of this mechanism among protozoa. For example, when viewed under a microscope, liberal protozoa from the New England states are the ones that always retreat from their original positions and begin swimming backward.

Kin investment is a function of lineage. Over evolutionary time, individuals who invest more resources in relatives of greater certainty than in relatives of lesser certainty are more likely to contribute more of their common genes to future generations, perpetuating favoritism toward direct descendants. Liberal Democratic politicians, of course, want to curb this practice; they prefer that everything be given to them personally for . . . distribution(?). In both humans and animals, the act of mating is a primary genetic imperative. And so is investing in kin. However, the first and most important genetic imperative is *eating*.

Is the liberal instinct for kin investment, as with other of their instincts, to some degree diminished? Do the majority of liberals have only moderate concern for the well-being and success of their progeny? The answer, in my opinion, is yes;

---

[464] Are "progressives" trying to infiltrate the comic book industry? If so, why? To try to make the superheroes look like themselves and their friends? So they can dress one another up and put on capes to wear at the Gay Pride parades? The original Green Lantern, a DC Comics superhero for the past seventy years has suddenly been revealed to be gay, so he was drawn kissing a boyfriend. The Hulk has changed drastically, too. Instead of being likeable, as he once was, he's a big green evil creep—in other words, *"he bad."*

[465] Physically deformed midgets are now being encouraged to have babies.

however, additional research is needed. Until then, we must rely on the opinion of a forensic psychiatrist and the author of the only major book on the subject (see footnote #159). He would say, "Yes, and without a doubt."

Biological Imperatives

Here's something else to think about. The entire field of psychology revolves around the concept of psychological problems stemming from an inability to achieve biological imperatives. One of the most important of these is obtaining a mate. For males, the ability to obtain mates is often related to social status, so achieving one's *normal* position in society at the highest level possible on the existing hierarchal scale (which is generally based on one's ambition and abilities) can also be considered a biological imperative. That means that an adverse political system such as communism, which inarguably prevents ambitious people from becoming rich and successful, causes not only mental distress but conceivably also an accompanying change in body chemistry, which results in psychological problems—and perhaps drinking large quantities of Stolichnaya. It seems reasonable to conclude that preventing hardworking, ambitious people from living their lives at a level that reflects their abilities, which are vastly superior to those of someone who prefers sleeping, can actually result in a mental sickness. In other words, he who climbs the coconut tree should be allowed to eat the coconuts. (This pertains to financial rewards, too.)

Political Puppets and Puppeteers

Speaking of coconuts, why have die-hard left-wing loons constantly compared President Monkeyshines to Franklin Delano Roosevelt, Abraham Lincoln, Ronald Reagan, James Bond (and other cool people), and even Jesus?[466] Why does the Left so often try to impart larger-than-life, quixotic, even holy biblical characteristics to their elected representatives? Conservative Republicans don't do it. Presidents Nixon,[467] Ford, Reagan, Bush I, and Bush II were all self-sufficient, take-charge individuals.

---

[466] *Re: Cool People*. "Cool" is smiling, talking, laughing, and perhaps dancing with your friends—but all the while being alert and prepared for danger. "Cool" is not sitting all alone on a barstool with half-lidded eyes and a grin, zonked out on drugs and swaying to the music, as though everyone in the world adores you, so you haven't got a care.

They didn't need to be propped up with false praise and patted on their backs—or on the tops of their heads like dummies, either—by yammering, beady-eyed financial supporters pulling their strings. They didn't need to be operated by crafty, money-hungry political ventriloquists, setting them on one knee and speaking out of the corners of their mouths while secretly manipulating their heads, arms, and legs to make them behave properly. So what's going on? The reason is that conservative Republicans vote for *leaders* but liberal Democrats vote for *champions*. What's the difference? A champion only talks the talk, but a leader talks the talk and walks the walk.

Politicians in Congress seem concerned only for themselves. Don't they see what's happening to our country as a result of suboptimal liberal *multiculturalism?* America is fast becoming divided, confused, and unrecognizable (an L.S.D.er's dream). That's because unchecked immigration, as many other countries have long known—but, apparently, have forgotten—doesn't just mean multicultural clothing, food, language, and music. It means multicultural I.Q.'s, multicultural primitive religions, multicultural bad judgment, multicultural lack of hygiene, multicultural serious diseases, multicultural medical practices,[468] and multicultural apathy toward human and animal life. The influx of illegal immigrants into the United States of America is causing the number of cases of tuberculosis, chicken pox, dengue fever, and leprosy, along with the reported number of birth defects, to rise.[469] Those children with mental or physical abnormalities who survive will likely vote Democratic when they reach the age of adulthood, with the expectation being, of course, that the U.S. government will take good care of them.

> "Foreigners covered with skin cancer (or diaper rash) have figured out what to do. All they have to do is come here to the United States and the government will pay for it. That's why they're in such a rush to get here before Obama leaves office." —Anonymous

> "But that's really just the tip of the multicultural iceberg. Multiculturalism also helps explain the growth of crime and violence in

---

[467] Many Republicans thought of Richard Nixon as a "crook" because of his demeanor, but still, most of us liked him—or tried to—because he was a president with conservative family values who only did things that were in the best interest of the United States of America.

[468] We're not just talking about witchdoctors here. We're talking about pleasant-looking "doctors" with degrees from Internet Web sites that you never heard of (e.g., the University of Boeotia) pretending to know things that they know almost nothing about, then checking *multiple choice* boxes on a small preprinted prescription form. Watering down expensive medications and reusing syringes is also commonplace.

[469] *Re: Illegal Immigrants.* Infectious diseases are a real danger to American children with low immunity residing in hospitals.

all our major cities. Rape and murder—including a few beheadings—are now beginning to seem commonplace. Child molesters and drug abusers are running free. So why don't we ever hear anyone angrily complaining about this situation on the evening news? Is it because we've all gotten so used to abnormality and crime—including stabbings, shooting rampages, and machete attacks—that we consider it *entertainment?*" —John Hayberry

"We see so many damn reports on the news about the violence around here and in the Dominican Republic that we think it's just the way life's supposed to be—killing people left and right. It's in the movies, too. So, now, everybody thinks murder is no big deal. Just wait'll it happens to them!" —Anonymous Italiano

"Is it just a coincidence that 95 percent of the crimes reported on national television appear to involve people who, if they were registered to vote, would choose Democrats exclusively?" —Concerned Mother of Five Boys

"Why do the police have to spend so much of their time on the job trying to be friends with multicultural losers and no-goods? To solve crimes and keep from being attacked—that's why. So why not just put all of Obama's illegal aliens in small neighborhoods surrounded by eight-foot-high cement block walls with broken glass beer bottles on top, just like they do in Mexico?" — Anonymous

"People whose ancestors were notorious for committing atrocities against their fellow man are now coming into the United States of America by the truckload, riddled with diseases, then getting free food, shelter, and clothing from our government. But why? What good does that do any of us? All it does is weaken the United States and help keep 'L.S.D.ers' in power." —J. H.

"Why are there so many lawsuits these days? Minority members are taking everyone to court. Somebody must be rounding them up, organizing their community, and giving them instructions, just like President Obama did. Why are *real Americans* being subjected to the abuse of foreigners? Only other foreigners could be behind such a thing." —Jen

"Multiculturalism, of course, includes everyone, including the Australian aborigines. We already have a few Australian Aborigine Americans. One of them, who was adopted and brought back to the United States, grew up here and then raped and strangled an attractive blonde woman living on the east coast of Florida." — Concerned Floridian

"The following seems to be the Democrats' secret plan. Pass legislation that attracts foreigners to the United States of America -- and, of course, offer lots of free stuff. Then secretly aid and abet millions of foreigners to break our laws by sneaking into our country. Then also pretend that it's a great big surprise but still really nothing to worry about. All the while, keep acting like everything's okay because Congress hasn't yet made a decision about something called `amnesty.' Also, argue vehemently and with all your liberal might that any fool should be allowed to vote for a U.S. president without identification. To top it off, let anyone stay here even if he or she (or it) is arrested for criminal activity. This fools the average American because practically nobody believes that anyone born and raised in our country would ever even consider behaving like a traitor or an enemy. The result is that hundreds of thousands of stupid foreigners who don't speak English and don't even like us are now casting votes for liberal Democratic asses." --C. G.

"Virtually everything in this country that is going wrong can be traced to liberalism." —The Big Guy (2013)

"Social Schisms"

Just recently, the president has begun using the phrase "social schisms." But why? A schism is defined as "a split or division between strongly opposed sections or parties, caused by differences of opinion or belief." Is this what liberals mean by their new attempts at *multiculturalism?* Wild animals (of the same type) don't have "social schisms"—except when it comes to their *territory*—so why would human beings? Why would we patriotic Americans? Gee, I wonder.... Is this what liberals really want? Hmm.

The phrase "divide and conquer" is derived from the Greek *Diaírei kaì basíleue.* It is attributed to Philip II, king of Macedon (382–336 B.C.), and it describes his policy toward the Greek city-states. In politics, sociology, and economics, divide and rule—also known as divide and conquer—refers to a strategy of gaining and maintaining power based on the fact that smaller opponents ("two Americas," for example) are easier to subdue and manage than one larger one. So what, pray tell, is the solution? Is there any way for the United States of America to regain the worldwide respect that it once had? The answer is, in the opinion of most conservative Americans, *yes, we can.* If we do not, our unique culture risks death and even extinction, just like the ivory-billed woodpecker, the Tasmanian wolf, the passenger pigeon, or the dodo bird.

President Obama's Immigration Policy

What exactly is the Obama Doctrine?[470] Is it "Leading from Behind"? Is it "King-for-a-Day Executive-Order Implementation"? Or is it "Let's Repopulate the USA with Illegal Aliens" (so that Democrats will win elections)? Each time the president is asked about it, he is unable to provide an answer. However, as time goes on, things become more and more clear. Now, he's flying planeloads of South American men, women, and children to different cities around the United States so that their relatives can come live here, too. But the unfortunate truth is this: In an open-border multicultural society, our normal constitutional protections *will have to be violated* by law enforcement

---

[470] *Re: The Obama Doctrine.* What is it? No one really knows for sure. Other presidents have had doctrines, but when asked about it, our president just talks about other things. Is it because there really is no Obama Doctrine? Or is it because he believes that he was elected to entertain everyone? Maybe he was. But what he does, instead, is go hopping and skipping around the world like a pansy. Then, with his chin raised high, he paternalistically pats the shoulders of other country's leaders (many of whom are alpha males), indicating that *he,* President Barack Hussein Obama, understands. But why does he act like this? Is he trying to start a goddamn war? What is he, anyway, the Antichrist? Or a cocky half-Kenyan with a I've-got-the-drugs-and-money-and-women grin? Does he really believe that he, Barack Hussein Obama, self-proclaimed "citizen of the world," is now the supreme leader of the entire human race? What does he want us to do next, build a fake Greek Temple, a marble statue, or Egyptian pyramid in his honor? Or is he just trying to start a game of fisticuffs with other world leaders? If he is, why doesn't someone try to arrange one between him and Angela Merkel? The good German Chancellor, with her arms akimbo, could jump around like a cartoon character and maybe throw a few punches to the side of his head, followed by a big left uppercut—and it might knock some sense into him. *Biff! Bam! Boof!* This would be a lot less costly for our children, the next generation of brave American men and women.

personnel in order to maintain the safety of all U.S. citizens. So we Americans have an important decision to make. Do we want to adhere to the bylaws of our U.S. Constitution—the one that the president of the United States has publicly sworn to uphold—or do we want more high-dollar primetime entertainment: packs of stupid foreigners and nincompoops wandering around the country, some like zombies, looking a place to vote? Do we want our prison cells emptied to make room for new criminals? Do we want our entire nation to suffer from Montezuma's revenge? Or do we want to live our lives in peace?

The choice is clear, so we Americans must soon make a decision.

Multiculturalism is why people aren't as friendly with their neighbors anymore. But why should they be, when their neighbors don't look, act, think, or speak the same way they do? Maybe that's also why so many conservative politicians don't care anymore, either. Apparently, the Republicans now think that our country is so screwed up that nothing they do is going to make any difference. For years now, apathetic *career politicians* have sacrificed our well-being to maintain their politically correct status quo. Liberal-fueled political correctness is what the Republicans believe at this point—and perhaps correctly—is what they need to use every time they speak, in order to keep their jobs.

> "Everyone in Congress acts as though they're afraid to call for a special prosecutor and they're afraid to use the word impeachment. You'll notice that Republicans are always very careful not to say what they obviously think. That's because females have the right to vote, so if a man is impolite, or raises his voice, or gets angry, or yells loudly at someone, he's liable to lose the next election." —Anonymous

> "Everyone keeps talking about impeaching the president, but impeachment only means a public reprimand. Nothing else ever happens. Bill Clinton was impeached and nothing happened. He's still smiling about it. It doesn't solve any problems. Everyone in Washington continues doing business as usual and making the same amount of money. It's a joke. The Democratic Party knows it's a joke. That's why they don't care. They're probably laughing about it right now." —J. M.

> "How come every time a Democratic politician is asked a question, and no matter what it is, he uses the words 'children' and 'kids'—even if he's homosexual and isn't married and doesn't have any? To try and make himself look good?" —Concerned Mom

Now, people are chanting, "Where were the Republicans? Where were the Republicans? Why didn't they do anything? Didn't they know what was going on? What are we paying them for?"

So now the United States of America is being populated with some of the worst of the worst available worldwide, and unfortunately, that is exactly what liberals want: *more multicultural liberals* to help vote them back into office. Why would anyone in his or her right mind be talking about "amnesty"? Since when do we offer amnesty to foreigners who think it's funny to taunt our border patrol agents and break our laws? There's a very simple solution to the so-called immigration problem. It's not complicated at all. But no one seems to want to talk about it. So here it is—printed in black and white—for everyone to read:

THE ILLEGAL IMMIGRATION SOLUTION

PROSECUTE TO THE FULLEST EXTENT OF THE LAW ON THE BOOKS ANY U.S. CITIZEN WHO PAYS A FOREIGNER TO DO ANYTHING (INCLUDING SHINING HIS SHOES), EVEN IF THE FOREIGNER CLAIMS TO BE A TOURIST, BECAUSE WHEN THE FOREIGNER RUNS OUT OF CASH, *THE FOREIGNER WILL LEAVE THE UNITED STATES ON HIS OR HER OWN AS QUICK AS A JACKRABBIT BEING CHASED BY A SWARM OF AFRICAN BEES.*

So why would anyone with half a brain want to continue to waste time talking about this subject?

This is not what "We the People of the United States" want, so how did it happen? Maybe it has something to do with today's voting rights. The inarguable fact is this: If a country wants to (1) guarantee life, liberty, and the pursuit of happiness to its citizens, (2) protect itself militarily without help from its neighbors, and (3) continue to exist, only those who are *provably conservative* should be allowed to run for political office, obtain a job with the U.S. government, and/or vote.

You see, LIBERAL SOCIALIST DEMOCRATS ARE THE MOST DANGEROUS ENEMIES OF THE UNITED STATES OF AMERICA.[471] Why? Because they don't make friends with other people, they make lifelong foes. This is the first time in U.S. history that we've allowed them to get this far. But

---

[471] For more, read *Shut Up and Sing: How Elites from Hollywood, Politics, and the UN Are Subverting America,* Regnery Publishing, 2003.

why? Have our lives become so comfy that the only entertainment we have now is watching all of the political shenanigans, chaos, and rampant crime on television? That's not entertainment; that's borderline sick.

"A good tree does not bear bad fruit." —Anonymous "Religious Nut"

"What everyone needs to understand is that silly liberals are great entertainers because they're often fun to watch and listen to, but they just don't belong in government, because they always screw everything up." —J. M.

"Liberals are like all of the exotic pets that people let loose in the United States. They're unusual and make our lives more interesting. But when they become a problem, like the jumping carp in Lake Michigan—that invade and decimate native species—something has to be done about it." —Anonymous

"Why is President Monkeyshine still campaigning for the job that he was elected to do three years ago? Is somebody else running for president, too?" —John Hayberry

"Social Justice" (Wealth Redistribution)

The seemingly, on the face of it, noble aspiration to take from the rich and give to the poor is considerably less admirable and humanitarian than it sounds. For one thing, prosperity, by definition, fluctuates. The rich and the poor are not precisely defined. A man who is rich today may be poor tomorrow, and vice versa. Of course, the unstated but implied assumption is that the rich are somehow bad and the poor are somehow good, even though ironically, the opposite is usually true—which explains why there are far fewer rapes, murders, drug busts, and acts of theft and vandalism in upscale neighborhoods than in the public housing projects. Consider this: What if "the rich" included someone like the child star Shirley Temple and "the poor" included a deranged psychopath like Charles Manson? Who the hell (excuse my frequent French) are liberals to decide that any wealth needs to be *spread* between these two people—or anyone else, for that matter? Why should liberals make decisions about who gives money to whom? Are they people of superior judgment? Do they know better than the rest of us? If so, where is the proof of that? Certainly not in any *unbiased* historical records, most of which were written prior to the Carter administration.

Blind, misguided, red-breasted, liberal quasi-Robin Hoods taking money from weary hardworking people to pay the bills of apathetic, drug-addled losers is similar to a farmer taking chicken feed away from all the birds that lay eggs and giving it to the ones that don't. The result is a pen full of distressed flapping fowl that produce nothing but lots of crap, and thus a business that can't sustain itself without massive government subsidies. That is quickly becoming a thing of the past. Why? Because the government is out of money.

> "Supposedly, President Obama wasn't in the Situation Room during the attack on the U.S. consulate in Benghazi, Libya. But of course he was. Where else would he have been? Standing on his head in the Oval Office and spitting out half-chewed gobs of our hard-earned tax money?" —Daffy Duck, Psychoanalyst

Politically Correct Kin Selection

Now that the problem with government interference has been correctly identified, maybe a practical solution can be offered as to what we are going to do about it. What kind of future presidents do we want to run the government and protect our country? Before deciding, every voter should go to the public library and take a close look at all of the pictures and drawings in *The Icon* (1982, Alfred A. Knopf, N.Y.). Then browse through *An Anthology of African Art: the Twentieth Century* (2002, Distributed Art Publishers, N.Y.).

Do you see the big difference? That's the reason the 2008 presidential election had its consequences.

> "This country's founders made a big mistake. They did not state in the Preamble to the Constitution, probably because they took it for granted that future Americans would always know, that a democracy can only survive when men are the ones who do all of the voting. That's because women, when given a choice, will

---

[472] To liberals, *communism* is the "C word." That's why they rarely use the term in public.

always vote for pretty-boys who act like children, pets, and 'pussies.'" —Name Withheld, Pending Notice Of Next Of Kin

When a person of sound body and mind is prevented by government from satisfying his or her instinctual psychological needs—one of which is having a social status greater than that of the average imbecile—the effect is similar to that of tying a ten-pound weight around the neck of the dominant male in a wolf pack. The lead wolf will be relentlessly nipped, bitten, and tormented by the weaker and less capable of its species without fear of reprisal—which, you'll note, is clearly the goal of not only today's pious liberal Washington, D.C., politicians but also of their fair-weather friends, relatives, campaign supporters, and associates: multicultural anarchists, terrorists, and communists.[472]

In conclusion, when a government forces the populace to live in an unnaturally structured society that operates counter to common sense and instinct, it can cause not only psychological distress but also severe mental problems. *Government* is not a divine entity separate from and above all of mankind. That is why President Obama's entertainment powers are limited. Unfortunately, it took him almost three and a half years to stop reading his teleprompter and begin to realize that fact.

Remember, man invented government to make his life easier, not more difficult.

What right does any government have to obstruct any man or woman's ability to—ethically—achieve his or her natural biological imperatives? None. Forcing intelligent, ambitious, hardworking people to live at the same level of comfort and security as those who are physically and/or mentally inferior can even cause a psychosis. For example, imagine how a six-foot-six, 350-pound N.F.L. football player would feel if, no matter how well he played the game, he was forced to live in a small, cramped, and crowded apartment complex populated by skinny bookworms with thick eyeglasses and badminton rackets. The question is, why haven't the consequences of governmental interference in people's lives been publicly acknowledged and discussed by the world psychiatric community? More—*liberal*—political correctness, perhaps?

Maybe political correctness should be made illegal.

The Death Tax

Tax policies, particularly with regard to estate ("death") taxes, are only one of the many insidious ways a government can negatively affect human evolution. Forcibly

---

[473] Liberal black people have been getting free support from the U.S. government for decades. That's why no reparations are owed to anyone for past injustices. They've already been paid.

taking the work product of one individual and using it to aid another actually tricks Mother Nature into believing that the dumb are the smart, the apathetic are the capable, and the inanimate are the industrious. When people die, they leave their money to their relatives and to other people that they like, but the government forces them to pay estate taxes. That essentially means that they are indirectly leaving a lot of their money to liberal black people.[473]

Evolution favors survivors—or at least those who *appear* on the surface to be such.

Whenever a government takes from one person and gives to another, that government is, in effect, deceiving nature as to who is the fittest. You see, nature is not some grand celestial Mother of All the Planets high on hallucinogens. Nature is an unthinking process—a result, if you will—and its laws are based on the concept of time, physics, chemistry, biology, and mathematics. Nature has no eyes, ears, or brain. Nature is an end product, a sum, a total, a consequence, and when the "fittest" men—or animals, or plants, or insects—are the ones receiving the benefits of confiscated property and capital, mathematics begins to favor those recipients of "spread" wealth by increasing the prevalence of their genetic information. This is a simple fact. Nature has no way of knowing that the recipients of lifelong aid and charity are neither self-sufficient nor survivors, unless one counts the ability to learn how to game a political system as a positive evolutionary trait. When a government automatically confiscates property from he or she who has much and gives it to he or she who has little—regardless of how worthy any of the individuals may be—the government has, for all intents and purposes, overruled Creation, the laws of nature, human evolution, and the natural order of things. The result is that those with little or no suitability for reproduction may increase rapidly, leaping and bounding in never-ending hordes. And they all smoke marijuana.[474]

> "Marijuana is illegal because most people don't like it. All of that inhaling, huffing and puffing, and coughing is creepy. It's kind of like sharing a big smelly glass of whiskey with a bunch of sycophantic people you don't know and then, when you're finished, licking the inside of the glass to make sure that you get every last drop. Next thing you know, a bunch of horrible-looking pimpled

---

[474] Always remember the old proverb: "If you lie down with dogs, you get up with fleas." Whenever a person has anything at all to do with wacked-out liberals who use illegal drugs, including marijuana (which is still illegal under federal law), he or she will *always* pay a price. One way that perverts manage to reproduce is by having sex with minors after heavy marijuana use. Today, marijuana laced with hallucinogens and various other drugs can drastically reduce a young person's inhibitions. Naïve teenage girls, for example, who decide to try illegal drugs under pressure from peers and/or an older male or female, then have to depend on some person—who, nine times out of ten, is a *liberal*—to provide her with those drugs, so a relationship inevitably ensues. It's also a fact that, in some families of liberals, incest occurs.

perverts are living in your neighborhood, rubbing up against one another and having group sex like slimy fish or something." — Anonymous (S.F.P.D.)

Male and Female Preferences

It should come as no surprise that women prefer, on average, slightly older, socially high-ranking men as mates. Men, on the other hand, generally prefer blonde fashion models who race beside them down the highway in red Ferraris—and so do liberal actors in their (soon-to-be decimated) movies. The fact is that when government, through legislation, artificially increases the hierarchal standing of socially inept liberal male dorks, those individuals become more attractive to females.[475] Unfortunately, when government helps those who are unable to help themselves, the result is the same as it would be if the helpless and nonproductive were fruitful go-getters who had what it takes to be successful financially. Clearly, by any measure, the ultimate human (and thus societal) consequences would be a highly dark and foreboding *evolutionary abomination*.

Liberal Democratic Kin Investment

The well-known, often stated, and fiercely debated liberal Democratic desire to increase taxes on the rich so as to give money to the poor (who, coincidentally, are mostly Democrats) is, in reality, a kind of instinctual vicarious form of liberal Democrat kin investment, whereby the material wealth of energetic, productive

---

[475] According to a nice guy named Ralph, a conservative, he once had a fun date with an attractive liberal female, but when they went back to her place, she just plopped down on a small sofa and sat motionless, smiling, and staring. It almost seemed as though she was waiting for him to manipulate her head, arms, and legs in order to have sex. Disappointed because he sensed there was something odd about her, he just gave her a kiss on the lips, promised that he'd call her again sometime (but didn't), and said good-bye. To this day, he still doesn't understand exactly what happened. Coincidentally, the very same thing happened to another acquaintance of mine named Betty, also a conservative. She once had a fun date with a handsome liberal man whom she thought she liked, but when they went back to his mother's house and sat on the hardwood floor, he suddenly stopped talking, went limp like Pinocchio, and smiled politely, as though waiting for her to take all of his clothes off. She gave him a quick peck on the cheek instead and hurried out the front door. Multiple accounts such as these are all *so* strange and perplexing. What would cause liberal males and females—or anyone else, for that matter—to act like this? DNA? Drugs? A venereal disease? Who knows?

people is transferred to those who eat nothing but cellophane-wrapped honey buns and then snore from midnight until noon. By using congressional legislation to, in effect, force successful people to support unsuccessful non-kin rather than allowing successful people to follow their instincts and support the kin of their own choice (which normally includes unrelated persons having both physical and mental characteristics similar to their own), the process of human evolution has literally been turned upside down, held by the ankles, and shaken until all of the "hope and change"—nickels, dimes, and quarters—has fallen out of its pockets: federal subsidies, food stamps, free cell phones, welfare checks, miscellaneous entitlements, sundry handouts, non-taxpayer tax rebates, etc. . . .

> "What's with all the free cell phones, anyway? What are they [the Democratic Party] going to do, call everybody on Election Day who's on welfare and getting food stamps and tell them that if they don't vote right away for so-and-so, their neighbors will find out and then be mean to them, and the government will also stop paying their phone bills?" —Major Rat Fink
>
> "You can be sure that the Democratic Party is going to do everything that it can to win elections, even if it means bribing voters with checks from the U.S. government. That's what welfare is—right?" —Anonymous (N.Y.P.D.)

Hamilton's Inclusive Fitness Theory–

The fact that no one to date has made the connection between governmental tax policies and Hamilton's Inclusive Fitness Theory is simply beyond understanding.[476] Note that inclusive fitness, unlike strict kin selection, requires only that the shared genes be identical by descent; it is not limited to cases where kin are involved. The ultimate effect is that when rich and successful individuals die, a large part of their confiscated wealth is used to help pay for programs to aid

---

[476] On December 8, 2010, former Rep. Anthony Wiener, D-New York, in an interview on FOX's *America Live,* vigorously defended the "death tax," dismissing progenitorial inheritance as nothing more than getting "very lucky in a casino." Poor Neanderthal man. If only he had lived long enough to learn how to play poker, he might've bred successfully with a Las Vegas hooker. Then there would be lots of little Neanderthals running around all over the place.

their antitheses, the unsuccessful—which is great if you happen to be slothful, inept, or an incurable drug addict. If anyone else has made this connection, then why haven't they stood up? Why isn't the subject of governmentally subsidized preternatural human genetic-pool contributions being publicly debated? More *political correctness,* perhaps? Or something worse? *(Shh . . . quiet. Don't say anything.)*

> "Life is not a matter of holding good cards, but of playing a poor hand well." —Robert Louis Stevenson (1850–1894)

That's why liberal socialist Democrats always have to cheat by dealing from the bottom of the deck.[477] They just don't play the game of life very well. Now we know why: F.A.D.

All of this leads to a particularly inescapable conclusion, which appears to conform to scientifically accepted modern evolutionary theory (liberals will angrily hee-haw when they read this): The higher the taxes a government imposes on its populace and the more wealth that government redistributes, the more it negatively affects human evolution. (F.Y.I.: The United Nations now seeks to create a global tax, which will enable our UN friends to redistribute the earnings of any Americans at all—wealthy or otherwise—to, say, people squatting on their hindquarters and eating insects in Nairobi.)

Altruism and Worker Bees

Kin investment also involves the quality of *altruism,* which is an unselfish interest in helping another person.[478] The purist forms of prosocial behavior are motivated by altruism, which is taught by Christianity, the most widely practiced religion in the world. The circumstance likely to evoke altruism is a feeling of empathy for an individual in need, or a close relationship between the benefactor and the recipient. Many prosocial behaviors that appear altruistic are, in fact, motivated by reciprocity, which is the obligation to return a favor with a favor—you know, like lots and lots of taxpayer funds in exchange for votes. Hamilton's concept of inclusive fitness explains how nat-

---

[477] There are only fifty-two playing cards in a deck. That's not very many scandals. Some more are probably on the way.
[478] For more, refer back to Chapter 7, "Altruism," page 106.

ural selection can perpetuate altruism. If an altruism gene or complex of genes influences an organism to be helpful or protective of relatives and their offspring, this behavior would increase the proportion of the altruism gene in the population. That is because relatives are likely to share genes with the altruist because of common descent. (Question: Does a pseudo-altruism gene exist in those who fake it?) Altruists may also recognize altruistic behavior in unrelated individuals and be inclined to support them.

Darwin was initially troubled by altruism. Worker bees that sacrifice their lives to protect their hives, for example—perhaps the ultimate illustration of non-human altruism—bothered him. If increased reproduction is driven by natural selection (survival), then common sense tells us that altruists will eventually cease to exist. However, they do exist. Darwin was so puzzled by this fact that he feared it was fatal to his entire theory. Eventually, however, he found the explanation. Darwin hypothesized that natural selection might favor altruism at the blood-kin level. In his *On the Origin of Species,* he proposed that the perceived problem with his theory of natural selection producing individuals that often risk their lives to protect others "disappears when it is remembered that selection may be applied to the *family,* as well as the individual and may thus gain the desired end."[479] Blood kinship and interactions among relatives, it turns out, are the key.

A century later, Hamilton formalized Darwin's ideas, but the path from Darwin to Hamilton was a difficult one, which isn't very surprising, considering the fact that the nature of *altruism*—which is, perhaps, the origin of goodness—has both religious and political implications. That fact may also explain why it apparently took more than one hundred years for even the simplest mathematical models of the kinship-altruism relationship to, finally, be formulated. (Coincidentally enough, human social evolution seems to be as controversial among "nonpartisan" scientists as federal income tax rates are between Democrats and Republicans.) If altruism, the selfless concern for the well-being of others, is the psychological source of all "good" in mankind, then it follows that *lack of altruism* is the source of all "evil."[480]

Is Parental Investment Genetic?

Readers might be interested in another tidbit of information: Apparently, there is a gene associated with parental investment, and it contributes to inclusive fitness. Certain species or populations exhibit parental care—crocodiles and some spiders, for example—whereas *closely related species* or populations lack it. This indicates a

---

[479] Charles Darwin, *On the Origin of Species,* 1859, John Murray, London, p. 204.
[480] For further insight, read *Demonic,* 2011, Random House, N.Y.

heritable trait that may also be present in humans—inattentive mommies, for example.

Of one thing we can be certain: When those in charge shun reality, the consequences will *always* be detrimental to whoever is in their care, custody, and control, whether that be an infant or a nation, so we must forever be on guard. Liberal suboptimality is especially risky and even downright dangerous when these immoral genetic ancestors of criminals, slaves, and domestic servants are allowed to serve in positions of power. The weakened state of our country's economy today is evidence of that. Remember, the establishment of the United States of America is a relatively recent phenomenon, and our nation is not a permanent fixture on earth; neither is the Constitution, the Bill of Rights, or our liberty, so we must forever be on guard.

It is the (D) evolution of man.

Chapter 16

Do They Belong In A Zoo?

Anthroposuboptimality: The New Normal

What accounts for the so-called coarsening of society? What explains modern human behavior (or lack thereof)? More importantly, is any of it reversible? Well, there's an old saying around the swamps and bayous way down south: "The more you feed a turtle, the more it shits in the pond."[481] (Pardon the precise French-English translation.) I heard it said once by a one hundred-year-old woman with only three yellow teeth who lived in a rotted fishing shack in Louisiana. She was throwing scraps of food to a big alligator snapper. The prehistoric-looking turtle was half buried in mud.

But that was many years ago.

Just recently, while passing through a small town in northern Arkansas, I saw a reasonably intelligent-looking, inoffensive, and, from all appearances, normal teenager—a white kid with a baseball cap and a bicycle—who had some peculiar mannerisms and body language. The only way I can describe his posture and gestures is to say that they were similar to those of a common chimpanzee *(Pans troglodytes):* quick jerky movements, a bobbing head, and overly relaxed hands and wrists. I had never seen such a thing before—not outside of a zoo, anyway—and could hardly believe it, so I watched, fascinated. A few minutes earlier, I had heard

---

[481] "Today, the United States of America is like a 100,000-gallon aquarium tank that hasn't been cleaned in three-and-a-half years. It's full of sheepshead droppings, bull shark paddies, and seahorse manure." —John Hayberry (1999)

this same kid speaking Ebonics,[482] the crude ghetto dialect that we so often hear with surprise these days coming from the mouths of white people. I had seen many strange things over the years, but nothing quite like this. The kid had to have learned these simian mannerisms from someone else; he wasn't living in the wild with bonobos, which means that there must be other human beings just like him. The only other possible explanation is that he was a throwback to the missing link.[483] And, no, he wasn't mentally handicapped, just neanderthalic. (Oh, I'm sorry, that's the same thing, isn't it?)

Then I noticed the kid again when he began staring strangely at a grasshopper, exhibiting the characteristic movements of a dumb animal that has spotted something to play with. My first thought, of course, was that his behavior was an act put on for some friend's amusement. But it wasn't, because there was no one else around. The kid was just being himself.

What is this, *the new normal?* What in tarnation is going on? Kids that age should want to be friends with other people—preferably with those who have a modicum of class, not with dull-witted, arm-and-hand–gesticulating apes. Is this kind of behavior what makes a kid popular these days? Is this what impresses females? I have a hard time believing it, but it must be true. Can you imagine if someone like him had suddenly appeared in a small farm town a hundred years ago? Why, the townspeople would've chased him away with brooms and tree branches. Either that or they would have coaxed him into a closet with some banana pudding, locked the door, and called a vet.

Do teenagers today actually *want* to be thought of by their peers as dumb? If so, why? Because it's considered uncool to be smart? Boy, do they ever have a big surprise coming when they get older and have to go looking for employment. Do they think that acting like chimps will increase the likelihood

---

[482] Ebonics—a blend of the words "ebony" and "phonics"—is a term that was *originally* intended to refer to the language of all enslaved Negroes. However, since the controversial 1996 decision by the Oakland, California, school board to denote, recognize, and respect the primary language of poor African American children who attend school, the term Ebonics is now being used to refer to so-called African American Vernacular English. The following word definition appears in a (Gangsta) Ebonics dictionary online: "Ganked—Dis what when some Mutha Fucka steals yo shih!" (Screamingpickle.com).

[483] Robert Louis Stevenson once quipped, "Each has his own tree of ancestors, but at the top of all sits Probably Arboreal." He was referring to Darwin's controversial description of the ancestry of mankind: "A hairy quadruped, furnished with a tail and pointed ears, probably arboreal in its habits" (Charles Darwin, *The Descent of Man*, Volume 2, 1st edition, 1871, John Murray, London, p. 389). Darwin also wrote, "For my own part, I would as soon be descended from that heroic little monkey . . . as from a savage who delights to torture his enemies, offers up bloody sacrifices, practices infanticide without remorse, treats his wives like slaves, knows no decency, and is haunted by the grossest superstitions" *(Descent,* pp. 404-405).

of a sexual opportunity? Is that what kids these days believe that it takes to achieve their biological imperative? Years ago, a neighbor told me that he thought evolution had reversed and that everyone is turning back into monkeys.[484]

> "Forced integration works both ways. Black children begin behaving like white children to be popular, and white children begin behaving like black children for the same reason. Then when they grow up, they talk the same and begin dating." —Karen

Presumably, that kid is going to get a job someday—but only if conservative Republicans and conservative Tea Party members are elected who make job opportunities available. The question is, what will he become—a butcher, a baker, a candlestick-maker? Maybe he'll be the one who installs the faulty smoke detector—you know, one of those small, round, plastic things outside someone's bedroom door that help keep people who are asleep from burning alive. Or maybe he'll be the one who rotates the tires on somebody's car and makes sure that he tightens the lug nuts so the front wheel doesn't come off when the car is going down an interstate highway doing seventy-five miles per hour.

Actually, the options for this kid's employment are endless. He's liable to get a job doing just about anything, including working at Miami International Airport, so don't ever think that just because you're careful, anthroposuboptimality can't harm you. Don't make the mistake of thinking that bad things happen only to other people, because next thing you know, a twin-engine Cessna will land in your lap while you're snoozing, lop off your head, and fling it into a neighbor's plastic backyard pool.

Suboptimality in our society is now threatening to become the rule rather than the exception. Those of us who have jobs today dealing with the public know this to be true. It has almost gotten to the point that many of us feel as though we're living in a foreign country. Each of our lives is affected negatively by dozens of

---

[484] The human lineage separated from that of the great apes about 5 million years ago (other estimates, based on fossil evidence, vary substantially: from 4 to 10 million), yet human and chimpanzee DNA differ in sequence by a mere 1 percent. In fact, humans have more in common with chimpanzees than chimpanzees do with gorillas, whose genomes differ from chimps by a whopping 3 percent. How could so little genetic change account for the substantial difference between man and chimpanzee—Tarzan's pet? The answer is that most of the important evolutionary changes occurred in the DNA that controls the switching "on" and "off" of genes. In other words, nature can create very different creatures by simply orchestrating the same genes to work in different ways (Watson, with Berry, *op. cit.*, pp. 234–236). To better visualize this, imagine Mother Nature putting corks in the holes of a Renaissance bass flute so it sounds like an Australian Aborigine's didgeridoo.

examples of suboptimality and unexceptionalism—everything from substandard products (made in China) that fail, don't fit, or break for no good reason, to people who can't speak, spell, or add correctly. Is it China's secret plan that everything in the United States suddenly fall apart, disintegrate, wear out, break, or stop working in the year 2020, thus making our country ripe for takeover? At the end of the day, we plop down in our chairs and sigh, then take a deep breath and try to rest up in preparation for tomorrow's battle against the forces of ignorance. Then the chair collapses.

This chapter was written, however, with the full realization that relatively few readers' attitudes will be altered. Our normalcy bias prevents most of us from heeding warnings until things get so bad that we simply can't ignore them anymore. The problems associated with substandard products and substandard thinking, both of which stem from extensive liberal influence in our country's affairs, have permeated Western society to the point that our personal safety may soon be on par with that of people living in mud huts in Africa. Unfortunately, not enough of us seem to care. It's only when the airplane runs out of fuel and crashes into our *own* living room that we realize what awful things really can happen—and by that time, of course, it's too late.

The following is an excerpt from *Anthropology for Dummies:*

Is the human species still evolving?
One of the most common questions asked of anthropologists is whether the human species is still evolving. Have we reached a pinnacle? Will we become giant-brained, fragile-bodied space-dwellers, using only a single finger to press buttons in the far future?

The simple answer is that yes, we're still evolving; if we have offspring (replicate), if those offspring aren't clones (variation), and if not all of our offspring survive to sexual maturity (selection), then by definition, the human species is evolving. But it's natural to ask whether we're still evolving because—in developed countries, at least—humanity has used medicine and other means to eliminate a lot of the pressures that once took so many of our children. With so many selective pressures defeated (at least in the short term), you may easily conclude that significant genetic evolution has stalled in developed countries in the last century or so.

But what's still evolving, and very quickly, is human culture, and this process is just as important as human genetic evolution.

Human culture changes very rapidly, and the changes affect millions. Imagine the differences between the United States of America (say, in clothing and musical styles, concepts of race and religion, and the ethnic diversity of the population) in 1950 and in 2000—some pretty major changes occurred in the late 1960s (for example, the success of the civil rights movement). Whether the changes are good or bad is another matter; for the moment, the important idea is that yes, humanity is still evolving and in a very significant way.[485]

Make no mistake, the kind of world we live in today—i.e., our evolutionary environment—is partly determined by government legislation, and it greatly affects man's evolutionary path. But never fear; our liberal friends are in charge, so we're all going to have plenty of "hope and change" pretty soon. Just give it a few more years. It's on its way. It'll be here eventually. But what kind of change are they talking about? Arm length, body hair, and loping gait?

Bella Vita[486]

No comprehensive discussion of liberalism would ever be complete without a few words said regarding the subject of abortion, for abortion rights are what many liberal females essentially live and breathe. Remember, the planet Earth is only so big. Its size is finite, as is the number of human beings it can support. (For further insight, visit an Iowa chicken farm.)

Now, the first question that comes to mind is this: If all animal species instinctively try to increase their numbers, how do we reconcile that fact with the liberal love for abortion and unlimited abortion rights? It's a given that most aborted babies (but certainly not all) are the offspring of women with liberal

---

[485] *Anthropology for Dummies,* 2008, Wiley Publishing, Indianapolis, Indiana, p. 40.
[486] *Bella vita,* the Italian phrase for "beautiful life," is what the Florida woman found innocent of murdering her two-year-old daughter paid a tattoo artist to put on her back after her child inexplicably disappeared (and died). Constant exposure to liberal attitudes has inarguably cheapened human life in the eyes of us all, including juries. Not surprisingly, some new-wave demented female oafs actually believe that killing one's own child under certain circumstances is justified. After all, it's just a really late late-term abortion, right? And if a woman is granted the power to kill her child, who has the right to take that power away from her? Men? *Before* the child is born, or *after* the child is born—what difference does it really make? Some women perceive, perhaps correctly, that there is no difference.

attitudes, but how many abortions are actually taking place in the United States? That is difficult to say for sure because it is not a question that is included in the U.S. Census. Democrats must not want anyone to find out, but I think we can safely assume that it's a holy hell of a lot. Many liberal females are viewed as pro-abortion fanatics. Apparently, there are few things they dread more than being puffed up and misshapen for nine months, then having to give birth to something that screams in their ears and wants to be fed day and night. Because giving birth to and raising a child involves so much work, liberal females seem to believe that they should have the right to kill their own young. The Supreme Court, in its wisdom, fashionably agreed. Now liberals consider it settled law (just like former vice president Al Gore's settled science—and we all know how that turned out).

But how, you may ask, can any group that kills its own young propagate so successfully? Well, for one, men and women with sexually liberal attitudes tend to breed like Tabanidae horseflies. A woman who gets pregnant ten times and has three abortions, then has two of her children fatally shot in a bar fight and has two more killed by the police still has three children left who can eventually have children of their own. If one of them dies from a drug overdose, that still leaves two—male and/or female—who, together, are easily capable of achieving or producing at least twenty more pregnancies.

The number of people with far-left liberal views has increased substantially in this country as a result of immigration policies and the ensuing influx of those who commit murder, rape, burglary, and a host of other crimes, and who are also partially responsible for rising out-of-wedlock birth rates.[487] Despite the fact that abortion helps keep Democratic voter registration rolls in check, all of their political opponents are still demanding an end to the practice. This fact by itself is clear proof that conservatives generally think less about themselves and more about others than do their liberal counterparts. The right to have an abortion, which liberal females hold so very dear, is actually the only thing—besides the homicide rate—that's keeping the number of liberals in our country from skyrocketing. The fact is, abortion kills liberals, so Democrats are their own worst enemy. Yes, the Democratic Party itself has been

---

[487] Here's an idea: Instead of "undocumented immigrants" from Mexico taking over the United States of America, why don't we the people of the United States just take over Mexico, instead? For example, why doesn't the entire membership of some conservative organization like, say, the National Rifle Association (N.R.A.), just pack up and move *en masse* to Mexico City? Then, instead of Mexicans illegally voting to change our way of doing things, maybe N.R.A. members could vote illegally to change the Mexican way of doing things. That way, the path to citizenship in Mexico could easily be cleared for about, say, 50 million happy Americans waving U.S. flags who could drive down there and buy up property real cheap all the way from the Rio Grande to Guatemala. Then these ecstatic new Gringo-Mexicans could level everything in sight, burn the debris, and declare the entire country of Mexico a drug-free zone! They could even change Mexico's official language to English. (To join the N.R.A., visit nrahq.org.)

Human (D) Evolution

diminished by its own secret, decades-long wars on three fronts: (1) their *War on Children*,[488] their *War on Women*,[489] and their secret *War on People of Color*—all of which they strenuously and furtively purport not to be engaged in. It appears to be a war against nice people in general.[490]

The only good thing that can be said about abortion is that the DNA of people with a low regard for human life is now quite possibly being gradually eliminated from the human gene pool. However, the way in which it is being accomplished is nothing short of an abomination. What is being done in some women's healthcare clinics is unspeakable.

The big problem with liberals when it comes to reproduction is that they have two conflicting biological imperatives: (1) to produce offspring and (2) to feel good (which means having no annoying kids running around). More often than not, the second goal seems to take precedence over the first. Nevertheless, the mass quantity of government-supported pregnancies has helped fuel an explosion of liberal growth. It wasn't too long ago that a woman was ostracized and considered a disgrace if she got an abortion for any reason other than her physical health. Today, the procedure is spoken of matter-of-factly around cafeterias and Laundromats in female chitchat (often in barely intelligible English) and sometimes with a certain degree of pride for having "taken charge" of her own body and life—as if hers was the only life involved.

It's no mystery why women get abortions. Every teenager knows the reason. It's not because of any "danger to the woman's life," except in rare instances;

---

[488] Liberal economic policies destroy the economy and lower the standard of living for everyone, including children, so many kids grow up living in poverty. Sometimes, their parents divorce because of arguments about money. When it gets to the point that hospitals can't afford to buy incubators, some premature infants may even have to be discarded as medical waste. (The lucky ones who live will probably owe the government fifty trillion dollars.)

[489] When a competent woman attains a certain level in management with a company run by male liberal socialist Democrats—most of whom are closet misogynists—those liberal males do not like her. Why? Because liberal males simply cannot stand competent women. They feel threatened. They want women who can't think for themselves, won't ask questions, and will obey their orders blindly because independent, intelligent, women make liberal males look like "pussies." So L.S.D.er males often conspire against those women to make them look bad or quit their jobs. Sometimes the liberal boss will increase a woman's workload to the point where she has to spend all of her time on a computer, day and night, and even during vacations and holidays. If she doesn't quit, the boss may even lose his temper and yell and stomp his feet. Sometimes, the liberal boss may even resort to trickery. For example, he may tell a woman that she needs to reach some impossible statistical goal, then secretly monitor her, slyly looking for any insignificant mistake. If he finds one, he will gleefully fire her without hesitation—but will display compassion. (Hopefully she'll find a better job working for Republicans.)

[490] *Re: The Democrats' War against Nice People* (men, women, and children alike): It has often been noted that (paid?) liberals "vehemently protest," "attack," and seem to want to "harm" other people—not only conservatives, but people of any race, color, or creed who verbally oppose their agenda. Why? The reason is simple: because such people threaten to "blow their high." Question: Can a liberal's "high" include becoming president of the United States of America and then controlling the world?

it's because of the extreme inconvenience, discomfort, cost, and, worst of all, embarrassment. What some women today consider family planning, others call murder, but modern liberals want to do what modern liberals want to do, despite the consequences it has for others, particularly the helpless child, who, of course, has no vote. There are laws against harvesting some saltwater animal species when they carry eggs, and yet it's okay to destroy a human fetus. Which is more important: human beings or soft-shelled crabs?

Don't liberals think that children are more important than animals? Conservatives certainly do.

Most of us, I believe, would be repulsed by a woman who, upon discovering a possum in her house, chopped it to death with a machete or stuck a pair of shears in its head rather than gritting her teeth and making an effort to humanely shoo it out the front door. Yet today, when it comes to killing a human fetus, we all act as if such behavior is normal. But it's not; it's ignorant jungle savagery. Society seems to have become numbed to this fact. Hopefully, that numbness will soon wear off.

Cash for Castration

At the risk of causing any on the far left to have conniption fits, tear out their multicolored hair, freak out, or explode into tears, I'm going to suggest that the simplest solution to the increasing percentage of P.P.J.s, people of poor judgment, in the United States is *voluntary castration* (i.e., removal of the scrotum, similar to pet neutering). Long-term governmental assistance should be offered only to those who are willing to permanently lose their family jewels. Any mentally weak but able-bodied, perpetually destitute male who doesn't particularly care to work for a living and can't support a child but keeps fathering babies anyway because he much prefers "sleeping around" should be an adult about it and agree to be *sterilized in exchange for cold hard cash.*

Now, if someone has a simpler and more practical solution (other than all liberal socialist Democrats being required to obtain a certificate before breeding—which, of course, they'll refuse to do), please, let's hear it. We have met the enemy, and the enemy is us.[491] Humanity is now reaping what it has sown, and the reapers' sickles are slick with Democratic donkey dung. (That's why everything stinks.)

---

[491] "What is man's chief enemy? Each man is his own." —Anacharsis, (?–600 B.C.), Scythian philosopher.

Human (D) Evolution

"My dawg be done got castrated two time and he still be's havin' a lotta sex!" —Female African American, Name Unknown

The Difference between Males and Females

Imagine what it would be like if your father ran the federal government. Now, imagine if your mother ran the federal government, instead. Is there anyone alive who doesn't see the big difference?[492] But "progressive" liberals apparently want everyone to believe that all men and women were created equal. This suits their liberal purposes, even though men and women are clearly *not* the same. Males and females serve two very different functions. That is why two different sexes evolved in the first place. Believe it or not, one likely theory is that the opposite sexes of all animal species developed as a means of creating new gene combinations that are unpredictable to parasites. (Now there's a great wedding toast.) You see, sexual reproduction between normal males and females—as opposed to, say, test-tube reproduction by unsmiling, neuter-gender "progressives" with burnt-orange hair smelling of marijuana, government-issued cell phones, and T-shirts that say, "I LOVE SAN FRANCISCO"—provides a means of random chromosomal mixing that can change the human immunological capacity in ways that are unpredictable to societal bloodsuckers. That is why the development of differences between the two sexes is a natural evolutionary strategy.[493]

---

[492] *Re: Women in the Workplace.* Men who work for females normally do what they are told as long as things are going smoothly, even in the U.S. military, but when things begin going badly, men will always stop listening to women. Only liberal "pup-P.E.T.S." will continue to listen and blindly obey. That is because no *real man* will allow himself to be controlled by a woman; he will only do it if he loves her.

[493] A Brief Note on Unisex "Progressive" Liberals: The so-called emasculation of males and masculinization of females in modern European and American society, with its increasingly "progressive" liberal populace, has often been noted, albeit with no real understanding of the root cause. Most men and women normally tend to do the things that are necessary to leave no doubt as to their gender, except in the case of an intersex condition. Sometimes, we may even exaggerate our physical and/or emotional differences to attract the opposite sex, but throughout history, male and female slaves have had little or no choice as to whom they mate with. That's why, in any given enslaved population, the natural human instinct to establish either a male or female physical/emotional sexual identity is predicted to eventually disappear, resulting in a "*genderless*" *unisex culture* in which it's sometimes impossible for others to distinguish between the two sexes. Furthermore, *hierarchies* of any real significance cease to exist among an enslaved population because the males have little power over the females, so they share whatever power they have *equally*. The only ones with any power are their captors/masters/"puppeteers."

"Most liberal males don't seem to really like females, and most liberal females don't seem to really like males. Why do they even bother to get married? Most of them probably don't." —Mike

As we know, the function of the human male is to protect women and children; the female function is to bear and feed her offspring (i.e., not dispose of the fetus in a plastic garbage bag). This is what ensures the continuation of our species. Although males and females have different responsibilities, both share equally in the biological function required for successful reproduction. If anyone doesn't know this, he or she should probably watch something other than *The Ellen DeGeneres Show*. Liberals despise such talk because it reeks of so many things they abhor: responsibilities, obligations, and, worst of all, duties. Body piercings, butt-cheek tattoos, and unisex jewelry are so much more fun!

Unfortunately, an elected government can grant its citizenry any kind of illegal rights it demands. Abortion is one of them. Why? The reason is very simple: No one can hear the unborn child scream in pain. If the yelps of startled innocents having their brains sucked out with vacuum cleaners or having their spines snipped with shears were loud enough for a woman's friends and neighbors to hear, *Roe v. Wade* would be ripped from the law books in *less than twenty-four hours.* Then any dark, horned, hunched and slippery, cadaverous-looking human reptile attorney who tried to throw up a legal roadblock against pro-life legislation under the guise of "American civil liberties" would either be summarily executed or mysteriously disappear, never to be found.[494] Only in a so-called *bipartisan* world influenced by liberal illogic can a person who murders a baby go to prison for life or die in the electric chair—but if he had done it a few hours earlier, before the child was delivered, he could've earned five hundred bucks for the job.

"Pro-choice" infanticide must end now.[495]

---

[494] It's notable that Roe (a pseudonym), the woman of *Roe v. Wade* fame, announced on January 17, 2005, that she had changed her mind about abortion and now wants to see the S.C.O.T.U.S. ruling overturned—*millions* of dead babies later.

[495] Of course, the flip side of the coin is this: If mean-spirited, subnormal, or mentally underdeveloped females do not want to give birth to their mean-spirited, subnormal, or mentally underdeveloped babies, why should anyone stop them? Someday, their spawn may accidentally slam his speeding FedEx truck into a California tour bus loaded with high school students, killing half of them. So it's a moral dilemma whether to abort or not to abort. The only reasonably humane solution, given the state of liberal society now—i.e., in lieu of any religious beliefs—is the "mourning" after pill, which can be purchased for only ten bucks.

Chapter 17

What Should We Do?

The Dilemma of the Good Samaritan

1. Consider the Good Samaritan, A, who has two suboptimal neighbors: B and his wife, C.

2. The charitable A provides aid to his neighbors, B and C, enabling them to survive.

3. B and C procreate and have suboptimal children, D, E, and F (with corresponding school grades).

4. Eventually, D, E, and F will grow up to become adults who also require the support of Good Samaritans.

5. The Good Samaritans who support them may be A+ and A-, the children of A (who plans to retire).

6. Thus, by providing unconditional charity to B and C, the Good Samaritan, A, has—without realizing it—*severely burdened* members of his own family.

7. That's not a very lucky family, is it?

The process doesn't stop there, however. No, unfortunately, over time, it gets exponentially worse. Imagine what it will be like a hundred years later. There will be a million Z's sleeping on the ground, in piles of clothing and garbage under bridges, and all over the place. There won't be enough Good Samaritans alive to provide all of the Z's with food and shelter, so the only way to put a stop to the problem is to require that, *in exchange for aid,* B and C will agree never to propagate.

There are many different methods of birth control. The decision about which one to choose can be left up to B and his wife, C—so, of course, it would be voluntary. If B and C decide to opt out, there's no problem. Instead, they can both return to eating tree leaves, drinking canned rainwater, and sleeping in a cardboard box, so Good Samaritans don't have to feel guilty about the situation. The choice is all up to B and his wife, C.

All of our liberal democratic friends are "pro-choice," right?

Oh, so liberals think this is too harsh? Too mean? Too "extremist"? Well, *tough toenails.*

No one has a right to force their neighbors to support them with hard-earned tax money. In fact, no one has a right to their neighbor's blood, sweat, and tears at all. Liberals are wrong about this, so they should just admit it and leave the rest of us alone. A human being's right to "life, liberty, and the pursuit of happiness" ends where another person's *same right* begins.

So the moral of the story is this: If you can't feed yourself, don't breed yourself.

What (the Hell) Does the Future Hold?

"Our American way of life is under attack by liberal socialist Democrats (L.S.D.ers), a rainbow coalition of *Homo sheepiens,* terrorist sympathizers, Mexican leaf blowers, Jewish organ grinders, and dancing African American political puppets!" —John Hayberry (2013)

Human (D) Evolution

The Regressive Advance of Civilization

Will today's modern society be considered the peak of civilization *a thousand years* from now? (It's doubtful.) Is man still improving biologically, or is he slowly degenerating, thus requiring more and more advanced medicine to live a normal life? Is mankind really all that civilized? (Maybe our stupid Neanderthal ancestors thought that they were civilized, too.) Are we human beings experiencing a forward or backward evolutionary change? Is our average I.Q. increasing or decreasing? If our species is improving, then why do we continue to spend so a big part of our lives in a seemingly endless battle against the loud, the irresponsible, the dishonest, and the ignorant? Why do the commercials that we watch on television so often seem designed to appeal to the lowest common human denominator? The rapid advance of medicine and of modern surgical techniques has far-reaching implications (especially when it comes to removing lead slugs from Mexican Negritos). People who used to pay the ultimate price for their mistakes—like forgetting to tie the other end of their pink bungee cords to the bridge railing—are now being stitched back together and living to breed another day. (Stupidity is a terrible thing to waste.)

The fact that a *true* conservative has any trouble at all winning an election these days shows just how far down the road to ruin we've actually traveled. Fortunately, there is a very simple way to end the scourge of unchecked liberalism: Simply make it a *felony* for a Washington, D.C., politician to lie to the American people about *anything*. If he cannot answer a question without lying, then he should just grit his teeth and keep his mouth shut. At first, many Republicans would find it stressful having to *always* tell the truth, so it would take a bit of effort for them to comply. But after a while, when practically all of the Democrats are locked up at San Quentin, Republicans could begin showing some gumption, telling the truth, and passing legislation that they *know* is good for the country, without fear of losing the next election. Today, the American public is so overwhelmed by misinformation from the government and the liberal (anti-truth) media that, half the time, most people have no idea what's really going on politically, economically, or culturally. They're all too busy working twelve hours a day to pay off all of the enormous bills they suddenly have.

In many ways, America the once beautiful is now becoming more like a backward Third World nation.[496] This has to stop. The fact is, as human civilizations advance on the planet Earth, there is an increasingly greater opportunity

---

[496] South Africa in many ways is very much like the United States. That is because it is industrious. The country is not generally considered Third World, even though half the people can neither read nor write. It has a populace that is 75 percent black, 13 percent white, less than 10 percent "Coloured" (mixed race), and 2 percent Indian. Only about 1/17 of the people of Africa live in South Africa, yet that country produces 40 percent of Africa's total manufactured goods. In other words, it's no Detroit.

through humanitarianism for the suboptimal to propagate, so what should we all do, just ignore the implications of this? Should the topic of human devolution, like so many other subjects that our liberal friends detest, be considered "politically incorrect"—or possibly even "hate speech" worthy of fierce condemnation? No, of course not.

We had better wise up.

An odd metamorphosis has occurred in modern man over the course of our relatively short 6,000-year recorded history: (1) the *charitably enabled* became (2) the *legislatively empowered*, and then they turned into (3) the *rights-entitled*. If left unchecked, what will blood-and-money-sucking L.S.D.er parasites become next—the ordained all-knowing Imperial Masters of Mankind? Not likely. So don't despair, for there's always *hope and change*. Technology is rapidly advancing in the field of neurometrics. Soon, deciphering what a person is really thinking by reading his or her brain waves will be possible. That should help put an end to all of the liberal nonsense. Political candidates need to wear beany caps with wires and electrodes.

"Progressive" Liberal Multiculturalism

Why are "progressives" so intent on achieving multiculturalism? Don't they know that America is already multicultural? We have always welcomed people from other nations—as long as they act right. British culture had a formative influence in colonial America, along with English, Scottish, and Irish settlers. Other major influences from parts of Western Europe include the Germans, French, and Italians. America also has the African people and the American Indians. Other foreign countries have also influenced the variety of cultures found in many of our states. There is Chinatown in Los Angeles, for example. In fact, there are Chinatowns all over the United States. There are even strong elements of the Haitian vodou (voodoo) culture in New Orleans, Louisiana.[497]

So, is multiculturalism what "progressives" really want? No, probably not, because we already have it here in the United States of America. What "progressives" really seem to want to do is divide and/or weaken the United States. By that, I mean they want to turn our "melting pot" into a *bowl of mush*. "Progressives" don't really want multiculturalism. What they want to do is create a *conglomeration*

---

[497] Other spelling variations include voudou, vodon, vodoun, and vaudoux. (Third World orthography is a beautiful thing.)

of unassimilated foreigners and minorities of virtually every available kind.[498] That's because "progressives" are clearly America's enemies, and just like all other opponents of our way of life, they seek to conquer the United States politically by using the laws of our Constitution against us. No, "progressives" aren't really that interested in multiculturalism. What "progressive" liberals want is a New Age of *Multiethicalism*—which is essentially the same thing as animalism.[499]

> "Progressives look like the characters in old black-and-white futuristic science-fiction movies. What do they want, anyway? Don't they know that electric toasters and instant waffles have already been invented?" —C. G.

Liberal Mathematics

Math is based entirely on facts and logic. In math, answers are either *right* or *wrong*. For example, 1 + 1 = 2 (not 47,000,000). And 2 x 2 = 4 (not zero). And a $780 billion stimulus package does not equal "job growth" any more than pouring a big bag of shiny nickels out of an open car window while driving down a potholed street in Chicago equals "shovel-ready jobs" for all of President Monkeyshine's supporters who frantically hop around trying to pick them up. (Voters need to understand that probably 75 percent of all the money that our federal government has spent

---

[498] Are male liberal "progressives" attracted to the fundamentalist Islamic practice of adults marrying children? If so, that may help explain why some of them are so intent on expanding the bounds of multicultural activity here in the United States. Is this the reason for the odd alliance between these two groups, who are clearly natural enemies? Possibly. Or maybe they just don't like Christians. Or maybe they think that here in America, votes rule no matter what the consequences.

[499] This may be why people in the past have added the appropriate suffix "-ism" to the ends of descriptive words that even today accurately describe "progressive" liberals and virtually all of their ultimate (and secret) goals. The term *animalism* is defined as "behavior that is characteristic of or appropriate to animals, particularly in being physical and instinctive; religious worship of or concerning animals." Here are all of the examples of words with the suffix "-ism" added to them just as they appear in *The Merriam-Webster Dictionary* ("alcoholism" appears twice): "criticism, plagiarism, animalism, racism, sexism, barbarianism, alcoholism, giantism, Buddhism, stoicism, colloquialism, hypnotism, heterothallism, alcoholism, morphinism, mongolism" (Merriam-Webster Online: Dictionary and Thesaurus, n.d.). Mindless depravity would be the ultimate result of an Age of Advanced Liberalism. Never doubt it for a minute. When a person (or population) is fed daily doses of a slow-acting poison, he or she may notice that the food tastes bad but may still not realize what's happening until just few moments before choking to death and falling to the floor. That's why the United States of America needs to do something about it as soon as possible.

over the past four and a half years has been nothing but *waste* and *accumulated interest*. The question is, why do we Americans keep letting our representatives do this to us—especially when so much of the money being spent goes toward nothing more than *unconstitutional entertainment?*

In other words, nonsensical major laws are being enacted that will eventually have to be nullified. (It's kind of like paying a team of union workers to dig a hole for a swimming pool, and then, later, paying some teenage kids to help you fill the hole back up with dirt.) How many more of our hard-earned dollars are we Americans going to continue to allow the liberal socialist Democratic Party to dole out to their needy supporters? Payoffs. Bribes. Graft. Kickbacks. No-bid contracts. Under-the-table deals. Who is all of America's money going to—foreign puppeteers?

It's almost as though a wildly grinning, elaborately feathered, Zulu "black tooth fairy" king riding on a rented float at the head of the Mardi Gras parade is throwing bucketfuls of $100 checks and gold doubloons off the back to a jeering crowd, and the tractor driver, David Axlegrease (wearing no pants?) is sitting on his broken fun-house mirror. The Reverend Wright, chanting, *"God damn America!"* is sitting on the front of the float, handing out some Chinese trinkets. Radical Bill Ayers, wearing his famous little earrings, is squatting on the king's throne and holding a time bomb. He's surrounded by midgets and drag queens. (Maybe the musician Bob Dylan could put a good tune to this.)

In basic math, there are no so-called common-ground answers or dissenting opinions. There are no decisions based on personal feelings rather than on correct information. In math, there is no such thing as polarization, bipartisan support, or much-needed debate. If any one of these things played a part when adding, subtracting, or multiplying numbers, then absolutely every answer would be *incorrect*. (Sound familiar? That's liberalism for you.) Furthermore, if political decisions were ever made based on *real math*, as opposed to warm and fuzzy liberal socialist Democrat math, there is no doubt whatsoever that the American people would be far better off. You see, numbers—unlike the liberal public servants who manipulate them to convince us that the financial scene is rosy—never lie.

So here's a *conservative* mathematical prediction for the future:

$$\frac{Z}{XY^2} = M$$

where Z equals the normal range of human intelligence; X equals the human survivability rate (which is constantly increasing, thanks to charity, government aid, and advances made in medicine, including life-saving surgical techniques); Y equals the number of P.P.J.s (people of poor judgment) in the world population—who, by the way, are breeding profusely even now as you read this book; and, M, as in monkey, is the *future average intelligence quotient* (I.Q.) of man.[500]

How to Solve Problems That Are "Too Complicated"

Please consider the following:

> With conservatives, if x = y, and y = z, then x = z.
> With liberals, if x = y, and y = z, then x = *"[sigh] Oh, unfortunately, there are no easy answers. . . ."*

Obviously, this kind of spineless, evasive, unscientific reasoning will not accomplish anything at all in the fields of math, physics, chemistry, or engineering—or even help a left-wing loon to count his change on the street corner after an illegal drug transaction. Liberal fraud in academic and scientific circles appears to be on the increase, for it is continually being exposed and it likely runs rampant in the fields of psychology and psychiatry. You see, problems are impossible to solve if people don't face facts. Then the problems become permanent. "Kicking the can" is a childish game for little kids. It's not worthy of any adult, not even dopey adults in the Senate and Congress, who behave as though they were born yesterday.

The Final Piece of the Puzzle

Why do so many liberals appear to disdain the United States? Why do they constantly belittle their own country? What is the reason for the national disloyalty of newspapers like the *New York Times*?[501] The reason is simple: Many liberals do not like America because they do not like their fellow Americans. They do not like the way we think. They do not like the way we live our lives. They do not like us.

---

[500] Readers should be aware that even Einstein's theory of relativity has its critics and it will undoubtedly be improved upon, so any suggestions here are welcome.
[501] Read *Journalistic Fraud: How the* New York Times *Distorts the News and Why It Can No Longer Be Trusted,* 2003, W.N.D., Nashville, Tennessee.

It may be difficult to accept this conclusion, but it's true.

"How can that be?" you may ask. Why don't they like us? What is it about strong, independent, self-reliant individuals that liberals don't like? Don't they know that without such men and women to protect them from harm, they wouldn't even be alive to wander around complaining about everything? Why, without the strong to feed and shelter them, L.S.D.er donkeys would not even exist! So what exactly is it about dominant individuals that subordinate individuals resent? Our charity and generosity? The kindness we show them? Our haircuts? Why is it that liberals just cannot seem to stand that the United States is the most powerful country in the world? Would they rather we be the weakest? Here in the United States, everyone has a vote, but that's not good enough for liberals. They don't just want to vote; they want a different political system—one *without* conservative Republican presidents.

"How can someone who is anti-America be considered an American?" —Rob

It's no secret that many liberals much prefer the lifestyle of other countries, such as Holland, Sweden, Denmark, and Finland—or at least they think they do until they realize one day that there's no U.S. military there to protect them. They will change their minds in a flash if war breaks out and foreign troops show up at their doors and tell them to get out of town or they will be removed forcibly.

The success of the United States of America is what prevents the advent of communism and socialism, and there are many people, not only outside but inside this country, who continue to do all that they can to see that we fail. It should be obvious that those who constantly denigrate America prefer our country's enemies. They seek to be smiled upon by such as Hugo Chavez, Kim Jong-il, Ahmadinejad, Putin, and Castro. Is every American who is angry at the United States an enemy of this country? No, of course not, but without a doubt, many such people, especially the ones who like to publicly burn the American flag, have a definite preference for other political systems—or at least think they do. Our founding fathers, the laws of our Constitution, and the concept of American exceptionalism will forever be foreign to our liberal friends; for them, patriotism does not come naturally. But never, ever question a liberal Democrat's patriotism publicly, especially if he or she is a senator or congressman, because if you do, you'll immediately be called every dirty name in the book. This has always been a raw nerve for the Democratic Party, and it always will be. Why? Because the truth hurts them politically.

"Why wouldn't anyone want to say the Pledge of Allegiance, unless they detested their own country or were ignorant of its greatness?" --Sean Hannity, conservative political commentator, FOX News channel television host, radio host, and bestselling author.

"Why wasn't Michelle O. ever 'proud of her country' until her husband was nominated to be president of the United States by the Democratic Party?" —Proud Mother Of A Paratrooper In The U.S. Army

"What kind of mind in the White House would release five mass murderers?" —Mark Levin, well-known conservative commentator, radio talk-show host, and one of America's preeminent constitutional lawyers[502]

(The following extremely derogatory quote regarding the liberal socialist Democratic Party, although accurate, has been redacted in the interest of National Security.)

—Anonymous C.I.A. Agent (just kidding)

Woolly Mammoth Resurrection

In 2005, *National Geographic* reported that a team of Japanese genetic scientists was planning to bring woolly mammoths—and perhaps big Republican elephants—

---

[502] In his interview on FOX News, June 13, 2014. He was referring to President Obama's Guantanamo Bay prisoner exchange, in which five of the worst Islamic terrorist murderers in custody were swapped for an American hostage suspected of desertion.

back to life and create a Jurassic Park-style refuge for resurrected species. Now, according to a report in Japan's *Yomiuri Shimbun*, scientists from Japan, Russia, and the United States hope to clone a mammoth *(Mammuthus primigenius)* that lived more than 12,000 years ago during the ice age. The research scientists say their goal is to produce a baby mammoth by extracting DNA from a mammoth carcass that has been preserved in a Russian laboratory. They will insert the DNA into the egg cells of an African elephant in hopes of producing a mammoth embryo. The team is utilizing research by a Japanese genetic engineer who successfully cloned a mouse from cells that had been frozen for sixteen years; however, the mammoth-cloning plan faces numerous obstacles, including the relatively low success rate of cloning from frozen tissue. Cloning can be a frustrating process requiring hundreds of attempts. The American researchers are *in vitro fertilization* experts and will work with a Kinki University professor to implant the mammoth embryo into the female African elephant. After the baby mammoth is born, they will examine its ecology and genes to try to figure out why the species became extinct, something that cannot be determined from museum skeletons. (Maybe, once the little behemoth grows up, he can become a mascot for the Republican Party.)

Hopefully, the information in this book—now that it has been made public—will help reduce the workload of the Federal Bureau of Investigation, the National Security Agency, and all other divisions of law enforcement, including U.S. foreign affiliates, so everyone can relax and maybe take a nice vacation. The Pentagon has also had its share of problems with its new liberal multicultural military. Why, for example, are so many fine soldiers and veterans reportedly committing suicide? Is it because of mental problems, or illegal drug use, or both? Does it have anything to do with homosexuality? (Sometimes, when the bodies are discovered, it looks like *no foul play* is involved.) Here's something else for everyone to think about. Why are spies, traitors, and defectors always skinny little runts instead of great big tough guys? Is it because these liberal losers want to get revenge on society and, at the same time, look like big shots to their drug-addled liberal mommies? Unfortunately, the United States of America is being overrun with the kind of people who were once given dirty looks, then shot with revolvers by Clint Eastwood in the old spaghetti westerns.

Remember when everyone in the audience used to *clap and cheer?*

Afterword

Fantasy addiction disorder is genetic. Various forms of slavery of the unambitious and unwary are the cultivating mechanism for F.A.D. That is why F.A.D. and the decreased ability to mentalize and thus understand what other people are thinking seem to go hand in hand. The precepts of Darwinian evolution state that species change is a function of environment. F.A.D.'s origin lies in an overwhelming need for "hope" and a strong desire for "change." F.A.D. is used by affected persons as a defense against intense feelings of pain and despair—and perhaps even madness—under long and agonizing man-made conditions that, in some dark corners of the world, still exist as a result of human barbarity. Human barbarity can include slavery, extreme cruelty, torture, and suffering because of long-term political oppression under a tyrannical dictator. In cruel environments, symptoms of F.A.D. propagate among those who are unable to escape and to free themselves but continue to survive and somehow tolerate the deplorable conditions.

It is plain to see that the P.E.T.S. hypothesis explains not only the existence of that which we refer to as liberalism but also its exponential growth. The ironic thing about being nice to other people because of their suboptimality is that when we allow these liberals to vote and elect other liberals to serve in public office, then those liberals who were elected always pass more legislation favoring their liberal financial supporters *almost exclusively*—and to the detriment of normal hardworking taxpayers, who are mostly conservatives. That creates a man-made evolutionary environment in which liberalism flowers, breeds, and disseminates. The P.E.T.S. hypothesis also helps explain the pervasiveness of all mental disorders in society today. This endless circle, if left unchecked, can lead to only one thing: a liberal playground for "biblical evil" and, eventually, a *disaster.*[503]

Perhaps, the Apocalypse.

---

[503] *Notable Liberal Quote:* "Never let a good crisis [or disaster] go to waste." —The official motto of the Democratic Party

Addendum

1. <u>Only let men vote.</u> Most single women are looking for someone to support them—and that someone may be the U.S. government. This would not, of course, affect any equal-pay-for-equal-work laws, which, if violated by an employer, should be prosecuted to the fullest extent of the law. Married women, if they want to, could go to the polls and watch their husbands vote. If a wife does not like the way her husband votes, she knows what to do.

2. <u>Require a voter I.D. card. Immediately require all U.S. voters to apply in person for a new voter registration card.</u> It should be laminated and include that person's photo. (All scam artists should be summarily executed.)

3. <u>All voters should be at least twenty-five years of age.</u> That's because young people are spending all their time fiddling with computerized electronic equipment—like smartphones, tablets, and Blackberries—and they don't know what the hell is going on around them. (If an underage person has served five years or more in the military and that time wasn't spent in a prison or the brig, he should also be allowed to vote.)

4. <u>Voters should be required to read and speak English.</u> Nobody who can't speak English should be considered an American. (Slight foreign accents are okay, as long as the person uses deodorant and his breath doesn't stink.)

5. <u>Voters should be required to pass an I.Q. test.</u> The results of a simple, randomly generated multiple-choice political I.Q. test should be attached to his ballot to prove that he is not high on drugs and/or mentally retarded. The test should be so simple that if he changes his mind and makes a run for it, he must submit to a state background

check. Then he should have the word DEMOCRAT tattooed on his forehead.

6. <u>Only people who pay more in federal income taxes than they receive in benefits from the federal government should be allowed to vote in any election,</u> with the exception of Social Security recipients who have paid their fair share. *Public servants and government employees should also be prohibited from voting in any election that might, in any way, shape, or form affect their jobs or income.* If they don't like their jobs, then they can go find new ones, just like everybody else.

7. <u>No voting of any kind should ever be allowed by mail.</u> The votes of military men and women should be hand-delivered by a five-star general.

8. <u>Everyone who ever sold a convicted criminal an illegal drug should be forced to go to work and pay a portion of his or her income to that criminal's victim(s).</u>

9. <u>Tighten up the military.</u> Begin changing the military back to the way it used to be before the Carter administration. Let men do all of the fighting and let women provide care and support. No women should be allowed to fly multibillion-dollar jets. The liberal social experiment was entertaining, but it is ending now because it has failed miserably.

10. <u>Make two years of military service mandatory for all United States citizens.</u> This should go into effect immediately and apply to every male or female—or member of the L.G.B.T. community—between the ages of 17 to 21. They should serve two years in the Army, Navy, Air Force, Marines, or Coast Guard in some form or capacity. It would be each person's choice, depending on what that person is best suited to do. Military service would not include the Peace Corps—which just doesn't work.

11. <u>All employers who hire illegal aliens should be prosecuted</u> to the fullest extent of the law. This should go into effect immediately. (Any illegal alien who is hired for work by a citizen of the United States should report it to the nearest police officer, so he can collect the $5000.00 reward.)

12. <u>All political candidates should be chosen randomly,</u> just like people who are chosen for jury duty. This should be followed by a drug test and a polygraph exam. This will help prevent Congress from being dominated by relaxed uncaring goofy-looking entertainers. They can communicate with their home computers and vote for pending legislation by telephone.

13. <u>No presidential candidate should ever be allowed to use a teleprompter in staged and televised performances before carefully selected "adoring" crowds,</u> especially those involving the military. If he does, he will appear to be something that he's not. The candidate should present himself on a stage before the American people and tell us what he really thinks about things, not what his handlers (Manchurian puppeteers, for example) wrote for him. If he can only *read words* and can't answer unexpected questions without consulting an attorney, then he doesn't deserve to be president of the United States.

14. <u>All politicians who want to serve a second term should have to take a polygraph test</u> to make sure that they have not knowingly done anything that violates their oath of office, the United States Constitution, or the Ten Commandments.

THE TEN COMMANDMENTS

1. *I am the Lord your God. You shall have no other gods except me.*
2. *You shall not make for yourself any graven image. You shall not worship them nor serve them.*
3. *You shall not take a false oath in the name of the Lord your God.*
4. *Remember the Sabbath day to keep it holy. Six days shall you labor and do all your work.*
5. *Honor your father and your mother.*
6. *You shall not murder.*
7. *You shall not commit adultery.*
8. *You shall not steal.*
9. *You shall not bear false witness against your neighbor.*
10. *You shall not covet your neighbor's wife, nor anything that is your neighbor's.*

A Short Final Note

We Americans now live in a country where people are hesitant and sometimes even afraid to speak the truth. Saying what we think used to be a source of national pride, but now liberals have taken over almost all of our media outlets --television, newspapers, magazines, etc.. For that reason, we Americans are headed toward becoming a population of Homo sheepiens. If the United States of America continues down this liberal road to ruin, our nation is predicted to become a vast morally diseased, multicultural metropolis and an example for the world. That is what our nation's enemies want and that is also what liberal socialist Democrats want, and if we do not do something about it now, they may all eventually succeed in attaining their goal. When they do, we Americans will then have to change our country's name to something more appropriate, like the "United States of Africa," but it won't be so bad. The government will provide us all with free cell phones, goatskin drums, and soul-food stamps. Perhaps, all of the world's compassionate humanitarians will also spend their time and money taking care of us, too. So look toward the future with hope and understanding and think about your children. Ask your kids to read this book carefully, and be sure that they understand everything that's going on. For those of you who think that what this book contains is mean or ugly, you should know that I've been in love many, many times, and a few of those women may have been liberals and a few of them may have been Democrats. That's why this book was so difficult to write, but it had to be done, so it was written in jest.

CPSIA information can be obtained
at www.ICGtesting.com
Printed in the USA
LVOW04s0712270316
480929LV00015B/96/P